FROM SELF-HELP HOUSING TO SUSTAINABLE SETTLEMENT

The Making of Modern Africa

Series Editors: Abebe Zegeye and John Higginson

From Self-Help Housing to Sustainable Settlement

Capitalist development and urban planning in Lusaka, Zambia

JOHN TAIT

Avebury

Aldershot • Brookfield USA • Hong Kong • Singapore • Sydney

© J. Tait   1997

Published by
Avebury
Ashgate Publishing Limited
Gower House
Croft Road
Aldershot
Hants GU11 3HR
England

Ashgate Publishing Company
Old Post Road
Brookfield
Vermont 05036
USA

British Library Cataloguing in Publication Data
Tait, John
    From self-help housing to sustainable development :
    capitalist development and urban planning in Lusaka,
    Zambia. - (The making of modern Africa)
    1.Urbanization - Zambia - Lusaka   2.Housing policy - Zambia
    - Lusaka
    I.Title
    307.1'2'16'096894

Library of Congress Catalog Card Number: 96-86691

ISBN 1 85972 425 6

Printed and bound by Athenaeum Press, Ltd.,
Gateshead, Tyne & Wear.

Contents

Figures, tables and pictures

Acronyms

AfDB	African Development Bank
AFS	American Friends Service Committee
ANC	African National Congress
BMZ	Bundesministerium für wirtschaftliche Zusammenarbeit (German Federal Ministry for Economic Cooperation)
CBO	Central business area
CBOs	Community-based organizations
CDG	Carl Duisberg Gesellschaft (Carl Duisberg Society)
CSO	Central Statistical Office
DAC-OECD	Development Assistance Committee (OECD)
DANIDA	Danish International Development Agency
DDCCs	District Development Co-ordinating Committees
DESWOS	Deutsche Entwicklungshilfe für soziales Wohnungs- und Siedlungswesen (German Development Aid for social Housing and Settlement)
EDF	European Development Fund
EPU	Economic Promotion Unit
EZE	Evangelische Zentralstelle für Entwicklungshilfe (A German church related NGO)
FNDP	Fourth National Development Plan
gate	German Appropriate Technology Exchange
GDP	Gross domestic product
GRZ	Government of Zambia
GTZ	Gesellschaft für Technische Zusammenarbeit (German Technical Cooperation)
HABITAT	United Nations Centre for Human Settlements

HPU	Housing Project Unit
HUZA	Human Settlements of Zambia
ILO	International Labour Organization
IMF	International Monetary Fund
INGOs	International non-government organizations
IYSH	International Year of Shelter for the Homeless
LDCs	Least developed countries
LGAZ	Local Government Association of Zambia
LUDC	Lusaka Urban District Council
MLGH	Ministry of Local Government and Housing
MMD	Movement for Multi-party Democracy
NERP	New Economic Recovery Programme
NGOs	Non-government organizations
NHA	National Housing Authority
NICs	Newly industrializing countries
OECD	Organization for Economic Cooperation and Development
ODA	UK Overseas Development Administration
RDCs	Resident Development Committees
RWG	Redistribution with growth
SAIL	Social Action in Lusaka
SEP	Small-Scale Enterprises Promotion Ltd.
Sina	Settlements Information Network Africa
SNDP	Second National Development Plan
TNDP	Third National Development Plan
UN	United Nations
UNFPA	United Nations Fund for Population Activities
UNCHS	United Nations Centre for Human Settlements
UNDP	United Nations Development Programme
UNEP	United Nations Environment Programme
UNICEF	United Nations Children's Fund
UNIP	United National Independence Party
ZCTU	Zambian Congress of Trade Union
ZNBS	Zambian National Building Society

Acknowledgements

This book would not have been possible without the cooperation and support of the Zambian and Lusaka authorities. In particular I would like to thank Mr M. Maimbolwa, Commissioner for Town and Country Planning; Mr Mwiinga, Assistant Commissioner at the Ministry of Local Government and Housing, and Mr M.Y. Mwanza, Dep. of Decentralisation. From the Lusaka Urban Council I am grateful to Mr Lungu, Director of City Engineering Services; Mr Suuya, Director of Peri-Urban Housing and Social services; Mr I. Mwendapole Director of Housing and Social Services; Mr T.L. Mwanamonze, Assistant Director of Housing; Mr Mukupa, Planning Officer; Ms M. Nkhoma, Senior Community Development Officer; Mrs Siavuta and Mr Matawe, Senior Field Officers in Kalingalinga, and Mr Kapatwe, Senior Field Officer in Matero.

I greatly appreciate the joint research work made possible by Mr O. Saasa, Director of Institute of African Studies (IAS), Mrs I. Mwanza, and the IAS research team that conducted the interviews.

My field work was greatly supported by the understanding of leaders in Kalingalinga and Kanyama. In particular I would like to thank Mr. Phirie, Kanyama Ward Councillor; Mr E. Kabinda, Chairman of UNIP Youth Organization in Kalingalinga, and Mr Kapenga, Old Kanyama Section Chairman. I was impressed by the patience of the people of Kalingalinga and Kanyama townships (including the members of Keemba Small Scale Industries, Old Kanyama) to answer my endless questions.

Information and support was also readily provided by Mr H. Jere and Mr F. Ndilila both of Human Settlements of Zambia; Mr S. Nienhuys, and Mr S. Mulenga of the UNCHS office in Lusaka; Mr Körner (LUDC); Mr Subryan and Mr W. Chabaputa from the National Housing Authority; Mr Mirah, Central Statistical Office, Lusaka; Mr M. Funcke-Bartz (CDG), and Mr McGrath from Irish Aid.

Finally, I would like to extend thanks to my teachers Prof. R.Tetzlaff and Prof. H. Harms who were truthful companions during the completion of this study.

Preface

The idea for this book was suggested during the International Habitat Conference in Berlin in 1987. In discussions with colleagues working with the Lusaka NGO *Human Settlements of Zambia,* the wide spectrum of national, international, and bilateral housing activities in that city appeared an ideal setting for field work that satisfied two conditions: first, that it should be representative of urbanization in Africa, showing typical problems and solutions to housing provision for low-income groups; second, that it should make it possible to evaluate the outcome of large housing projects and to compare them with the conditions in 'unauthorized' settlements in the same city. While Lusaka fulfilled both these criteria for the empirical side of research, the appropriate theoretical background gave more concern. For a sociologist/political scientist 'converted' to town planning after working on developmental and rural problems in Africa, the systematic study of Third World city concepts displayed deficiencies compared with the standards of developmental theory. Thus, in due course, the theoretical part of the research began to live its autonomous life far removed from the African setting, instead becoming largely devoted to the more advanced and better researched Latin American urban situation. In the end these efforts explain (and justify) the more universal title 'From Self-Help Housing to Sustainable Settlement'.

The aim of this book is both theoretical and practical, with *planning issues* taking an intermediary role. In other words, urban theory was deployed and developed with a focus on implications for planning and developmental strategies without any intention of submitting a comprehensive concept of the Third World City. In the methodological unfolding, the issue of *self-help housing* appeared as the natural and logical starting point for discussion. Since the emergence of development programmes some thirty years back, devoted to housing the poor, the self-help 'solution' has quickly become a central element in feasible and affordable approaches to housing provision. At the same time the societal and developmental implications involved in this concept go to the heart of controversial discussion among planners. Chapter I discusses both the evolution of self-help housing concepts and their critical reassessment in the mid-1970s and early 1980s, notably by the Colombian architect and social scientist E. Pradilla. In the tradition of Friedrich Engels, Pradilla defined the social character of housing as part of the reproduction of the labour-force, leading to critique of self-help advocacy in capitalist developing countries. From the point of view of political economy, the questionable outcome of self-help housing by low-income builders implies a possible dual exploitation: first by the lowering of labour costs through the workers' self-provision of housing instead of the inclusion of housing costs in wages; and second by the unavoidable process by which capitalist markets and commodification gain control over the final housing accomplishment. This often involves the displacement of self-help builders who are usually unable to fully recoup their investments, in particular with respect to the labour invested. As a result, self-help is seen to provide the capitalist markets with cheap housing rather than truly solving the housing question for low-income groups.

As Mathéy notes, this academic critique of self-help housing was at its peak in the 1980s. It has since then lost relevance and been replaced by discussions on the concrete problems of housing projects (Mathéy, 1992). This shift from theoretical to pragmatic orientation has occurred for various reasons. In part it reflects the heterogeneous local circumstances in housing projects (cultural, geographic and political aspects) that are not comprehended by a single theory. Moreover, the shift seems associated with the depoliticization of developmental theory in the past decade, reflecting the lack of alternatives to the capitalist growth model. But a final reason appears in the deficiencies of the academic critique itself that, isolated from developmental theory, has proposed abstractions incapable of embracing the totality of Third World urban development and housing. Among the most important neglected or omitted aspects were the internationalization and globalization of capitalism, the particular role of the Third World state, and the inconsistencies in the spatial formation of capitalism itself.

This last argument is the operational base of this thesis. It proposes a concept that revives and retains the analytical merits of an approach critical of capitalist development, but reconceives it as *an instrument for appropriate planning*. Chapters II and III attempt to criticize the simplistic and economistic early postulates of political economy of housing. This entails the introduction of aspects that have been elaborated by developmental theory in the past 10 years. At *macro level* these include theories on the internationalization of capital and new global and regional models of accumulation. Likewise with urbanization, post-moderniz-ation concepts of Third World urban development have been proposed that now differentiate between the European capitalist cities and cities in the capitalist periphery. This allows the analysis of 'World Cities' in terms of their mode of integration into the global economy and as part of the spatial and territorial dimensions of capitalist formation. At the *meso level* these concepts correspond to a differentiated analysis of the informal sector, underpinned by new modes of household reproduction at the *micro level* that transcend the conventional class conflict between capital and labour. These perceptions reflect growing informalization in the relations of production and new modes of surplus appropriation stemming from the specific form of Third World urbanization.

Broadening conventional comprehension, it is proposed to view self-help housing as no longer adequately analysed by the circumstances of housing production and the reproduction of labour-power alone. With decaying municipal and state functions in the Third World, self-help housing also comprehends alternative informal means of delivery of land, property, and infrastructure as well as the provision of the socio-spatial environment required for the functioning of informal sector activities. Accordingly, social conflicts do not simply arise over the capitalist appropriation of the values incorporated in housing and labour-power: distributive, spatial, and political conflicts also arise in urban social reproduction vis-à-vis the state and the municipality, which in strategically important World Cities may have international dimensions. Chapter IV is devoted to reincorporating these conclusions into a more adequate framework of the political economy of housing by extending proposals by Burgess and Moser to define the informal sector in terms of petty commodity production. In its newly proposed *peripheral form* it appears not only as a sphere of production but also as a relation of production sustained by *collective* workers who are part of a household reproductive unit that maintains specific forms of redistribution among its members. It is further argued that this relationship is actively reproduced within the capitalist peripheral growth model, thereby adding new forms of exploitation as yet inadequately distinguished. The relevance of this approach for appropriate planning is shown by the fact that these proposals differentiate between various forms and modes of exploitation/appropriation, denoting their potential social repercussions in dependence on the reproductive situation of household units and the prevailing societal structures.

A different matter altogether is whether or not the terms of housing projects and the social and political circumstances of their implementation allow this type of approach. This is investigated in Chapter V, which is devoted to planning transfer and the sociological dimensions of planned interventions in settlement processes. As shown in the history of international housing programmes in Latin America, the satisfaction of basic needs in dwelling was seldom more than a sideline to politically motivated interventions in the 1950s and 1960s in order to 'pacify' the urban masses and to 'stabilize' political regimes. Genuine efforts to deploy feasible and affordable housing policies for the urban poor can, however, be seen in the World Bank's housing schemes in the 1970s. One of the positive outcomes is that appropriate housing schemes, like upgrading, have come to be accepted by most Third World governments as partial solutions at project level. Nonetheless, these housing programmes have not matured into solutions with mass replicability at national policy level, and they have achieved little change in the social and political perception of the 'squatter problem' by Third World governments. Instead, a legacy of the World Bank's intervention is the conversion of housing for the poor from a politically biased problem of unequal urban service provision into an economic one of cost-recovery and the introduction of the market economy to low-income housing provision. Actions of national states towards the regularization of unauthorized settlements within this policy are shown to vary according to economic or political circumstances, but with a growing segregatory tendency at the expense of the lowest-income groups.

Thus, prospects for comprehensive solutions instead of short-term project interventions, such as the 'enabling approach' proposed by the UNCHS - with NGOs as intermediary agencies between planners and residents' organizations - would depend on the questionable cooperation of the state. So far the design of feasible housing strategies has idealistically omitted considerations of the specific functions of the state in dependent economies and the class alignments underpinning them. Steps towards realistic schemes would instead have to start with a politicization of planning procedures and reforms in the planning bureaucracy. Besides reinforcing autocratic attitudes, planning transfer from the First World has implanted an inappropriate orientation of Third World planners to the European city, diversionary to the requirements of seeking indigenous solutions that realistically correspond to the needs of residents and the availability of national resources.

Housing projects of bilateral development programmes are shown to have a generally better record of adjusting to their target groups. But here too planning technocracy may prevail over cautious monitoring of the social and economic dynamics stimulated in planned development. All too often short-term project schedules create different levels of opportunity for resident fractions once a settlement is legalized and opens itself up to the regular housing market. Filtering processes of housing stock and displacement of the weaker and less adaptable dwellers might be avoided if a preassessment of the sociological and economic situation were included in the project design. Overambitious standards and too rapid implementation are only two crucial cases in point. Other suggested post-project protective measures deal with various forms of communal control over achievements, which, if necessary, allow individual aspirations that might become harmful to the communal equilibrium to be curbed.

One planning instrument that would help in predetermining developments and would guide planning is suggested in the systematic analysis of a settlement's consolidation process. According to data from various international studies, consolidation of housing and settlement is seldom the result of incremental development by the same group of households, but rather involves a dual dynamic of 'consolidation and displacement'. The occurrences of housing stock filtering processes and waves of displacement are shown to relate to dominant aspects in consolidation patterns (i.e. territorial, physical, commercial and legal consolidation). Each stage produces typical features in the internal structuring of settlements that ultimately define the limits of socioeconomic sustenance for their resident households. As demonstrated for the Lusaka case, this type of analysis could be used by planners to control negative displacement and the usual filtering-up effects of regularization. For instance, undesired gentrification could be discouraged either by legalization at an early stage of a settlement's development to freeze up the filtering process, or by devising appropriate improvements that divert territorial and physical consolidation *away* from middle-class housing standards and preferences. The consolidation model also suggests that lowest-income groups, on account of the special role housing plays in their survival strategies, have little chance of improving their housing situation once physical improvements and upward filtering set in. As displacement is inevitable without some kind of cross-subsidization and protective measures, comprehensive housing policies would need to address these groups by specific programmes that control the pace and form of consolidation according to their capabilities and needs.

With few exceptions, the urbanization of black Africans was introduced under the auspices of colonial authorities who built cities designed for administrative purposes and to fit the residential needs of their European populations. But the notorious 'colonial city', modelled on racial and segregatory principles, is more than a physical and spatial heritage for postcolonial urban development. In fact, most of these principles have been retained by the new African elites for their own political rule. The political and developmental background leading to this failure to decolonize planning in Africa is analysed in Chapter VI. In Zambia one of the keys to understanding contemporary urban developments lies in the history of the contradictory requirements imposed on the colonial authorities: namely their inability to reconcile the official dual policy of 'native rural' and 'white urban' development with the *de facto* African urbanization of mine workers after the introduction of a migratory labour recruiting scheme. Still little recognized, this contradiction in effect produced the indigenous solution of unauthorized African settlements as early as the mid-1930s, when these were 'tolerated' by mining companies and authorities as they helped to lower wage costs and functioned as labour reserves without requiring the enfranchisement of Africans.

Although Lusaka is not a mining town, the illusion of a white urban settler development and the reality of gradual African urbanization has also characterized its development since its selection as colonial capital in 1935. Town planning was guided by the idea of spacious European settlement in a 'garden city' that systematically omitted adequate planning provision for its growing African population. Following Zambia's independence in 1964, the abolishment of colonial influx ordinances confronted Lusaka with unprecedented migration from rural areas. The degeneration of agricultural production schemes that had not recovered from the colonial migratory labour systems continued to cause rural-urban migration in Zambia, giving rise to one of the highest urbanization rates in Africa. In Lusaka the inability of planning (and lack of political determination of the government) to cope with this situation left migrants little alternative but to reside in the already existing unauthorized housing areas close to the city centre. With more than a 50% rate of squatters by 1970, unwilling to be relocated to the Lusaka periphery, an upgrading solution was finally decided upon, jointly financed and implemented by the Zambian Government and the World Bank.

The experiences of this project to upgrade two-thirds of Lusaka's squatter population are the background to the field study of two of the town's low-income settlements. Unexpectedly, the project has not matured into a politically acceptable solution to low-income housing provision, and a planned second project stage to service the remaining unauthorized housing areas was never realized. At the end of the 1980s, the heavy bias of public spending on government middle-class housing had not been reversed. Despite continuously growing unauthorized settlements in Lusaka, some with severe hygienic and physical deficiencies, there is at present little political dedication to deal with the problem. Planning action is additionally paralysed by the unsolved problems of cost-recovery and affordable housing standards with appropriate building codes, and by lack of municipal land delivery and housing finance schemes. All this is aggravated by the economic crisis of the past 20 years that has cast Zambia back into the group of 'least developed countries'.

The situation of Lusaka's low-income populations in 1989 was analysed by comparing an integrated project of German Technical Aid (GTZ) implemented in the early 1980s - at that time the only successor to the World Bank scheme - with the living conditions in Lusaka's largest unauthorized housing area. The critical assessment of the integrated project addresses both the material improvements and the experiences with new forms of participation and self-administration that were intended to have 'model character' for Lusaka. Some of its novel components, namely the successful local economic promotion programme and the revolving loan funds, appeared to have made an impact on municipal policies and were to be extended to other legalized low-income settlements. However, under the prevailing political structures, hardly conducive to the devolution of responsibilities to residents, participation in housing issues has been prone to misuse by influential local groups and has not mobilized the self-help capacities of the community.

This is contrasted by the situation in the second unauthorized settlement that was intermittently threatened by eviction due to its disadvantageous geophysical conditions. The township's systematic neglect by the urban council to discourage settlement has enhanced community-based organization and self-help activities of residents. With the help of local and international NGOs these have led to self-provided basic infrastructure, efforts which have at the same time strengthened the community's political acceptance by the municipality. The settlement is also an interesting case of a thriving informal rental housing market as a vital subsidiary source of income, a factor that also determines the valorization of housing and the physical development of the housing stock. In view of the crisis of public finance and Zambia's poor economic prospects that are highly dependent on copper exports, already decaying council functions are unlikely to recover in the future. Moreover, international policies on urban development now strongly favour the deregulation and privatization of local state functions. In this respect the already advanced degree of informality in the provision of housing and infrastructure in this unauthorized settlement may be the prototype for coming urban policies and for realistic solutions in Lusaka with less involvement of the state. It shows that instead of waiting for the council to take initiatives, low-income residents must organize and with the help of NGOs take community matters into their own hands. Wherever required, they must urge disengaging authorities to comply with community-based planning and action.

Recommendations for new urban policies in Lusaka are proposed in the final chapter. Additional comparisons that are drawn with the urban situation in other African countries in this chapter, however, show that the urban crisis has become a general feature on that continent and that no ready planning solutions are available without fundamental structural reforms of the political and administrative systems.

Postscript: The study outlined above was completed by 1994. It was based on two visits to Zambia in 1988/89. Field work in the two Lusaka settlements was conducted in 1989. With politically-oriented research, taking years to put on paper, the greatest problem for an author is to be overtaken by history. This has happened with the introduction of a multi-party system in Zambia and the election of a new president in 1991, which put an end to the 25-year rule of President Kaunda and his UNIP party. Democracy has brought about considerable changes in the institutional structures of Zambia and led to some new policy orientations. A third visit to Lusaka in late 1995 gave the opportunity of studying the new political and economic developments and verifying some of the original conclusions. The results of this restudy have been incorporated into the manuscript with an additional subchapter added on 'The Urban Situation Under The Multi-party System 1991-1995'. Since the empirical data-base stems from the days of a long-term UNIP single-party dominance, many of the recommendations made for political and institutional reforms of that particular system have been retained in their original form in the Chapters XI and XII (the field studies of the two settlements) for two reasons: first, they are part of the evolution of human settlement in low-income areas and add to the understanding of established leadership roles and forms of communal participation; second, the strong intermeshing of urban planning with party politics in council bureaucracies is shown to be a lasting heritage that is not simply overcome by the replacement of senior office holders or by the administrative reforms proposed by the new government.

Constitutional reforms and changes in the political superstructure have only had limited effect on the politics of planning. Under the new government, major reforms and planning initiatives in the urban development of Lusaka have yet to materialize. Although some international NGOs and bilateral aid projects have appeared as new urban actors in infrastructure provision, the inferences drawn in 1989 on the crisis of planning and urban policies are still valid today. The council has been unable to take any steps towards addressing the issues of planning and infrastructure provisions for the ever-growing low-income settlements of the city. As to the validity of the 1989 field study, visits to the settlements showed that physical standards in housing and the situation of low-income households have remained unchanged or even deteriorated since they were analysed last. On the trajectory already denoted and predicted in 1989, the displacement of vulnerable low-income residents has increased, and there is growing competition on the unauthorized housing market due to privatization of the former state-dominated economy and the introduction of the market economy in the housing sector as more and more formerly privileged dwellers in state-subsidized housing are now forced to satisfy their housing demand on informal housing markets.

I   The self-help housing debate

1   Introduction: the research situation

Marxists are latecomers to research into urban development in the Third World. Not surprisingly, this circumstance has handicapped the production of an adequate theoretical framework capable of handling the emerging issues of housing and shelter as part of the developmental problematic in the Third World. Moreover, early materialist theories of the 'capitalist city' proposed by Lefèbvre (1972) and Castells (1973) were strongly biased by experiences of Western urbanization then thought to express a universal pattern of capitalist development (Slater, 1986, p. 10). This failure to analyse urban development in relation to the emerging world economy and its differentiated functions and spatial requirements has produced an atrophied concept of cities degrading them into the 'spatial image' of the capitalist mode of production. Once regarded as an isolated phenomenon, this in turn allowed the internal structures of cities to be deduced from abstract capitalist laws assumed to reflect the exigencies of capitalist expansion (Friedmann/Wolff, 1982, p. 328). This disorientation of Marxist urban analysis left considerable conceptual gaps between theory and social reality of Third World cities. In particular it led to a wide disregard of urban aspects related to the uneven territorial formation of national capitalism and related to the historic specific mode of integration of cities into the emergent global capitalist economy.

The appearance of the Latin American 'Dependency theory' was a first important step towards modifying the general framework of capitalist development to make it fit the historical situation on that continent.[1] Nonetheless, 'dependencia' remained fixed to a high level of macro-economical abstraction making it partially inadequate in addressing the newly emerging phenomena of development in urban metropolises. However, this characterization was probably true for most of the Marxist discussion at that time that was trapped in an abstract and conceptually dogmatic perception of society making it incapable of matching Third World reality with the requirements of class analysis and the determinants of capital accumulation. In a word, these approaches were unable to provide genetic explanations for the phenomena of marginated or structural heterogeneous urban development within a materialistic framework.

Therefore it was not the Marxists but self-critical 'modernists' who, in the late 1960s and early 1970s, provided fresh conceptual ideas to the debate on Third World urban development. The main topics of discussion were put on the board by the ILO (largely adapting Hart's 'informal sector' approach), the World Bank (the 'basic needs' approach), or by individual experts such as Mangin and J. Turner who proposed self-help housing as a 'solution' to the habitat problems of the urban poor.[2]

If the contemporary Marxist discussion on urban development may have finally overcome theoretical stagnation, we must credit this to the large number of empirical studies conducted during the past two decades that critically readdressed neo-modernistic propositions on low-cost housing - thereby disclosing the 'hidden' economic rational of self-help housing programmes. Despite our now greatly enlarged knowledge on life and work in squatter settlements and the greater insight into the governmental perception of the problem, some points should be borne in mind as criteria for further research proceedings and priorities.

Lacking public support for research, many of these studies had to be based on small-scale surveys, or even on individual case studies. Furthermore, the findings cover a great variety of countries, each of them representing a specific stage of development and type of housing policy, and each directed to social groups of specific social composition who again react individually to the programmes implemented (cf. HABITAT, 1982). All this sets limits to the extent to which we may generalize the available data. For the reasons mentioned above, the emphasis of research, towards formerly neglected and misconceived sides of social reality can only be a first and necessary step in the direction of a more comprehensive understanding of the nature of heterogeneous urban development. What remains is a considerable uncertainty on part of Marxist researchers as to how social phenomena reflected in the non-Marxist concepts of 'dualism', 'hyper-urbanization', 'marginality', 'informal sector', etc. are to be properly conceptualized in materialistic theory.

Amid all these problems and uncertainties - which have proved injurious to professional action in the field of habitat improvement - the self-help concept must have attained sheer irresistible attraction as an escape from these predicaments. Initially the idea of self-help not only promised a practical approach to the housing problems of the urban poor, directly adapting to their financial capacities and 'felt' needs. For all those who were critical of the prospective outcome of capitalist development and simultaneously frustrated by the perspectives of a struggle against it, the organizational terms of self-help measures (e.g. self-control over the building process, self-consumption of the product, familial and communal forms of work cooperation, application of appropriate technology) necessarily suggested a unique form of developmental effort capable of uniting various aims put forward in the recent discussion on development planning. These included the following:

- Housing programmes could be directly oriented towards the needs of a definable and accessible target group without the bulk of resources being drained away unproductively by intermediate agents and institutions as is the case with many government development projects.

- Low-cost housing projects could claim top priority in the strategy of basic-needs satisfaction propagated by international development agencies in the early 1970s.

- Housing projects were credited with having favourable indirect impacts on development projects such as increased utilization of underemployed family labour, promotion of occupational opportunities, increase in the rate of consumption, general promotion of social aspirations, mobilization of untapped capital reserves of the extended family, and ready extension of monetary income through renting out rooms in the newly built houses (cf. World Bank, 1982, pp. iv-xv).

- Successfully conducted self-help projects were expected to be positive demonstrations for sceptical local authorities and state housing policy-makers that would bring publicly-financed infrastructure into formerly marginal residential areas. In the end it was hoped that such projects might even promise a complete reconsideration of attitudes towards low-cost housing projects, leading to their acceptance as an integral part of planned urban development with economic prospects of cost-recovery.

- Finally, and not to be underrated, the engagement of professionals in the politics and practice of squatter settlements could, by them, be perceived as a direct involvement in the political grassroots movement emerging in low-income urban quarters. Specifically the influential writings of Castells in the early 1970s[3] nourished hopes and expectations that people's frustrations over housing and settlement circumstances might crystallize into an alternative form of political mobilization, superseding the stagnation of highly suppressed class struggle in Third World countries.

As we now realize, many of these expectations have turned out to be illusions. Irrespective of the specific content, or the practised forms adopted in self-help measures, the general fallacy seems to have been that an individual solution was held possible for a problem that is created by the specific terms of social reproduction in Third World countries.

2 Self-help housing - a reactionary policy?

Opposing the notion of possible individualistic solutions to the housing problem, Pradilla was one of the first to insist that in societies dominated by capitalism all aspects of social reproduction, including housing, may only be appropriately analysed and understood in the context of Marx's theory of labour-power reproduction. According to Pradilla, the now well-known conclusions to be drawn for self-help programmes would entail that:

- Houses built in this manner may be seen to prolong the working day over its socially average, i.e., its necessary duration.

- Self-help tends to preserve both the low states of productive forces employed in the building process as well as a low standard of housing for the labour-force.

- Public self-help programmes lead to an increasing dependence on the state due to the involvement of the latter in the legalization of squatter settlements and the provision of infrastructure. Specifically the ideological state power is reinforced by these processes.

- Self-help supports the compulsion of the reserve labour-force to maintain a subsistence mode of reproduction to the benefit of capital that is responsible for its existence.

All these mechanisms have a direct bearing on the general wage structure. As housing is a socially necessary part of reproduction, Pradilla concludes that self-help housing advocacy will only lead to a lowering of the exchange-value of labour: the fraction of wages that is usually dedicated to covering housing expenses may be withheld by capital, thus enlarging the appropriated surplus. The alternative to self-help housing advocacy would be to demand appropriate housing for the labour-force as part of the price for labour-power (cf. Pradilla, 1984, pp. 164-165).

These rigorous conclusions have not failed to make their mark on advocators of self-help strategies as a solution to the housing problems of the urban poor in Third World countries. But even if we concede that the position of Pradilla has been extensively discussed in theoretical analysis, the impact on professional practice seems much less significant. There are obvious reasons for this situation that can be attributed to underlying disparities between the generally postulated theoretical perception of the housing problem and the practised forms of self-help in specific socioeconomic contexts.

In the first place, the actual magnitude of self-help practice seems to have been greatly exaggerated. The perception that self-construction and self-consumption of houses are the dominant form in the provision of housing for the urban poor only seems to fit reality for the early 1950s. Data presented by Mangin (1963) and Lloyd (1980) for Lima, or Perlman

(1976) for Rio de Janeiro suggests that commercialization in low-income settlements has expanded rapidly in the provision of housing and land as well as in subletting. True self-help construction in combination with self-consumption of the house is increasingly seen to be the exception rather than the rule. A similar development pattern is reported by the local housing authority of Nairobi (cf. Wetter, 1984, p. 83). Here, the rate of self-constructed houses in squatter settlements declined from 60.5% in 1967 to 40.8% in 1973. Finally, the World Bank's evaluation report on their sites and service and upgrading programmes in El Salvador, the Philippines, Senegal and Zambia shows an unexpectedly high rate of wage-labour involved in the construction of housing in a programme that was initially designated as a progressive self-help measure (cf. World Bank, 1982, pp. i-xv).

Due to the apparent erosion of the self-help category, various researchers have proposed more specific technical concepts such as 'self-build' (equivalent to the Spanish 'autoconstrucción'), 'autonomously-produced housing' (cf. Connolly, 1982), or 'auto-organization of shelter' (Canel/Delis/Girard, 1984). However, these alternatives tend to reduce the social dimensions of housing provision. Even if the content of self-help may have changed, now no longer necessarily incorporating self-production, we suggest that 'self-help' remains the most appropriate concept if conceived in a contextual dimension, i.e. in relation to the socially dominant form of housing. Accordingly, we will define self-help housing as a means of supplying housing with predominant use-value character under circumstances that must seek ways to bypass the legal, financial, and societal constraints set to its provision under prevailing housing and land market conditions. Thus the specific forms of self-help that people adopt for housing provision are subject to variance depending on the given conditions of the local market, and/or the given administrative constraints. For instance, the off-market, irregular terms of self-help housing provision might be defined by its illegal character, e.g. with respect to land invasions or dubious land titles, violations of building codes or disregard of official minimal plot standards, substandard hygienic conditions in the settlement, or lack of basic infrastructure. Legalization, on the other hand, does not automatically exclude a possible self-help component. In legal housing schemes the self-help context may be defined by the conflicts involved in developing the individual plot and house according to project time schedules, or rather according to material standards that are appropriate to the housing strategies and the needs of the builders and not to those of the implementing agency. As we will demonstrate later, the sharp division initially assumed to exist between subsistence (i.e. self-help) and market forms of production was in fact a misperception on part of planners. For poverty groups, interrelations between subsistence and commodity forms of reproduction are indispensable for urban survival. Changes in this interrelation, such as the implicated use of construction labour or subletting for income generation, reflect modifications in the applied strategies of sustenance or changes in the urban economy. They do not necessarily deny the self-help character of housing accomplished within this framework.

5

As Harms (1982) has pointed out, the discussion on self-help housing has produced two rather antipodal lines of interpretation in which confusions concerning the character of the self-help concept are apparent. According to publications of J. Turner and his followers in the 1960s and '70s, the self-help discussion was very much oriented to the pure material and physical aspects of squatter housing and slum-settlements. They argued that in a social situation in which the socioeconomic system is unable or unwilling to satisfy the housing demand for specific low-income groups, dynamic, self-determined individual action would more than compensate for the prevailing social constraints of adequate housing provision: in combination with appropriately adopted measures, this would also open altogether new perspectives for autonomous action. In this vein, self-help housing was seen as a vital part of a new spontaneous, self-determined, neighbourhood-based, and non-anonymous ways of living. Thus, in the idealistic impetus, self-help housing subversively generated new dimensions of autonomy, e.g. 'the freedom of community self-selection; the freedom to budget one's own resources and the freedom to shape one's own environment' (J. Turner, 1968, p. 357).[4]

In the face of Third World reality, this approach reveals an euro-centric projection that fundamentally mistakes the phenomena of 'marginal' existence in Latin American metropolises for a niche in the capitalist system. We have already provided some evidence showing the contrary, hereby indicating that the propensity of capitalism to undermine autonomous forms of reproduction was just as seriously underrated as were the desire and motivation of people to participate in self-help measures misconceived. As Harms aptly puts it:

> The ideological slogan 'freedom to build' confused freedom to act with the necessity to survive. It implies an actual freedom of choice when in fact there is little or no choice (Harms, 1982, p. 18).

In contrast to these pragmatic or idealistic approaches to self-help housing, critics have instead emphasized the inescapable social determinants in practice and theory of the concept. The roles the actors (builders, agents, state) play in housing provision are seen as clearly defined by the concept of political economy of capitalism - whether the participants realize this or not. One of the crucial aspects is that in a commodity-based society, housing, as a socially necessary good with use-value, simultaneously becomes an economic good, i.e., it becomes an object with exchange-value relating to the process of capital accumulation and capital valorization.

But political economy also depicts internal contradictions within capitalism itself. Whereas one of its objectives would be the maximal expansion of the sphere of commodity circulation into the housing sector, this tendency is counterpoised by the capitalist interest of lowering the reproduction costs of the labour-force in which housing costs play a considerable part. As the contrasting solutions to this conflict in capitalist core countries and capitalist peripheries show, much depends on the concrete historical circumstances. The logic of political economy may work in both ways. In the developed capitalist countries commodity production and circulation of housing are controlled by landlords, housing estate agents, commercial craftsmen, and building industries. All these stand for firmly established fractions within the formation of ruling classes and are tightly interlocked with vital interests of capital. Here urban self-help housing in the true sense of the word is the rare exception. It is virtually made impossible to the extent that urban land-use plans and contemporary building regulations enforce complex construction systems, requiring industrially produced building materials, and qualified craftsmen.[5] Accordingly, in developed capitalism the general level of rent as a capitalist-based source of revenue is maintained at a high level with public subsidies on rent provided for low-income groups. Also, the scope for possible self-help housing would be limited due to its necessary accentuation of internal conflict between the different fractions of capital involved. For dominant industrial capital, the interest in lowering labour costs by self-help building after office hours would only be secondary to the maintenance and regeneration of the full work capacities of its highly qualified labour. But in the case of increasing unemployment and economic crisis in the capitalist centres, self-help may, even there, be revitalized as a reaction to declining income security and dwindling state subsidies.[6]

Considering all these aspects, a theory delineating the determinants of housing provision and specific self-help strategies in Third World countries will, obviously, turn into a project of considerable complexity. What must be considered is no less than (1) a methodical assessment of the extent to which abstractions of political economy and the concept of the capitalist mode of production are valid instruments in the analysis of underdeveloped and dependent capitalist societies, (2) an analysis of the interdependence of the two conflicting strategies of capital valorization (expansion of commodity circulation in the housing sector and/or lowering of reproduction costs of labour) in a specific historical situation, and (3) the assessment of self-help measures in social formations that integrate capitalist and non-capitalist forms of production, exchange, and valorization of goods.

The problems this kind of analysis poses to researchers are very clearly demonstrated in the writings of E. Pradilla, who was the first to present a Marxist critique of the self-help debate in Latin America. A critical discussion of his influential alternative framework for housing analysis will be the subject of the next chapters.

3   The determinants of housing provision in dependent social formations

As a general framework for analysis Pradilla adopts a double level of abstraction: (1) the capitalist mode of production that is dominant, thus determining the structure of development in Latin America, and (2) the dependent social formation in which the dominant capitalist mode of production is articulated with other historically preexisting modes of production

(Pradilla, 1979, pp. 2-3). This double point of reference applies to every specific social object of investigation, meaning that

> ... the 'housing problem' can only be defined as an object in thought inside the determined social form in which it occurs and ... it must be understood ... in relation to a theory that at one and the same time takes account of the real movement of the historically dominant mode of production and the particular form that it assumes in the concrete society in which it is located (Pradilla, 1979, p. 3).

As an 'object in thought' the character of housing may be derived from the dominant social relations in capitalism with regards to its inescapable commodity form. The capitalist domination works to the effect that irrespective of the specific modes of construction or consumption of the house, all aspects of housing are ultimately submitted to a process in which they acquire the form of commodities or potential commodities. Pradilla distinguishes three ideal types or forms in which the production, exchange and consumption of housing can take place:[7]

1   With the *industrial production* of housing, capital valorization takes place in its most advanced form, i.e. involving a high level of productivity, a high content of building machinery, and fixed production installations. The valorization of constant capital becomes the preeminent aspect in the mode of surplus extraction from wage-labour. The production process is dedicated to serving a high-standard housing market. In this exchange-value form of capitalist commodity production of housing, additional commercial profit will accrue to the housing agents involved in the sale of the product.

2   In the *manufactured production* of housing, money is invested for self-consumption and, therefore, only indirectly becomes part of the process of capital circulation. Investments are primarily directed to hiring wage-labour, or to engaging building contractor firms working under the supervision of the architect or the builder. Generally this mode of construction, combining skilled and unskilled work, will be more labour-intensive than the industrial form. It will, nevertheless, still greatly rely on the acquisition of raw materials from the capitalist commodity market. The manufactured house built for self-consumption will only attain commodity character if it is utilized for commercial subletting.

3   In the *self-constructed* form of housing the producer and the consumer are identical. The determining factor for progression in the construction process will be the availability of personal work time of the builder or his family and cash for the acquisition of building material. Usually this will involve the readiness to prolong the work day, if necessary,

8

at the cost of a temporary lowering of sustenance standards. Market-available building materials are substituted as far as possible, often by utilizing throwaways that are revalued in the production process. Ideally no capital relations are established as the product is designated for self-consumption and will not involve wage-labour (Pradilla, 1979, pp. 7-9).

Although intermediate forms of production have always existed combining the three 'ideal types', according to Pradilla, the empirical evidence of the last 10 to 15 years displays an increasing dominance of the capitalist related forms within the housing sector. This is held to express the general tendency of expanding capitalist development. Under the specific conditions of dependent capitalism, however, this development takes the form of an articulation - with industrial capital in dominance. As a result, the industrial capital is not only the driving force behind development in the housing sector; it also imposes the limits to which other forms of production may continue to exist or are dissolved. By this logic the continuing reproduction of the manufactured form is only explained by the constraints set by dependent development to industrial capital's capacity of expanding in the housing sector. The limiting factors are the scarcity of circulating capital, the restrictions on the importation of building machinery, equipment and materials, and finally the limits of 'solvent' demand in the housing market. Another supporting element for the manufactured form is seen in the abundance of cheap wage-labour from the ranks of the unemployed.

Finally, Pradilla explains the persistence of the self-built form in housing provision as the consequence of labour-force over-exploitation. This results in the deterioration or non-availability of financial capacities to afford housing of commercial standard. For the reserve army of unemployed with only sporadic monetary income, self-help measures, therefore, become a means of subsistence in which the necessary costs of reproduction are borne by the individual members of the labour-force and their families. In this context, state interventions directed to these groups (e.g. self-help programmes for lowest income-groups) merely have the intention of preventing an excessive deterioration of living conditions that might be injurious to their general ability to function as labour-power on the market.

In a critical commentary on Pradilla's framework I would like to concentrate on two aspects that are hardly specific for the housing problem alone. The first problem concerns the general relationship between the theoretical concept of capitalist mode of production and the reality of a particular social formation (reflected in terms of dominance and determinativeness or of articulation between different forms and modes of production). The second problem addresses the appropriateness of Marx's theory of reproduction of labour-power - once it is removed from the 'ideal' context of developed capitalism - to explain the specific social relations of production in Third World countries.

A first indication of a possible methodological bias is conveyed by a closer look at the way the different forms of housing production are seen as united in a single process but bound

9

together by relations of determination (cf. Pradilla, 1979, p. 13). The concept adopted by Pradilla for the analysis of this relationship - as mentioned - is that of articulation of the capitalist mode of production with preexisting forms of production.

In general discussion the concept of articulation was proposed as a more appropriate approach to the analysis of existing heterogeneous structures of social formations. This was conceived in contrast to the conventional line of thinking that supposes necessary antagonistic contradictions between capitalist and non-capitalist forms of production (cf. Foster-Carter, 1978). In contrast to this, the principal conceptual notion of articulation is a defined mutuality and reciprocity in the relations established. In this form the dialectical development of capitalism would not be only the gradual dissolution of preexisting structures, it must at the same time also actively reproduce them to some extent. This gives rise to several consequences for the analysis of social structures. Assuming that the capitalist mode of production is articulated with other forms of production, this would imply that the dominant mode of production is for its own reproduction partially dependent on forms of production alien to its own laws of motion and structural properties. Further, once articulated relations are considered functional parts in the total reproduction of the social formation, this requires that the dominant capitalist mode of production enables the non-capitalist forms to exist according to their own structural properties and reproductive requirements.

At first glance, Pradilla's statement that the industrial form of housing production determines the entire sector - thereby articulating all other production forms in defining the limits of their survival and how they function - seems to conform with the general definition given above. However, as the following quotation demonstrates, his attempt to structure the determinants and dynamics of production, exchange, and consumption of housing by 'articulation' is obviously contradicted by various suppositions concerning the theory and practice of the movement of the capitalist mode of production in dependent social formations:

> If in the transition phases between the predominance of a past productive system and the use and development of a new one, the non-correspondence between the dominant and the determinant form occurs, the inherent dynamism of the new form will not only let it become determinant, but it will also occupy the dominant role, by subordinating all the other forms, articulating and subordinating them to its laws of development and gradually dissolving them. This is in fact the existing relationship between the industrial and the manufactured and artisan forms in the existing conditions of capitalist development (Pradilla, 1979, p. 10).[8]

In this case the relations between the 'past productive system' and the 'new' one are clearly conceived as contradictions between systems (hence inter-systemic contradictions). However, this would require that the relationship between the systems be necessarily characterized by opposition rather than by relations of mutuality. This would, of course, still be a perfectly

10

acceptable approach to the analysis of historical conflict between different modes of production. But the point at issue is whether this kind of framework is appropriate for the current historical situation in which the expansion of artisan and self-constructed forms of housing production is determined and stimulated by the action of the capitalist mode of production according to its reproductive needs for cheap labour. Therefore, it hardly comes as a surprise that in his concrete approach to the housing problem, the theoretical notion of contradictions between systems is dropped and instead replaced by the concept of intra-systemic contradictions (i.e. indicating relations of causal and functional reciprocity). This is apparent from the manner in which the different housing production forms are conceived as bound together by articulated relations of determination within one and the same social formation. Without this implicit methodical revision, Pradilla's thesis would be self-contradictory in that the expansion and increasing dominance of industrial production systems and the simultaneous expansion of artisan self-built forms are merely divergent appearances in the unitary process of capitalist reproduction in dependent social formations.

The second serious omission in Pradilla's framework concerns his assessment of class analysis and the reproduction of the labour-force in disregard of aspects of capital reproduction on a global scale. Orthodox perceptions of class formation, seen as modelled according to the classic materialist positions of capitalist development in a solitary national framework, have far-reaching consequences for the assessment of the housing problem and its solutions.

His approach implies that the established structures of articulation among the three forms of housing production cannot be more than a transitional or intermediate expression of capitalist development in time. No attempt is made to discuss the repercussions of international divisions of labour, contemporary global modes of capital accumulation, or the emergence of new capitalist relations of production that incorporate informal production - which all necessarily undermine conventional definitions of exploitation or even concepts of the 'working class' and 'class struggle'.

With respect to the formation of social classes, Pradilla contends that the potential or propensity of groups other than the proletariat to develop progressive forms of class struggle can be 'objectively' ruled out from the very start. With regards to self-help advocacy, only a class-conscious proletariat could grasp the ideological content of this policy - though the given material conditions for class struggle in Latin America may prevent this at the moment. By contrast, all other social fractions, including the reserve army of the unemployed and migrants from rural areas, are prone to ideological inhibition by self-help policies due to their own individualistic petty bourgeois social ideologies (cf. Pradilla, 1984, pp. 153-155).

We will question the validity of these arguments in the light of recent work on the international capitalist system. This body of research, elaborated in the next chapters, shows in essence that the current structures of the capitalist world system are not equatable with the spread of the capitalist mode of production to a world scale. Instead differentiation is required between: (1) the globalization of capitalist production and commodity exchanges

11

on the world market, and (2) the relationship between the capitalist centres and the periphery, which is structured by a specific hegemony within the internationally operating capitalist system. The latter would be appropriately defined as imperialistic. It relates to an economic totality in which the laws of motion are not based on the operations of 'regular' capitalist relations alone. Additionally, the imperialist system is structured by political subjugation on the part of capitalist centres and corresponding internal class relations in the periphery (cf. Amin, 1980, pp. 131-181). (3) With national peripheral economies being supplanted by supranationally operating capital, the economic laws concerning internal dynamics and self-regulating mechanisms would have to be reassessed in terms of their modification by supranational determination. As explained in the next chapters, these modifications concern factors such as the rate of profit, capital accumulation, the organic composition of capital, the productivity of labour, and the extent to which quantitative labour inputs in production are equated by values. Finally, modifications imposed by the internationalization of capital do not exclude conventional theories of labour-power reproduction (at national level). Pradilla's uncritical orientation to Marx on this issue is a crucial cornerstone of his analysis of heterogeneous housing production systems, class formation, and dependent capitalism.

4   Labour-power and concepts of social reproduction at national level

In materialistic theory the social reproduction of man is defined as the process by which the members of a given mode of production produce/reproduce their material conditions of existence. This encompasses the given means of production and the social relations of production in their relation to the specific form in which nature is appropriated by productive work. It is important to notice that for reasons specific to the logic of capitalist political economy, Marx elaborates the problem of social reproduction at a level of abstraction in which (1) the complete capitalist transformation of the relations of production is already presupposed, and (2) the general mode of the renewal process is analysed in terms of its simple and not expanded reproduction.

According to these suppositions found in Marx's systematic presentation of political economy, the concept of capitalist social reproduction refers to the mode and the conditions by which the prerequisites of production, including the labour-power commodity, are continuously provided for in time. This process is seen as necessarily governed by the same laws of value and motion as the production process itself. Hence, individual reproduction is presupposed as an integral part of this social process, because the private terms of consumption of necessary goods by workers merely lead to the renewal of the compulsion to reappear on the labour market as an object of exploitation for capital and as buyers of commodities. Inevitably therefore, the conditions determining labour-power reproduction were analysed by Marx in relation to the process of capital accumulation and not in relation to the reproductive needs of a specific labour-force.

Realizing that a concept based on simple reproduction cannot explain the phenomena of social reproduction which accompany the uneven dynamics of contemporary Third World social formations, let alone the disparities of capitalist expansion on a world scale, many writers, including Pradilla, have turned to Marx's analysis of the relationship between the general law of capitalist accumulation and the progressive creation of an industrial surplus population. This poses the questions (1) if on a scale of enlarged reproduction there are distinct and deterministic relations between the rate of capital accumulation, population growth, and the internal socioeconomic composition of the working population, and (2) whether the logical tendencies apparent in the historic development of European capitalism can be trajected to contemporary Third World capitalist development.

Marx's overall analysis of the social conditions for the process of extended capital reproduction seem to indicate relations of *correspondence* and *functionality* between the development of the economic base and the reproduction of the working class population. The mechanisms of this process are mediated by economic crisis and socio-political adaptations rather than by direct determinations by the laws of political economy: as the quantitative demand for labour is not determined by the absolute volume of capital but by its fraction operating as variable capital, the process of expanding accumulation will have an ambiguous rather than a linear effect on the conditions of labour-power reproduction - very much depending on the force and velocity of capitalist development:

1   At the level of individual capitalist enterprise, the intrinsic logic of expanded capital valorization is an increase in the organic composition of capital (the substitution of labour by machinery in the production process) striving to develop the productive forces of labour, providing a higher rate of profit is attainable. Following this line of reasoning, the surplus population is necessarily produced as a complementary and colligated part of the general tendency of the accumulation process.

2   But as the development of the productive forces and the rise in the organic composition of capital is a function of the rate of profit and not an end in itself, the tendency to produce a surplus population is counterpoised if the price of labour drops below its value due to its availability exceeding the demand by capital. Moreover, Marx indicates a general self-regulative tendency in the event that a disproportion between capital and exploitable labour occurs: if at a given stage of accumulation the demand for labour exceeds its availability, the price of labour will rise - the result being either a rise in the organic composition of capital, or, if this is not possible, a general depression in the rate of accumulation. In both cases the obvious effect will be a decline in the demand for labour

and a lowering of wages that triggers off anew the cyclical movement as rising rates of profit will stimulate the general rate of accumulation (Marx, *Capital,* Vol. I, p. 641).

3   Finally, quite a number of economic mechanisms are in operation at the level of social capital and the reproduction of capital-in-general relations that are decisive for both the magnitude of the surplus population and the social conditions of its reproduction. Affected are also wage rates, labour demand, mobility, and disposability of the labour force in general. These mechanisms include (i) the cheapening of the necessary commodities for labour reproduction and the introduction of new commodities to the 'basket' of necessary goods; (ii) the continuous expulsion and repulsion of labour by the expansion of capital into new sectoral and spatial areas of production; (iii) the impact of class struggle on the material conditions of reproduction (including the duration of the working day); (iv) large-scale migrations of parts of the surplus population in reaction to poor labour conditions, and finally (v) state interventions in the social reproduction of the labour-force directed at maintaining the interests of capital in general.

To sum up, Marx's solution to the surplus population problem, contradicting the Malthusian theory of absolute surplus population, could in practice be that of a 'relative' surplus population in which the latter acts as a reserve labour-force facilitating the movement of capital. Marx's familiar subdivisions of the surplus population into floating, latent and stagnant forms of the reserve army, therefore, tend to mark out the different terms of their *reintegration* into the production process rather than question their respective functionality for capitalist reproduction in accordance with the accumulation process (cf. Marx, *Capital,* Vol. I, chap. 23).

In contrast to this, Pradilla's reading of '*Capital*' on this issue is not only that Marx's solution may be generalized for contemporary Latin America. Additionally, the concept of relative surplus population is viewed as providing a fundamental aspect in the explanation of underdevelopment itself. Pradilla argues that the enormous size of the industrial reserve army in combination with the stagnation of industrial development has in most countries led to a situation of saturated labour markets, weak unionised labour movements, and subjection of the proletariat to severe political repression by the state. Hence, wage rates have been lowered far below the value of labour, and over-exploitation has become the predominant form in which capital reaps its profits (Pradilla, 1984, pp. 127-132).

In terms of social reproduction and housing provision, Pradilla sees the large mass of the industrial reserve army left outside the sphere of circulation of industrial or manufactured goods. With respect to housing, this part of the population must either resolve their needs in other sections of the market (subsidized state sector, slum tenements), or self-produce their houses. However, the 'marginalist' approach to this phenomenon is rejected on the ground that this section of the population may seem marginalized with respect to the dominant modes of production and consumption from which it is excluded; but due to their social function as labour reserve, they are in fact principal supports for the maintenance and functioning of a society that is economically based on exploitation and over-exploitation. The capitalist relations of production in their dependent form dominate society and govern the social forms of existence for the unemployed and sub-employed groups therein (Pradilla, 1976, p. 25).

Nobody could contest that those mechanisms of wage depression are in operation. But Pradilla's proposition that the specific conditions of labour-power reproduction (i.e. the excessive size of the surplus population) are characteristic for the functioning of the capitalist law of value in a dependent social formation, seems inappropriate to explain the totality of social reproduction. Even if we concede that the current situation is aggravated by capitalist recession, distorting a clear perception of salient features, the overt appearances of social reproduction under capitalist domination in the peripheries rather indicate conditions in which the self-regulative mechanisms assumed by Marx are no longer in operation - or at least not at the level of a single capitalist nation.

As a number of authors have pointed out, these features of social reproduction in Third World countries can lead to the very opposite conclusions. According to their assessment, the inability to determine a functional (i.e. self-regulative) connection between the accumulation process, the development of productive forces and the price of the labour commodity on a national basis would, instead, necessarily signify a breach in the functional relationship between the relative surplus population and the capitalist accumulation process. Accordingly, this *breach* and not functionality is seen to condition the forms of existence for these population groups in capitalist Third World countries. The alternative explanation given by this approach for the forms of social reproduction is that only a minority of the population are actually subjected to proper capitalist relations of production, whereas the majority are to some extent 'resisting' complete subjugation by maintaining traditional modes of production (cf. Senghaas-Knobloch, 1979, pp. 224-225).

But the matter at hand should not be precipitately polarized into unitary vs. dualistic perspectives. The global spread of capitalism has penetrated and transformed even the remotest parts of the world. What are sometimes referred to as traditional modes of production mostly prove to be folkloric illusions. In reality they only exist as vestigial and undermined forms of production surviving by adapting to the capitalist social and economic environment. Consequently, any notion of a breach between capitalist and non-capitalist reproduction can, ultimately, only refer to functional disparities within the same entity. But contrary to Pradilla's assumption, Marx's labour-power theory fails to explain these functional breaches or disparities. As shown, Marx's concept was *integrative*: a reciprocal system of capital valorization and labour-power reproduction precluding excessive segments of the workforce becoming absolute surplus population. By contrast, in peripheral capitalism it is precisely the non-correspondence of the terms of capitalist production based on wage-labour relations and the contemporary forms of social reproduction that creates this system of excessive

15

lowering of labour-power costs for certain segments of the labour-force (such as the informal sector). All this cannot be deduced from the original theoretical framework proposed by Marx.

However, my conclusion is not that Marx's theory of labour-power reproduction is wrong. It was based on the premises of auto-centred, nationally developing capitalism. Obviously these premises have changed in peripheral capitalism. To arrive at a consistent theory of social reproduction at national level, the concept would need reformulating to incorporate the impacts of the internationalization of capitalism. As a result, new international divisions of labour are created interrelating the law of value to the global movements and operations of capital.

5   The internationalization of labour-power reproduction and heterogeneous labour in the Third World

The recent discussion on the world systems theory has tried to overcome the deadlock of nationally-based approaches by postulating that international capitalist development now signifies the wide and irreversible supersession of geographical barriers and national markets in a 'functionally unitary global economy' (Walton, 1985, p. 4). Spurred by economic crisis in the capitalist centres, a 'new international division of labour' is appearing. It reflects the new strategy of capital to reallocate and reorganize international production in terms of a worldwide sourcing for cheapest labour at a comparable level of work productivity (Fröbel/Heinrichs/Kreye, 1986, p. 101). Again some doubts remain as to whether this line of reasoning goes to the heart of unequal capitalist development on a world scale. A. G. Frank, for example, queries if this type of analysis does not tend to overestimate the significance of its empirical data, thereby mistaking short-term appearances of capitalist crisis and recession for a fundamentally new structure of capitalist development (Frank, 1980, p. XV).

Burgess has drawn attention to some of the more obvious analytical deficiencies of this concept in comprehensively explaining the determinants of the housing problem (Burgess, 1987). In his critique he has pointed out that the international labour-power reproduction theory exclusively regards housing as a 'necessary good' that 'directly or indirectly enters into the production of all other commodities' (Molina, 1976, p. 4). As Burgess argues, this type of abstraction is important for understanding the part housing provision plays in determining wage differentials between capitalist core countries and the periphery. However, it cannot provide more than a partial explanation as it neglects two other sides: housing is also a 'fixed good' attached to a piece of land that is a scarce commodity not producible at will, and it is also a 'commodity' that is subjected to the given conditions of accession to products within the commodity circulation. Burgess concludes:

> The lack of attention paid to the role of housing as a fixed good and as a commodity leads to an underestimation of the significance of national structures and their

16

contradictions for the nature and scale of housing and settlement problems and policies. In other words the reproduction of labour power theory tends to establish direct lines of determination between international structures and local phenomena whereas in fact this is more likely to be a more complex and highly mediated process (Burgess, 1987, p. 131).

Nonetheless, as long as the theoretical issues are not confused, we consider the world systems theory a perfectly valid approach to the analysis of accumulation and to understanding the operation of the capitalist law of value in its contemporary form. Since the unity of the commodity, capital, and labour markets, which constitutes the framework for the law of value, is no longer restricted to one capitalist nation as at the time Marx first analysed the problem, we can agree with Amin who concludes that:

> The globalization of the productive process implies the globalization of the space within which the law of value operates. The theory of imperialism must therefore be constructed on the infrastructural basis of the theory of value operating on a world scale. In these conditions, the law of value must account for the different levels in the selling price of labour in the different segments of the imperialist system (Amin, 1980, p. 226).

The important emphasis put forward in this quotation is the necessity to differentiate between the concepts of imperialism and that of the capitalist mode of production. As Amin emphasizes, to analyse the imperialist system is to analyse a system of social formations and not the capitalist mode extended to the world. The current practice of international capital of exporting parts of its commodity production to the periphery reflects the conditions that (1) products are increasingly being turned into world commodities with only one price; (2) capital is mobile on a world scale in search of an average rate of profit, but (3) labour is immobile with different levels of remuneration at the centre and the periphery (Amin, 1978, p. 60).

It has not always been realized that the internationalization and globalization of capital have considerable modifying implications for the theory of labour-power reproduction and the related concept of 'working class' in the class analysis of Third World countries. The problem arises from the specific character of labour-power as a commodity the price of which is fixed by a dual mechanism: a) in relation to national average costs of reproduction and b) in relation to social aggregate levels of productivity. With dependent development and internationalization of capitalism, the unity and interrelation between both mechanisms assumed by theory have probably never existed in a Third World country. Due to its submission to the capitalist centre and productivity deficits compared to First World production, the labour process in Third World countries has been relieved of its function of determining the valorization of its products.[9] The unity of productivity and labour prices

17

has now become an exclusive operation of international circulation, setting the price determination of Third World labour in accordance with the uneven relationship between centre and periphery. Accordingly, the reassessment of the theory on labour-power reproduction then becomes closely associated with the rise of heterogeneous labour markets and the determination of their function for global capitalist accumulation.

In general, the specific character of the labour-power commodity is determined by its remuneration, not according to its productive potentials to create values for capital but by the social costs of its reproduction in a specific national framework. In the first instance this gives rise to arbitrary fixing of wage levels in dependence on class struggle between capital and labour and the formation of labour as an organized class. This, obviously, is the first possible source of heterogeneous labour. Bowles and Gintis (1977) have suggested that unequal rates of labour exploitation are conditioned by the heterogeneity in the formation of the labour force.

> Divisions within the working class allow the capitalist to bargain separately with each group of workers. Any individual capitalist, or the entire class, may combine with one group of workers against another. The resulting disunity of the workforce may allow the capitalist to impose lower wages or more unfavourable working conditions upon the workforce as a whole, while surrendering only part of the increased profits to the colluding workers. To this end the capitalist will, should the occasion warrant, draw on whatever racist, sexist, nationalist, credentialist or whatever divisive sentiments are found, or can be created, in a working class culture. The outcome of a successful manoeuvre of this type is a fragmented work force, higher profits and unequal rates of exploitation among labour segments (Bowles/Gintis, 1977, p. 178).

But the dissociation of wage levels from the levels of productivity is conditioned by a second economic factor requiring an objective interrelation between wages and productivity. With reference to the closed, auto-centred capitalist model, profits can only be realized to the extent that the consumptive capacities of the labour-force approximate the productive capacities of capitalist enterprises. Moreover, for reasons of dynamic capitalist growth, it is required that labour returns should not be heterogeneous between different branches of production, that is, not directly linked to their specific productivity. Therefore the general movement of capital and the reproduction of social capital relations will only be facilitated if the uneven development in the productive forces between different branches of production is compensated by a national average value of labour-power. Obviously these premises are not applicable for economies that have been developing subordinated to the needs of central capitalism and are now assigned specific functions according to global divisions of labour. As development theory has pointed out for Third World economies, it is precisely the internal lack of backward linkages between wage-labour remuneration, productivity levels, and capital accumulation that explains the structural difference between dynamic capitalist development in the centre and stagnation in the economically fragmented capitalist periphery (cf. Janvry/Garramón, 1977; Portes/Walton, 1981, p. 68).

Thus, heterogeneous labour is created by the sectoral disarticulation of peripheral capitalism and the heterogeneity of productive forces deployed in line with global determinations of the law of value. While arbitrary wage determining mechanisms, using the disunity of the labour-force, may act upon these structural conditions, they do not generate or explain them. Third World wages can be pressed down to minimum levels of sustenance because dependent economies do not require the national equilibrium between production and circulation - conditions that are resolved at the level of globally operating capitalism.

This brings the discussion back to its starting point: the central proposition of Pradilla that self-help housing, as part of labour-power reproduction, is instrumental in lowering wage levels. But given that prices and values are determined internationally and not by national terms of production, Marx's theory on labour-power reproduction, on which Pradilla has extensively based his conclusions, could only partially apply to peripheral capitalism. While it is undeniable that the self-provision of housing lowers the bargaining power of the workers and that state housing programmes tend to enhance the segmentation of the workforce, Pradilla fails to assess the problem of heterogeneous housing and labour markets in relation to the dimension of structural dependency indicated. His identification of the enormous size of the industrial reserve army and the lack of organized class struggle as the main sources of low wage levels, thus, confuses cause and effect. It mistakes the national process of wage arbitration for the actual price allocating mechanism for labour-power. While national conditions contribute relatively to the lowering of wages below the value of labour, low wage floors are posited in absolute terms by the structural conditions given for the national reproduction of labour under international dominance.

This leads to the first conclusion that even for strong unionised movement, Pradilla's political conviction to generally reject self-help housing and to instead demand appropriate housing as part of the price for labour-power would appear to overestimate the economic and political autonomy of national employers. At best, union demands for appropriate housing provision could be a valid strategy for *formal sector employees* where arbitrary wage levels are indeed fixed below the price for work performed at a productivity level comparable to First World standards. The second conclusion would be that Pradilla's political statement towards housing provision is even more doubtful with respect to informal sector workers. As shown, Marx's theory on labour-power reproduction, on which Pradilla bases his class analysis, in fact makes no reference to the formation of heterogeneous labour. Consequently, heterogeneous production forms are necessarily taken by Pradilla to be 'articulations' between pre-capitalist and capitalist modes: non-industrial and non-manufactured forms of housing production and provision are seen as intermediate stages in the transformation of pre-capitalist forms of production to the fully developed capitalist mode of production. It is probably no

19

coincidence that Pradilla made no explicit reference to the informal sector concept. This dismissal of aspects concerning the possible internal heterogeneity of production in peripheral capitalism allows to align all workers with an orthodoxly defined working class. According to these questionable class distinctions, the particular political struggle of informal sector workers becomes unidirectional with that of wage labourers. Thus, even under the particular conditions of reproduction in the informal sector, self-help housing advocacy is, once more, deemed an illegitimate policy.

In conclusion, the issue of self-help housing in the informal sector can only be discussed appropriately by a careful assessment of the role heterogeneous production systems perform for global capitalist accumulation. The frame of reference would necessarily have to supersede orthodox deductions from the capitalist mode of production and include the following:

1   A concept of exchange between the modes of production or different segments of capitalism involved differentiating between: a) direct forms of capitalist penetration of non-capitalist modes in which the production or labour process becomes directly linked to the process of capitalist accumulation with exchange taking place under commensurable terms of valuation and b) indirect forms in which capitalist penetration takes place by way of the commodity circulation, i.e. by uneven exchange of money and commodities but without interventions into the mode of simple production itself.

2   A concrete analysis of the ways by which exploitation and surplus appropriation take place by non-capitalist classes that are interrelated to the capitalist system. Here differentiation is necessary between the form of surplus product and the mode of exploitation in order to discriminate the specific mechanisms by which non-capitalist produced surpluses are channelled into commodity markets and are transformed into values and profits for capitalist accumulation.

3   An analysis of the political, economic, and ideological state functions in dependent social formations that are no longer assessable according to the classical fundamentals of the Marxist approach. These were elaborated with reference to a social class formation determinately structured by contradictions and struggle between two national classes (bourgeoisie and proletariat) and the provision of infrastructural and material conditions of reproduction for a homogeneous mode of production. The articulation of relations of power and legal ownership between the various national exploiting classes, their extensions to international class alliances and the indebtedness of Third World states are only some of the factors that impose contradictory conditions and limits to the postulated general functioning of national state apparatus in the periphery.[10] A comprehensive discussion of the role of the peripheral state is beyond the scope of this book as it represents an extensive discussion in its own right. However, selected issues

pertaining to labour-power reproduction and class-biased housing provision will be discussed in a later chapter on urban planning and in the case study of housing provision in Zambia where special reference will be made to the case of the African state.

As is apparent, the comprehension of heterogeneous production systems also raises problems concerning the general appropriateness of Marx's theory to analyse the contemporary global capitalist system. Confusions of levels of abstraction and the invariant use of Marx's different conceptual levels (historical materialism, mode of production, political economy, capitalist mode of production, social formation, etc.) pose the question which of these strands is most suited to address the developmental problem in its contemporary complexity. Both these issues, heterogeneous (or informal sector) production and the methodological complications of Marx's theory, will be the main subjects of the next chapters.

Notes

1   Compare Stavenhagen (1969); Cordova (1973); Frank (1969).
2   cf. Hart (1973); Mangin (1967); Turner (1968).
3   See Castells (1983) for a self-critical assessment of his earlier position.
4   Comparing First and Third World forms of self-help, Harms has suggested distinguishing four forms: i) self-help based on individual family management of limited resources and time budgets to achieve house-ownership and housing quality; ii) self-help housing as a form of collective group action and/or innovative resistance the political aims of which go beyond housing, i.e. are parts of social urban movements, for instance against demolitions, removals or technocratic planning; iii) self-help housing as a form of creative and self-determined work outside the formal structures of industrial society; iv) self-help as a form of societal solidarity work in collectively preserving, maintaining or rebuilding environmentally or socially valuable buildings that would otherwise be destroyed or fall into disuse (Harms, 1989).
5   The historical perspectives and policies of self-help housing in capitalist core countries, e.g. USA and Germany, are discussed in Harms (1982, pp. 17-53).
6   Examples of contemporary European, First World cases of semi-legal self-help housing are to be found in Rome, Naples, Barcelona and Lisbon.
7   Similar sectoral models are proposed by Drakakis-Smith, 1981 and Lea, 1979.
8   In an important distinction, Pradilla refers to the dominant form in terms of quantitative importance in relation to the totality of activities, whereas the determinant position is ascribed to the dynamic pole in society determining the structure of articulation and subjugation (see Pradilla 1979, pp. 9-10).

9   The economic and political mechanisms involved in this process are discussed in more detail in chap. III.2.

10 cf. Elsenhans, H., *Abhängiger Kapitalismus oder bürokratische Entwicklungsgesellschaft. Versuch über den Staat in der Dritten Welt*, Frankfurt 1981; Evers, T., *Bürgerliche Herrschaft in der Dritten Welt*, Frankfurt/M. 1977; Singer, P., 'Capital and the National State' in Portes/Walton (eds.), *Capital and Labour in the Urbanized World*, London 1985; Castells, M., *City, Class and Power*, London 1979; Slater, D., 'Territorial Power and the Peripheral State: The Issue of Decentralisation', *Development and Change*, Vol. 20, 1989; Tetzlaff, R., 'The Social Basis of Political Rule in Africa: Problems of Legitimacy and Prospects for Democracy', in Meyns/Nabudere (eds.), *Democracy and the One-Party State in Africa*, Hamburg 1989.

II Housing, subsistence and simple commodity production in theories of dependent urban reproduction

1 The political economy of the informal sector

The emergence of the 'informal sector' concept in the early 1970s reflects the fundamental crisis of developmental theory and policies after the second international decade of development. In the late 1960s the state of affairs was characterized by:

- an obviously growing conceptual inability of the dualist perception (neatly segregated into traditional and modern production sectors) to grasp the dynamics and determinants of social reality, specifically with reference to the economically and socially deteriorating situation in most Third World cities;

- a rather embarrassing failure of statistical approaches and methods, due to their First World methodological bias, to even produce a correct empirical quantification of the developmental achievement that was taking place outside the modern sector, the most apparent case in point being the assessment of 'traditional' sector workers as 'un- or underemployed'; and finally,

- the widely realized ineffectiveness of Third World development programmes such as the World Bank's 'accelerated growth' model. According to this, investment priorities on the industrial sector were supposed to expand employment in the wage-earning sector, thereby both absorbing underutilised labour, migrating from the traditional sector, as well as gradually redistributing income and capital into the more 'backward' segments of the economy ('trickle down' effect).

Sponsored by the ILO and the World Bank, the discussion on the 'informal sector' provided the conceptual backbone to a major attempt on the part of international development

23

agencies to comprehensively reassess the situation in Third World countries and to formulate new development policies. In a series of ILO expert missions, e.g. to Columbia (1970), Sri Lanka (1971), Kenya (1973), and in a number of related city studies (Abidjan, Calcutta, São Paulo), the new paradigm of the urban developmental problem gradually took shape. No longer as a problem of unemployment but as one of employment of the 'working poor' in the informal sector.[1]

The findings of these various ILO missions, including their attempts to classify the nature of the 'informal sector' and to determine its importance for national economies, are well covered in concise form, for example by Sethuraman (1976), Weeks (1975), Mazumdar (1975) or - with additional critique - by Senghaas-Knobloch (1979), Moser (1978), and Portes/Walton (1981). Therefore, it seems justifiable to direct our debate to some of the unresolved conceptual problems.

As many critics have already pointed out, as a new line of approach the informal sector does not really overcome the old deficiencies of dualism. In principle, the economic system is still conceived in terms of a dichotomous structure (see Moser, 1978, p. 1052). In whatever terminology, the attempts to define the nature of the informal/formal sector interrelationship have not gone beyond a mixture of conceptual and descriptive terms. The proposed features of the informal sector (seen as low level of productivity, low wage levels, small-scale enterprises, economic activities unprotected by state and law, etc.) all only become arbitrarily definable in relation to their concrete given opposites in the formal sector. Or, to put it more bluntly, 'informality' is defined as a residual vis-à-vis all those economic appearances that do not fit into the pattern of formal activities.

The 'informal sector' approach also tends to completely disregard different terms of integration into the capitalist mode of production, for instance whenever the concept is indiscriminately applied to rural and urban contexts alike. Surprisingly, many observers have failed to notice the fundamental contrast the case of rural transformation represents to the analysis of capitalist subjugation: even in industrialized Europe, agrarian development has predominantly taken place by integration of simple commodity production via market mechanisms and not by direct penetration and organization of the production process by industrial capital (cf. Rey, 1973; Vergopoulos, 1974).

This severely hampers all attempts to define anything like an 'in general', structural significance of the informal sector in developing countries. Moreover, conceptual deficiencies cannot but affect the reliability of possible policy recommendations: so far, advocates of the informal sector approach have not been able to decide whether the general relationship between the formal and the informal sector is to be conceived as exploitative or benign. In practice the propensity to promote the informal sector or not seems to depend on the concrete available country-specific data, rather than on reliably established policy criteria. As a concept, the informal sector remains strongly imbued with concrete specific and empirical phenomena. For example, this is most apparent in the way informal theory formulations are

24

proposed selectively for each of the three Third World continents while very little cross-continental, comparative discussion is taking place. In its present form, therefore, it seems questionable if this line of approach really represents a true analytical concept with more than descriptive properties.

As Moser quite rightly states, the unsatisfactory point in the informal sector approach is that the empirically described multitude of linkages and dependent relationships between both sectors are analysed in terms of a two-sector division of the economy whereas a continuum would be the more appropriate model. The more pertinent focus for economic analysis should lie on the 'relationship between the different elements of the ensemble' rather than on the definition of the two sectors (Moser, 1978, p. 1055).

The framework Moser proposes as an alternative is that of petty commodity production. In contrast to the capitalist form of commodity production based on social divisions of labour, this concept refers to production based on work of private, self-determined character, either as self-employment, or by sale of excess use-value products as commodities. Additionally, petty commodity production is viewed by Moser as a transitional or intermediary form that may only exist in necessary articulation with the socially dominant mode or modes of production.[2] Thus, petty commodity production is not conceived as a 'quasi' mode of production equipped with logically necessary tendencies of development and self-reproductive properties. Instead instability in form and dynamics is to be expected following the nature of its interaction with the determinant mode at the level of productive forces and relations of production given for its existence (for a more explicit discussion see Moser, 1978, pp. 1055-1062).

Although some cases exist that have used this approach for comprehensive analysis (cf. Gerry's 1974 study on urban petty commodity production in Dakar), the proposed framework has for various reasons failed to make an impact on informal sector studies. In the first place, as Portes/Walton have noted, the classic definition of petty commodity production does not encompass the totality of informal sector operations. Informal sector households will, besides petty commodity production, also base their income on a variety of strategies for gaining access to means of consumption including subsistence production, rents (from land and housing), transfer payments (gifts, alms and free subsidies), and wages (Portes/Walton, 1981, p. 86).

Second, the underlying notion of petty commodity production as a transitional or intermediary form of production seems to deprive the concept of a vital necessary characteristic: i.e. it would have to be shown as a systematically reproduced feature of the contemporary process of capital accumulation in the periphery. Simply perceived as a pre-capitalist residual, 'petty commodity production' tends to replicate the problems criticized in the informal sector concept. Contrary to Moser's claim of providing a base for the analysis of a continuum of interdependencies, the assumed structural interdependencies tend to be reduced to simple relations of subordination, constraint, and transformation vis-à-vis the prevailing interests of industrial capital, the state, and the world market.

Although the contribution of petty commodity production to explaining the dynamics of the peripheral accumulation process is limited, it would display other striking merits if conceived as a concept in explaining how the productive workers are integrated into the capitalist commodification process under social conditions of selective and incomplete proletarianization and commodification. Trapped in the notion of deducting all relevant categories from developed capitalism (the result being always subordination), the debate on petty commodity production has failed to realize that the concept provides an important inductive aspect to the proliferation of Third World capitalist. From this perspective petty commodity production becomes a powerful conceptual tool in explaining the social and economic forces underpinning the basic logic of urban domestic reproduction in peripheral capitalism, which are only partially governed by capitalist principles of valuation of labour-power or products. The basic orientation of the individual domestic units towards simple commodity forms of reproduction performs vital functions for peripheral capitalist reproduction. (1) For the mass of workers outside the formal sector, a certain degree of participation in commodity circulation appears as a compulsory condition for urban sustenance, thereby integrating the productive workers into the capitalist labour-force and commodity circulation. (2) In the specific economic terms of the articulation of capitalism with simple commodity production, however, the valorization of the labour-process becomes related to individually determined minimal levels of sustenance and not to social prices of the labour commodity. This process allows capitalism to appropriate unpaid portions of labour through the operations of the informal sector. (3) Finally, the reproduction of labour-power and the production of market commodities dissociated from capitalist cost and price structures concerning wage, profit, and rent becomes a necessary economic component for the utilization of Third World labour and commodity markets under internationally defined terms of capital valorization.

The further elaboration of this line of approach in the next chapters will necessarily shed new light on the housing and self-help problematic, as illegal and squatter settlements overwhelmingly house those who work in the informal sector. In a concept in which the existence of reproductive subunits with defined relations with the dominant mode of production is acknowledged as part of the entire dynamics of development, housing issues would necessarily attain multifunctional character for informal sector workers and petty commodity producers:

(1) a potential site for a production process or store room (i.e. a means of production), (2) a means of access to land, enabling subsistence production of crops and small livestock, (3) a means of spatial unification of the extended family household working as a reproductive unit but often split up in town in the process of its rural-urban

26

migration and in the search for housing, (4) a means of establishing wider network relations to members of the local community, thereby raising the social productive forces of the group for its survival, (5) a means of access to commodity circulation and monetary income by sale or rent of a self-produced house or plot, and (6) access to work in petty commodity production, informal trade or services, the opportunity for which - contrary to the conventional notion of 'easy entry' - is usually quite restricted by locational aspects, such as local informal and personal communication connections or the physical and social proximity to clients and customers.

These proposals raise the question how far the notion of a simple commodity production, reconceived as structural component of contemporary capital accumulation in the periphery, is still conforming with the theory of capitalism.

In their related writings on this issue Marx, Lenin, and Kautsky have considered petty commodity production as a mere transitional form in the expansion of industrial capitalism. Moreover, in one of his rare explicit comments on the subject, Marx seems to spell out something like a necessary structure in the process of capitalist development and in the decomposition of petty commodity relations:

> Wherever it takes root capitalist production destroys all forms of commodity production which are based either on the self-employment of producers, or merely on the sale of excess product as commodities ... Capitalist production first makes the production of commodities general and then, by degrees, transforms all commodity production into capitalist production (Marx, *Capital,* Vol. 1, as quoted by Moser, 1978, p. 1057).

Considering these classical assessments of petty commodity production, some provisos must be made concerning the historical situation when they were analysed by Marx. First, seen in global terms, capitalism itself has deviated considerably from the originally anticipated straightforward course of development that would have, indeed, made petty commodity production an obsolete phenomenon. Second, the specific forms of capitalist territorial formation and the rural-urban relationship in Third World countries have introduced altogether new socioeconomic facets, only in part directly determinable by the logic of capitalism. Contemporary capitalist formation in the periphery has become a complex process in which global, national, and local aspects form an overlapping structure. In particular it is necessary to revise the framework of materialist theory in order to accommodate new forms of societal appearance beyond orthodox preconceptions and to address the problem of heterogeneous production systems.

International terms of capital valorization and accumulation do not necessarily require the dissolution of simple forms of commodity production as anticipated by Marx. While changing global valorization and regional developments may give rise to New Industrializing

Countries (NICs), most of the Third World nations continue to extensively base their accumulation on simple commodity forms. Consequently, contemporary petty commodity production cannot be considered a vestigial, pre-capitalist mode designated to become dissolved. Instead it has become an integral part of the system enabling pertinent forms of exploitation and value transfers.

In its historical form, petty commodity production referred to an inter-systemic relation between two opposing production forms and not to relations of reciprocal causality within a social totality.[3] As political economy deals with the laws of motion (i.e. intra-systemic relations) regulating the movements of capitalism as an epoch in history, petty commodity production, as referred to by Marx and others as a historical form, has no part in this, simply due to its socially undetermined and unsystematic form of production and coincidental terms of exchange (Marx, *Grundrisse*, p. 179). Consequently, the modern case of petty commodity production in the manner presented by Moser and others tends to give rise to unjustified generalizations and faulty parallels.[4] In reality there is little resemblance to the case analysed by Marx. Instead it would be necessary to reconstruct the category of petty commodity production in terms of a 'determinate form', i.e. its incorporation as a logical, intra-systemic part in the dialectical development of contemporary capitalist production and commodity circulation. In the following sections we will amplify this line of approach, proposing a peripheral capitalist form of petty commodity production as a structural, intra-systemic feature of contemporary capitalist relations of production.

2 Modes of production and political economy in the analysis of dependent social formations

As is probably well known, Marx himself, under the immediate impression of triumphant British capitalism, was firmly convinced that a global expansion of capitalism was inevitable alone by virtue of its very nature. In the words of the Communist Manifesto:

> The bourgeoisie cannot exist without constantly revolutionizing the instruments of production and thereby the social relations of production, and with them the whole relations of society ... The bourgeoisie ... draws all, even the most barbaric nations into civilization. It compels all nations, on pain of extinction, to adopt the bourgeois mode of production.

In other words, the distinct intrinsic notion assumed by Marx for the capitalist mode of production was its tendency of expanded auto-development according to the categorical genetic and dynamic properties postulated in '*Capital*'. The obvious divergence between the reality of Third World capitalist development and Marx's scientific prophecy has been

28

the source of considerable disputes over consequences for an appropriate methodological approach. Levels of abstraction are a focal point in this discussion. The object of analysis in '*Capital*' is, in Marx's own words, an investigation of its general form. It necessarily presupposes that the real relations correspond to their categorical expressions, which is only another way of saying that real relations are only accounted for to the extent they represent their own generalizable image or type (cf. Marx, *Capital*, Vol. I, p. 152). By abstracting, Marx also disregarded all those concrete aspects that more or less 'coincidentally and insignificantly' determine the real historic development of the mode (world market, cycles of production, politics, state, crisis, etc.). Thus, Marx's rendition of capitalism is predetermined as 'internal organization of capitalism in its ideal general or average form' (ibid.).

The 'exegetical' problems of Marx's concept of political economy become paramount when dealing with undeveloped capitalist formations subjected to developmental dynamics far removed from the postulated model conditions. Aiden Foster-Carter, in his discussion of various approaches to the analysis of the Third World, presented something of a programmatic outline of necessary conceptual elements and issues related (1) to the problem of transition to capitalism and (2) to the manner in which dependent social formations become inserted into the wider system of capitalist world economy. According to this,

> ... capitalism (in general, in the abstract) must be distinguished as a level of analysis from its concretizations, plural, as capitalisms (e.g. national and rival); that capitalism(s) should be seen as not merely processual and developmental, but also relational and interactional; and above all that there was and is a crucial distinction between where capitalism arose internally within a social formation (typically analysed by Marx as the 'normal case', i.e. the European model), and where it was imposed from outside (the colonial and hence the Third World case, hitherto inadequately theorized by Marxists (Foster-Carter, 1978, p. 66).

I am inclined to agree with T. Evers that the disputes between theorists representing the world systems approach and those representing the dependencia model largely reflect a disunity over the question of appropriate level of abstraction (Evers, 1977, p. 49). Whereas the former accentuate the general conformity of global capitalism, the latter make reference to the differences in particular. Under this premise it can be accepted that different theoretical approaches to Third World analysis do not necessarily mutually disqualify each other. Their potential degree of complementariness is, however, conditioned by an appropriate assessment of levels of abstraction and procedures of deduction involved.

For our own framework on development theory we will extend these arguments, proposing a general hierarchy of abstraction and deduction/induction in the logical reconstruction of Third World capitalism. For analysis this implies that when moving down the hierarchy towards the more concrete and historic specific, the details added by more specific concepts are in each case implicitly conditioned by the more abstract or general anterior level of comprehension.

Thus, in delineating *Third World formations*, the primary aspect of analysis would be directed to the internal variance in the development of the capitalist mode of production itself. As not even metropolitan capitalism is homogeneous, deviations from the general form would first have to be explained within the framework of incomplete and uneven formation of capitalist relations of production with respect to its sectoral and territorial formation.

At the level of the *historic specific*, imperialism and the history of colonialism have introduced the element of extra-economical force by grafting specific production systems onto subordinated countries oriented to the needs of the core economies. At the same time developments related to the incipient expansion of capitalism are diverted by political means (i.e. the containment of the wage-labour system, limitations on indigenous commodity production, control of class formation, racist dual systems of legislation, etc.).

The contemporary *capitalist world system* approach indicates both the generalizations of capitalism to a global scale and the terms of dominance and subordination imposed in meeting the requirements of capital accumulation and valorization. This includes the growing impact of supranational institutions towards controlling the unimpeded circulation of world market commodities and the related mechanisms of reinforcing uneven international divisions of labour between nations of the capitalist core and periphery.

Finally, dependencia and peripheral capitalism comprehend the most concrete and specific *totality of Third World capitalism*. Due to its specific history and defective capitalist genesis - reinforced and reproduced by the imperatives of world market dependency - internal structural heterogeneity now figures as a functional aspect of Third World social formations (Cordova, 1973). Uneven and heterogeneous development of capitalism is related to the different and contradicting requirements of the economy imposed by: (1) the integration of developed capitalist enclaves into the world-market, and (2) the maintenance and/or creation of a multitude of simple production forms aligned to serving the reproduction of the dominant capitalist sector under the specific terms of capital accumulation in the periphery.

Working towards a framework for the analysis of Third World urbanization, we will first analyse the general form of peripheral capitalism, showing its historical constituents, the process of gradual integration into world market mechanisms and the model of its internal economic reproduction. Although this indicates the principal contradictions and dependencies of the peripheral growth model, it does not, however, explain the genesis of the specific Third World urbanization itself. Additionally, spatial concepts are required that add their own specific contradictions to the process of urban formation. Thus, in a second step, after discussing concepts of urbanization, a more detailed reconstruction of the process of uneven and incomplete capitalist territorial formation of peripheral capitalism will indicate the nature of specific urban contradictions arising from the urban form itself.

30

3   The emergence of peripheral capitalism in the world system

Colonial conquest and subjection of peripheries to imperialist relations are fundamental to the explanation of how dependent capitalism was continuously reproduced in the Third World. But at the same time we must acknowledge that for contemporary analysis an important change in paradigm has occurred. Capitalist dominance, formally externally enforced in dependent social formations by 'extra-economic means', is today established as '... dominance directly within them; the metropolitan mode of production reproduces itself, in a specific form, within the dominated and dependent formations themselves' (Poulantzas, 1975, p. 46).

Within this form, transition to capitalism has taken a completely different character than theoretically anticipated: instead of homology between the agricultural and the industrial production sectors and homology between the industrial departments producing consumer goods and capital goods, Third World economies are distorted in three ways.

1   Most essentially, after an initial decomposition of indigenous artisan production by merchant capital, the peripheries were fully integrated into the capitalist world economy at a point in history when central capital had already attained an advanced level of productive forces. Promoted by foreign investment seeking higher rates of profit and sourcing for cheap raw materials for industrial expansion, the peripheries were forced to specialize in production sectors offering profitable conditions for export production. Thus, exotic agriculture and mining became the fulcrums of dependent economies. With the higher level of productivity in capitalist centres, the continuous provision with cheap labour became a precondition for the valorization and expanded reproduction of invested capital in the peripheral export production sector. These conditions were supported by rural exploiting classes and the emerging comprador bourgeoisie by all available economic and extra-economic means. By these mechanisms, export-oriented production is inextricably bound into terms of unequal valuation of labour. To the extent that productive forces develop in the centres, peripheral export production as part of the worldwide accumulation process becomes dependent on social conditions that maintain unequal levels of income. For capital the

> ... products exported by the periphery are attractive to the extent to which the gap between the returns to labour is greater than the gap in productivity. ... the principle articulation that characterizes the accumulation process in the centre - which is translated by the existence of an objective relation between the returns to labour and the development of the productive forces - completely disappears. The returns to labour

in the export sector will be as low as the economic, social and political conditions allow (Amin, 1980, p. 134).

2   Both the low levels of labour remuneration and the appropriation of surplus by central capital limit and bias the growth of the internal market in the periphery. Wherever export production creates a contained internal commodity market, it is also subjected to a process of polarization: the low level of income from wage-labour restricts the growth potential of a mass consumer market whereas the social stratum allied with international capital creates a demand for luxury goods. Luxury demand, initially satisfied by direct imports, was later to become the predominant object of import-substituting industrialization.

3   In the model of capitalism elaborated by Marx, the determining relation of development is that of an equilibrium between the departments of the economy producing mass consumer goods and capital goods. Accordingly production, distribution, and consumption are developed as corresponding intra-systemic relations, reciprocally interlaced by the operations of the capitalist law of value. The dynamics of growth are based on backward linkages between the various productive elements. Although the principal motive for development of the productive forces will be the private appropriation of additional surplus values (i.e. extra-profit) by individual enterprises, any change effected in the productive forces becomes part of the general social terms of capital valorization once the technological innovation spreads and becomes the new average standard for production. In this case any gain in productivity will not only effect the level of capitalist reinvestment in the capital goods sector. It will also influence the consumer goods sector and wage rates as a necessary condition for the promotion of solvent demand for the additionally produced consumer goods. Hence, the principal intrinsic property of this system may be determined as 'auto-centred'. In contrast to all this, the contemporary growth model of peripheral social formations, following Amin, is rather determined by a structural link between (1) the primary sector (mining and agriculture) oriented to exportation and (2) the luxury consumption of the middle and upper classes. The impact on the economy is twofold. As part of the surplus is externalized by investment in imported capital goods, no adequate capital-goods sector can develop, and as demand promotes an industrialization of luxury-goods production at standards comparable to those of the centre, this type of production will absorb the bulk of available capital and skilled labour, leading to neglect of the mass consumer products (cf. Amin, 1980, p. 137). Since capitalism is not attracted to the mass consumer sector, productivity in the agricultural sectors - not related to export production - remains stagnant. Accordingly, impoverishment of rural population, mass migration to the cities, hypertrophic urban growth, and urban unemployment are all reflections of growing

32

inter-sectoral disparities within the distorted peripheral growth model. True, to some extent, these phenomena were also characteristic of certain historic stages in the formation of today's central capitalism. However, we must look beyond superficial resemblance and come to an adequate understanding of the completely different economic framework given for development of peripheral capitalism, where

> ... the weight of the unemployment keeps the returns to labour at a relatively rigid minimum and blocks both the export and the luxury production sector. Wages are not at once a cost and an income that creates a demand essential to the model but are only a cost, with demand originating from outside or from the income of privileged social groups (Amin, 1980, p. 138).

All these distinctions discern a fundamental difference in the manner in which the general theoretical framework of the capitalist system may be applied to the analysis of peripheral capitalism. The dominance of the international system is not equatable with the expansion of the capitalist mode of production. Instead, capitalist conquest and subordination of peripheral social formations create reproductive conditions of a different systematic order. They phenotypically create an internal economic structure characterized by modified capital-capital and capital-labour relations, imperfect competition, distorted value-price proportionalities, and constraints on capital and labour mobility within a modified capitalist mode of production.

Thus, finally, we can differentiate two orders of determinants applying to the analysis of capitalist peripheries. (1) Central and peripheral capitalism, obviously, share the same generic character. This mutual relationship, in which central capitalism occupies the dominant position, is defined by intra-systemic contradictions. The organic composition of capital, average rates of profit, technological arrangements, and commodity price structures are posited at a global level. The dominance of international capital determines limit functions and developmental constraints on the properties of the peripheral economic systems. Specifically, it curbs and fragments the development of the productive forces as the central aspect of self-centred capitalist growth, and it imposes relations of production modelled on the interests and exigencies of international capital valorization. Therefore, structural constraints in the development of the productive forces and relations of production and not value transfers by unequal exchange are seen as the fundamental source of underdevelopment of peripheral capitalist formations. (2) Since a mode of production is principally defined in terms of its own intra-systemic contradictions between given forces and relations of production, peripheral capitalism will, within limit functions, also constitute its own relatively autonomous structural properties defined by the relations and forces of production imposed. These are internally determined by economic relations of reciprocal causality, i.e. laws of motion and self-regulative properties specific to its own defective reproduction that are only partially derivable from capitalist relations in general.[5] These dimensions need to be analysed in terms of a conflict-laden, inter-systemic relationship between the dominant capitalist world system and the peripheral capitalist formations. In this sense, peripheral capitalism becomes a totality *sui generis* in which contradictions of two kinds coexist in mutual articulation. On the one side it is intra-systemically bound into the dominant global process of capital accumulation and expanded valorization. On the other side, inter-systemic aspects of relative autonomy are introduced to its state of aggregation by uneven capitalist formation and expansion that is based on surplus production and class-specific appropriations related to the distorted and blocked growth model.

Finally, dependent capitalist development is not assessable in terms of a capitalist mode of production in general situated in a specific social formation. Instead it would have to be theorized as a totality structured by the articulation of inter- and intra-systemic contradictions, partially of irreconcilable and repugnant character: with the preeminence of inter-systemic contradictions, the ability of Third World countries to find immanent solutions to social demands of any kind, or to solve class conflicts at national level, is absolutely constrained by the requirement of functioning according to the exigencies of the international capitalist system both in economic and political terms.

Extended to the analysis of Third World urbanization, this approach leads to important conclusions concerning the character of urban conflicts and their possible solutions. Obviously urban development is not adequately accounted for as part of the process of territorial formation into rural-urban divisions and regional disparities. Instead migration has transplanted irreconcilable developmental contradictions to the cities where vast parts of the population are now deprived of means to afford adequate housing and are unable to pay for urban services. The repressive class structure made up of rigorous social cleavages, hegemonic power structures, and the authoritarian state apparatus will make it possible to fend off most of the 'excessive' demands of squatter populations and to some extent politically control the situation. But while the urban structure remains heterogeneous, as the urban economy is unable to find ways of supplying adequate income opportunities and urban services for all its inhabitants, a countercurrent aspect exists that arises from the spatial urban formation. Both the social and political impact of the urban congestion and the spatial unification of conflicting interests will set limits to the disregard of the squatter problem. In order to curb the squatter encroachment and to maintain basic urban functions - e.g. with respect to labour systems, minimal housing standards, social and physical infrastructure, space use - the urban system must seek ways of selectively coming to terms with its squatter populations.

4 Concepts of urban development in dependent capitalist formations

a) The modernization approach to urban development

To the theorists of urbanization the salient features of Third World cities prove an awesome challenge to viable developmental alternatives. Even a very summary glance at the available urban statistics shows that the sheer size of populations living in poverty-stricken slum and squatter settlements represent a situation to which no solution seems feasible in terms of conventional urban development strategies. No imaginable amount of restructuring of urban policies - or, for that matter, even the immediate and complete implementation of the 1976 'HABITAT declarations' of the first United Nations conference on human settlements (United Nations, 1976) - would suffice to cause a perceptible change in their housing situation. What, according to some accounts, is still perceived as a problem of urbanization and habitat in a specific stage of social transformation, in reality express antagonistic contradictions pertaining to the peripheral form of capitalist economic development. Third World metropolises are stricken by far more than intramural growth disparities. These cities have in fact now become the spatial imprints of fundamental contradictions in the dependent development of the entire society. In this situation there can be, strictly speaking, no separate urban solution without a complementary agrarian and industrial reform aiming at a complete restructuring of the growth model of these countries and the establishment of a new relationship between the First and the Third World.

Deprived of easy answers that stand up to the complexity of problems and solutions described, both materialist and modernist theories of urbanization have largely adopted an analogous rather than an analytically penetrating approach. Categories derived from western experiences were seen to reflect constant factors in every possible society (cf. Slater, 1986, p. 10). Thus, the classical European case, characterized by a mutual and balanced pattern of industrial-urban growth, was considered the prototypical frame of reference for the determination and evaluation of emerging Third World urban growth patterns. According to this, the historic lesson to be learnt from the European or western model spelt out a ubiquitous, progressive function of urbanization in two dimensions: as an accelerator both of economic growth and of corresponding socio-cultural change.

Whereas the urban congestion and concentration of human and social resources - providing the indispensable material and spatial arrangements for capitalist industrial development - have self-evident economic functions, empirical research in the 1950s went one step further. The modernization approach attempted to substantiate that the process of urban formation also provides a benign socio-cultural environment for capitalist development. According to the very influential works of Daniel Lerner, both the exposure to and the cultural contacts with the urban way of life and its social values were seen as invariant promoters in the proliferation of social attitudes and dispositions closely related to the urban-capitalist growth model. At that time the empirical verification of this thesis in Third World cities seemed to prove a causal nexus between the rate of urbanization and a multitude of other factors that were directly related to the set of developmental issues discussed in the modernizations approach. These included economic growth, income, education, dispersion of adaptability, and innovative potentials ('empathy'), extent of mass-communication perception, social differentiation and division of labour, social mobility, etc. (cf. Lerner, 1958).

Nowadays, critical discussion widely agrees that dualist and modernist approaches are theoretically out of date and disproved practically. In the past three decades patterns of Third World urban development have changed considerably, and growing rates of urbanization no longer go hand in hand with economic development. But in a striking contrast to critical academic reasoning, the modernistic and dualistic line of thinking is very much alive and painfully kicking among policy makers and urban administrators - and still finds ample theoretical support.

Neo-modernist concepts of urban development still tend to iterate the basic premises of dualism, albeit in a amended state of presentation. The earlier crude version of rural-urban dualism reappears in a form related to the apparent unbalanced structure of urban formations. With the failure of cities to become catalysts for development, the city itself has been identified as a problem. Concepts like 'over-urbanization', 'hyper-urbanization', or 'pathology of urban growth' discern the new problem perception according to which cities are suffering from excessive in-migration and its detrimental effects on urban development. Failing to analyse the process of spatial expansion of capitalism in terms other than those derived from the supposed western universalism, these concepts are, again, unable to account for the 'historic specificity of social development in Third World regions' (Slater, 1986, p. 10).

b)   The Marxist approach to urban development

Although the categories underpinning the Marxist vein of research are derived from the totality of social and economic relations, meaning that concepts of urban development would also have to be put into the context of the concrete social formation, urbanization has in fact been widely discussed at a more abstract level, i.e. as the 'spatial image' of the capitalist mode of production (cf. Friedmann/Wolff, 1982, p. 328). This notion is close to Marx's own perception that the palpable spatial dimensions of the capitalist mode of production develop a strong natural affinity to the urban form (cf. Lefèbvre, 1972). And indeed, more than any other anterior mode of production, capitalism seems by precondition affiliated to the urban form for its own development. Thus, in theoretical accounts, transition to capitalism has widely tended to be identified with urbanization of the society as a whole:

- Excepting mining and agricultural production physically tied to specific locations, urban agglomerations and not the proximity to raw materials figures as the natural spatial precondition for the capitalist production process. Preferences for sites of production are given by enterprises to those urban areas rendering maximal conditions for capital valorization. These conditions include the access to abundant, disposable and cheap labour, a centralization of production that provides economies of scale, the spatial concentration and unification of commodity and capital markets, and the partial externalization of overhead-costs to state funds for necessary infrastructural provisions (roads, transportation system, energy, water, sewage, communication facilities, etc.).

- Aspects of urbanization also promote the general social and material conditions for the reproduction and maintenance of the labour-force. The urban social structure is characterized by a high degree of social differentiation, divisions of labour, social mobility, and aspiration. With its corresponding impact on the structures of family socialization (e.g. social individualization and loosening of family ties, complemented by the expansion and increasing importance of public education) this greatly enhances a complex, urban-based process of social restructuring. Braverman and others have analysed this in terms of the 'habituation of the worker to the capitalist mode of production' (Braverman, 1974, p. 139; Bowles/Gintis, 1976 and 1977).

- Since transition to capitalism demands that the natural prerequisites and elements of production (land, labour, means of production, and capital) all attain commodity form and become primarily subject to capitalist relations of production, the movement of capital and its requirements for expanded valorization will necessarily become dominant for the entire spatial arrangements of society. This includes the formation of hierarchical divisions of labour and exploitative relations between the metropolis and rural areas, just as much as the internal fragmentation of urban reproduction into heterogeneous systems of labour-power remuneration by divisions of the working class (Bowles/Gintis, 1977, p. 178).

Following these basic findings, the Marxist approach has proposed a line of determinate analysis of the urban problem directly related to the laws of motion underpinning the expansion of the capitalist mode of production. Cities are seen to develop as the spatial image of the capitalist mode of production, indicating social and spatial arrangements that are functionally related to the requirements of the valorization process. Once commodity production is generalized and occupies the dominant role in urban formation and social differentiation, capital is seen to attain ubiquitous allocating functions for the hierarchical alignment of production, distribution and consumption and the corresponding spatial arrangements. Moreover, these terms also determine how commodities are produced, how

37

they become socially valued, and how the various systems of production define the limits of access to their products for different income groups (cf. Baross, 1978, p. 45).

For the European, auto-centred case of urban development where industrial promotion of the productive forces functioned as the prime accelerator of rural-urban transformation and the expansion of the capitalist relations of production, we can agree that the spatial image theory is *de facto* verified by the history of urban development: by all accounts the rates of urban intake of migrants from rural areas seem to have closely corresponded to the urban growth rate and the effective demand for industrial labour-power. Demographic 'pull' rather than 'push' factors have dominated the process of social restructuring. Hence, in the European case, urban agglomerations were not the given prerequisites for industrial growth, but, inversely, urban environments were created under conditions in which they provided locational advantages to the process of industrial and commercial expansion.

As contemporary urban research now widely acknowledges, the contents of the Third World urbanization process are only partially identical with those of central capitalism (cf. McGee, 1971; Davis, 1972). Essentially this means that the peripheral urban growth model would need to be analysed as a historically specific entity. Specifically with the 'principal city' type of urban development, the magnitude of demographic growth has by far outstripped the growth rates of the industrial sector and its demand for labour-power. This situation is aggravated by the specific structure of industrialization in Third World countries that has become subject to the global determinants of capital valorization and prevailing technological standards (Frieling, 1984). Despite the abundantly available cheap labour, indigenous national capital is found to employ capital-intensive methods and standards of production in accordance with the given technological linkages to the world market. In the case of multinational capital, the operational terms of these enterprises are based on direct importation of their own First-World-born technological means of production. Although the lower wages paid for equivalently qualified industrial labour are still an important economic and locational aspect to attract capital, the lower level of labour-power remuneration in Third World countries is no longer able to establish the original dynamic backward link found in classical capitalism where low wage rates were important regulators for capitalist development and rates of accumulation (cf. chapter I.4).

Historically, the social costs of labour-power figured as a decisive factor to individual capital when considering whether to substitute labour by machinery or not. Today, the organic composition of capital comes to Third World economies already predetermined by production standards laid down in the capitalist centres. This explains why there is so little scope for the sometimes proposed alternative strategy of industrialization based on labour-intensive production methods that might utilise the given lower wage standards in expanding the formal labour sector.

This significantly different process of capitalist transition in the periphery necessarily entails modifications in the approach to the analysis of urban development. Predisposed to disparities and diachronies in the formation of peripheral capitalism, the functions of urban agglomerations are no longer directly attributable to those distinctions assigned to them in the European auto-centred model.

c) The world city approach

As Friedman/Wolff have noted, Marxist theory has made little attempt to synthesize its global capitalist analysis with urban studies. Marxist analysts widely still treat the city as an isolated phenomenon assuming that its internal structures can be directly 'determined' by abstract capitalist forces (Friedman/Wolff, 1982, p. 328). In an effort to bring together the world system approach of Wallerstein, Amin, and Frank with urban analysis, Friedman and Wolff have suggested that the contemporary urbanization process would be more adequately analysed by the mode of its integration into the world economy. According to the economic role assigned by capital to cities that lie at the junction between the world economy and the national state, this has given rise to an urban hierarchy of influence and control. At the top of this hierarchy we find urban regions defined by Friedman/Wolff as 'world cities'. Their mode of integration into global economy has two aspects: (1) the *form and strength* of the city's integration (e.g. the extent of its function to serve as a location for transnational headquarters, as a site for 'safe' investments such as real estate, its importance as world market production centre, or as an ideological centre); and (2) the *spatial dominance* assigned to the city corresponding to the global structuring of capitalism into core, semi-periphery, or periphery. According to this, the operational scope of world cities may be either global or regional with respect to the financial and/or market control, or may be defined as articulating a peripheral national economy with the world system (Friedmann/Wolff, 1982, pp. 310-11; for similar global models with more emphasis on the capitalist centres cf. Wallace, 1990 and Feagin/Smith, 1987).

In a process of urban restructuring the functions of world cities are to spatially articulate the interests of transnational capital with those of national states who have their own historical trajectory. This inevitably gives rise to new forms of conflict and contradictory planning requirements in reaction to global tendencies of capitalist formation (Friedman/ Wolff, 1982, pp. 320-326). Four processes of concurring urban restructuring are identified:

- Economic restructuring may be seen in terms of a changing occupational clustering. The dynamics of urban development are largely defined by the *primary cluster* of high-level business services and professionals of the transnational elite. A *second clustering* of growing importance is found in ancillary occupational groups serving the first (e.g. construction, real estate, luxury goods retailing, hotels, domestic services). A *third cluster* tied to the performance of the world economy is international tourism, considerably overlapping with the second. The expansion of these first three clusters is

39

taking place mainly at cost of the declining *fourth cluster* of manufacturing employment. While cheap labour provision still may act as an incentive to select 'world city' locations, capital-intensive production and automatization will gradually displace the mass of employees in this line of occupation. The *fifth cluster* of government services concerned with the reproduction of the world city and the provision of items of collective consumption (such as infrastructure, land, public housing, transportation, etc.), is generally quite large in world cities. Its political character and technological backwardness, however, tends to make it a bloated urban sector with much overlap and redundancy in employment. Large numbers of people are employed with low productivity levels and on a low wage scale. The *sixth cluster*, the largest in Third World cities, comprehends informal sector activities. Often an extension of the household economy, it requires little or no overhead, and is defined by low and uncertain labour returns, lack of protective labour legislation, long working hours, and possible illicit character. Due to its function of taking up the slack in the formal economy, it is usually tolerated by the state. Finally, the full-time unemployed represent a residual cluster, however not made up of more than 5-10% of the labour-force.

- The primary aspect of social restructuring in the world city is the polarization of social class divisions. The transnational elites and the dependent middle sectors enjoy permanent employment, security, and complete legality in a cosmopolitan surrounding well served with urban provisions. As Friedmann/Wolff put it, for all practical purposes these groups *are the city* with the underclasses living at its sufferance. The traditional working class is disappearing, replaced by a class with mimetic propensities. Outside the formal sector, class formation is fragmented with internal divisions emerging among the workers in the ghetto of the poor along racial, ethnic, and nationalist lines. Violence and high crime rates have become a typical feature of world cities, countered but not contained by police repression and private security guards in the upper city. But conflicts are not a sign of impending revolution. With opposition groups lacking a political centre, world cities are practically immune to revolutionary action.

- Physical restructuring brings forth new dimensions of size and internal spatial structures divided into a secluded 'citadel' and a 'ghetto' reflecting inequality and class domination. The topography of land values is ever-shifting, complying with the dynamics of capitalism and its inequities not mitigated by considerations of basic needs, social justice, or equal access to power. The enormous size and wealth of world cities put strains on the natural resources and rouse conflicts with its hinterland, as need for water and energy results in an expansion of intake far beyond the city boundaries. Waste disposal and pollution are becoming critical to a point where health is endangered. Solutions are sought at high-tech

40

level making the cities even more vulnerable to problems resulting from sophisticated and expensive methods.

- Urban restructuring necessarily involves political conflict over the distribution of costs and benefits. World cities tend to magnify contradictions. Lacking counter-forces to capital expansion, complex feedback mechanisms tend to destabilize the system, and localized conflicts may erupt into a worldwide crisis. Economic space and life space are increasingly becoming contradictory. With economic space obeying the logic of capital, individual profit interests dominate society as a whole and clash with territorial needs for life space. The motions of the dominant economic space produce conflicts with territorial space for livelihood. Jobs may be relocated, or labour markets are reoriented to new international divisions of labour, intensifying competition amongst workers over good jobs. The requirements of economic space may extend to housing areas with people defending their neighbourhoods from the intrusion of capitalist logic. People may campaign for environmental protection or more social facilities. Poor people will struggle for the right of access to social provisions, the right to organize, or demonstrate for sources of livelihood or housing areas, for higher income, etc. All these conflicts occur simultaneously and are engendered by the social form of the city that links heterogeneous aspects together.

Although transnational capital desires freedom from state intervention in the movements of capital, information and commodities, it is interested in having the national state assume as large a part as possible of the costs of production including the reproduction of the labour-force and the maintenance of 'law and order'. From this it follows that political conflict is not only structured by the classical struggle between capital and labour. Additionally we have struggles between transnational capital and the national bourgeoisie, between politically organized national states and transnational capital, and between the people of a given city and the national polity (ibid., p. 312).

Although only a few Third World cities such as Cairo, Bangkok, Mexico City, and São Paulo can be considered world cities in-the-making, the perspectives of expanding global capitalism unite world cities in a common fate with cities in the semi-periphery or on the periphery of the global economy. States and territorial planners must understand the disastrous consequences of the dissolution of life space into a vast economic space controlled by transnational capital. The world city perspective may contribute to a structural understanding of specific local problems that ultimately only have global solutions. But as Friedmann/Wolff emphasize, planners need not yield to a supposedly inevitable process. Due to the reciprocal relationship between world cities and the international economy, local actions and urban struggles may have global consequences. The political leverage is that world cities are essential for the management of international capital that has 'little choice but to settle there and come to terms with local populations' (ibid., p. 330). In realizing the functional importance of world cities for capital, partisan planning can adopt a political partiality towards defending territorial interests or supporting political action. Local battles over sites for economic space-use may, for example, be seen as 'extracting a price from capital which inevitably needs space for its activities' (ibid.). A new role for political planning would be to enlarge the scope for political action of community groups by supplying information and organizing its exchange or by actively coordinating policies and actions curbing the domination of capital over life space.

While the political implications for planning suggested by Friedmann/Wolff may only have practical significance for First World cities that are in a position to initiate popular support for anti-capitalist policies, the analytical perspective of the world city encompasses First and Third World cities alike. One obvious advantage of this approach is that its framework is able to incorporate expanding informal sector activities, including self-help housing, in the economic role assigned to Third World cities in global capitalist expansion. Amplifying this line of argument, Portes has shown that uncontrolled settlement forms, illegal occupation of land, and self-construction of habitat are not the consequence of excessive urban demographic development, or in-migration to the metropolis. They increasingly express functional aspects of the global economy. The unemployment rates in these settlements are not higher than for the total urban labour-force. Moreover, most of the recent studies indicate that the internal occupational diversity is quite considerable. It extends far beyond the conventionally claimed subsistence and informal artisan economic activities - actually ranging from skilled and semiskilled work in the formal sector to white-collar jobs and to government employment (Portes, 1985, p. 113; cf. also World Bank, 1982; HABITAT, 1982, pp. 115; and Lloyd 1980, p. 122).

Consequently, the emergence of squatter settlements can be seen to reflect the given structure of labour remuneration (poverty-in-employment) in which wages bear no relation to the market costs of housing and shelter as basic consumption items. The self-provision of housing figures both as a subsidy to employers in the formal sector and as a means 'to perpetuate returns to labour that exclude the real market costs of a place to live in the city' (Portes, ibid.).

The point is that accelerated migration and the 'hyper-urbanization' of Latin America and Caribbean countries are not symptoms of the breakdown of the economic system. Instead, they are integral components of that system and routine aspects of its operation. This pattern of urbanization fits the requirements of the existing model of development and the short-term needs of different classes and institutional factors (Portes, 1985, p. 116).

While the functionalist perspective of a worldwide, unitary evolving socioeconomic system has added new insight into urban development, it also inevitably raises some methodological considerations concerning meta-theoretical reasoning and the involved levels of abstraction. Nagel's critique on this kind of approach in social science is a point in case edifying that the functionalist postulate will have no substantive content unless,

> ... the state that is allegedly maintained or altered is formulated more precisely than has been customary. It also follows that the claims functionalists sometimes advance concerning the 'integral' character or 'functional' unity of social systems produced by the 'working together' of their parts ... cannot be properly judged as either sound or dubious or even mistaken. For in the absence of descriptions precise enough to identify unambiguously the states which are supposedly maintained in a social system, those claims cannot be subjected to empirical control, since they are compatible with every conceivable matter of fact and with every outcome of empirical inquiries into actual societies (Nagel, 1961, p. 530).

Obviously, we need to draw two conclusions concerning the appropriate application of the world city concept to the analysis of larger urban systems in transitional processes. First, as Friedmann and Wolff have pointed out, conventional urban studies directed to individual cities have hitherto suffered from fragmentation of their findings and urgently need reorientation towards a more comprehensive outlook. But second, it would be insufficient to merely reinterpret the available data in order to make it fit the new functionalist global perspective. According to Friedmann/Wolff the problem focus of urban studies should rather be the 'restructuring of economic, social and spatial relations, and the ensuing political conflicts in the world city formation' by a dialectic model of interpretation

> ... in which the territorial interests of particular world cities and the national states within which they are situated are seen as both united and opposed to the interests of transnational corporations that are the principal actors in the world economy. ... every world city, being integrated along both functional and territorial lines, has a dual but contradictory aspect (Friedmann/Wolff, 1982, p. 329).

As suggested, this complex subject should be analysed as an articulation of inter-systemic and intra-systemic aspects. Urban formations need to be conceived as a relationship in which both existing forms of the capitalist mode of production - the dominant central and the subordinated peripheral, each retaining autonomous genetic properties - provide formative aspects to urban development according to their respective preponderance within the peripheral social formation. Ultimately then, growth patterns of Third World cities would be governed by more than the functional imperatives of the expanding capitalist world system. The economic, political, social, and physical heteronomy of cities in capitalist peripheries would, rather, have to be understood as images of the fundamental developmental contradictions the contemporary urban system spatially unites.

d) The political economy of petty commodity housing production

The deeper significance (and possible controversial potential) of the notion of changing spatial appearances and restructuring of capital according to the global requirements of valorization can best be clarified in comparison with the more conventional Marxist approach to urban analysis. Here analysis starts from two fundamental aspects that are usually seen to typify capitalism:

- In contrast to other preceding modes of production, capitalism is based on the generalization of commodity production and the expansion of corresponding relations of production that draw more and more segments of the population into a mode of reproduction in which capital is in direct command.

- The objection of production, circulation, distribution, and consumption of products with use-value has as its end the expanded valorization of invested capital and the reproduction of capitalist relations of production and not the satisfaction of needs.

Extending these basic premises to the housing problem, both Burgess and Pradilla have concluded that in Third World formations the question of existing heteronomous production systems must be posed and solved in terms of the operation of a total system and the imputed relations of dominance and determination. Any crude or arbitrary separation of use-value and exchange-value would merely reproduce the bourgeois perception of the urban question in dichotomous conceptions whether official/popular, formal/informal or institutional/self-help (cf. Burgess, 1982, p. 67). Since capitalism is seen as

> typified by generalized commodity production which has as its end the valorization of capital ... the critical question then is whether the forms of production of the housing commodity can best be identified on the basis of user-control, and the systems of construction of the housing object; or whether they can be best understood in terms of the different ways they assume this status as a commodity and valorize this capital (Burgess, 1982, p. 64).

We begin the discussion of these propositions with the less controversial aspect: the valorization of capital as an essential determinant to the problem of housing provision and production. Within this discussion we will try to point out that the valorization process in

44

the periphery is subject to specific conditions that modify the postulated general tendency towards the generalization of commodity relations.

The significance of 'valorization' as a concept extends far beyond the conditions that impel production under direct capitalist command to function as an inseparable unit of the work-process/capital-valorization process. Before capital can dominantly determine the social terms of production, this presupposes that preceding production/self-consumption cycles (in which the producers are still in control of their product and their means of production) are decomposed and reassembled according to capitalist requirements. Capital must either be in direct command of the social means of production or effectively control the way in which they are socially utilized in subordinated production systems: it must determine the forms of appropriation and distribution of the social product, and it must determine the economic rationality of the system. Since this rationality - at least in its fully developed form - operates as a self-regulating price and value system, this necessitates that the capitalist law of value must be extended to the production/reproduction of all productive elements that directly feed into, or are related to, the capitalist production process. This law of value entails that other forms of capital (nonproductive merchants and finance capital), labour, means of production, and - specifically important to the case of housing - landed capital/ground rent are reproduced in terms of social valuation and self-valorization equivalent to those of capitalist production itself.

As the following analysis will show, both aspects of capitalist expansion - the initial decomposition of productive elements and their sequential reunification in the process of territorial formation - are not necessarily congruent. Instead they tend to create and inflict a multitude of contradictions upon those specific urban locations that become the site of their conglomeration. As the basic cycle of production/consumption is dispersed both in time and in space, capitalism, more than any other mode of production, becomes typified by the proliferation of production, circulation, distribution, and consumption into separately existing social entities. This gives rise to the need for affiliated social agents who earn revenue according to their function and position within the valorization process.

In housing commodity this has been elaborated in detail by Pradilla, showing the extent to which the provision of housing involves a multitude of interlacing actors and intermediate agents: owners of productive capital, landowners, building material producers, technical and commercial agents, productive labourers, unproductive wage workers, etc. all necessarily become involved in the production, exchange, and consumption of the product (Pradilla, 1976, pp. 12-18).

The issue behind all this is that once capital dominantly determines the social terms of production and the social divisions of labour, its economic laws of valuation will be in operation no matter whether the specific production process is under direct command of capital, or is informal sector production working at a lower level of productivity. In economic terms the amount of labour-power, hence value added, in a production process, is valorized not according to the working hours but to the extent that these represent socially average levels of productivity. Since the socially average levels of productivity are determined by the most advanced, i.e. most productive, mass forms of commodity production in the industrial branch in question, the working hours needed to produce the same amount of exchange-values must be expanded when the labour process is conducted at a lower level of productivity. In peripheral, heterogeneously developed capitalism this economic law has two dramatic effects on the internal conditions of national reproduction:

1   Due to the historical deformation of national structures of production and the hierarchical economic links with the centre, the mechanisms that would have normally worked to generalize the most advanced forms to all other branches of production are blocked in peripheral economies. Capital is merely attracted and allocated to specific areas of production that are predetermined and reinforced by the international division of production according to the productive needs and consumption of the centres.

2   In contrast to the situation in central economies, the labour-power invested in peripheral non-industrial forms of production will lose its immediate determining relation to the valuation/pricing of the product it produces. Most labour processes may be performed at low levels of productivity in the traditional or manufacturing branches of production. But in terms of valorization, the totality of existing production has invariably become linked to the most advanced national and international industrial levels of productivity. For these mechanisms of valorization to be in effect, it is not even necessary that production takes place in elaborated commodity forms. Conditioned by socially preponderant mechanisms, the valorization process already functions by way of its potentiality alone. Once the social terms of national production have by exchange, competition, and comparison with the world market products become part of the capitalist world economy, the self-regulating economic logic entails that all invested labour becomes valued (and remunerated) in accordance with the highest levels of (mass) productivity. Therefore, as long as capitalism dominates the social process of production and reproduction, it is not the concrete amount of labour spent in a specific production process that counts economically but the socially reckoned part determined by the valorization process (cf. Schoeller, 1976, p. 246).

Accordingly, the self-help producer of housing may conceive the social relations involved in his own production process as outside capitalism. They enable him to cheapen the costs of his accomplishment by avoiding the surplus increment that accrues when hired labour, market-bought building materials, or other overhead costs become involved. But any conception that regards this as truly autonomous and self-determined decisions of the

46

producer/builder, fails to notice that all these elements have already been subjected to external and prescient terms of valuation/devaluation.

Therefore, we must conclude that the whole productive ensemble of self-help - i.e. the costs of housing rendered affordable, the choice of construction technology, the building materials utilized, the choice of building site, and the labour arrangements used in the construction process (utilizing and probably combining the work of hired craftsmen, the family, or adapting forms of work cooperation with members of the local network) - are within certain limits already predetermined as a form of production/consumption complying with those conditions assigned to it by the process of capital valorization. Although it will only become obvious in case of direct commodification of self-help products, either by subletting, or the sale of the housing product, all potentially increment value arrangements are pre-fixed in relation to the socially preponderant economic mechanisms of surplus production and appropriation, irrespective of whether such bearings seem visible in the initial terms of construction/utilization of the house or not.

In this sense production, circulation, and consumption can be defined as different instances of a unitary relationship - functionally and spatially dispersed but *bound together as a valorization process.* Corresponding to these separate instances of valorization, we find a wide range of distributive relations required to ensure the social conditions of expanded surplus production and realization: intermediary agents, different fractions of capital, the labour-force, unproductive proprietors of land, and finally the state, which all perform vital functions for individual capital. After all, for various reasons individual capital cannot itself produce the labour-force, it cannot produce land, urban centralized space, or the material and social infrastructure required by social capital as general prerequisites of its reproduction. In fact, it is an essential condition for the mobility and competitiveness of industrial enterprises that productive elements are reproduced and held available for them by conditions in which individual capital plays no direct part if unproductive ties of capital curtailing its profits are to be avoided. These conditions would include the availability of an adequately qualified, disposable and mobile labour-force, urban service provisions, as well as the question of integrating landowners into the capitalist class formation in such terms that conflicts between real estate as a commodity and the need for reasonably priced urban space do not become counterproductive to the expansion of capitalist enterprises.[6]

Walker (1974) and Harvey (1974) have shown that the state's role in the system of urban land allocation and valuation is not merely one of a neutral advocate in a free, competitive market. In collaboration with influential urban power groups and banks, planning-decisions of public administrations structure or restructure urban space into different partial markets to encourage speculation and to enable proprietors to realize a 'class-monopoly rent' (Harvey).[7] Moreover, state action towards infrastructure provision, land-use plans, and residential zoning in specific urban locations does not only provide differential ground rent to landowners, but it may actively produce a new category of 'redistributive rent' (Walker,

1974, p. 55). In urban fringe areas, or in newly legalized settlements, urban services (including land development) are often provided by the state at rates far below the actual costs, either for socio-political reasons, or in order to make up for the locational disadvantage. With the gradual integration of these settlements into the urban land and housing markets, price increases complying with market demand will then allow the capitalization of 'redistributive rent' by landowners, i.e. the differential between land development at real costs and the public-subsidized provision by the local state.

e)   The uneven international spatial formation of capitalism

Having put forward the argument that capitalist terms of production/valorization determinatively underpin the economic rationality of the social system, the strict application of these distinctions to Third World economies points to an intricate aspect: global levels of determination have led neither to the generalization and uniformity of the concrete conditions of valorization nor to the universal assimilation of given material standards of production. As shown, capital has merely selectively penetrated and transformed Third World social formations. Moreover, all capitalist production must come to terms with the national conditions given for valorization in an articulated peripheral capitalist mode of production. We are now able to phrase this economic condition in its spatial dimension: the basic postulate of political economy, that the terms of production also determine the mode of exchange and consumption, will not apply to peripheral capitalism in its full sense as the cycle of production/consumption is in reality only partially unified in the periphery. Instead:

> The contradiction between the capacity to consume and the capacity to produce is resolved on the level of the system on the world scale (centre and periphery) through the growth of the market in the centre, with the periphery playing a subordinate and limited role. This dynamic leads to a growing polarization in wealth to the benefit of the centre (Amin, 1979, p. 135).

Future analysis must renounce oversimplified concepts that attempt to directly read off comprehensive patterns of urban formation from the inherent logic of political economy. Specifically, with the posited tendency to identify all, even self-help, forms of production, as an integral part of the 'generalization of commodity production', differentiation is needed before we may conclude that these forms are adequately understood as part of incessant capitalist expansion.

A study presented by Mingione on the 'peripheralization' of capitalist centres underscores our point. In Italy economic crisis has given rise to a decline of industrial employment and a parallel diffusion of informal activities signifying a decommodification process with decreasing direct command of capital over the social organization of reproduction (cf.

Mingione, 1983, p. 312). Thus, much of what has formerly been exclusively discussed as a topic of peripheral capitalism - the various functions of subsistence-based forms of production subsidizing global capitalist accumulation - would, according to Mingione, in fact apply to First and Third World urban formations alike. With rising rates of long-term unemployment in capitalist centres, labour markets are becoming structurally discriminating with respect to economically backward regions, to regions dominated by industrial branches now being technologically downgraded, to specific occupational and ethnic groups, gender, age, educational standards, etc. In this process, sections of the labour-force are being increasingly denied regular and adequate monetary income. Social security and public welfare, which are in any case not designed for mass unemployment and which are suffering from fiscal crisis in the most effected areas, are unable to compensate for the individual loss of income. Consequently, for the effected groups the mode of satisfaction of needs itself must change - much resembling the situation in Third World countries. Needs that were formerly satisfied by monetary acquisition will either have to be substituted by domestic familial activities, or, wherever substitution is not possible, income has to be derived from informal work involving substantially increased working hours per consumption unit (for a model of different modes in the satisfaction of needs cf. Mingione, 1983, pp. 313-319).

What emerges from this is that the process of commodification is not an end in itself. The formerly observable tendency of capitalist centres to expand commodity forms of consumption to virtually all facets of everyday life in an endless 'sourcing' for new areas and objects for expanded valorization of capital has been misinterpreted as an absolute and necessary feature of capitalism. Although commodification is a precondition of valorization, it would be a serious mistake to conflate both processes. This appears to be one of the specific points Wallerstein has captured in his concept of emerging World Capitalism. Wallerstein shows that the global expansion of the capitalist valorization process does not go hand in hand with the generalization of commodity terms and related spatial arrangements. What appear to some observers as contrarotating economic tendencies could, according to Wallerstein, be more adequately conceived in terms of the structural formation of a tripartite capitalist world system into core - semi-periphery - and periphery (cf. Wallerstein, 1979). This approach contradicts the conventional perception in which the economic development in the centre, including its changing spatial arrangements, can still be equated with absolute and irreversible expressions and tendencies pertinent to maturing capitalism - as it was, a process merely temporarily interrupted by economic crisis. Obviously, with changing global terms of valorization, even the capitalist centres can be submitted to partial peripheralization. Then social reproductive functions are burdened on private and domestic activities, or on state welfare whenever economic conditions for adequate capital valorization are no longer met and social restructuring of capital becomes inevitable (for a critical discussion of the 'inevitability of uneven spatial development under capitalism' cf. Browett, 1984, p. 155).

49

A basic frame of reference comprehending this type of analysis for the urban situation (i.e. the combination of political economy with the spatial perspective) has been elaborated by Henri Lefèbvre (1970). In his classical rendition of urbanizing societies, any precipitate notion of a unilateral determination of urban development is rejected. Instead the social and economic proliferation of urban structures are seen as highly interferential or overlaying processes requiring careful analytical differentiation of their *form* and *content*.

Following this approach, the problem for urban research would be to distinguish more clearly between the centralistic propensities pertaining both to form and content of cities developing as capitalist metropolises. As Lefèbvre points out, irrespective of its specific content the urban form is endowed with the natural property of condensing and unifying the given material conditions of society simply by submitting these to the urban situation. It spatially concentrates the social productive forces and means of production, and it creates an urban potential that relates given social and material entities to one another. Due to this aggregative potential, the urban situation will naturally support and promote the process of capitalist development. The urban form provides the spatial unification of capital, labour, and real estate markets; however - and this is the point - it does not become identical with it.

The centralizing function also impacts on the hierarchical formation of rural-urban relations. Thus the city interrelates the regional and the national commodity markets, and the agrarian and industrial markets, and links all these with the world market. Although these urban functions are indispensable for the development of capitalism, the urban form would be incorrectly perceived as the motor of development. In other words, the analysis of form is not to be confused or conflated with the analysis of the content (cf. Lefèbvre, 1970, p. 125).

Notes

1   The World Bank has suggested that the 'unprotectiveness of labour relations' is the most characteristic feature of informal sector activities whereas the ILO seems to have favoured 'low productivity' as the most distinctive criterion. In practice, however, both approaches boil down to using the size of enterprises and low wage rates as an empirical indicator for informal sector economic activities (see Senghaas-Knobloch, 1979, p. 55-190).

2   Similar proposals are submitted by Bienefeld, 1975 and Mandel, 1975.

3   For a more extensive discussion of relations between different modes of production and the internal relations of the capitalist mode of production cf. Tait (1987, pp. 314-325). Both types of relations imply quite different concepts of dialectical unfolding in thought. While the 'dialectics' between forces and relations of production

and the dialectics in the relations of consecutive modes of production are Kantian 'real oppositions between repugnant properties' (Colletti, 1977, p. 8), the logical reconstruction of capitalist reality by political economy is based on modified Hegelian dialectics. Marx himself accounted for both types of movement invariably in terms of 'dialectical development', thereby confusing the issues for his later interpreters (Godelier, 1972; Friedman, 1974; Sartre, 1967).

4   The analysis of the urban petty commodity production in Dakar, Senegal by Lebrun/Gerry is a case in point. The authors conclude that in petty production there exists a mechanism of dissolution-conservation. The dissolution aspect dominates in the European case whereas the conservation aspect typifies the Senegalese, Third World case (Lebrun/Gerry, 1975, p. 29).

5   In concepts of capitalist underdevelopment advocated either as the 'world capitalist system' (Frank, 1969 and 1981; Wallerstein, 1981), as 'peripheral capitalism' (Senghaas, 1977), or 'blocked capitalist development' (Baran, 1957), the notion of two-dimensional analysis is absent. Instead underdevelopment is conceptualized straightforwardly as a structural relationship stemming from the forced subjugation of peripheral economies by the capitalist centres. As this relationship is seen as mediated by the circulation of international capital, it is the circulation process and not the determinants of production that is held to provide the appropriate level of abstraction for the categorical analysis of dependent economies. Following this line of reasoning A. G. Frank, for example, has explained that the postulate of primacy of production over exchange, or the distinction between endogenous and exogenous conditions of development, become insignificant for proper analysis of underdevelopment, once a global capitalist mode of production and a single worldwide process of capital accumulation are assumed (cf. Frank, 1979, p. 80).

6   The case of ground rent, if conceived as a genuine capitalist category, exemplifies our argument that abstractions figure as a one-sided dimension/aspect of the social formation subjected to further concretization with respect to the complex reality they relate to: although the fact is acknowledged that real estate is a very specific commodity (e.g. with restricted availability and not reproducible at will), the conventional notion - following Marx - has rather been to unconditionally consider ground rent as intrinsic to the capitalist law of value/price determination. Recent discussion on the various aspects of rent, however, demonstrates that no strict economic inter-systemic determination of the rent question is feasible (cf. Amin, 1978; Rey, 1973; Walker, 1976; Harvey, 1974). Rey has discussed the emergence of absolute ground rent and its supposed valuation according to the capitalist development of the productive forces in alternative terms: i.e., as the outcome of class alliances cutting across different modes of production. Because capitalism, due to internal economic constraints of capital valorization in the agricultural sector, is only

able to transform agriculture gradually, it becomes dependent on the integration of pre-capitalist forms of production and the affiliated landed classes into its own mode of expanded reproduction. Therefore, capitalist ground rent can be seen as the social product of an articulation between the capitalist and the pre-capitalist mode of production. Amin's searching account of the problem supports the notion that the specific terms of absolute rent should be conceived as a category of distribution and not of production. It necessarily reflects social relations of power and class struggle that impact on the economic terms of its reproduction within capitalism (cf. Amin, 1978, p. 45).

7   It should be noted that the collusion of class interests between state, land speculators, and banks to some extent expresses a necessary condition for the organization of urban land markets in a market economy. Speculators have the 'positive' function of determining the right moment for changes in land-use according to the process of urban development to ensure the appropriate valorization of capital invested in land and buildings. To fulfil the positive function of coordination and stabilization of capitalist investments, individual capital owners or organizations need the institutional support of planning legislation to minimize the risk of high capital investments on a competitive market (cf. Harvey, 1974, p. 63).

III Third World uneven territorial formation and incomplete transition to capitalism

The basic distinction between form and content of urban formations is a particularly valuable instrument in analysing aspects of Third World urbanization that are only crudely and superficially defined by other concepts like the Marxist 'spatial image' theory, or the 'hyper-urbanization' approach introduced by Bairoch:

In the *spatial image* approach, the uneven spatial formation of urban-rural relations is conceived as a replication of the global relations between capitalist centre and periphery. The relations between peripheral cities and rural areas are not only those of urban-rural divisions but the preponderance of cities over their rural hinterlands through a process of unequal exchange and appropriation. Although the spatial image approach overcomes the perception of urban development in isolation from exogenous factors, the proposed urban-rural polarization is directly ascribed to the specific circumstances of peripheral capitalism but is not derived from the tendencies of capitalist development. As Läpple notes, this tends to explain uneven spatial formation as uneven development between capitalist (urban) and pre-capitalist (rural) production.[1] Although such relations exist, they would be a part of and not the primary cause of capitalism's uneven territorial formation. In the process of capitalist development, spatial formation is constantly subjected to changes in the organization of the social reproduction process. This both reinforces the existing spatial disparities between and within cities and creates new ones (Läpple, 1978, p. 28). Another crucial point with the 'spatial image' approach is that urban structures are not entirely social representations of one capitalist valorization process, nor can they *in toto* be reduced to functional requirements of capitalist valorization. Besides meeting locally determined functional requirements, Third World cities are simultaneously formed by the requirements of international capital, by the impact of uneven territorial formation, and by specific exigencies in the organization of the urban situation (see below).

The thrust of the 'hyper-urbanization' concept is less structural and again isolates urban development from its wider causes. Arguing at a phenomenological level, the concept has

53

in particular addressed the role of the urban informal sector for the urban economy, albeit in a form focusing on the nonfunctional and harmful aspects of excessive migration to cities. Thus, hyper-urbanization is conceived as an anomaly within capitalist development and not as an intrinsic aspect of territorial formation of peripheral capitalism. In operational terms of policies on urbanization and employment, this anomaly is seen to impair sectoral balanced growth leading to a hypertrophic, unproductive tertiary sector.[2]

Crucially both concepts, in one way or another, fail to analyse Third World urbanization in terms of its contradictory tendencies and dysfunctions pertaining to the territorial formation of peripheral capitalism. According to this, uneven peripheral capitalist development imports contradictions and heterogeneous aspects of its territorial formation to the cities where they are reshaped and interrelated with prevailing capitalist structures helped by the spatially unifying properties of the urban situation. A more comprehensive approach would, therefore, require distinction of three instances in the process of peripheral urban formation:

First, in Third World metropolises, the dominant impact of international and associated national capital will shape the urban core functions according to its economic and infrastructural requirements. Based on corresponding political and financial power structures, priorities in urban planning and tenure arrangements in 'world cities' are designed to accommodate multinational enterprises and their employees. General state action will safeguard the operations of international capital and the different affiliated national enterprises and proprietors of urban land. Conforming with dominant capitalist terms of valorization, urban markets, price structures, and consumption patterns are set at internationally defined cosmopolitan standards. Corresponding to these conditions, the urban structure is highly segregationist with respect to employment, settlement, housing, provision of urban services, etc., reflecting the degrees of proximity of its different populations to the core of the economic and political system.

Second, outside large cities the capitalist penetration of Third World societies remains a highly uneven and selective process. To mobilize and exploit indigenous resources, colonial and peripheral capitalism has decomposed pre-capitalist production systems but only partially reintegrated the uprooted masses into capitalist relations of production. In particular it has distorted the rural-urban demographic balance leading to an urbanization pattern disjunctive from the capacity of the urban economy to absorb all its population into wage work and urban provision systems. Following Läpple (1978, p. 31), these contradictory aspects of urban development need to be analysed from a double perspective: (1) as part of the general uneven territorial formation of capitalism, structured by *intensive* urban and *extensive* rural socialization regarding the organization of production and labour; and (2) the specific articulation of both intensive and extensive forms of socialization, spatially counterpoised in Third World cities by the asynchronisms of peripheral capitalist development.

54

Third, in an effort to distinguish clearly between urban form and content, the process of urban formation should be analysed strictly as a moment of its contemporary history, whatever its previous historical determinants and conditions. An example of the appropriateness of this approach is found in the analysis of functions performed by the urban form in the spatial reorganization of societies during the transition process set in motion by capitalist penetration. In an earlier section we have outlined a first important spatial aspect related to the formation of capitalism. As a mode of production alienated from its natural productive requirements, capital must to some extent remain detached from the social processes that provide the essential productive elements. This condition can be inverted: to the extent that capital is obliged to assign reproductive functions to other sectors of the social formation, it must also come to terms with the historically given set of national, regional, and local conditions of production. Within limits defined by valorization and commodification, local production systems must, therefore, be given space and means to reproduce according to their own properties. With reference to the urban formation, this gives rise to the notion of sociospatial conflicts and incongruities emanating from the centralizing functions of large cities and the self-contradictory aspects imposed on them by the capitalist content. Hence, although the capitalist mode of production must be held responsible for exerting the decisive 'pull factors' - attracting and reallocating the human and material resources of society - it will not take direct responsibility for their sustenance. According to the logic of political economy it is essential that individual capital retains its mobility to respond to changing terms of valorization - i.e., it does not become irreversibly tied to the production of a specific commodity or location for its production process nor to the reproduction of a specific part of the labour-force.

In the necessary socialization of means of production and productive requirements the state plays an important role in providing capital with 'gratis' productive forces that may be privately appropriated. The urban space itself is a vital productive force, engendering the intensive socialization of production, circulation and services. In this sense it is both a location and a field of employment in which contradictory interests come together. Besides those functional aspects directly related to capital valorization and accumulation, the urban space also has to accommodate the demands of its residents for adequate social living space. Thus, state interventions in the form of town planning, infrastructure, housing, economic and social development polities do not simply represent functional requirements of urban growth: instead they are urban and state-disposed social *gratis* productive forces subject to class struggle over who controls them. The predominant character of urban conflicts in the capitalist city is therefore appropriately defined by the process in which private capital appropriates social space and the social productive forces. Capital not only monopolizes specific favourable locations for its production; it also privately appropriates the state-provided infrastructural prerequisites of production (Läpple, 1978, p. 42).

1 The urban congestion of productive forces

For social capital the urban congestion provides the solution to all these contradictory conditions by interrelating and spatially unifying capital, labour, and commodity markets, maintaining them in the urban situation and holding them at the disposal of capital. It is in this sense that municipalities and petty commodity forms of production suffer from the contradictions of capitalist reproduction: on the one hand we find that the bulk of urban resources and facilities are primarily allocated according to the infrastructural and productive needs of capital. But on the other hand, specifically with regards to the material reproduction of the labour-force, the urban formation must deal with the ramifications arising from the fragmented structure of employment and the affiliated problems of housing provision and urban survival.

Beyond the unifying functions required for the operations of the capitalist mode of production, the urban congestion not only spatially unites and interrelates heterogeneous aspects. This also applies to social matter of an altogether different order. Seen from the wider frame of the urban situation, not all aspects can be entirely equated as actions and conflicts within a reciprocally defined system. Rather, urban dynamics will also be structured by a complex interferential articulation of intra-systemic *contradictions* and inter-systemic *real oppositions* (cf. chap. II.1). While the economic rationality of the total social formation is dominated by the capitalist law of value, the lasting contradictions of incomplete and uneven capitalist transformation have led to the survival of pre-capitalist and to the creation of new petty capitalist economic forms, each generating semi-autonomous reproductive properties. Conventional conceptualizations that, for example, support the notion of 'disparities' between the dominant dynamic capitalist and the resilient pre-capitalist forms of production and reproduction, therefore seem inadequate. What makes the proper assessment of these semi-capitalist forms most difficult is that, besides their subordination to capitalist terms of valorization and commodification, they will also become subject to specific determinisms that are generated by their own material existence within the urban situation. Within the limits of economic commensurability set by the dominant capitalist relations of production, all semi-capitalist and petty capitalist economic forms will also reflect the specific urban conditions of their existence. This entails a process of continual internal restructuring according to dynamics generated by their own spatial conglomeration and concentration in the urban situation.

Considering the brief history of the proliferation of unplanned settlements, informal forms of reproduction, and self-help housing, too little consideration has been given to the aspect that new forms of production and reproduction are maturing in the process by which poor urban dwellers adapt to a changing and deteriorating social environment. As far as the deprived urban groups are concerned, their struggle for survival will necessarily be structured by contradictions and unreconciled articulations with capitalism, symptomatically producing political conflict and frustration. But this process will also be accompanied by new alliances, collusions, social segmentation, and internal differentiation emerging amid the newly forming peripheral urban fractions. In this respect we propose a distinction between transitional processes that are (1) true adaptations and assimilations to capitalist relations of production and (2) intermediary and interstitial new urban forms in which subsistence forms of production would have to be conceived in terms of their adaption to the urban form. The observable forms of 'urban subsistence' and 'informal network activities' - not yet capitalist but necessarily specifically interrelated with capitalism - will develop and be structured in dependence on the specific reproductive conditions given for their existence in the urban form (cf. Stuckey/Fay, 1980, p. 159).

The genealogy of contradictions and real oppositions between modes of production must be systematically traced back to the specific conditions under which peripheral capital comes to reproduce itself in a national context. This includes the dissections of both (1) aspects arising from the historic formation of the peripheral mode of production, and (2) the national reproduction of Third World economies working as functional parts of the contemporary international capitalist system. As a result we can now distinguish between *contradictions* and *real oppositions* arising inter-systemically from the incomplete and asynchronous capitalist transformation of Third World social formations.

In the auto-centred form the process by which the original relations of production are torn apart and reassembled by developing capitalism is synchronous, i.e. more or less a simultaneous process of disarticulation of the pre-capitalist modes of production and reorganization of the given productive elements according to the newly emerging capitalist requirements. As European history has shown, auto-centred transition to capitalism often includes aspects of uneven territorial formation. Social restructuring will be pushed forward selectively and unevenly; but it will be closely related to the dispersion of technical innovations among different branches of production, to the emergence of industrial mass production, and to the gradual creation and stimulation of mass consumption. All this involves a constant process of economic and spatial restructuring of capital and the proliferation of related state functions. These are accompanied by social adaptations, changing socio-spatial arrangements, and regional disparities, not to mention the impact of economic crisis and political class struggle. All this is unlike the type of uneven development encountered in the periphery. To make this point clearer we shall distinguish between 'primary accumulation' and 'real capitalist accumulation'. In the case of First World capitalism both are interrelated and sequential processes whereas in the periphery they are not.

2 Primary capitalist accumulation and the uneven rural-urban formation

Marx's concept of primary or original accumulation (sometimes misleadingly referred to or translated as 'primitive accumulation') relates to the socio-structural and generic prerequisites for the incipient formation of the capitalist mode of production. In this historical process capital subordinates and concentrates the historically given and the, to some extent, already socially developed prerequisites essential for its own 'take off': these are a social surplus production, crude social divisions of labour, a labour-force fraction liberated from personal liabilities, circulation/exchange of money, and, finally, accumulated capital. Since it is a precondition that capital is able to create and reproduce these prerequisites out of its own means, this necessarily calls for the controlled decomposition of existing modes and forms of production, dividing the original producers from their means of production (thus creating the proletariat) and transforming social production into various states of commodity production.[3] The decisive formative aspect in this process is that production and circulation are restructured as a unit in which capital now becomes the dominant instance (cf. Marx, *Grundrisse*, p. 226). As far as the mere generic determinants of the capitalist mode of production are concerned, the capitalist relations of production, following Cohen, can be sufficiently defined as 'proprietal relations of production', i.e. legal rights or relations of power socially bestowed on capital for the private appropriation of surplus products (Cohen, 1978, pp. 216). Since at this stage of development the historically given productive arrangements are merely formally subsumed by capital, this means that the extraction of surplus production will, in principle, be limited by two factors: (1) the physical bounds set to the expansion of the working day (therefore termed 'absolute surplus production'), and (2) the only rudimentarily developed divisions of labour in a production process based on work cooperation within otherwise unchanged technical modes of production.

Quite distinct from formal subsumption are the real dynamics behind the expansion of capitalist accumulation. Once deployed these will lead to a fundamental transformation of all given social prerequisites and forms of production. The velocity of capital accumulation and surplus production will then be determined by the rising organic composition of capital and the productive forces fostered by capitalist competition. Here the proprietal relations of production only figure as a precondition for the appropriation of what has now become 'relative surplus production' - i.e., surplus produced under terms entailing the complete restructuring of the technical and social relations of production. On this proper capitalist basis, the development of the social productive forces will appear as a faculty of capital itself. Accordingly, individual capital can realize and appropriate productive potentials on a private base that are in reality engendered socially by divisions of labour and large scales of economy. This is the process that defines the terms of 'real capitalist accumulation' with its higher rate of capital accumulation and pace of social transformation, the seizure of more and more sectors of production, and the drawing in of more and more segments of the population into its specific mode of reproduction.

As to Third World social formations we can now explain why capitalist transformation will be structured by asynchronisms. Since capitalism is imposed externally on colonial or peripheral social formations according to the advanced state of capital accumulation and to the consumptive and productive needs of the centres, primary accumulation must be pushed forward in advance and indeed far off balance from the requirements and dynamics of real capital accumulation on the given national base. Capitalist transformation in the periphery will be asynchronous because it lacks the self-regulative economic articulation between 'primary accumulation' and 'real accumulation' specific to capitalist development in the centres. All this can be exemplified by capitalist colonial history. Once imperialist conquest had taken place, the newly implemented colonial production systems were faced with immediate and rapidly growing demand for labour. At the same time, in the face of intact rural subsistence systems, colonial capital found indigenous populations very much reluctant to work as wage workers. Forms of primary accumulation had to be devised and by force imposed on these societies by various political and economic means.

In colonial regimes political measures employed included taxes, seizure of land and livestock, conversion of conquered people to slaves, compulsion of peasants, and conquest of trade routes, whereas the economic means involved a system of overexploitation of labour and unequal exchange (cf. Cliffe, 1976, p. 114). In the postcolonial stage the problem of labour provision was 'solved' in Latin America by the strengthening of a politically installed capitalist land-owning class and the associated 'hacienda system' as a means of surplus extraction from rural peasants (cf. Furtado, 1970, pp. 14-15). In colonial Africa, labourers for plantations, farms, and mines were mobilized and recruited predominantly by political and military force, undermining or irreversibly destroying traditional peasant systems and paving the way for the postcolonial dependency of rural populations on additional income from wage-labour and migrant labour systems (cf. Nzula/Potekhin/Zusmanovich, 1979; Cohen, R., 1976; Amin, 1974, pp. 65).

The social restructuring and transformation of pre-capitalist formations take place in a way that allows capitalism to mystify its real productive relationships (i.e. the contradiction between social terms of production and private appropriation of the product). This happens to such an extent that they reappear on the surface of society in what Marx has called the 'trinitarian formula' of sources of social revenue: capital/profit, landed property/rent, and labour/wages (cf. Marx, *Capital*, Vol. III, cap. 48). In the ideological content of this social mystification, capital, landed property, and labour now come to appear as the independent and indispensable 'natural' factors of production from which corresponding sources of value and revenue are derived. Thereby revenues will not appear as an arbitrary social relationship entailing a specific value distribution determined by capital, but rather as an allotment to the independent owners of capital, land, and labour-power to which they are entitled in proportion to their contribution in the making of the value incorporated in the product.

The outcome of this mystification is that whatever the extent of palpable economic contradictions and disparities in Third World countries, they will not appear as the adverse product of their historical conditioning and subordination by capitalism. They are perceived as shortcomings in the functioning of the 'naturally' given material base between independent owners of capital, land, and labour-power. As Lefèbvre emphasizes, the 'trinitarian' character of capitalism is not only the *de facto* result of the expansion of commodity relations and the generalization of exchange. It also expresses a necessary formative property of capitalism. In order to masque its social sources of wealth, the natural elements and means of production are dispersed by capital, only to be reallocated and centralized in the urban space in a state of separation. For its functioning the capitalist mode of production sustains capital, labour, and land in a state of socio-functional and spatial detachment, mediated by class divisions and discriminative state politics as their ultimate unifying instances (cf. Lefèbvre, 1972, p. 115).

According to these statements it is not surprising that despite the sectoral disparities in most Third World countries, territorial formation of capitalism is governed by a comprehensively deployed class formation with well institutionalized and personified capitalist relations of power. Wedged between the processes of uneven primary and real capitalist accumulation we find the victims of incomplete capitalist transition and modernization, or, in the words of Marx, those whose work ability is without value for capital, condemning them to exist without social and material conditions for their existence, therefore becoming a 'mere encumbrance' (cf. Marx, *Grundrisse*, p. 502).

In the rural areas of peripheral formations, contemporary capitalist transformation and modernization of agrarian production, committed to exportation, have irreversibly inhibited and supplanted existing peasant production systems still in command over their means of production and with access to arable land (cf. Feder, 1978; Griffin, 1974). The contradictory result of displacement is an increasing de facto proletarianization of the rural masses. But while the proprietal status of the migrants pressing into urban areas has changed in relation to the social means of production their socioeconomic position within the distorted system of social reproduction has not. The capitalist transformation of rural areas has not only displaced families from their subsistence base and deprived them of their means of production. It has also trajected a particular form of subsistence production to the cities in a process engendering unparalleled dimensions and varieties of form in urban reproduction.

The separation of family labour from its means of production or the loss of control over their product is the essential leverage by which labour is integrated into the system of proprietal relations of production. The outcome of primary capitalist accumulation is that workers are cast into the circulation of commodities. They have become private owners of their own labour-power with a specific potential exchange-value that, in theory, is determined by the socio-cultural costs of reproduction within a given national level. To the extent that capital is in command of the means of production and determines the mode of consumption, workers are faced with the problem that they have become socially dependent on the materialization of the commodity form of their own labour-power. Before the worker can realize his own real productive potentials, he is not only compelled to offer his labour to the market: he must ultimately also be successful in selling his own labour-power commodity.

The specific terms of this exchange are vital to understanding the way in which labour-power comes to be utilized by capital: the social transformation of labour-power into a privately owned commodity is a precondition for the capitalist appropriation of the social forces of production that are set to work by individually spent labour. Accumulation and surplus production are not only based on the appropriation of an unpaid portion of the working day. They also involve the appropriation and control of the social productive forces engendered in the production process when individual labour is subjected to work cooperation and divisions of labour.

3 The informalization of labour-power reproduction in the urban situation

As shown in various accounts for Latin America, the labour-force working in industrialized relations of production protected by labour legislation has remained stagnant at a rate of about 14%, with less than 8% occupied in 'big industries' (Quijano, 1979). Data from Columbia, typical for Latin America, suggests that the non-formal labour segment of the urban workforce was still expanding during the 1970s. Informal sector activities accounted for 45% of the urban workforce, self-employment comprised 25%, leaving a substantial balance of unpaid family labour and unemployed to make up the total.[4]

The situation in other Third World countries shows that developments in Latin America reflect global structures of peripheral urban labour markets. In Asian metropolises the rate of formal labour had declined to approx. 10% in the 1970s (H. D. Evers, 1981; Sethuraman, 1976). African labour statistics show a much lower ratio of non-formal labour (albeit with growing tendency). Nonetheless, considering its submission to comparable terms of integration into the global capitalist economy and with growing poverty and unemployment, the African situation should only be considered temporarily untypical because labour markets are still partially controlled by extra-economic means. This is explained by the dominant role of governments and parastatals in Africa who act as the major employers and by the heritage of recent colonial history in relation to labour market structures and on labour legislation.[5] Accordingly, the Latin American situation, which provides the assessment presented in detail below, will be taken as prototypical for Third World labour markets - at least if we include prevailing tendencies and anticipate ongoing developments towards growing informalization in Africa. An illustrative separate account of the situation in Zambia will be provided in the second part of this book.

The question how capitalism utilizes and exploits the different non-formal labour fractions and to what extent the prevailing forms are functionally related to capital valorization, i.e. represent an integral part of capital accumulation in the periphery, is an issue of considerable complexity. We will restrict discussion to the urban situation, first reviewing recent empirical evidence on developments in the informal sector and then going on to complete the picture from the viewpoint of household reproductive strategies that have developed in response to the constrained economic situation.

Although the evidence is still not conclusive, recent developments tend to disprove the perception of marginalization of urban masses forced to survive by autonomous interstitial economic activities and to function as a reserve army of unemployed.[6] If anything, the relation between the formal and the informal sector is complementary, although broken down into different modes and degrees of interrelationship in which the real nexus very often remains concealed.

Concerning informal production and commodity circulation, Portes/Walton have raised the interesting point that the very slow expansion of formal labour, even in relatively industrialized Third World countries like Mexico, is not alone explained by capital-intensive production methods. A widespread practice is the delegation of more labour-intensive and unqualified sides of the formal production process to informal producers. This strategy allows formal work regulations to be bypassed, avoids the frictions of labour dismissal, and keeps the ranks of tied employees at a minimal rate (Portes/Walton, 1981, p. 98). The arrangements made by firms with informal producers are usually indirect and make excessive use of the wage-depressing mechanisms inherent to the informal production system. To give a typical example, raw materials would be supplied to an intermediary informal broker who takes responsibility for the delivery of a specific product. The broker then subcontracts small workshops or home producers. For the home producer, paid below minimum wages, the delivery according to schedule usually requires, on top of working hours exceeding the industrial standard, the help of the family that adds unpaid portions of work to the value of the final product.[7]

The distribution of formal sector products by the informal sector works along comparable lines. In street vending, firms in the formal sector sell their products by *commission sellers*. These are supplied with sales equipment and are helped in getting trading licences. In return, commission sellers, exclusively selling products of their sponsors, are obliged to work with pre-fixed retail prices and profit margins (Bromley, 1978).

Petty commerce in low-income settlement areas, making use of the spatial and social proximity to its customers, is usually no less dependent on price-terms dictated by wholesalers. Lacking working capital, informal retailers are forced to pay higher prices for goods and high interest rates for commodity loans. Despite higher sales prices, marginal profits can still be accrued through breaking bulk and selling in very small quantities in shops, street stands, and local markets (Portes/Walton, 1981, p. 102). This practice corresponds to consumption patterns of customers who gain their income on a day-to-day basis and for whom buying in central commercial areas would involve additional commuter costs. Consumption credits offered by shopkeepers to regular customers are another incentive to buying in local shops, supporting their competitiveness with shops in the city centre.[8]

All these cases exemplify the fact that informal production/retailing is to a large extent openly controlled by the formal sector. Although these producers frequently use their own means of production (e.g. sewing machines, equipment, tools, stands, store rooms), the terms of contract imposed leave the dependent workers virtually no control over production or their products. Here nominal self-employment merely signifies that the activities of producers/ retailers represent a disguised wage while they are burdened with the risks of production.

Of course interstices exist that in particular allow the informal sector to perform important service functions for the reproduction of the labour-force. The gap between high-price world market commodities and low wage rates in Third World countries has given rise to thriving informal activities, supplying the economy with cheap services and consumption products. Repair workshops, household products recycled from scrap materials, domestic and personal services, food products, clothing, etc., are all in high demand not only by low-income groups. Reaching clients in the higher income brackets, informal production also greatly contributes to the general cheapening of the social costs of reproduction in the formal sector. Representing direct contributions to the reproduction of the formal sector, these informal activities may be accounted for in terms of open or disguised wages. In one way or another these are derived from the formal capitalist value circulation but under terms of exchange that subsidize capitalist labour-force reproduction.

Informal housing and land delivery are other examples of this type of subsidiary function, though in a somewhat different context. On the one hand, self-help housing provision is related to the capitalist commodity cycle and labour-power reproduction in the manner defined earlier by Pradilla and others. The self-construction of housing lowers rents, provides a housing market for middle income groups, or allows the externalization of housing costs from wages altogether by reassigning the social responsibility for housing provision to individual workers. On the other hand, the social function of self-help housing is not exclusively defined as a production process. Self-help housing also collaterally serves to provide social means of production and distribution. It substitutes missing or inappropriate state functions, in particular towards the demands of low- and middle-income groups (such as the failure of the state to devise appropriate forms of housing provision and land development, to extend urban community functions for labour reproduction, or to supply social living space). Due to the almost complete lack of government land delivery systems for low-income residence, illegal land invasions and informal land markets have turned into a customary form of urban land provision not only in Latin America but in most Third World countries.

Although not recognized by the state and thus officially violating prevailing legislation, evidence shows that the occupation of land by squatters is not a real threat to social order. On the contrary, if squatting takes place on difficult to develop land with little speculative value, a convergence of interests of squatters, landowners, the state, and politicians is a quite probable configuration (Collier, 1976):

- In the political field, pro-squatting campaigning has been a frequently used strategy of rousing populist party support. For landowners, invasions of low-value land will transform their premises into land of speculative value if invaders succeed in converting it into a permanent residential area.

- Land values will rise even higher if squatter actions can pressurize the state and local municipalities into legalizing the area and providing it with urban services and infrastructure.

However, in Latin America organized land invasions and spontaneous extensions are more and more forestalled by growing speculation with informal land markets. In Bogota, Mexico City, and San Salvador clandestine subdivisions are now reported as the dominant form of land provision. Remote urban land without basic services and with very low residential value (on steep or rocky hillsides, on river banks susceptible to flooding, or industrially polluted areas, etc.) is bought by middlemen and sold with high profits with dubious ownership titles (Portes/Walton, 1981, p. 96). For Buenos Aires, T. Evers has shown that illegal subdivisions are a deliberate strategy of landowners and real estate agents to evade the official minimal requirements concerning plot size and basic infrastructure. Cheaply developed plots are sold without cadastral registration of the subdivisions, leaving buyers in a legally insecure position with respect to their land ownership status. Most dwellers face an arduous struggle for official recognition that comes as a precondition for the provision of urban services (T. Evers, 1980).

Squatting may be initially tolerated by authorities as a cheap solution to acute housing problems and be used as a means to forestall social conflicts. But squatter problems have low state priority, and the state will do little to protect the dwellers' claim to residence if contested by more powerful pressure groups. In the case of a long-term illegal status, municipal policies towards squatters thus tend to become divided between integration, repression, force, and concessions depending on several factors. (1) With Third World economies racked with hyperinflation, land acquisitions are one of the last resorts of secure investment for capital owners. If invasions are successful in delivering land to the urban market, they may subsequently rouse the interest of investors and convert plots in squatter

64

areas into a highly speculative capitalist commodity. (2) With growing self-organization and political awareness, squatters are inclined to become a disruptive pressure group when they appear as competitors to public budgets and start voicing demands for settlement legalization and provision with urban services. In the absence of general state programmes and legal protection, the squatters' struggle for land and legalization very much becomes a regular part of class struggle, e.g. with respect to the distribution of state resources and services, access to urban space and housing, and over the issue of who determines municipal policies and planning.

In spite of the official disregard of social functions incorporated in squatting, the self-organization of the housing and settlement process by its residents provides a social and spatial aspect vital to the reproduction of the labour-force not catered for under the prevailing system of capital valorization and associated state policies.

> ... the constitution of the settlement brings together workers employed in the formal sector and those employed in informal petty production and trade. The settlement as a social community, is the context in which networks of exchange and mutual support are created. It is also in this context where the articulation of money wages with informal sources of supply permits the simultaneous reproduction of the different segments of the working class. Subsidized illegal settlements and the gamut of informal activities based on them are ultimately appropriated by capital in the form of lower wages. Squatter settlements and land invasions do not represent an abnormality or a contradiction in peripheral economies but are, instead, an intrinsic component of the process of capitalist accumulation, as it occurs in them (Portes/Walton, 1981, p. 97).

Coming back to the general assessment of informal sector activities, most of these have displayed a strong notion of *functionality* for capitalism. Nevertheless, the informal sector concept resists any easy integration into defined capitalist relations of production. Portes/Walton's attempt to account for the informal sector as part of peripheral accumulation and of working class reproduction may serve to prove this point. Portes and Walton have quite rightly argued that customary wage depressing mechanisms, in the formal and informal sectors alike, would be inadequate to explain the low wage floors in peripheral capitalism. Additionally, according to Portes/Walton, extramarket means are needed for the cost reduction in reproduction of the fully proletarianized working class segment. By utilizing unpaid family labour, the informal sector is able to produce an output of goods and services at prices lower than could be offered by formal production arrangements. Hence, the informal sector attains the vital function of maximizing surplus extraction by reducing labour reproduction costs for firms in the formal sector by providing direct subsidies (Portes/Walton, 1981, p. 86 and 106). As these informal activities are based on a wide range of strategies for gaining access to means of consumption, e.g. subsistence production, transfer payments, rents, and wages, and at the same time are coherent with the demands of the economic system, this leads the authors to the following proposal:

> As defined here, the concept of informal sector thus encompasses all income producing activities outside formal sector wages and social security payments. To a greater extent than the concept of petty commodity production, it enables us to examine the interplay between such multiple activities and their impact on the reproduction of urban labour (Portes/Walton, 1981, p. 87).

Without questioning Portes/Walton's conviction that the informal sector has indeed become a characteristic component of peripheral capitalism, some reservations towards the conceptual proposal submitted seem pertinent. In the first place, a social analytical concept should be more than the aggregation of individual cases. Higher levels of abstraction necessarily account for more phenomena; but they are not necessarily analytically more penetrating. It seems that the mere agglutination of analytical features into a presumed social totality of 'informal sector' hinders rather than assists the task of distinguishing the intra-sectoral relations involved. Precisely this kind of assessment would, however, be a crucial requirement for a framework working towards the design and implementation of appropriate developmental policies. In particular the informal sector concept of Portes/Walton, following its ubiquitous notion of functionality for peripheral accumulation, conflates the observable variety of exploitative relations, invariably reducing them to expressions of unequal exchange. Instead the intra-sectoral relationship can be seen to encompass a wide range of different forms: (1) *commensurable valuation and exchange*[9] such as in the appropriation of surplus labour from informal labour contracts, or market exchanges stemming from different levels of productivity in producing comparable specific commodities; (2) *uneven exchange* when surpluses of subsistence production from family work are offered to the market; and finally (3) the *appropriation of social productive forces* engendered by reproductive strategies within the urban situation. Although we agree with the view that all these means of exploitation and appropriation are ultimately bound together into a specific unitary structure of the capitalist urban periphery, their respective internal dynamics and interrelations will differ according to given social and urban circumstances. Moreover, not all informal production/reproduction is automatically part of capitalist relations of production. In part it will be, for example, subject to class struggle over its reappropriation by capital.

To express these last points more principally, the disarticulation of social relations in peripheral capitalism will not lead to their reunification according to requirements of capital valorization alone. Parts of the supposed functional contributions of informal production to capitalist accumulation must in fact be attributed to the urban situation of the workforce, i.e. be related to territorial, urban, and social circumstances of reproduction and not directly to requirements of the capitalist economy. With respect concern to the reproduction of the workforce, the fundamental condition of peripheral capitalism is the contradiction between the limited demand for labour-power, accompanied by low aggregation of capitalist commodity circulation, and the compulsion of urban residents to reproduce through participation in commodity and monetary forms of exchange.

- In peripheral capitalism the valorization process is no longer self-determined on a national base. Under the globally operating law of value, the organic composition of capital has lost its function of being economically regulative between productivity levels deployed and labour prices (cf. page 46). With a relatively small segment of capital operating at high international levels of productivity in the formal sector, only the fraction of labour-force incorporated in this sector has been able to organize as a class with bargaining power and enjoys protection by labour legislation.

- As international terms of valorization depress the national volume of capital and commodity production, peripheral capitalist production has become disproportional to its populations uprooted by the primary capitalist accumulation process. Simultaneously, since only limited scope exists for the expansion of the capitalist commodity cycle while the demand for labour-power is restrained, the urban situation will for its residents act as a reinforcement of the compulsion to reproduce mainly by commodified and monetary forms of production or labour. In the search for income opportunities, the terms of informal reproduction have become highly competitive. The social disarticulation between production and consumption has led to divisions in the informal working class that allow capital to bargain separately with each group of workers and depress wages by direct liabilities (cf. Bowles/Gintis, 1977, p. 178). On top of this, capital can take advantage of informal activities prompted not directly by capitalism but by the participation in urban commodity circulation of goods and labour-power. These emanate from the compulsion to expand the reproductive base of the individual worker in the urban situation and from the conditions under which the labour-power commodity can be realized on the market, if necessary by selling below market prices. Therefore subsistence, petty commodity production, and networking activities are passed on to the commodity markets but are subjected to production under non-capitalist terms of labour- and product-valuation. In this process, the urban economy is supplied with necessary goods not provided by capitalist commodity cycles. It thereby *de facto* subsidizes formal labour reproduction.

Accordingly, in the determination of labour rates, various factors combine in the result. In the first instance, wage-labour arrangements (open or disguised) and exploitative relations are inflicted by the structural constraints of expanded capitalist valorization and by its reduced need for wage work. In this respect, wage level determinations may be conceived as a direct, undisguised capitalist relation of production complying with the given terms of capital valorization in the periphery. As a revenue, the wage stems directly from the (formal) capitalist production or circulation process. In part the wage rates in the informal sector may be adequate to sustain the worker and his family at a minimal level of subsistence, or above, by market means. But for a large part of informal sector wage workers conditions apply that enable/enforce the lowering of individual wages below the level necessary to sustain their entire families.

The point is that these wage structures, with the additional requirement of providing cheap goods and services by informal means, in effect presuppose the existence of mode of labour-power reproduction *disjunctive* from capitalist principles. The operations of this reproductive system reflect the fact that peripheral capitalism, as a permanent feature, sets absolute limits to the capacity of its labour-power intake while it fails to develop a mass consumption sector with affordable commodities. In compliance with these fundamental constraints of peripheral capitalism, the corresponding mode of reproduction has developed two significant modifications. (1) It has the mutual reproduction of an extended family or reproductive group as its enlarged base and not that of single workers or core families as in industrialized capitalist countries. (2) The productive activities of the family or the reproductive group will be partially disintegrated from capitalist principles of work valuation. Instead they will reflect the economics of urban survival. From capital's point of view, the labour it employs is subsidized by the unpaid family labour that helps to sustain it. In terms of a mode of household reproduction, wage work, subsistence, petty commodity production, etc. are all merely options within household divisions of work, inevitably constrained by the limits of urban subsistence production and the need to achieve a substantial market exchange and monetary income for survival.

4 Labour-power utilization and collective survival strategies in the informal sector

Although the household group's choice of economic activities pursued will, for the most part, depend on the specific opportunities offered by the market, the rationale behind decisions is, ultimately, not to be found in the capitalist objectives of income- or profit-maximization. Under conditions that will mainly only provide sustenance at a minimum level of existence - constantly endangered by arbitrary price movements on commodity and labour markets - the key to understanding poverty groups' reproductive logics is to be sought at the level of domestic strategies rendering *maximal security of survival in time*. On part of the household unit, this type of strategy involves a specific adaptation to the wider urban and local social environment. The strategic mixture of productive activities pursued will be derived from feasible forms of subsistence and petty commodity production. Household strategies will make use of given locational advantages, access to and utilization of available resources,

68

mobilization of internal familial divisions of labour, networking, and informal economic activities, as well as formal sector wage-labour arrangements. In appropriate combination, all these factors can become part of a specific economy of survival within the given urban situation (cf. Elwert/Evers/Wilkens, 1982).

The internal operations of this collective reproductive system will be based on three elements. (1) The specific assessment and valuation of those activities considered necessary for the reproduction of the entire group. (2) The corresponding allocation of tasks amongst the group members, enabling effective divisions of labour in the pursuit of their specific reproductive strategy. Within these mutually agreed upon divisions of labour, the activities of specific group members may be economically valuable without necessarily directly or immediately contributing to income generation (e.g. time spent in the search for jobs, acquisition of information, negotiating, maintenance of networking activities, etc.). Finally, this requires (3) a specific mode of internal redistribution of the mutual income as not all economically active group members can actually acquire income or use-values from the specific task assigned to them (cf. Polanyi, 1978, p. 77).

These basic domestic reproductive strategies are simultaneously modelled by articulations both vertically towards the capitalist economy and horizontally in relation to other segments of the informal sector. The major *vertical articulation* requires that the market valuation of informal labour-power or products imputes its potential competition with advanced forms of production (either capitalist or informal). In other words, independent of the amount of labour time advanced for the production in question, it will only be valorized and exchanged on the market according to the extent to which it represents socially average terms of production. Within the time budget available to the individual worker or to his family, the marginal benefits derivable from informal work may, thus, lead to a situation in which it can be more beneficial to substitute domestic work of low productivity (e.g. self-help building, informal commodity production) by hired wage-labour if subjectively higher valuated jobs (both in terms of wage rates and job security) are accessible to him.

The production or retailing of exchange-values for the market also incorporates several risks for the petty producer/petty trader. Depending on the specific product offered, there are limits to the extent to which it can be self-consumed, i.e. made an interchangeable part of sustenance in the event that the commodity cannot be sold (perhaps this is one of the main reasons why trade or production of foodstuffs is one of the major informal economic ventures). In other words, although the specialization on a specific product or activity (enabling higher labour productivity and potential mass of producible values) seems more opportune, the advances spent on labour and outlays might be lost if the product is not sold and is without use-value for self-consumption. Consequently, flexibility and non-specialization in performing varying activities might be considered a safer contribution to the immediate maintenance of sustenance - even if it means working at much lower levels of productivity.

The offering of labour-power to the market may avoid some risks of self-production. But it is prone to a similar line of subsistence-strategy reasoning. The time spent on the search for jobs may be a deduction from possible alternative subsistence activities in the event that employment is not found or a job is not paid adequately to maintain sustenance. Moreover, the pressure on the individual worker to find sustenance within constrained time budgets, or to satisfy urgent monetary needs, will allow employers to take advantage of the job seeker's specific predicament by lowering the wages. In this case the wages paid bear no relation to the socially average price of this kind of labour-power on the market. Instead, it will be determined by the worker's bargaining power that, in turn, depends on the economic situation or degree of distress he finds himself in. This will often leave him no alternative but to accept underpaid jobs until alternatives can be found.

Finally, the maximizing equilibrium of work allocated to necessary domestic activities and wage-labour can become distorted in a fundamental way for the household. This might be the case if monetary income drops below the minimum level needed for market-dependent survival. In this situation access to monetary income under whatever conditions will have precedence in strategies of reproduction. This explains why under certain conditions of economic vulnerability it may be completely rational to sell products below their actual production costs if this contributes to survival, or this option provides urgently needed money to start other reproductive schemes.

To mitigate the pressures and insecurities imposed by vertical articulation with capitalist markets, *horizontal expansions* of the reproductive base have become an important new feature of urban survival. The striving to enlarge the domestic reproductive base has given rise to networking activities that surpass the demographic limitations of kinship relations. Lomnitz has defined the purpose of networking activities as the 'flow of reciprocal exchange of goods, services, and economically valuable information' the intensity of which will be determined by various degrees and forms of socioeconomic distance and proximity (Lomnitz, 1977, pp. 132-133). Unfortunately, an adequate discussion of this complex subject, moving far into ethnology, is beyond the scope of this book. However, it should be noted that research in this field is of growing importance for the assessment of planned interventions into habitat and settlement of low-income groups. The point in networking is that precarious conditions of survival can be mitigated by a social foundation providing a continuum of stability within the reproductive unit. This involves social closeness to others in networks with symmetric face-to-face relations and intensity of reciprocal exchange. To some extent this might, at first glance, seem to resemble rituals and cultural values that serve to reinforce the traditional group cohesion in an alienated urban environment. Contrary to their appearance, however, these are not to be mistaken for pre-capitalist modes of production or traditional systems of patronage. Instead we should come to consider them genuine 'modern' adaptations of poverty groups to Third World urban capitalism that must be acknowledged and not undermined by external interventions and planning procedures.

Another important aspect in the adaptation to the urban situation, seldom found in traditional pre-capitalist forms, would be the openness of the group to means of strengthening their reproductive base by cooperation with others, thereby surpassing the bounds of particularized group interests. In this way the establishment of urban-rural circuits and networks of exchange between regionally divided low-income households or between suburban and rural communities will provide a *territorial expansion* of the reproductive base. The scope of available resources (productive knowledge, means of production and reproduction, money, information, etc.) can be pooled together and allocated between families according to mutually defined economic objectives. These will allow larger scales of economy and a more intensive utilization of given productive resources (cf. Wallerstein/Martin/ Dickensen, 1979; Maennling, 1984). Community based habitat organizations (CBOs) and self-help projects are other good examples of horizontal network expansions. They not only mobilize economic potentials but add to political group cohesion as well. As a rule, the concentration of resources and the coordination of mutual actions in settlements or communities will be to the mutual benefit of all dwellers. The position of the entire settlement is strengthened more effectively than it would be by spontaneous solidarity actions, e.g. in the event of external hazards or harassing by urban authorities. Again, all this is far removed from the sometimes supposed resilience of pre-capitalist, peasant forms of production within Third World cities.

According to estimates of the United Nations and the World Bank, in any given Third World country large sections, or even the majority, of the urban population will be found without adequate provision for their livelihood by the market (cf. World Bank, 1983; UNFPA, 1986). Wherever reproduction on an individual or core family base is not feasible, economics of survival become indispensable entailing the concentration of means and the utilization of the higher productive potentials engendered by the formation of a larger reproductive group. In a constantly changing urban environment this will require that external constraints are integrated and flexibly transformed into corresponding actions and appropriate internal divisions of work. The productive forces of the reproductive group will be determined not so much by their social cohesion and proximity but by their ability to adapt and respond to changing income opportunities by way of internal reorientations and reallocations of their collective work stock.

This demonstration of versatile associations among informal sector members should not prompt us to assume that absent class distinctions, cleavages, or exploitation in their internal relations are absent. The necessary market-related and monetary based mode of reproduction also reflects itself in the internal process of exchange among informal sector members. According to Santos (1979) the essential instances of exchange are mediated by credit, money, and middlemen. The market acquisition of goods by low-income groups for self-employment schemes very often involves consumption-credits that are only attainable by personal means. This not only implies extraordinarily high rates of interest; it also leads to direct personal dependencies and liabilities towards credit-providing middlemen (mainly retailers, transport agents, and money lenders). As these agents operate both in the formal and informal sectors of the economy, they have access to formal credit and are also provided with the means and personal relations important to the expediting of market transfers between informally produced goods and the corresponding demand in the formal sector (cf. Santos, 1979, pp. 123-124).

As reproduction is subject to a situation in which the vertical articulation of the informal sector with capital determines the forms of social production, i.e. the ways it utilizes labour-power according to the requirements of capital valorization, owns and operates the social means of production, and controls the price structure of commodity markets, the *reconquest* of means of production/means of subsistence can become a paramount issue for the future safeguarding and amelioration of urban living conditions for low-income groups.

Within the search for economic security by the combination of various sources of income, it would be wrong to consider subsistence-based production a mere 'last resort' for household reproduction when everything else fails. According to estimations in Jakarta, Indonesia, urban subsistence production on average contributed 17.6% to household consumption, a ratio rising to 30% for a significant fraction of 13.2% of households (H. D. Evers, 1981, p. 66). Various accounts from all over Latin America show the continuing importance of subsistence gardening and animal husbandry for urban dwellers (Roberts, 1978; Mangin, 1967; Portes, 1972). Of course, true subsistence production in the form of urban agriculture, livestock, consumer goods production, self-help housing for subletting, etc. will also find limits in the urban social environment. For example, transport-cost-saving inner city habitat rendering better access to jobs, will usually go hand in hand with high population densities in these locations. This will tend to curb subsistence production (possibly excepting subletting), or restrict the scope for the spatial unification of the extended family as a means to concentrate and centralize reproductive networks. On the other hand, recent research has shown that wherever urban space allows access to higher monetary income this does not automatically mean a decline in the significance of subsistence production as a contributor to household sustenance. On the contrary, in many cases planned forms of urban subsistence production can only be initiated *subsequent* to the market acquisition of the prerequisite means of production. Since official bank credits are virtually inaccessible to low-income groups and informal credits are subjected to excessive rates of interest, any kind of investment into means of production only becomes feasible, or can be ventured, from an economic position in which stabilized and continual provision of monetary income is already ensured (cf. Elwert/Evers/Wilkens, 1982, p. 14).

The realization of survival strategies by domestic-based means of production may not only be hampered by a multitude of market restrictions, including credit facilities and access to monetary income: housing programmes introduced by state and international development agencies may frequently act in the same way by disregarding locational, spatial, and territorial aspects vital to informal reproduction. Following the conventional perception of housing and employment as spatially and functionally divided activities, squatters have been relocated to site and service or housing schemes on the urban periphery under terms of spatial provisions of house and plot designed to serve the basic housing needs of core families only. Opposition to resettlement, decline in income, and subsequent deterioration of housing conditions in the new habitat environment have been the logical consequence of such programmes. In the official view, the failure of resettlement schemes has often been wrongly perceived as a problem of lack of social integration. Instead it most probably exemplifies once more that subsistence production (urban agriculture, animal husbandry), or domestic based production/trade are more than marginal aspects of sustenance for squatter populations.

Habitat planning for low-income groups, either professional or by dweller's self-help, still also underestimates and neglects the specific needs of women, whose domestic and informal sector work plays a most important part in securing sustenance for the family. Specifically in Latin America and South East Asia the contribution of women to informal production, services, and petty trading - often using domestic infrastructure - is quite high, reflecting the fact that it is the women who carry the main burden of the new urban familial and networking divisions of labour (Moser, 1994). According to Boserup, between 40 and 50% of informal activities in Latin America are accomplished by women involving total working hours considerably exceeding those of the men (Boserup, 1982, p. 156). In the urban informal sector of Africa similar developments are observable. There women are no longer only responsible for urban agriculture and domestic activities, as required by their traditional role. Within new domestic divisions of work and the expansion of informal activities, women have, for instance, occupied the former domain of men in street and market vending.

Having pointed out striking aspects of production/reproduction of Third World urban survival, this still leaves us with the question of how to place the issue of reproductive efforts, including self-help housing and land provision, in the perspective of developmental policies and theories. Accordingly, the next chapter will be devoted to the problems of reassessing self-help housing and the associated reproductive activities as a part of peripheral accumulation and urban formation.

Notes

1   For an extensive critique of conventional Marxist and dependencia accounts of urban-rural disparities and polarizations see Läpple (1978).

2   cf. Bairoch (1973).

3   This does not exclude that capital will, for some time, continue to rely on pre-capitalist forms of production most typically in the provision of agricultural products. The question of ground rent discussed in note 6 in the last chapter has already become the classical controversy in this field concerning the necessity of building these forms of production into the capitalist system of valuation (cf. Rey, 1973 and Amin, 1978).

4   Romero, 1980 quoted by Portes/Walton, 1981, p. 83.

5   Major changes to this structure are imminent under the various structural adjustment programmes in Africa that are pressing for deregulation and privatization of state functions.

6   The assumed wage depressing function is not supported by data presented by Tokman. It indicates that productivity gains in the formal sector have been handed down to employees in form of higher wages, even if they are still markedly below wages paid in capitalist core countries for comparable jobs. The explanation given by Tokman for wage rises is the interest of companies in stabilizing their workforce and the impact of labour legislation (Tokman, 1978).

7   Contract terms in clothing production by seamstresses are a typical example for this practice: for Mexico cf. Lomnitz (1977); for Argentina cf. Schmukler (1979).

8   For an account of the very similar practice of informal retailing in Zambia, Africa cf. chapter XI.1.

9   A theoretical exposition of commensurable exchange of invested working hours in production performed at different levels of the applied productive forces will be given in the next chapter.

IV Reconceiving urbanization, self-help housing, and social reproduction in peripheral capitalism

1 The self-help debate revised

Since the start of our discussion of the self-help housing problem, this issue has been presented in different contexts. Starting with Pradilla's modern adaptation of Engels' classical exposition of the working-class housing question,[1] going on to global aspects like the internationalization of labour-power reproduction, then considering intermediate concepts such as the informal sector, and finally coming down to the level of reproduction strategies of domestic households. In terms of consequences for concrete planning the question arises as to whether it is now possible to see the self-help housing problem from a different perspective.

As recalled, Pradilla had given support for self-help housing projects a distinct implicit negative connotation. Mass forms of self-help housing not only allow the reduction of wages by the income-fraction normally dedicated to rent. They also lower the entire social exchange-value of labour-power by reducing the social standards of average housing. The advocacy of self-help housing programmes reinforces an ideological perception of social disparities: the failure of state or market to provide affordable housing is, by self-help programmes, *politically* reassigned as a private commitment to labourers and their families to be accomplished outside paid wage-labour activities in their recreation period.

Although Pradilla's elaboration of the housing problem, conceived as part of labour-power reproduction, is still an important analytical approach, shortcomings in the economic comprehension have appeared. As shown, Pradilla's theoretical perspective was narrowed by his exclusive reference to the classical form of capitalist development and its conceptual assumptions. Choosing an 'ideal model' approach, deliberately abstracting from aspects of world market integration, he was unable to present his case in terms of contemporary accumulation models working on global scales that have disproved the Marxist concept of a 'reserve army' of unemployed. New international divisions of labour assign new functions both to labour reproduction and to self-help housing in capitalist peripheries. Recent empirical evidence has shown considerable differentiation of the Third World labour-force and the modes of its incorporation into capitalist relations of production. Peripheral accumulation functionally requires heterogeneous structures of reproduction: formal sector production and its labour-force are maintained by open and concealed informal wage relations, by the delegation of production through intermediate informal agents, and by the provision of cheap necessary consumer goods by informal production. Additionally capital can appropriate surplus from the informal commodity cycle shown to pertain to the urban mode of reproduction. In its specific articulations with capitalism, the domestic mobilization of productive human and material resources by economics of survival and subsistence expediently offers commodities and services to the market virtually exempt from capitalist cost calculations. But the social functions of self-help housing go beyond these economic contributions.

Besides being a process of production and a means of labour-power reproduction, vital urban and communal functions are performed by the social circumstances of the self-organized settlement process. Squatter communities constitute an urban situation in which the functional constraints imposed by peripheral capitalism on the urban economy can be mitigated. The squatting process delivers land and housing, and provides social space for the vertical and horizontal articulations required for the simultaneous reproduction of different segments of the urban workforce. This process is shaped by state action that, on the one hand, is strengthening international capital, and, on the other, is struggling to alleviate its consequences for national reproduction and emerging class conflicts (cf. Walton, 1985, p. 10).

This goes some way towards explaining why migration, uncurbed urban concentration, unplanned settlements, and self-help housing activities are increasingly conceived and accepted by Third World states as a functional response to changing economic situations. Accordingly, urban politics and attitudes have gradually changed in the last two decades, swinging from slum clearing and eviction to *laissez faire*. Migration or illegal settlement are not encouraged, nor are more than palliative efforts made to integrate the residential areas of low-income dwellers into the framework of urban planning. Whenever the situation permits, unplanned settlements and squatter movements are widely left unregulated and uncontrolled by the state in an attempt to forestall political conflicts, costly interventions and planning. Exceptions are those cases where direct capital interests become involved, or difficulties in maintaining capitalist conditions of production seem imminent.

With regards to the self-help problem, Portes/Walton's approach to the informal sector, although more extensive than Pradilla's, lacks conceptual conclusiveness. In particular their global definition of the informal sector, as a functional alignment of peripheral accumulation and reproduction, fails to open new developmental perspectives. As long as all operations of the informal sector are merely seen to subsidize the worldwide process of capitalist accumulation, any effort to strengthen self-help activities by providing financial, technical, and material support would indeed only add to the exploitation of low-income groups. It

76

would also deepen uneven international divisions of labour and reinforce the productive functions assigned to peripheral capitalism within this system. But the impression given by Portes/Walton of an inescapable vicious cycle is less conclusive than might seem.

An assessment of self-help activities in terms of appropriate developmental measures hinges on a more differentiated analysis of capitalist accumulation and the modes of value production and appropriation deployed. This analysis would have to cover and conceptually reassess three concurring aspects of capitalism and the informal economy, relating to (1) the historical specific indigence of capitalist accumulation in the periphery, based on social conditions of production that draw on intersectoral value transfers, (2) the reproductive situation of the working class within this system, and (3) aspects of urban formation introduced by squatter activities including the terms of their partial integration into the legal urban framework. The core intent of these propositions will be outlined below, showing the terms under which support for self-help may be defined as appropriate.

The undifferentiated notion of functionality derived from what appears as the empirically evident in the informal sector conflates the contemporary historical state of uneven global formation of capitalism with the inherent dynamics of capitalism itself. The alternative lesson to be learnt from the current formation of the world system is that, under specific national conditions, the dynamics of capitalism can indeed be mobilized as is happening with the so-called New Industrializing Countries (NICs). This does not deny the tendencies of growing internationalization of capital and the changing patterns and stages in spatial divisions of global capitalism.[2] To reiterate a previous distinction, the capitalist world system - as a theory of imperialism - is not the capitalist mode of production extended to a global scale. Thus, informal production represents a mode of exploitation serving the needs of internationally operating capital. But as a form of production based on retarded development of the productive forces, it can only be *relatively* functional for indigenous capitalist accumulation insofar as national capital is compelled to operate within internationally imposed terms of valorization. Therefore, the design of developmental measures should surpass status quo reasoning and be posed in terms of the dialectical unit of historical specific capitalism and the latent general developmental tendencies of the capitalist mode of production.[3] For development practice, this means that measures directed to the improvement of informal production systems should be carefully scrutinized with respect to the potential effects of increased commodification and enhanced productivity. For instance, who will be the main beneficiaries under the prevailing structures of appropriation, and what are the effects of market expansion on the social equilibrium of settlements? Does it encourage the intrusion of alienating capitalist powers, will it lead to self-exploitation or to the internal exploitation of other informal workers?

With regard to the reproductive situation of the working class, Portes/Walton's failure to differentiate between the modes of appropriation involved in the exploitation of informal production by capital obscures rather than clarifies its social character. The necessary determination of the class-specific relations of production involved in informal activities is supplanted by the notion of relations of unequal exchange. However, to some extent the assumption of unequal exchange appears counterfactual in that it presupposes the existence of an urban pre-capitalist sector subject to arbitrary terms of valorization and not the unitary urban economy in question that is structured by disparities in the development of productive forces and retarded generalization of commodification.[4] In peripheral capitalism the different degrees of integration of the working class require specific terms of reproduction of formal and informal labour that are made possible by the existence of a new category of sustention underpinning it. The widely generalized practice of households to combine wage-labour, petty commodity production, networking activities, and subsistence into an expanded, reorganized base of work cooperation has not yet become fully realized as a novel relation of production within peripheral capitalism: not vis-à-vis individual workers but in relation to what we suggest calling *collective workers* acting as members of expanded reproductive units. Importantly, the appropriation of surplus from collective workers is not entirely defined by socially commensurable terms of valuation and exchange. Additionally hidden or disguised class struggle over extramarket terms of surplus usurpation will occur. Depending on the aggregate state of sustention and the more or less organized bargaining power of collective workers, prices and wages can be reduced complying with levels of minimal subsistence that bear little or no relation to the potential market value incorporated. The uncertainty of realization of the commodity character of labour-power and informal products is a powerful mechanism in reinforcing this type of structural relationship. Seen from this vantage point, support for self-help activities of collective workers would, for example, seem appropriate under two conditions: (1) if it contributes to achieving a true market price for products or labour instead of a subsistence-oriented valuation, and (2) if the terms of self-help support warrant producer control over the product and include protective measures, e.g. legal or political, against its dispossession by external forces.

In the manner previously described, squatter activities are a positive contribution to urban development. Their settlement process overcomes institutional and market disparities in the delivery of land, housing, and social living space. In this sense the squatting process must be considered an alternative means of providing the *infrastructural* prerequisites for peripheral capitalist development comparable to those provided by the state. But like all prerequisites of production that are necessarily produced outside direct capitalist command, these are subject to class struggle over their appropriation and utilization: appropriation may take place directly by capital and market forces, or indirectly through the interventions of the municipality in the settlement. Accordingly, measures designed to strengthen communal coherence and self-control over settlement affairs, either with or without municipal cooperation, may also cause a change in the asymmetries involved in the capitalist appropriation of assets deployed by communal self-help action.

2 Informal production and peripheral capitalist accumulation

What is lacking in most assessments of informal production as a contributor to capitalism is a clearer distinction between the inherent logical tendencies of capitalist accumulation and valorization, on the one hand, and the national base of capital reproduction that has evolved in response to the limit functions imposed on capitalist development in the periphery, on the other. Due to this misperception, underdevelopment comes to appear as an irreversible state in accordance with the international valorization process and the functional divisions in global capitalist production. In the export-oriented growth model 'informally channelled subsidiaries' (Portes/Walton) have, no doubt, become a permanent structural feature of peripheral accumulation. From the viewpoint of economics, intersectoral transfers of labour and resources invariably support the global accumulation process. But the perspective of development policies requires a closer examination. It would reveal that the transfers in question are effected along two different lines, the differentiation of which is relevant to the question of appropriate support to self-help and petty commodity production schemes. These are

- the discriminate appropriation of productive elements and resources by means of *unequal* commodity exchange between different branches and sectors of the economy, and

- the appropriation of productive elements produced under modified but completely *consistent terms of value-production* complying with the internationally determined capitalist law of value and conditions of valorization.

The argument of unequal exchange, implying an intersectoral flow of subsidies, will be explored first. It contends that a specific quantity of labour produced within one system or sector is transferred to another under social terms of valuation that allow the appropriation of unpaid portions of values incorporated in the product. For the industrial sector of developing countries data is available that indeed supports the assumption of unequal exchange. Despite comparable levels of labour productivity, average wages are only a fraction of those paid in industrial core countries, allowing international transfers of surplus labour (Portes/Walton, 1981, p. 72; ILO, 1970). By combining cheap national labour with imported productivity standards in production, multinationals can sell products at (high) international prices, thereby achieving high rates of extra-profit. Without touching the ongoing dispute as to whether these extra-profits accrue directly from the terms of exchange within the commodity circulation, or express disparities in the relations of production, the point is that in any version the context of unequal exchange of values will be limited to products of specific character: i.e. to Third World goods that are produced and exchanged on the capitalist world commodity market and are subject to internationalized price structures.

Thus, the impact of unequal exchange seems to have been grossly exaggerated for global capitalist accumulation. Although asymmetric exchange may adequately describe the exploitative relations between core and periphery with world market products, it is of limited value in explaining the absolute logical tendencies of capitalist dynamics and the part the non-industrialized sectors of peripheral economies play in the accumulation process. As a category of circulation, it also fails to define the basic relations of production that make unequal exchange possible. Although uneven exchange or extra-profits are an appropriate *relative* accumulation strategy for international capital under given terms of valorization in the periphery, they must be dialectically related to the limits they impose on *absolute* capital accumulation. The accumulating potentials mobilizable by uneven exchange are naturally limited by the productive potentials it can draw on. With absolute surplus production already brought close to its physical limit in most Third World countries, unequal and asymmetric exchange would, in the last instance, seem incapable of substantially increasing the appropriable surplus needed for the expansion of capital accumulation at national level.[5]

Studies presented by A. Pinto and Quijano illustrate this argument. Their data reveal vast differences in work productivity among the various economic sectors of Latin America. In comparison to the 'modern' industrial sector, technologically linked with international capital working at a productivity of 100%, the 'intermediate sector' (mining, export agriculture, manufacturing, and artisanal production) produces at a rate of 25%; whereas the 'primitive sector', encompassing 40% of the population deploying small-scale and subsistence production, is only able to achieve 8% of the productivity rate of the modern sector (cf. Pinto, 1973, p. 6; Quijano, 1980). As surplus production is the expansion of the working day beyond the level of basic sustenance, and the valorization of labour time is strictly bound to market values of the product, it is difficult to imagine how capital can, in the end, extract a substantial and sufficient mass of values by maintaining primitive forms of production - however susceptible to exploitation they may be.

In analysing exploitation, the point is not to confuse surplus appropriation with the appropriation of unpaid working hours. There is a fundamental difference between value quantities (estimated in socially necessary units of work representing social average levels of productivity) and the real labour time incorporated in the production of a specific commodity. In Third World countries the objective link between national profits and wages has been supplanted by international predeterminations. The amount of time spent on the production of a commodity no longer directly represents the value incorporated in the product. Instead the labour invested is valorized according to the amount of social labour its product represents in direct comparison with the most advanced international capitalist production systems (cf. Schoeller, 1976). In other words, it is the internationalized market and pricing system that decide the extent to which imputed labour figures as exchange-values and not the absolute amount of labour hours spent on production. Whereas for international capital, subjected to internal competition, the development of the productive forces of labour and the means of production are the essential mechanisms by which an expanded rate of accumulation can be achieved, this condition can only apply to the small section of industrialized Third World capital.

This leads to the paradoxical situation that while 'intermediate' and 'primitive' forms of production are compelled to expand their working hours in order to compete with the superior productivity of internationalized industrial production, vast amounts of Third World labour time spent in this process are actually lost for the national and international capitalist accumulation process. This results from the circumstance that the *international* framework determines the socially necessary labour time to produce specific commodities at *national* level. Accordingly, Third World conditions of production, structured by low productivity levels that achieve the necessary rate of profit by utilizing cheap labour, can merely be functional for the dependent national mode of peripheral capital accumulation. But the failure to develop means of relative surplus production that are competitive by international standards inevitably means a potential loss in terms of absolute capital accumulation.

At the same time as the gap between First and Third World productivity is growing, physiological and socioeconomic limits are emerging in the extent to which this gap can be compensated by increasing exploitation by absolute surplus production: the workday cannot be extended beyond biological limits, and wages paid outside the formal sector have been depressed close to the minimum level of survival made possible by the expansion of urban subsistence networking.

What follows from this is that the national process of production must be seen as a response to distorted price/value proportionalities complying with the terms of a globally working law of value and not as an intrinsic function of the capitalist mode of production as such. In any given peripheral economic system the existing homogeneous aspects of internationalized capital valorization are counterposed by internal national modifications and fragmented conditions for the production of values. Following Schoeller (1976, p. 78) these include:

(1) the continuing coexistence of a variety of technical and social modes of production, ranging from industrial to simple commodity and subsistence production in both urban and rural areas; (2) a low and uneven dispersion in the development of the productive forces between different branches of national production; (3) a very low level of social divisions of labour and concomitant proliferation of wage-labour relations; (4) the continuation of personal dependencies and liabilities in both in rural and urban areas; (5) socially inhomogeneous rates of surplus production and a low state of aggregation in capital circulation; (6) a low level of capitalist mass production without

social uniformity in the value-producing potential of labour, non-standardized national rates of profit, and non-standardized commodity prices in all sectors of the economy.

Without the backward linkages between productive sectors essential for the development of national average rates of profit and the emergence of wage structures related to the organic composition of capital, the capitalist law of value will only operate under modified terms of deployment within heterogeneous social forms of production.[6] In a situation in which the national shaping of capital reproduction blocks the development of the productive forces and limits the absolute rate of accumulation, capitalist expansion will merely reproduce and deepen the given internal structural heterogeneity and disparities in productivity. As Quijano has put it, the result of the grafting of industrial production onto the given artisan and domestic forms of production will not be their displacement or dissolution but merely their internal modification and increasing depression of their economic plane of reproduction (Quijano, 1974, p. 302).

With regard to the role of the informal sector in capitalist accumulation, we fully agree with the statement of Portes/Walton that it is impossible

> ... to assimilate the informal economy as it exists today in peripheral countries to the earlier 'transitional' stage of advanced capitalism, for the present situation is the deliberate and continuously reproduced consequence of a new worldwide structure of accumulation. Thus, informal enterprise is not a vestigial presence, a lag from pre-capitalist times but rather a very modern and expanding creation. It is an integral component of peripheral capitalist economies and its development is mandated by the conditions in which these economies are incorporated into the contemporary world-system (Portes/Walton, 1981, p. 104).

But apart from our earlier reservations towards Portes/Walton's use of 'informal sector' as an analytical category, we also disagree with their perception that the informal sector is *in toto* subject to unequal exchange, i.e. is 'subsidizing' the formal production sector. Instead, under modified terms of global expansion of the capitalist law of value, vast parts of informal production are, by their vertical articulation with the capitalist sector, based on *commensurable* terms of value production. The devaluation of informal work is, as shown, principally the result of its estimation in comparison with advanced capitalist production. As a corollary, subsistence levels have been lowered by the networking efforts of the expanded reproductive unit, the benefits of which are *additionally* appropriated by capital, cheapening the labour-power of the collective worker even further. Hence, wage-labour relations (partially concealed) and costs of labour-power reproduction remain the valid economically determining categories, which makes the assumption of uneven, arbitrary terms of exchange and transfers a misleading proposition. These definitions are not contradicted by the circumstance that informal sector activities also comprehend commodity production and circulation. Instead they are integral parts of a modified petty commodity production system; a concept perhaps precipitately dismissed by Portes/Walton as inappropriate to comprehend the totality of informal sector (Portes/Walton, 1981, p. 86).

3 Peripheral petty commodity production

An abstract conceptualization of the informal sector requires the incorporation of its manifold appearances into an integrated structure, not excluding socially necessary aspects of workers' self-perception and class-based ideologies. In this sense the notion of unequal exchange is perhaps a necessary misperception. It stems from the functional requirement of the informal sector to *appear* as an independent sphere of production in order to fulfil its productive role in peripheral capitalism as a concealed relation of production. These social requirements very much resemble the properties depicted by Marx in the assimilation of petty commodity production by developing capitalism. Referring to petty commodity production Marx explained that the

> ... exchange of equivalents proceeds; it is only the surface layer of production which rests on the appropriation of alien labour without exchange but with the semblance of exchange. This system of exchange rests on capital as its foundation, and, when it is regarded in isolation from capital, as it appears on the surface, as an independent system, then it is a mere illusion, but a necessary illusion (Marx, *Grundrisse*, p. 510).

These social properties of petty commodity production reappear in the structures of the informal sector providing we regard it as a potential new type of capitalist relation of production. The point is not to empirically see informal activities in isolation - many of which are in fact borderline cases already representing petty capitalist enterprises (of course using informal labour), or are stabilized wage labour relations. Instead, when conceived as a relation of production, the informal sector refers to an economic substructure capable of sustaining workers and their families under conditions of partial disintegration from labour and commodity production markets. Seen from this social perspective, all informal activities have as their mutual core the reproduction of the expanded domestic unit. Accordingly capital-labour relations are no longer established with individual workers but are negotiated with collective workers who are part of an expanded reproductive unit. Although wages are paid to individual workers they are, in return, transformed into a different category: that of a contribution to the group's *reproductive funds* and subject to specific terms of redistribution amongst its members. Within this internal relation, other activities of the reproductive group pursued according to internal divisions of labour, including commodity production, vending, subsistence, networking, and subsidies of various kind (welfare, state grants, etc.) are, in spite of their different material fabric, economically part of the same reproductive structure.

Leaning heavily on the original concept of petty commodity production, we propose the delineation of its peripheral form, i.e. *peripheral petty commodity production*, expressing a new relation of production - appropriate to the exploitation of collective workers and their specific mode of reproduction. The versatile properties of 'petty commodity production' were first elaborated by Marx, Lenin, and Kautsky for the peasant mode of production (cf. Marx, *Capital*, Vol. 3 and *Grundrisse*; Lenin, *Collected Works*, Vol. 1 and 4; Kautsky, 1970). The economic roots of this production form were seen in the patriarchal subsistence mode of production, based on small-scale means of production and the exploitation of family labour. Most importantly this underlying economic logic continues to determine production even when petty commodity production arises from this form. For Marx, the peasant, in this case,

> ... regards the expenditure of labour as the indispensable prerequisite for the labour-product which is the thing that interests him above all. But as regards his surplus-labour, after deducting the necessary labour, it is evidently realized in the surplus product; and as soon as he can sell the latter or use it for himself, he looks upon it as something that cost him nothing because it costs him no materialized labour. Even a sale below value and the capitalist price of product still appears to him as profit. ... The absolute limit to him is no more than the wages he pays to himself, after deducting his actual costs. So long as the price of the product covers these wages, he will cultivate his land, and often at wages down to the physical minimum (Marx, *Capital*, Vol. 3, pp. 805-806).

As the historical European case, in which developing capitalism extensively coexisted with petty commodity production without need of its dissolution exemplifies, the relationship between both production forms is non-contradictory, even complementary. This is explained by the fact that petty commodity production shares, in undeveloped, embryonic form, basic categories with capitalism, allowing its easy integration into capitalist commodity circulation. Stated in terms of political economy, compatibility is achieved by three features of petty commodity production.

- As an essential formative abstraction in determining the structure of capitalism, simple commodity production represents the first and simplest social totality in which the logical unity of use- and exchange-value may come to exist interchangeably in every product: subsistence products with use-value are either self-consumed or may attain potential or real commodity form when the use-value of the product appears as a prerequisite for its subjection to the capitalist commodity circulation. In this case the use-value for the producer becomes use-values for others and is transformed into a commodity with exchange-value.

- By the terms of exchange between what appear as independent modes of production on an intermediate market, petty commodity production integrates the original producers into commodity circulation without requiring that the capitalist law of value be fully applied to their terms of production or to the valuation of products sold on the market.

- It provides the logical base of synthesis between petty production, conceived as private and independent, and the dominant social relations of production in which the circulation of capital determines the movement of what appear on the surface as a self-regulating price and value system of equivalents.

The social perception of exchange inherent in petty commodity production serves economy in a double fashion: retaining the pre-capitalist self-valorization of expended labour as equivalents without exchange-value, it allows the integration of simple production into capitalist commodity circulation in a situation in which- as yet- undeveloped capitalism must, for its own reproduction, partially rely on pre-capitalist forms of surplus production. For the preservation of this complementary sphere of production, still unattractive for capitalist penetration and generalized commodification, it is essential that the involved relations of production yield an ideological perception that permits the notion of social detachment and self-containment on the part of petty producers to be maintained.

In contrast to these classical determinants, the major modification of petty commodity production in its contemporary peripheral form concerns the content and social form of subsistence on which it is now based.

- In the first case, the base of urban subsistence is no longer exclusively land or static traditional production forms performed by isolated units - although ties of informal producers to their urban locations may be just as fundamental as that of peasants to their land. Instead, subsistence is now organized according to the changing social, material, and environmental conditions offered by the urban situation. According to the diversity of productive opportunities, subsistence is subject to highly differentiated divisions of labour, flexibly responding to given external economic circumstances. These include networking activities and territorial expansions of the reproductive base.

- Secondly, the production form in question is no longer pre-capitalist, or a subordinated, vestigial petty capitalist occupation as sometimes associated with petty commodity production. Peripheral petty commodity production has developed in close association with the expansion of capitalism in Third World cities, interstitially responding to the

85

contemporary contradictions of the peripheral growth model. In this sense it represents an intra-systemic relation of production appropriate to the given terms of capital valorization and accumulation.

- A third difference is that urban subsistence necessarily incorporates compulsory exchange with capitalist-dominated labour and commodity markets. Thus, subsistence is no longer related to the organic unit of contained private production and consumption. It has become a social category in which the necessary illusion of an independent production system is retained by the character of the collective work system: in an economic situation where wage-labour or market production is unable to grant full and secure sustenance, market-related economic activities appear to the reproductive group as *one* means of subsistence among others, thereby concealing their character as a capitalist relation of production.

For peripheral capitalism the original category of petty commodity production has been subject to a determination of form, modified according to its contemporary function within the global process of accumulation and reproduction of the workforce. Therefore, peripheral petty commodity production has retained old functions and acquired new ones: it continues to rest on subsistence, but is internally modified in form and character and now articulated intra-systemically with the capitalist law of value and the urban social environment. The *collective worker* is the key to understanding how combined labour strategies and networking activities have become part of a capitalist relation of production. Contrary to the self-perception specific to this form as independent producers or owners of their labour-power, the price that the producer/owner receives is

> ... no longer a pure category of exchange, but a category, that is, a relation of production, a concealed wage. ... subsistence production now figures, under this system, as the specific form of reproduction of labour-power within a capitalist process of production (Banaji, 1977, p. 34).

In the notion originally put forward by Marx and Lenin, petty commodity production reflects embryonic stages of capitalism at a time when it is still struggling to dominate and transform independent pre-capitalist systems. Peripheral petty commodity production of today is conceived as an intrinsic and semi-permanent response to distorted terms of valorization and to the incomplete and unevenly developed capitalist mode of production. The self-imposed conditions of 'overwork' and 'underconsumption' (Kautsky) typical of simple commodity forms of reproduction of the labour-force, comply readily and flexibly with the various limit functions imposed on peripheral accumulation. They reproduce a disposable workforce and supplies the economy with necessary consumption goods that are unprofitable for capitalist production. At the same time these specific fields of production are instantaneously dissolvable, if changing market conditions should make them attractive to capital.

- The labour-process, even if no longer necessarily strictly patriarchal, but today increasingly determined by mutual group actions and decisions as collective workers, has preserved its predominant orientation towards self-sufficient simple reproduction at socially imposed minimal levels of sustenance.

- The households, as independent units of production, still have their 'freedom' to allocate their work funds between use-value production for immediate needs and commercial activities when offering their labour-power to the market, or engaging in private commodity production. In each case decisions depend on the price acquired on the market and the magnitude of absolute monetary needs at 'any costs' for reproduction.

- According to the retained subsistence-orientation, costs of production or labour remuneration will not be exclusively assessed in terms of capitalist prices or profits, unless the household becomes firmly established in productive and properly remunerated capitalist relations of production.

- The semblance of exchange between what appear as independent systems, works both ways. It does not only allow the capitalist appropriation of surplus dissociated from cost-calculation; it also fragmentizes the working class and facilitates the expulsion of collective workers from labour and commodity markets if the economic situation requires. The ideology of independent production systems effectively conceals the social character of the relations of production involved, dissuading collective workers from participation in class struggle.

In retrospect, many difficulties encountered in understanding the self-help housing process may now be attributed more precisely to its character as peripheral petty commodity production. Ambiguities in the proper determination of the social character of self-help housing arise from two distinct features: (1) it is based on the specific interpenetration of use- and exchange-values in terms of both housing production and consumption, and (2) it gives rise to the semblance of an autonomous production system required for capital valorization in this specific production form. As Burgess has shown, the failure to conceive self-help housing in these terms has led to wrong polarizations between housing forms seen to represent use-values as direct, autonomous expressions of human needs, contrasting with institutional housing forms based on exchange-values. This means that

... social science has persistently attempted to understand housing and social realities through the evolution of partial, one-sided and falsely polarized categories and the reconstruction of this reality in terms of these false polarities. In this way the crude separation of use-value and exchange-value becomes the false opposition in practice between institutional and self-help housing (Burgess, 1982, p. 67).

The question of self-help housing's social character is not a matter of mere academic debate. Wrong polarizations between use-value and exchange-value have been the obvious source of illusions concerning the autonomy and the actual stage of market integration involved with self-help housing projects (Burgess, 1982, p. 68). The frequent failure of squatter housing policies and projects - implemented through national governments, international agencies, or bilateral development aid alike - are manifestations of planning built on false premises. Planning for Third World low-income populations is not a discipline confined to technical details of construction and organization defined by isolated status quo assessments. Instead the entire framework of planning and implementation is enmeshed in a socially dynamic, highly politicized, and conflict-laden process. Disregard of the social and political context in planning inevitably leads to a dilution or complete corruption of nominal project aims at the expense of sustainable solutions for the target groups. Although planning may not always be able to control or even anticipate factors embedded in the structural problems of urban formation, three fields are identifiable in which developmental theory and political economy can help to overcome technocratic-biased planning approaches. Therefore, more appropriate sustainable planning should include the following.

- The integration of the micro-economics of housing and settlement into planning with regard to the functions assigned to the squatting process in the urban economy, including the mode of reproduction of collective workers.

- A flexible and open approach of planning towards the vulnerable legal and administrative position of squatter settlements. With politically arbitrary interferences and bureaucratic conflicts being the rule, planning must seek means of strengthening dwellers' organizations rather than rely on institutional and political benevolence.

- An acknowledgement that changes in the legal status and material standards of former illegal settlements open the door to a host of unpredictable market forces, some of which may benefit dwellers (e.g. rise in house and land value, new sources of income), while others may prove detrimental to the social integrity of the community if housing market speculation and displacement gain the upper hand. Conventionally, such results are beyond the scope of project concern as they usually take place after the withdrawal of the implementing agency. Nevertheless, they are immediate and, within limits, predictable outcomes of the initial project arrangements as they partially arise from project-imposed building standards, terms of cost-recovery, time schedules, forms of dwellers' participation, etc. Accordingly, efforts should be made to expand the framework of planning to incorporate all these aspects if nominal project aims and more sustainability are to be ensured.

Notes

1   Engels, F., The Housing Question. Moscow 1975.
2   For an account of the changing appearances of internationalization of capital cf. Läpple, 1985. According to Läpple, early imperialism, characterized by internationalization of the realization of surplus value, was followed after the Second World War by the internationalization of productive capital based on direct capital investments in Third World processing industries. These transformations in international divisions of labour have since the early 1960s integrated Third World countries into the world economy as exporters of manufactured goods. In its most recent stage the internationalization of surplus production attains the form of worldwide sourcing for the most profitable conditions of production on a world market for production sites. Footloose industries seek to extort maximum surplus value in the shortest possible time and will run away in the event of local restrictions (Läpple, 1985, pp. 59-69).
3   For a similar critique of self-help housing, informal sector and cheap reproduction of labour-power for capitalist accumulation cf. Gilbert, 1986, p. 179. In particular, Gilbert emphasizes the potential conflict between the subordination of informal production systems and the necessary tendency of capitalism to expand commodity markets.
4   A general critique of the theory of unequal exchange is given by Busch, 1974 and Schoeller, 1976. The contradictions involved in using unequal exchange as an explanation of uneven territorial formation and urban disparities are discussed by Läpple, 1978.
5   We are, however, aware of the fact that mobile international capital can sidestep these constraints by temporary production arrangements like those offered by free trade zones in Third World Countries. "This form of production is mainly characterized by the temporary nature of employment. The high intensity of work and the very long working days, combined with the low wages, imposes a constant replacement of labour force. The supply of labour is inexhaustible. If local restrictions occur, in the shape of increasing labour costs or of workers' resistance, industry will run away to the next country awaiting its turn" (Läpple, 1985, p. 68).
6   cf. Janvry/Garramón, 1977.

V Exporting planning for self-help housing projects

1 The evolution of self-help housing projects

The Third World history of state-aided self-help housing schemes dates from the 1940s and '50s when US-agencies like the 'Housing and Home Finance Administration' and later the 'International Cooperation Administration' introduced pilot projects to specific Latin American countries (e.g. Puerto Rico, Columbia, Chile). But with short-term exceptions, such as populist left-wing interim governments, the *de facto* primary intention of family or mutual aid projects in Latin America was not to address the actual housing demands or to support self-help community development (De Kadt, 1982). Instead, housing and community action programmes were used as a diversionary political instrument to legitimize the state or to control opposition-groups by coopting their leaders and integrating recalcitrant communities into the political power structure (Gilbert/Ward, 1984a). Moreover, self-help housing schemes were condemned to remain isolated projects due to their disharmony with the prevailing dogmas of modernization (Burgess, 1988, p. 18). Housing finance was regarded as a consumptive expenditure not contributing to the maximization of incomes or to the promotion of industrial relations of production. Nor was self-help housing in line with the general policies of social and demographic transformation. Urbanization and in-migration to cities were promoted as part of the scheme to modernize social values and to stimulate a cultural transformation appropriate to industrial development. This attempt to imitate First World urban development patterns was viewed as incompatible with life in shantytowns where, according to conventional wisdom, traditional social relations and attitudes were bound to be preserved. The squatter 'housing problem' came to be regarded as a temporary issue that would automatically disappear with economic and urban transformation. Correspondingly, housing policies at that time remained fixed to conventional housing 'encouraged' by bulldozing and resettlement of squatters in modern, western-style housing.

These paradigms of modernization gradually began to crumble in the early 1960s. Following the Cuban Revolution in 1959, rural guerrilla warfare, and the general economic crisis in Latin America, the 'Alliance for Progress' was devised as a means to pacify social unrest and counteract the spread of communism (cf. Gilbert/Ward, 1985, p. 178). Self-help housing, and saving and loans programmes for lower income groups attained new significance, e.g. the US-AID 'Housing Investment Guaranty Programme' that sponsored various national housing finance agencies (cf. Harms, 1982, p. 23). After the momentum of the Alliance dwindled by 1966, state aided self-help housing received a fresh and more substantial promotion in the early 1970s through the engagement of the World Bank in this sector. Recognizing the failure of the modernization approach, 'redistribution with growth' (RWG) and 'basic needs' became the new poverty-oriented development strategies of the World Bank under its director McNamara.[1] According to Burgess these included policies

> ... to increase output, productivity and incomes and to alleviate poverty, inequity and unemployment; the redistribution of income and investment increments derived from growth; the search for labour intensive 'appropriate' technologies; the deregulation of the informal sector; improvements in the access of small scale enterprises to finance, markets, technical and managerial assistance; the elimination of factor-price distortions in labour and capital markets; the introduction of transfer strategies in favour of the poor in public service expenditures (water, sewerage, electricity, health, education, transport etc.); and the encouragement of self-help housing policies (Burgess, 1988, p. 5).

The conceptual foundation of the Bank's housing policy was derived from the various recommendations of J. Turner and Abrams towards more appropriate housing solutions for low-income groups (cf. Abrams, 1964; J. Turner, 1968). Largely conforming to the RWG approach, their proposals for low-income housing provision included home-ownership, legal security of tenure and land, principles of progressive development, a self-help contribution, the reduction of housing standards down to affordable levels, access to loans, and the use of appropriate technology and materials.[2]

Between 1972 and 1981, the World Bank has spent approximately 9% of its total budget on 52 urban projects. These included projects of urban development, water supply, sewerage, and small scale enterprises. In the field of housing provision the World Bank was to become the major single international investor. Between 1972 and 1980 it spent some US$2.5 billion on housing, providing 310,000 sites and service plots and 780,000 upgraded units in 29 developing countries (Linn, 1983, p. 170).[3] In 1985 the Bank agreed to nearly triple its financing of housing and urban development in the 1986-91 period up to a total of US$6.1 billion. As by far the largest financing agency in this field, the World Bank inevitably also became the international spear-header with respect to feasible housing policies and planning approaches in the Third World. The experiences derived from the four major World Bank self-help housing pilot projects (El Salvador, the Philippines, Senegal, and Zambia) and its sector policy recommendations were adapted by most state agencies of bilateral aid and international cooperation for their own development programmes.

Burgess has identified four 'main phases' in the World Bank's housing policies, largely corresponding to those implemented by other concomitant international development agencies (Burgess, 1988, p. 6). This policy evolution appears closely correlated with the aim of optimizing the World Bank's strategic goals of attaining affordability and cost-recovery.

- In *Phase one* (1972-75) attention was almost exclusively focused on sites and services as the politically most acceptable form of low-cost housing provision. The housing standards introduced, the orderly settlement layout, plot size and densities, controlled terms of project completion with visible progress and easy administrative integration, etc. all conformed best with the perception of most Third World governments of a housing solution not too far removed from that of conventional housing.

- *Phase two* (1976-79) marked a shift of priorities to upgrading with a complementary site and service component required for essential resettlement and dedensification of the upgraded area.[4] The new policy reflected the Bank's tightened commitment to principles of full 'cost-recovery' and 'affordability' for target groups (cf. Sanyal, 1987). Escalating costs for land, infrastructure, and services were counteracted by a substantial reduction in planning, design, and technical standards as well as by the introduction of higher housing densities. Confronted with increasing economic decline and uncurbed squatter growth, most Third World governments were successfully persuaded to accept upgrading of existing squatter locations as the preferential strategy of low-cost housing provision.[5]

- *Phase three* (1979-84) maintained priority on upgrading, but with additional components of integrated labour-intensive employment promotion, more emphasis on community organization and on dwellers' participation in project management (cf. Paul, 1987). These new elements can be seen as measures to improve the conditions of cost-recovery that had turned out to be a critical issue in most pilot projects. High repayment defaults in part reflected stagnating income development - but were even more severely affected by lack of efficient collection systems and lack of political will on the part of leaders to carry through this part of their responsibility (Keare/Parris, 1982, p. 64).

- *Phase four* (since 1985) pays exclusive attention to upgrading as part of 'programme' rather then 'project' lending. In this version upgrading appears in a more rational form than the project-by-project approach, which is isolated from the wider urban framework and will have only token impact and limited replicability (Burgess/Ramirez, 1988, p. 9).

Integrated urban development projects are also in line with the World Bank's structural adjustment policy striving to achieve economic costs of basic goods and services by the removal of national subsidies and government protectionism in domestic markets. Low-cost housing projects now figure as one element within the dual urban lending strategy of raising productivity of urban workers and making a more significant effort towards improving the market efficiency of municipal services by unblocking obstacles to the delivery of land, infrastructure and finance (cf. Mayo/Malpezzi/Gross, 1986).

It is beyond the aim of this book to offer a comprehensive analysis of the World Bank's policies of urban development and housing, which have already been extensively dealt with by many writers.[6] Critics have in particular drawn attention to contradictions between the nominal poverty orientation and the obviously politically biased economic and social allocation policies. According to estimates by Williams, an ex-World Bank official, no more than a million people in LDCs have been reached by its housing programmes (Williams, 1984). In terms of geographic distribution, lending had, according to Burgess (1987), concentrated on countries with high levels of US-capital investments in the semi-periphery (e.g. Brazil, Mexico, S. Korea, Indonesia). Within this allocation pattern, selection criteria for project participants had, despite the continuous reduction of costs and standards, excluded the bottom 40% of the national income distribution. Furthermore, project design made little effort to protect economically struggling project participants from being ousted from their plots by the middle classes during implementation and after project completion. In fact, middle-class encroachment has been detected as a typical feature of World Bank projects. In contrast to their nominal design as projects for low-income households, these have been predominantly dedicated to groups in a secure economic position, such as wage-labourers and civil servants (Bamberger, 1981, p. 60).

Although it may be argued that, due to the World Bank's allocation policies, its quantitative impact on Third World low-cost housing has not been very significant, the project principles implemented have, nevertheless, exerted a considerable influence on national housing programmes and planning approaches in the Third World. With regard to the present discussion on appropriate planning, three issues pursued by the Bank stand out as the most crucial: (1) cost-recovery and affordability, (2) reduction of housing, plot and service standards and (3) participation of dwellers in planning and management.

In line with World Bank principles, cost-recovery has been adopted by most national housing agencies as a standard arrangement for their low-income housing programmes. This introduction of the market economy into the housing provision for low-income households, however, is sharply contrasted by the usual practice of Third World governments of highly subsidizing middle- and high-cost housing (Hardoy/Satterthwaite, 1989, pp. 106; Sanyal, 1981). Not surprisingly, surveys of low-cost housing projects indicate that high default rates in loan repayment are predominantly a socio-political and not an economic problem. The

World Bank's own project evaluation has revealed that, excepting lowest income groups, there is no direct correlation between income and defaults in loan repayment (Keare/Parris, 1982, p. 63). The problem of creating a positive repayment attitude thus rests largely on project-external factors. It hinges directly on people's feeling of social injustice towards governments who may be insisting on full cost-recovery while they are not prepared to allocate more than a fraction of national housing budgets to low-income housing provision. The motivation to repay will drop even further when defaults in repayment (usually a package including service charges) lead to a decline in or withdrawal of community services by the urban municipalities.

This remodelling of a political problem (i.e. class-biased subsidization) into what now appears as an economic problem of housing projects (i.e. cost-recovery) is one of the most problematic ideologies reinforced by the design of World Bank projects. It also impacts directly on the interlacing policies of standards and affordability as the occurrence of high default rates is usually viewed by policy-makers in two ways. In the first case, it exerts pressures towards an even greater lowering of standards in housing projects down to what appear to be more affordable levels. But the constant lowering of standards, in conjunction with failure to consolidate the settlement, has in turn created rising problems of maintenance of poorly upgraded and cheap site and service housing stock (cf. Burgess, 1988, p. 6). Lusaka is such an example, where housing standards began to deteriorate shortly after project completion for these very reasons.[7] In the second case, low cost-recovery may also serve to justify the exclusion of poverty groups from future housing programmes on the grounds of 'affordability', instead of leading to questioning of the project arrangements. Reasonable and affordable low-cost standards should, as Steinberg/Mathéy suggest, be defined according to the paying capacities of low-income households and allow for gradual development instead of insisting on strict planning procedures or the observance of building codes (Steinberg/Mathéy, 1987, p. 6). The ignorance of people's financial capacities to develop their house and plot according to building standards will not only lead to high dropout rates of project participants; it may also lead to a further deterioration in their economic situation. In the event of legal sanctions like dispossession or the compulsion to sell the uncompleted house and plot to middle-class buyers, the unsuccessful builder often receives little or no compensation for his work and expenditure.

In the original recommendations of J. Turner and Abrams, adopted by the World Bank, many of these problems were foreseen. Their proposals to incorporate extensive participation and community self-responsibility in all stages of housing project planning were devised to reduce tutelage from the state and from the implementing agency and to ensure solutions appropriate to the needs and capacities of the participants. Support for and recognition of institutionalized residents' participation would also ensure progressive development of the community after project completion. Although the World Bank nominally accepted these premises - in particular with respect to the consolidation phase after project completion -

94

it has counteracted these aims by its introduction of a comparatively vestigial concept of participation and self-help. Largely reduced to an instrument of cheap labour provision and *ad hoc* planning support during implementation, community participation has dwindled everywhere once the projects terminated. Following its frequent misuse and the failure to develop an adequate organizational framework with real and not token decision-making capacities, self-help and community participation are now found difficult to mobilize for follow-up schemes. Instead dwellers' post-project expectations tend to rest entirely on the municipality to deal with any problems that arise.[8]

Having stated these critical points, it should not be overlooked that the World Bank and bilateral aid agencies have also supported the dissemination of progressive attitudes to the squatter problem. Third World governments are increasingly prepared to acknowledge the rights of dwellers living in unauthorized settlements to the provision of infrastructure and services. To some extent it is also officially appreciated that efforts of squatters to solve housing problems are reactions to inappropriate municipal planning and provisions that have excluded low-income households from legal land and housing markets. Accordingly, governments have within limits accepted upgrading as a policy of infrastructure provision and settlement regularization, often approving land tenure arrangements differing from those officially defined in land use legislation and housing bye-laws. Housing projects have further proved that illegal communities have considerable untapped capacities for improving their housing situation, if financial support and legal recognition are given. Finally, some governments have begun to support the production of cheap building materials using alternative technologies and locally available materials. However the necessary revisions of planning and building codes required to make alternative and innovative approaches work, still remain a sensitive issue and have not been extended beyond the level of demonstration projects (Hardoy/Satterthwaite, 1989, p. 121).

Despite these encouraging developments in government-sponsored housing approaches - at least in comparison to the earlier solutions based on inappropriate public housing with high unit costs - the agony of state aided low-cost housing continues. Not only has the project-by-project approach failed to make a significant impact on mass housing provision. The experiences with state low-cost housing projects, often implemented with the money and expertise of international aid agencies, have in most Third World countries failed to produce solutions with mass 'replicability' at the national policy level.[9] As the following examples show, the main obstacles to scaling-up feasible project solutions are found in political and economic decision-making, in the constraints of bureaucratic implementation, and in housing price developments after project implementation.

Economic problems may arise already as early as at the demonstration stage or as a corollary of the scaling-up of projects to programme level. German Technical Cooperation (GTZ) has, for instance, implemented a series of pilot upgrading projects in the late 1970s and '80s in cooperation with the national governments of Zambia, the Dominican Republic, and Columbia (GTZ, 1984; Goethert/Oestereich, 1987). At project level these upgrading schemes have been reasonably successful in demonstrating the merits of the 'integrated' approach. Going beyond the standard components of improvements to infrastructure and housing, and legalization, this type of project also includes job creation, capacity building of communities, the promotion of alternative technology, and self-production of building materials based on local resources. The financial inputs necessary to make these schemes work have, however, been in the range of US$1,000 to 2,000 per household, including more than 50% subsidization of total costs (Ziss, 1987, p. 8). The success of this type of project is somewhat mixed. With respect to its political aim of developing institutional capacities to deal with upgrading as a medium-term housing strategy, the projects have strengthened the national housing agencies involved in their commitment to upgrading. Similar projects are now spreading in Latin America and may impact on the political discussion concerning appropriate housing solutions. But with respect to the unit costs, integrated upgrading projects are considerably above the present politically acceptable threshold for turning them into a national, large-scale housing policy.

The Indonesian kampong improvement programme and the World Bank sponsored upgrading scheme in Lusaka, Zambia, are cases where the up-scaling of initially cheap projects have resulted in a rapid increase in related costs, seriously impeding replicability. Starting in 1969 in Jakarta, the kampong programme has turned into one of the largest upgrading schemes in the world, successfully reaching urban low-income groups all over the country. Recent research, however, shows that in its wake land prices have risen and cheap rental accommodation has decreased. Moreover, project design only foresaw the installation of infrastructure without making provision for its maintenance by self-help or by the local government (Hardoy/Satterthwaite, 1989, p. 126). In Lusaka land prices have remained moderate, but with citywide upgrading in 1978 the demand for 'modern' building materials has initiated a disproportionate and lasting price increase. While prices for building materials increased by 1,993% from 1974 to 1987, consumer goods in the low-income category have 'only' risen by 1,113% (GRZ, 1989, p. 279 and 16). Thus, despite its short-term success in upgrading two-thirds of Lusaka's squatter population, necessary maintenance and planned follow-up projects are beyond the financial capacity of local government. As Hardoy/Satterthwaite point out, the general problems with upgrading programmes are that they

> ... suddenly make a series of basic investments which should have been made on a continuous basis by the local government. It may improve conditions considerably at first but very rarely does it increase the capacity of local government to maintain the new infrastructure and services and to continue with the process of upgrading. Upgrading momentarily makes up for a deficiency in local government but over time, this deficiency returns (Hardoy/Satterthwaite, 1989, p. 127).

Political and administrative problems with upgrading are abundant. In spite of what appears to be a consensus between the institutions and implementing agencies involved once a project is decided on, the practice of upgrading is hazardous. As evaluations have shown, all main project phases (planning, implementation, cost-recovery, and post-project maintenance) are ridden with conflicts between the different sponsors, the project management, and the different municipal authorities. The latter are also often lacking clear internal divisions of duties and responsibilities. Slow bureaucratic decision-making, lack of adequate dwellers' participation, and external political interference are among the most frequently reported problems of project accomplishment (cf. Angel, 1983; Steinberg/Mathéy, 1987). Van der Linden has compared the circumstances of slum upgrading to a jungle: successful work in squatter areas really benefiting its residents, depends not so much on the intentions or technical competence of the implementing agency but on knowledge of 'gaps' in the system, or the ability to subversively bypass or outmanoeuvre deadlocked bureaucratic authorities (Van der Linden, 1980).

In comparison to the structural limitations of state-aided housing projects, nongovernmental organizations (NGOs) have, in close collaboration with residents' organizations, been much more successful in supporting and developing innovative self-help housing approaches in the past 10-15 years. NGOs are usually founded through private initiative on the part of independent local experts, or have evolved from community based organizations (CBOs). But particularly in Africa we increasingly find international NGOs that have become locally active. NGO activities are guided by two basic operational principles. The first is the 'reversed' approach towards the community on which projects are not, as a rule, imposed top-down. Instead NGOs will act as consultant, project manager, community developer or as mediator between the community and the state for active, self-organized CBOs only. Secondly, decision-making in all aspects is to be in the hands of the CBO, i.e. the pace of activities will be defined by the implementing capacities and the priorities of the community and not by the supporting NGO (Sina, 1987; IYSH-NGO Forum, 1987; CDG, 1987).[10]

Working along these principles, NGOs have been particularly effective in Asian and Latin American countries where people's self-organization and commitment to self-help has been pronounced and governments have been prepared to collaborate with this kind of initiative.[11] NGOs have received positive recognition and support from international bodies like the UNDP, OECD, the World Bank, and from bilateral aid agencies (Paul/Israel, 1991). However, their possible contribution to solving national housing and settlement problems is restricted by their inherent terms of operation, and NGOs are hardly without their own developmental idiosyncrasies (White, 1989, p. 6; OECD, 1988; Sanyal, 1989).

- The relationship between local NGOs and First World donor organizations has complicated with the rapid expansion of activities. Many NGOs find their autonomy threatened by the expectations of donors for bigger and more sophisticated projects, involving larger budgets, more trained personnel, and more and more administrative work. Betraying their initial integrity, based on structures of personal communication and a small-scale base of operation in dealing with CBOs, many NGOs have now turned to project management with emphasis shifted to public relations and elaborate documentation of progress. Pressed by donors into competition with government schemes for quick results, NGOs have in other cases overestimated their institutional capacities and lost public credibility by promising too much (Ruiz, 1989, pp. 23-27). The common wisdom that NGOs necessarily represent models of cooperation with local authorities is challenged by Sanyal (1989). As these organizations largely depend on grants and donations for their survival, the image becomes vital that they alone were responsible for success, even if cooperation between NGOs and the state (or other NGOs) was in reality the key factor. This lack of cooperation and the reluctance to work with the state, on the other hand, sets limits to large-scale replication of successful projects (Sanyal, 1989, p. 8).

- The relationship with the state and municipal authorities is a crucial issue for NGOs. NGOs are most effective when governments recognize the complementary role these organizations can play in housing programmes. They can fill in gaps where government programmes are not active, or can reach target groups more effectively if government agencies are prepared to recognize the function of NGOs as intermediaries between them and the people. Working in a more effective and less bureaucratic manner, they may also act as consultants or researchers for governments. All these possible roles, however, involve a certain devolution and decentralization of government competencies to the NGOs as private bodies. This condition is not easily accepted by the state as it means loss of control and involves admitting of previous shortfalls and deficiencies in their policies. [12] It is also often feared that people's confidence in the more democratically operating NGOs might rouse opposition to governments. In the event of this kind of development, the relationship between governments and NGOs has sometimes changed from 'negotiation to confrontation' (CDG, 1987, p. 130). As NGOs must manoeuvre along this narrow political ridge, this seems to dispel expectations that they might also be promoters of democratization, as suggested by Korten (1987). As a rule, NGOs are capable of strengthening and extending latent developments - but they cannot work against the tendencies of the political system.

- Participation has recently become an indispensable part of developmental rhetoric. But very few agencies, not even NGOs, can practise a genuine participatory approach. As White has pointed out, any true implementation of participation would for target groups mean 'their taking an active role in the process of development resources, the setting of priorities, the identification of goals and the planning of efforts to be made to achieve them' (White, 1989, p. 9). The complete surrendering of an agency's decision-making powers to target groups would imply a shift in its role better to one described as a passive catalyst - a condition that seems incompatible with social reality and with the requirements of project management. For instance, not even NGOs can cope easily with a situation in which project planning is virtually impossible due to the latent uncertainties about peoples' decision-making in terms of goals and time schedules. Very few donor agencies, obliged to justify their project-spending in public with respect to expected results and budgets, would be prepared to accept a complete uncertainness of project goals. Secondly, participation in the developmental process, in the full meaning of the word, would involve more than changing the project-specific decision-making structures. To really work, it would have to be backed up by a social redistribution of power and resources in favour of poorer groups at all levels, as suggested by the empowerment approach (Hardoy/ Satterthwaite, 1989, p. 136). Though NGOs have greater potentials than government agencies to adopt a participatory approach, the institutional and political constraints involved often result in compromises when NGOs offer a developmental package and 'participation' becomes the freedom of CBOs to take it or leave it (White, 1989, p. 10).Thus, contrary to some recent euphoria on the subject, the incorporation of NGOs into development schemes is hardly a guarantee that participatory aims are actually realized or even practised in their true sense.

Stripped from undue expectations, NGOs nonetheless have an important role in urban development. They could be particularly valuable in carrying out what has been outlined as the 'popular' or 'enabling approach' that aims at creating and supporting continuous programmes instead of short-term interventions (UNCHS, 1987a). According to this hypothetical scenario, a government would have to draw conclusions from all available experiences at project level and combine the progressive elements of recent housing policies with a complete reconsideration of stereotypical attitudes towards squatters. The change in attitudes would apply to four levels.

First, governments must accept that solutions to urban problems are probably not to be sought in foreign concepts. In a report on the situation of African cities Stren/White come to the conclusion that ultimately

> ... solutions to urban finance, housing, public transport, the siting and standards of urban infrastructure, public health and public cleansing services, water, electricity and numerous other urban amenities must be formulated locally, by local people, on the base of local experience and information (Stren/White, 1989; as quoted by Hardoy/ Satterthwaite, 1989, p. 137).

Second, governments have either by repression, inactivity, or inappropriate planning legislation been instrumental in creating the squatter problem. They must now use their considerable legislative and administrative powers to support squatters and protect them from market forces. *Third,* governments must move from short-term project intervention to long-term collaboration with citizens and their community or neighbourhood associations (Hardoy/Satterthwaite, 1989, p. 137). CBOs and NGOs working at settlement level must be legally recognized as positive consultants in the formulation of basic needs of dwellers. But it is not only essential that people's participation is recognized as a basic right. To enable active participation, governments must promote people's democratic organization and decision-making, e.g. by training and education, networks of information, and exchange of experiences. They must also institutionalize symmetric terms of cooperation between CBOs and the local government responsible in which the communities have an effective say in policy-making and in the use of available resources.

The *fourth* condition of the 'enabling approach' demands a reassessment both the potentials and the limitations of low-income households and communities in contributing to settlement projects. In this field research findings and the conventional wisdom of planners are at odds. For example, implementing agencies still hold on to the perception that informal workers and their families have ample time to contribute self-help work to the projects. With working hours in the informal sector largely exceeding those in its formal counterpart, the obligatory self-help component (often coming as a precondition for project implementation) may in fact unduly exploit people's readiness to participate by self-help. This practice is particularly questionable considering the customary terms of subsidized service provision to upper-class households without demands for self-help contributions. Community structures, too, are frequently wrongly perceived. For example the supposed collective solidarity of its members does not always match with the reality of settlements: developmental priorities and participation may vary considerably between house proprietors and tenants, or between settlement groups in different occupational and social brackets. As research in Latin America has shown, this is particularly the case after unanimously voiced basic demands for water and electricity have been satisfied. Thereafter support for and active participation in the accomplishment of secondary aims, like health centres and schools, tend to become highly selective (Gilbert/Ward, 1984).

As the proponents of the popular approach realize, it is above all institutional and legislative change that is needed to make the proposed scheme work. Changing the institutional structures and legal procedures implies much more than the rethinking of policies by local administrators, or hoping for self-critical insights on the part of government housing agencies towards improving the low effectiveness of their management and implementation. Unlike the situation in most industrialized countries, the problem of low administrative efficiency cannot be addressed as a separate issue in Third World countries, i.e. in isolation from the political structures underpinning it. Issues such as the decentralization of local government and democratization, which appear as essential prerequisites of the popular approach, are sensitively interlocked with prevailing structures of power and class closely associated with the state. Accordingly, experiences with decentralization in Third World countries have in the past not been very encouraging. As D. Slater concludes from his review of literature on decentralization in peripheral states, centralizing and decentralizing activities can easily coexist within the same polity. The devolution of power may even augment the dominance of those already powerful at local level, introducing an even more elitist, more ruthless attitude towards the poor (Slater, 1989, p. 511). Similar conclusions will be drawn for the Zambian case, showing that decentralization policies, contrary to their rhetoric, have been used in the past as a means to strengthen the control of central powers (Greenwood/ Howell, 1980 and Scott, 1980).

The problematic point of the 'enabling approach' is its complacency with its own planning premises. Its idealistic and technocratic message is that the approach is right, planning knowledge is available - only we have to wait till governments and administrators provide the right socioeconomic framework before we can implement. This can be called *idealistic* because it assumes that planning is a 'technical expertise' free of cultural, social, and ideological contents and may be exported invariably to all urban societies and deployed in the realization of appropriate solutions (King, 1980). And it is *technocratic* because it reinforces a self-perception seeking to isolate and depoliticize planning procedures from the social circumstances they must act upon. A critical review of the history of planning shows to the contrary that it has been used everywhere as collateral part of the economic and political power system. Its appearance as a socially and politically unbiased, technical discipline has helped in exporting planning to Third World countries where it has contributed to the capitalist transformation of dependent economies (King, 1980, p. 218; Harvey, 1973, p. 228). The problem with not wanting to look for 'foreign concepts' is that the professional rationale of the planning discipline has been shaped in the First World and already globally disseminated by planning export. With rising doubts about the blessings of western civilization and more critical public coverage of their activities, First World planners had, in the past 20 years, begun to realize the highly politicized, value-laden premise of their discipline (King, 1980, p. 219). But while confidence in planning has declined in the First World, it is now Third World planners who still follow the traditional perception of planning as value-free, 'technical expertise'.[13]

Thus, changes in planning policies do not only rest on innovative political decision-making. Reforms must start at the level of Third World planning bureaucracy itself, where the critical discussion on the societal role of planning has yet to begin. Exceptions from this pattern are indigenous housing agencies which have collaborated closely with progressive western planners. In this mutual effort, planners have gone some way towards sensitizing their approaches to the social circumstances of implementation, and pay growing attention to problems of environmental protection and use of natural resources. In comparison to most state housing schemes, projects implemented by international or bilateral aid agencies tend to be less socially discriminatory, more appropriate, and more scientifically oriented to criteria of successful achievement according to predetermined developmental aims. No doubt, the discussion on planning transfer and the devolution of planning competencies to residents' organizations has produced important new insights towards necessary reorientations. But solutions to Third World housing problems will not come out of rejection of foreign expertise, nor can the proposed say of residents' organizations in local planning be a substitute for the required new definition of the role of national planning. The devolution of certain planning competencies to residents and their organizations would be appropriate in fields where they know best how to cope with limited resources (Wakely, 1989, p. 20). But it cannot make up for deficits in essential central planning. As Heinrich has emphasized in his critique of master planning transfer in Tanzania, effective Third World planning would in fact require *higher* steering capacities and a *more diversified* conceptual framework than in First World countries, where planning is often reduced to giving private commercial activities 'a helping hand' (Heinrich, 1988, p. 354). Expanding and redefining competencies of Third World planners and reforming the institutional structures would encompass various breaches with conventional practice.

- Most Third World countries have adopted the planning legislation and the entire comprehensive planning system from their former colonial powers. The importation of a planning rationale from countries never confronted with problems of scarce resources and hypertrophic demographic growth automatically produces the appearance of quantitative and qualitative deficits in Third World national planning (Heinrich, 1988, p. 349). In particular the legally and technically imposed standards of comprehensive planning are at odds with the given low institutional planning capacities: the civil service is largely unattractive for competent national professionals, and national planning boards are suffering everywhere from lack of professionalism, manpower, resources, and accurate survey data. Low planning and implementing capacities are further reinforced by the subordinate position of planners in the hierarchy of political power. In many city councils the planning department is no more than a bureaucracy, with decision- and policy-making monopolized by top level political appointees. These political office holders often not only lack professional qualifications and tend to take decisions based on vested interests; their typical short-term tenure of office effectively inhibits politically 'risky' reformations of planning policies. Consequently, more adequate development policies could only be designed by national planners if they were endowed with wider implementing powers, and if planning offices enjoyed greater professional freedom in realistically assessing the needs, priorities, and available administrative capacities of the country.

102

- According to Sträb, the orientation of Third World planners to the European city as a model for their own urban design has created a highly inappropriate situation in dealing with contemporary problems of urbanization. In Africa the adaptation of geometric land use patterns, which disregard locational and environmental aspects, have, together with the high technological inputs involved in the provision of centrally-managed infrastructure systems (roads, electricity, water, sewerage, drainage, sanitation), added to excessive administration and expensive maintenance. Declining financial resources in Africa have made municipalities incapable of extending or even maintaining their infrastructure standards to meet population increases of up to 10% annually (Sträb, 1986, p. 22; Stren, 1988, p. 242). To accommodate the majority of low-income households, appropriate planning concepts would have to abandon the European-inspired rigidity in space use and building standards. Alternatives are offered by the African informal system of housing provision that could be integrated into the formal planning framework.[14] It would allow affordable solutions to land delivery requiring minimal surveying and legal procedures, if traditionally established communal land allocation systems were used and guided to conform with essential central planning. The traditional African one-storey house with plot and wall is ideally adopted to the needs and financial abilities of its dwellers. Its character as a low-density habitat area with gardening facilities avoids many environmental problems typically created by high inner-city densities. Following Sträb (1986, pp. 23-25), greater spatial spread would also enable 'organic' solutions to the provision of most urban utilities (e.g. wells and pit latrines; recycling refuse or transforming it into compost; drainage systems that make use of natural topographical features). However, it is important to note that a planned and encouraged urban sprawl would also require a reverse of the present concentration of economic and commercial facilities in the city centres. More local job opportunities and commercial facilities would be necessary to make peripheral housing areas acceptable for residents. On the other hand, decentralization would also have the positive side-effect of reducing the already severe problems of public transport to and from the centres of larger Third World cities. While we can agree with Sträb that a defined urban sprawl may be a corrective to excessive densification, an excessive sprawl is not without its own specific drawbacks. Some typical problems of finding a balance between necessary inner city densification within an urban growth pattern dominated by low-density residential sprawl will be presented in the discussion of the Lusaka case study.

- National development plans are quite often prepared to give low-cost housing certain nominal priorities. But master or development planning is rarely supported by clear directives as to how aims are to be implemented, nor does it realistically assess the capacities of municipal planners to submit concrete proposals (cf. Reichert, 1981, p. 97; CDG/GRZ, 1989, p. 20). There is also a striking discrepancy between the world market dependency of Third World economies, exposed to high world market price fluctuations, and the tendency of central planning authorities to favour comprehensive, long-term planning that would essentially require predictable and reliable budget allocations (Heinrich, 1987, p. 370). The practice of down-scaling national budgets to the real revenue situation regularly means revoking the allocations with the lowest priorities. Lacking a strong political lobby, low-cost housing is a typical candidate for this routine as town planners and squatters are rarely able to match other, more influential social groups in the scramble for resources. To bridge this planning gap, new instruments and survey methods are required that correspond to the cultural setting and the resource situation of the country. More incremental and spontaneous approaches would make town planning more flexible and responsive to given financial and administrative constraints.[15] Similarly, more participation and involvement of target groups in planning procedures would strengthen the position of town planners and municipal authorities in the competition for scarce resources. Stronger politicization and more public awareness over housing issues would increase pressures to step up necessary planning measures or to implement projects according to plan; moreover politicization could make centrally planned housing provisions less susceptible to local political arbitrariness.

First World planning consultancy has often been sought by Third World governments to solve their urban problems. As a rule it has not helped in the necessary reorientation of planning standards and approaches to more appropriate solutions. Exceptions are self-help housing projects implemented by bilateral aid and international agencies that have been a more effective leverage in supporting indigenous solutions by national housing authorities and planning boards (cf. Ziss, 1986). Nonetheless, the limitations of development-aid sponsored projects should not be overlooked. Western project planning is not without ties to the dominant indigenous political or social system, nor can it be free of political biases of project arrangements: project aims and terms come out of bilateral negotiations and are based on mutual agreements between governments that set diplomatic limits to possible criticism. As far as I can see, project experiences have seldom led to a fundamental reconsideration of the planning paradigm, even in cases of considerable target deficits. Western project-internal evaluations are illustrative in this respect. Instead of questioning the validity of the planning approach itself, they have repeatedly pointed to the 'corruption' of their target aims by local, project-external factors. Reinforced by the need to cooperate with local planning authorities, projects have depoliticized the planning process by largely adopting a technocratic approach to problems which arise. In general, short-term accomplishment has taken priority over considerations of the long-term sustainability of projects. This means in particular that

- technical issues of project accomplishment and completion according to schedule have taken precedence over critical monitoring and reassessing of project aims to changing situations, e.g. when projects become politicized in the course of their linkage with the established legal and commercial urban framework;

- interests of local politicians and bureaucrats have in many cases overruled dwellers' interests via the pressures put on the project management to reconcile conflicts and to compromise project aims with the constraints imposed by local authorities;

- the usual practice of short-term evaluation of implementation legitimizes the sponsors and the project management, but it fails to assess the post-project settlement performance and the sustainability of measures within its new socioeconomic and legal frame - evidence that might easily contradict the initial success of nominal aims fulfilled.[16]

As in many other countries, the German planning discussion had in the 1970s come to realize that planning could be more effective if it were based on a theory of society (Rodenstein, 1982, p. 42). It also realized that in pluralist societies effective planning (i.e. politics of planning) must incorporate the political circumstances and conflicts of its implementation (Scharpf, 1971).[17] As innovations are bound to cause anxieties on the part of institutionalized parties, it would be futile to look to governments to provide indispensable prerequisites of proposed planning procedures - but this is precisely what many policies, including the enabling approach, seem to expect. The by no means radical German planner Scharpf has made the crucial point.

> If resistance to changes stems from institutionalized interests, innovative planning must fail if it does not succeed in raising resonance and support outside of institutionalized politics. If politics directed to structural changes are to be successful at all, they need publicity, the politicization of problems, the mobilization of expectations, demands and readiness for action outside of institutions (Scharpf, 1971, p. 189 / translation from German: J.T.).

Considering the ominous role of foreign planning expertise in the past, it is indigenous planners who are best placed to move towards 'politics of planning' in rousing public support for new planning approaches. But development aid projects need not be affirmative. The integrated project approach goes some way in overcoming the containment and denseness of the conventional sectoral planning. By its multisectoral design, comprehending the horizontal and vertical articulations with issues related to the successful accomplishment of the core project goal, it necessarily raises people's awareness of problems (Kunzmann, 1981). At a *horizontal* level, for example, the integrated approach makes it clear that housing conditions cannot be alleviated by housing production alone, i.e. in isolation from aspects like the conferral of basic land rights, local job opportunities, markets, dwellers' rights to organize at settlement level, access to credit and urban provision systems, etc. *Vertically*, local target aims are defined according to national development aims and in interrelation with problem assessments ranging from the neighbourhood to regional level (Mathéy, 1984). A different question is if the organizational terms of project are able to fulfil the premises postulated. As Böhm/Stürzbecher point out, the integrated approach prerequisites astute knowledge of the society in question and complex functional delimitations with respect to defining the appropriate plane of planning. As a rule, agencies have simply implemented such projects ad hoc without conducting the essential preliminary studies on socioeconomic, spatial and functional structures (Böhm/Stürzbecher, 1981, p. 39).

2   Sociological dimensions of planned interventions in habitat

In dealing with illegal settlements, virtually all urban development projects display two built-in contradictions: (1) planning directed to 'development and change' will, in the course of its implementation, necessarily tend to lose control over the effects it has brought about; (2) the more comprehensive the approach, the more vulnerable it makes its participants to the conditions it exposes and orients them to. Planners of housing projects often fail to realize that their framework of planning and implementation comes to a functioning socioeconomic system as a major and possibly alienating intervention.

Although living in unauthorized settlements is hazardous in many respects, the illegal status to some extent also protects residents from the vagaries of urban economics, municipal services, and planning. The problem of housing projects is not only that settlements are transformed into a regular part of urban land and housing markets and that they tighten the commercial links with the capitalist urban economy. Particularly with integrated projects, any attempt to accelerate development at settlement level comes as a major intervention in the internal socioeconomic equilibrium that has grown out of the residents' mutual squatting history. With the introduction of new dynamics to the community, the course of development is seldom evolutionary and balanced. Gradual commodification and commercialization of housing are unavoidable aspects of housing projects. Often the new opportunities offered by the market are only realized selectively by dwellers, leading to a differentiated or even polarized pattern of aspirations that may counteract the premise of solidarity and mutual self-help on which most projects are founded.

Political economy has in particular emphasized the importance of these extra-functional aspects of projects, showing that the integration of housing projects into the wider socioeconomic and urban context will inevitably counteract many policy aims. Intentionally or not, self-help housing will become subject to the mechanisms of capitalist expansion, i.e.

the articulation of capitalism with informal structures. In housing policies the goals of this articulation have been described as

> ... the penetration, and consolidation of commodity markets for land, housing, building materials and finance; the generalization of the principle of private property in land and housing; the introduction or expansion of the capitalist division of labour and wage economy; and the lowering of the reproduction costs of labour power (Burgess, 1988, p. 7).

We have already addressed these problems at length. The question remains as to what consequences the critique of political economy can have for future planning processes. Obviously, project planning cannot create islands of bliss in a 'hostile' and exploitative capitalist environment. But in line with the conviction that planning theory cannot be separated from the theory on the object of planning (Harris, 1960), planning must respond to the contradictions imposed by development under peripheral capitalism. It must open itself to development theory and adapt its analytical critique to planning requirements. I agree with Fiori/Ramirez that the insights conveyed by developmental theory are not exclusively negative. Statements concerning the social character of self-help housing are very much dependent on the perspective of theoretical reasoning applied (Fiori/Ramirez, 1988, p. 14), and many findings remain ambiguous even within the same line of reasoning. For instance, the incorporation of informal production into the peripheral capitalist mode of production will always be typified by complex dialectics of reproduction/dissolution or of use- and exchange-values. In the same manner the advocacy of peripheral petty commodity production of housing is associated with the cheapening of capitalist labour-power and the expansion of housing commodity markets. However, by its dissociation from the constraints of dominant capitalist relations of production, it may also generate new resources and more productivity. Thus, from the point of view of planning the question is

> ... not one of choosing between these perspectives as if they were mutually exclusive. The challenge, in our view, is precisely to recognize the ambiguities of reality itself and the complexities they pose, accepting that on this issue generalizations one way or the other are impossible (Fiori/Ramirez, 1988, p. 14).

Ambiguities reflecting the specific terms of integration into capitalism or the urban environment pervade and typify all aspects of peripheral petty commodity production. They also necessarily underpin the entire framework of housing and settlement projects, although this is not often acknowledged. Ultimately only the transformation of the latent structures generated by projects into *contents of planning* prevents them from becoming prone to planning ideology. This is not to say that planning should be held entirely responsible for discrepancies between plan and the final outcome. With close monitoring, incipient ambiguous patterns of change and development would be observable at early stages of implementation. For example, the response of dwellers even to standardized, egalitarian project arrangements is usually socially differentiated with respect to terms of credit, self-help organization, participation in planning, building standards, applied technology and management. High dropout rates and selling of plots and houses in upgrading and site and service schemes are other indicators that squatter projects are themselves actively contributing to perpetuating the squatter problem.

Although internal social differentiation and dropouts are inevitable in housing projects, social differentiation should be controlled to the extent that tendencies towards community disintegration are forestalled. The propensity of wanting to do too much in too short a time, with low priorities on intermediate evaluation, are typical features of project implementation oriented to producing visible progress within tight time schedules. Step by step implementation in accordance with the abilities of participants, combined with monitoring of progress and incremental decision-making with respect to the further advancement, might be a more appropriate approach than comprehensive project design. In a more systematical fashion we will discuss these latent ambiguities of project components at three levels.

- The micro-economics at domestic level with respect to reproductive strategies that affect affordability, the role of self-help, participation, building standards, and appropriate building technology.

- The remodelling of community structures by project institutions and by legalization, newly introduced municipal administrative structures, and the penetration of communities by political parties and local political interests.

- The integration of project areas into urban markets for housing, land, and rent that will effect changes of the economic and social environment by commodification and commercialization, by speculation, and by dwellers' potential displacement by middle-class encroachment.

a) Domestic reproduction and micro-economic aspects of planned interventions

We have referred to the wide discrepancy between theory and reality of project assessments concerning affordability and self-help contributions. The failure to predict the performance of these key project components no doubt partially reflects the limitations of quantitative survey methods. Unable to go below the surface of basic demographic data and the observable physical state of housing, statistical surveys fail to address important determinants of household decisions regarding participation in housing projects. Perhaps the unexpected performance of some target groups even points to altogether divergent conceptions of the reality involved. For planners, project inputs tend to be conceived as part of a linear cost-benefit calculation in achieving defined standards of improvement. But for squatters, material and monetary inputs offered by projects can be incorporated in a dynamic, multifunctional context structured by the articulation of formal and informal economic realities and by different horizons of expectation and commitment to project aims.

Only in a social situation of stabilized wage-labour relations with steady income is it probable that housing will be conceived by households predominantly as a consumption good to which projects offer cost-benefit governed terms of participation. There are other aspects that might dominate in a dweller's project participation, leading to different attitudes as to what is deemed affordable, or may influence his self-help practice. For some dwellers the locational aspect may be more important than the improvement of housing conditions. Here, participation in a housing project merely becomes a precondition for expanding or starting local business activities, or it serves as a means of securing the required on-site premises. For lodgers and tenants, housing projects may offer the chance of attaining home ownership, whereas for absentee landlords (often disguised by nominal house and plot holding) housing projects may be a veritable object of speculation. Affordability, too, may only be arbitrarily assessed by the pre-implementation income standards. For residents whose income situation may have initially appeared to planners to be below thresholds of affordability, the problem may be resolved by consumption sacrifices, rewarded by a subsequent recovery of costs from the market, e.g. by renting out accommodation or the sale of the more valuable legalized house and plot.

As these examples demonstrate, the significance of one and the same project component can be perceived quite differently by planners and by each of the different population segments having their own separate aspirations and preferences in housing projects. In the case of planned self-help contributions, the matter becomes even more complicated. Self-help becomes not only related to social attitudes but also to the changing character of its economic content, the meaning of which alters according to the economic circumstances of household reproduction. The meaning may also depend on who can appropriate the products of self-help activities. With lack of specific assessment, self-help can be a very conflicting and counterproductive planning measure.

In his study of low-cost housing in Nairobi, Wetter has emphasized that a major distinction exists between self-help that is practised as part of subsistence and self-help that is already an integral part of informal commodity production (cf. Wetter, 1984, p. 66). In projects it would therefore only seem appropriate and justified to utilize or advocate self-help if household reproduction takes place under conditions in which the limited access to commodity and labour markets figures as the principal constraint to sustenance and the utilization of family labour. In this case the use of self-help as a project component can mobilize family labour lying idle, it can improve the productivity of use-value production, or may lead to the utilization of locally available resources.

Conversely, the misappropriation of self-help as a project premise may result in additional financial burdens on the target group once formal or informal commodity production has already become the predominant mode of reproduction. The frequently observed practice of self-help builders to selectively utilize wage-labour and market-bought inputs in the construction process clearly expresses the existing interdependence of self-help forms with the capitalist society in various economic, consumptive, and social aspects: the delegation of self-help activities to wage workers may, for example, reflect short-term economic considerations in a situation in which the labour-power of the builder and his family can be sold or utilized at higher levels of valuation on the market. Then the employment of wage-labourers as a substitution of self-help construction work minimizes the deductions from the family consumption funds. Even substituting self-help construction by other subsistence activities may be rational if the family labour is required for activities dedicated to the long-term security of sustenance. Under this condition, self-help builders will even be prepared to pay higher wages for self-help substitution wage-labour than they themselves receive.

This interpenetration of societal and private terms of valorization poses a difficult problem in defining appropriate inputs and adequate measures in self-help housing schemes. Reasoning of this kind will, in particular, apply if projects work with target groups in the lowest-income segments where household reproduction is bound to be based on some degree of collective work. The combination of formal, informal, and subsistence work pertaining to this form of reproduction has sometimes been precipitately equated by planners with unemployment, suggesting ample disposable working capacities for self-help. However, an expanded self-help component may be counterproductive for these target groups, as working hours of collective workers tend to be longer than those of wage-labourers. The real problem is not one of available working capacities but the low and irregular monetary income available to meet the financial and legal project requirements. Many municipal authorities show little flexibility in allowing terms of progressive development of the house and plot according to the paying capacities of lowest-income builders. Building to standards defined by building codes within a specific time schedule is often a basic requirement for the conferral of full title deeds. This is particularly the case in communities with mixed income levels where the progress of better-off families becomes the implicit standard of accomplishment. Difficulties in complying with these requirements may lead to the exclusion of unsuccessful builders, or prolong their illegal status if projects are not prepared to devise protective and complementary measures.

Integrated projects have addressed the problem of income inequality by experimenting with a wide range of income- and employment-generating programmes. Vocational training centres, small-scale industries, promotion of artisanal petty commodity production, and cooperatives are among the approaches most frequently tried (ILO, 1981, p. 90; Hammock/Lubell/Sethuraman/Rafsky, 1981). Their weak side is the unpredictable dynamics of the labour and commodity markets in response to project measures. Income-promotion schemes have a bad reputation of breaking down after the withdrawal of the developing agency and the phasing out of its institutional support. Contrary to expectations, evaluations of income-generating projects have shown that autonomous growth from the bottom is not hampered by lack of opportunities alone. As the low rates of return in most projects demonstrate, any amount of inputs, credits and assistance cannot create long-term employment if the formal economy itself is stagnant (Sanyal, 1989, p. 7). Expert advice on informal market opportunities often tends to exaggerate the possibilities and to underestimate the difficulties of entry to urban markets. After the project-stimulated building boom is over and local demand stagnates, business newcomers find it difficult to establish themselves beyond the island of their own community and to become competitive on the regular urban market. For example, production standards may be too low, or business faces institutional constraints like price control systems, anti-black market measures prohibiting the sale of essential commodities, and legal restrictions to street vending. Other market constraints are transport problems, a closed and protected informal market, no access to loans, low working capital, and limited financial capacities of selling to customers on credit (ILO, 1981, p. 94 and 182).

Thus, as a rule, the encouragement of community-centred, private business is an unreliable and risky measure for lowest-income groups if their activities are not integrated into cooperative community structures or receive post-project assistance from other established legal bodies like cooperative associations and NGOs, or unless they can participate in municipal programmes for small-scale business promotion (cf. LUDC, 1989). As community members already established in specific lines of business are inclined to be the prime beneficiaries of income-generating measures (profiting from credit provisions, newly built local markets, and enlarged demand), projects should make efforts to identify opportunity-maximizing schemes for individual socioeconomic groups (UNCHS, 1982). Feasible schemes for lowest-income groups would, for example, have to avoid undue exposure to competition by finding productive niches in the urban market. They should select fields of business with predictable growth perspectives like those arising from structural problems of the market. Growing urban transport problems have, for instance, encouraged profitable carpentry work in decentralized squatter settlements for the production of bulky commodities such as furniture (ILO, 1981, p. 182). If reasonably protected market activities cannot be found for lowest-income groups, project arrangements might alternatively make provision for the construction of additional rooms as an income source from renting. Space provision for subsistence gardening would be another appropriate measure, having a similar policy effect to that of renting for lowest-income groups: both measures centre the economic interests of the households concerned on the settlement economy. Thus, in the inevitable process of social and economic settlement differentiation, locational ties might act as a preventive measure to avoid the disintegration or displacement of low-income groups from the community. It also might help fend off middle-class encroachment, usually directed to the economically vulnerable low-income households in newly upgraded and legalized settlements.

The logical complement to income generating schemes are provisions to reduce costs for housing production and for service charges. Flexible building standards, the use of appropriate technology, and self-help maintenance of infrastructure have been offered as options in adjusting project costs to the individual paying capacities of households. While international implementing agencies have eagerly engaged in pilot schemes of alternative and cheaper production of building materials, their practical impact on projects has generally not been very significant. The problem is, however, only superficially related to dwellers' acceptability of new materials. Instead the various concomitant financial and social terms of projects seem to introduce countercurrent tendencies that block the potential of alternative or unconventional approaches. Stated formally, the principal constraint on appropriate and more affordable solutions is their orientation to use-values, whereas the aspirations raised by housing projects tend to enhance the prestige or exchange-value of housing. Even without compulsory building legislation, upgrading projects have tended to elevate the criteria for acceptable housing standards and building materials (Schlyter, 1988, p. 111). With the legalization of settlements, the criterion for 'good housing' increasingly becomes oriented to standards of the commercial housing market, usually closely associated with the legally defined minimal housing standards.

Thus, possibly disregarding criteria of affordability, decisions to use more expensive building materials (e.g. corrugated iron roofs, concrete blocks, metal doors and window frames), or to employ experienced craftsmen in self-help projects, often reflect long-term expectations and aspirations pursued even at the cost of indebtedness or underutilisation of available family labour. The choice of higher building standards may also have material reasons, e.g. to want more durability and safety of housing constructions, or more protection from burglary, or may reflect social aspirations in terms of the prestige value of the house when adapting to capitalist consumption standards. Finally it may reflect higher income expectations based on the perspective of growing commodity markets and commercialization in the settlement, not excluding housing. A good mud house may for low-income families have a similar use-value to that of one made of concrete bricks. However, with newly introduced minimal housing standards, the exchange-value of traditional housing will become near zero. For potential middle-class buyers of the plot, an existing traditional house will figure not as an asset but as a cost accruing for its demolition. Therefore, even for very low-income households, compliance with market standards becomes rational in upgrading projects, as it is the only way to retain a market value of the structure built in case of displacement or the need to sell.

Under these circumstances the advocacy of appropriate and intermediate building technologies and materials cannot escape its interrelation with real or potential market valuations. To be successful, appropriate solutions must not be only technologically equivalent to the conventional ones; they must also conform to acceptable standards, or work to achieve this status during project implementation. These criteria are not easily met by prevailing project arrangements.

- In the first case it is difficult for low-income communities to adopt to the inclination of 'rich' foreign sponsors to insist on cheap solutions below the expected or conventionally applied standards. This problem is aggravated when project management itself shows lack of dedication to these principles. This may be the case when supplementary contractors are hired to meet project schedules, or unconventional self-help project components, initially declared 'indispensable', are abandoned overnight if delays in implementation occur (Oestereich, 1986).

- Giving appropriate measures an optional status may also become a constraint in achieving their acceptability, in the event that intermediate technology is suspected of imposing a dual housing standard on dwellers. For example the self-production of concrete blocks with casting forms has become generally accepted because the product is near indistinguishable from factory-made bricks and can be made on-site at a much lower price. However, schemes aiming at introducing unconventional building materials and new techniques of processing often fail, not due to technical infeasibility but for lack of institutional support and timely preparation under local circumstances. Advance rather than parallel research would be required with respect to the technical, manpower, and commercial side of its introduction to projects if appropriate technology is to be available to meet current demand when the main implementation phase starts. Under the premise of equivalency of appropriate technologies with conventional solutions, their inclusion in projects on a compulsory or incentive basis should be considered. This could contribute to a wider dissemination and acceptability than is possible by the experimental and optional terms of introduction usually pursued - and often precipitately aborted if not readily accepted by project participants (cf. Ziss/Ziss, 1986).

- Decisions on terms of project consignment of building materials, either as an independent operation of dwellers or its controlled supply by project management, can be an important criterion for the promotion of appropriate solutions and support of the informal sector. The disbursement of credits to squatters for the acquisition of building materials may be an incentive to adopt cheaper appropriate solutions, or to acquire them from the local informal market (cf. Peattie, 1982). The catch is that this approach is more time consuming and susceptible to abuse than the direct delivery of materials by project management itself. Confronted with this problem, project managements interested in tight schedules of implementation, visible progress in physical terms of housing, and adequate building standards have become reluctant to provide building credits for the self-acquisition of materials, or for the hiring of craftsmen. Many agencies now favour bulk buying and the controlled allocation of industrially produced building materials. This erodes the original concept of promoting self-determination of the self-help process in all aspects, including the support for the local informal market. Whenever necessary for the progression of construction to proceed on schedule, subcontracting of experienced craftsmen or of petty construction enterprises has become the rule (cf. Rakodi, 1991; and the summary of German experiences with self-help housing documented in BMZ, 1986).

- In their endeavour to find income-saving measures housing projects tend to develop two preoccupations: they want to accomplish everything locally and exclusively with the target population, and they tend to become centred on the project-related construction process without scrutinizing the possibilities of appropriate or intermediate solutions from the local or even international setting. Often knowledge of appropriate income-saving devices may already be available in other parts of town, but these have not yet been brought up to a marketable standard or popularly accepted due to lack of institutional support. Promotion of these external schemes would immediately benefit the target population of housing projects. To give an example, in Zambia cooking with charcoal is devouring up to 25% of poor families' incomes. At the time of an upgrading project in Lusaka a cheap, energy-saving stove made from scrap metal was produced on an experimental scale in another illegal settlement. External support for this scheme and its integration into the project could have saved up to 75% on fuel consumption and immediately benefitted the population of the upgrading project where this device was still unknown. Similarly the reprocessing of amply available organic refuse could have provided a charcoal substitute if a simple carbonisation method already successfully used in other countries had been adapted to the local situation in Lusaka (cf. gate, 1991). Quite probably both measures combined would have had a much greater and more long-term potential of reducing living costs than the actually deployed scheme of producing appropriate building materials.

b) *State interventions and the politics of squatter regularization*

One of the principal aims of state aided low-cost housing projects, besides the improvement of housing conditions and the provision of urban services, is the regularization of tenure and usually the conferral of full ownership rights on the occupiers. But service provision and security from removal also have their price: occupier households formerly living without legal costs become liable to service charges and taxation of property, and tenants are confronted with marked increases in rent reflecting the rise in property value.[18] According to comparative evidence, the global impact of regularization and upgrading often involves increases in living costs and problems of affordability. Thus, for poor families who usually become indebted by participating in the housing programme, security of tenure often means less real security due the opening of the community to land and housing markets (T. Johnson, 1987, p. 175). The fragile household situation of residents is confronted with growing commercial interest from outside, fostered by a large, unserviced middle-class housing demand and land and housing speculators in search of safe investments in inflation ridden economies. Middle-class groups who are not eligible for low-cost housing programmes and deterred from illegal housing by the insecurity of investments, inevitably exert considerable pressures on newly legalized settlements. The result has been a considerable middle-class encroachment in low-cost housing projects, usually displacing the economically most vulnerable residents.[19] Within the given legislative and market framework, protective measures against involuntary displacement are difficult for the planning agency to implement without supportive cooperation with the municipal authorities who take responsibility for the community after project completion.

In order to analyse policies of safeguarding upgraded communities in the post-project phase, a change in perspective is required, i.e. an investigation of the growing tendency of Third World states to legalize and service squatter settlements in the past two decades. Since squatter settlements and the various functions performed by them for urban reproduction have been shown to appropriately express the given structural relationship between capitalist and informal production forms, this poses various questions: (1) What pressures or interests explain the recent shift in policies of Third World states from condemnation of squatter movements to selective interventions in this sector? and (2), is it possible to discern a predictable pattern of state interventions in low-cost housing sectors? Answers can be provided along two lines: first from the perspective of theories on state functions and second from empirical research into the intentions of the local state, showing the impact and changes induced by its interventions at settlement level.

As theorists of the peripheral state have noted, general state functions are considerably modified by the conditions of world market dependency.[20] Under First World conditions of a self-reproductive economic system, the state's relative autonomy from its economic base allows its activities to appear as the common interest, that is, 'the ruling class not only justifies and maintains its rule but manages to win the active consent of the governed' (Gramsci, 1975, p. 182). This congruence between the political and the economic spheres, however, does not fully apply to Third World states (T. Evers, 1977, p. 80). Although Third World states are formally sovereign, the relative autonomy of their political sphere is related to a heteronomously structured economy, the dominant part of which is extraterritorial, i.e. subordinated to central capital and shaped by the terms of their world market integration (Hein/Simonis, 1976, p. 223). This imposes contradictory functions on the peripheral state. It has to develop its world market integrated economy, while simultaneously counteracting

115

the generalization of capitalist commodity relations in economic sectors whose basic function is to provide the export sector with cheap resources. The maintenance of this crucial balance between capitalist and non-capitalist sectors requires permanent state intervention, which inevitably reveals its discriminatory character towards capitalist interests (T. Evers, 1977, p. 124). Thus, in contrast to its appearance as a strong, interventionist state, the failure to integrate all sectors and groups into the political and economic system will rather lead to a syndrome Myrdal (1972) has described as the 'weak state'. It is characterized by a chronic deficiency of legitimization, latent political and economic crisis or instability, and a biased usurpation of the state apparatus by state classes (cf. Hein/Simonis, 1976, p. 228; Elsenhans, 1977, p. 259).

Because growing state interventions have concentrated on cities, Castells (1979) has tried to analyse this in terms of a necessary and universal tendency of capitalist development. State interventions concentrating on infrastructure and urban services, according to Castells, reflect the need to compensate the falling rates of profit in the capitalist economy.

> ... the intervention of the state becomes necessary in order to take charge of the sectors and services which are less profitable (from the point of view of capital) but necessary for the functioning of economic activity and/or the appeasement of social conflicts (Castells, 1979, p. 18).

Evidence supplied by Gilbert/Ward (1985) refutes the transferability of these findings (derived from 1872-1971 France) to Third World countries. The main areas of state interventions in Latin America were, in fact, related to economic growth, i.e. directed to industry, commerce, and agriculture, with social policies mainly being an 'afterthought'. At the same time, infrastructure provisions predominantly served the needs of the economic growth sectors and were not even necessarily organized by the state (Gilbert/Ward, 1985, p. 132).[21] Moreover, the tendency of the state to take over urban services to meet growing demand reflects problems with the 'size, complexity and inherent monopolistic character' of provisions rather than their unprofitability for the private sector (ibid.). Cases of public subsidies to private sector provision of collective goods (e.g. public transport, refuse collection, telephone) are not uncommon. Recently, there has also been a strong trend towards the privatization of state service provisions in both First and Third World countries (Glade, 1986; Gilbert, 1993). Consequently, neither the increasing degree of state intervention nor the different patterns of its involvement in the field of urban services can be convincingly derived from general and universal functions of the state in capitalist development.

According to the theory of the peripheral state, the heterogeneous base of national production systems and the fragmented social class formation will even convert state provisions of infrastructure from a 'common interest' into a highly politicized issue. Forced to act as the prime organizer of the industrialization process, directly as an agent of capitalism, states themselves accentuate the sociopolitical contradiction between the development of a capitalist enclave and the relative exclusion of marginalized masses from this process. Permanent interventions in support of international and nation capital valorization have led to a structural deficit of state actions in the field of 'unproductive' social programmes, excepting spoils extended to members of the state class and to other strategically important groups.

The conclusions drawn in Gilbert/Ward's comparative study of three Latin American cities - one of the rare urban studies that incorporate the role of the state - clearly show the structural limitations of state programmes in their compliance with the expansion of capitalist markets. This pattern is only broken in cases of necessary political and ideological appeasement of the urban poor. According to Gilbert/Ward, state intervention on behalf of the poor is only likely

> (1) when the poor have raised a serious threat to social stability; (2) when the state has acted to foster capital accumulation (such as increasing the supply of electricity or water for industry), and the poor benefit indirectly from this action; (3) when assistance to the poor furthers state interest, an example being land-regularization schemes which have also had the effect of integrating many barrio residents into the tax base thereby increasing revenue (Gilbert/Ward, 1985, p. 243).

With few exceptions like Mexico, Colombia, Chile and Brazil, social movements for land, infrastructure and housing have not been very substantial or determined in addressing the obvious inequity in the state's delivery of urban services to its low-income populations (Gilbert, 1993, p. 125). In Africa social movements have almost exclusively been confined to issues of workplace (Mabogunje, 1990). As Gilbert/Ward (1984) have pointed out, the attitude of most low-income settlements is not opposition or independence but apathy in response to state action. Settlement programmes have frequently been used by populist parties to rouse political support from squatters. But the subsequent failure of the elected parties to take more than token action on their promises does not seem to have caused serious political repercussions. In general it seems as if the *toleration* of illegal squatter settlements in itself has worked as an effective appeasement policy towards low-income groups. Deficits of provision of low-cost housing programmes or land have not raised problems of legitimization in this specific field of state action. Serious mass political protest and riots have only been occasioned in the event of threats to more vital urban interests such as cuts in food subsidies. While it is true that authoritarian regimes, like in Chile, have responded to isolated squatter movements with repression, more liberal governments have been able to control demands of tenacious or militant squatter movements by limited community programmes. The cooption of leaders and the satisfaction of basic needs such as water, or in some cases electricity, have sufficed to establish effective social control and deterred further settlement action (Gilbert/Ward, 1984a and 1985).[22]

Reflecting the circumstance that states do not seem to have been pressurized by squatter movements or class struggle into expanding their urban functions to these settlements, and given that most community programmes have in fact been initiated by governments and not by low-income residents, various researchers have stressed the importance of underlying political and ideological objectives: besides being a cheap form of infrastructure and housing provision, state self-help housing projects also have an important function as instruments of regulation and control over the urban development process. They install political authority in unplanned areas of town and integrate settlement life with the political party and the institutional structures of the local state (Burgess, 1984, p. 50; Gilbert/Ward, 1982; Rakodi/Schlyter, 1981; Skinner, 1983). The process of regularization not only delivers new land to the urban market; it also necessarily disseminates capitalist values related to private property and commodity relations, whilst politically inculcates petit bourgeois values amongst former squatters (Harms, 1982). The precise significance of political and ideological motives behind preventive state interventions in squatter settlements, i.e. to head off potential social conflicts or movements, will necessarily vary considerably according to the character of the political regime or the economic situation.

Irrespective of what function prevails in interventions (the economic, the political, or the ideological), researchers have often tended to wrongly polarize the discussion between pre- and post-legalization periods. This implies that state interventions are seen as essential leverage in establishing market conditions and associated values. However, studies by Engelhardt (1988), T. Johnson (1987), Pfeiffer (1987), and Gilbert/Ward (1985) have revealed that market-related value dissemination and expanded commercialization are not necessarily mediated or initiated by legalization alone. Widely disregarded by planners, evidence shows that this process automatically occurs by upward filtering of the housing stock in relation to the ongoing consolidation of illegal settlement.[23] Parallel to the growing probability of settlements to become legalized, a thriving informal market for land and housing will emerge if urban residential land is scarce and illegal settlements are suitable residential areas.[24] In this case residential mobility gives way to gentrification, replacing large parts of the original poor squatters by wealthier residents. We will address the problem of policy implications of this presumably widespread process in the next section.

As T. Johnson (1987) and Baer (1991) have noted, little is still known about the chain of moves and the actual dimension of residential replacement processes due to lack of longitudinal data. Individual case studies in Mexico and Tunis indicate a post-upgrading displacement rate in the range of 25-35% (T. Johnson, 1987, p. 176). With respect to the motives of state interventions in illegal settlements, a more substantial data base would, thus, probably underscore the supposition that serving middle-class housing demand at low costs is much more than an incidental aspect of upgrading and regularization programmes. The

118

collateral aspect of this intent would be a reinforced division of the urban poor into the economically integrable (those who succeed in staying in their settlement), and non-integrable 'outcast' population segments (those who are forced to move into lower grade illegal housing). As Pfeiffer's study of favelas in Rio de Janeiro has shown, a selection process of this type emerged during the economic decline of Brazil in the early 1980s. Massive downward displacement took place between the serviced and economically consolidated 'A-type' favelas and the 'B-type' favelas on lower value land with poorer infrastructure and service standards. In a chain of moves the outcasts from these two favela types were forced into the new 'C-type' of unserviced shanty-town favelas in remote locations and/or on erratic lands unsuited for building (Pfeiffer, 1987, pp. 211-214).

These described intents of state interventions towards regularization largely conform to policies of international agencies that have attained growing influence on national states and urban politics in the course of growing economic decline and indebtedness in the Third World. In the early 1980s Burgess argued that the growing intervention of international agencies could largely be explained as a strategy to safeguard capitalist valorization in times of global crisis. Thus, international banks and aid agencies have pressurized recalcitrant national bourgeoisies to direct some of their public resources to self-help housing (1) as a means of integrating politically unstable low-income groups by the provision of basic needs, and (2) as a deliberate strategy to keep the reproduction costs of formal-sector labour low in the interests of high profits in Third World countries (Burgess, 1984, p. 49). In retrospect the argument of 'wage cost reduction' appears tenable in that self-help housing has allowed real wage declines and made their impact more socially tolerable. However, Burgess' expectations of a general support for low-income groups by basic needs provisions have turned out to be a very selective policy sideline. Once more taking the World Bank as a trend setter, the recent swing to market-oriented restructuring of urban politics means that stabilization of the urban poor by government housing and infrastructure programmes will probably only apply for the economically 'integrable'. By deepening the urban division of the poor, this process is inclined to single out those with untapped resources and productive potentials from economically vulnerable groups without the means even to stabilize themselves in the informal sector.

The broader policy implications of urban restructuring according to the principles of the market economy are clearly expressed by Linn in a background study for the World Bank's 1979 World Development Report. Linn has argued in favour of stronger state intervention designed to minimize the barriers to housing-supply by removing biases against increases in the private housing stock (Linn, 1983, p. 182). According to this argument, housing construction should best be left to the private sector. But interventions in the urban land market would be required to provide more serviced land and to dampen rises in urban land prices.

119

The urban land market, and in particular urban land prices, serve to allocate scarce urban land to the most productive uses. Artificially depressing urban land prices or other means of interfering with the functioning of the land market are likely to lead to misallocation of urban land resources. The main role of public intervention therefore is (1) to regularize land tenure where clouded titles are a major impediment to private housing investment; (2) to assist selectively in sub-division of new land, particularly for the benefit of poor urban households displaced from central city locations by expansions in commercial uses of land; (3) to limit private monopolies in urban land markets; and (4) to develop effective land registry and cadastral records. ... Public service provision is the major area for public intervention in the urban housing market. Extension of public services throughout a city is the most effective policy instrument for expanding the supply of urban housing, dampening land price increases, and stimulating private investment in shelter (Linn, 1983, pp. 182-183).

Linn argues that the housing stock could be increased by removing institutional constraints to the expansion of market housing supply (i.e. control of rents, regulation of land use, subdivisions, and building standards), by giving small improvement loans to home owners and by keeping regulatory intervention in the housing market at a minimum. Although Linn acknowledges that middle-class groups would no doubt be the main beneficiaries of an improved capital market for housing, it is suggested that an increase in the overall housing stock might also improve the supply for the urban poor in a process of downward filtering of old housing units. Another concomitant aspect of the conversion to market-based housing policies would be to discontinue general subsidization of urban services. This is justified by the detrimental effect of subsidization on efficiency, revenues and equity, resulting in a decline in housing provision for the poor (Linn, 1983, p. 162 and 184). Exceptions would be selective subsidies for poverty alleviation measures such as water supply by standpipes. Taxation on property is seen by Linn as having no significant effect on housing supply and may even be a disincentive for construction and maintenance. Instead user charges with efficient service pricing should play a major role in encouraging the allocation of demand, private location decisions, and investment patterns for public services (ibid., p. 184).

As Gilbert comments, this argument defends private property rights, encourages the investment and credit facilities in the petty commodity sector, accepts the need to relocate people from central city locations, encourages the functioning of market mechanisms, and advocates that the public sector leave housing construction to self-help processes (Gilbert, 1986, p. 185). While the result of expanded state intervention may be a larger supply of reasonably priced serviced land, this type of regularization is bound to be divisionary with respect to low-income populations.

In the first case it will amplify the basic internal division of poverty groups according to income levels, separating those who are able to afford serviced housing with full cost recovery

120

from those who are not. Second, with respect to differential patterns of housing preferences, it seems that lowest-income groups are additionally discriminated by their specific needs and their lower potential of adapting to conditions of spatial restructuring. According to Dwyer (1975, p. 28) and Linn (1983, p. 127) housing and settlement preferences of low-income groups follow a common, distinct pattern.

For the very poor, job and income security is the most vital aspect of urban life that also accentuates their specific locational preferences irrespective of its possible illegal character. Closeness to jobs, the saving of transport costs or walking time, or other esteemed socio-spatial advantages related to subsistence or networking activities in the settlement location make this group most vulnerable to resettlement or displacement.[25] With incomes mainly dedicated to food and basic needs, rises in housing costs by regularization and legalization will tend to make their residential areas no longer affordable to them. If central city settlement locations are affected, land regularization may make the area attractive to commercial development or speculation, inevitably resulting in displacement or even compulsory resettlement.

The next group is still poor, but its members have achieved a reasonably stable income making their locational interests in housing more flexible and less dependent on the specific occupational circumstances. Interests in housing are mainly concerned with security of tenure and space needs for which they are willing to pay, with lower priority given to urban amenities. Most importantly this group is willing to 'trade location for security of tenure' (Linn, 1983, p. 127).

Although the boundaries between these two groups are fluid depending on specific national or local conditions (e.g. with respect to land prices and access to land, labour markets, household size and space need, and requirements of economic reproduction of households besides income), the group of the very poor can be easily identified as the potential main victims of market-oriented and state regulated urban restructuring. Their ability to evade regularization and to find access to land might be further restricted by state action when land invasions are opposed in an attempt to plan for low-income residents (Gilbert, 1986, p. 184). Thus, inappropriate restructuring of low-cost housing policies, ignoring the needs and financial capabilities of up to 40% of lowest income groups, might easily achieve the very opposite: the aggravation of unequal life space and unequal chances of prosperity in 'slums of hope' and 'slums of despair', respectively (Stokes, 1962).

Reservations must also be expressed regarding the alacrity of preferential states to restructure urban distribution patterns in defence of life space of the poor against economic space use. In the past, states were not able to control land prices, or were inclined to take action even if such policies were proclaimed. In Latin America public land has often been used for speculative purposes and not for low-income settlements. Wherever the state bureaucracy came into contact with the poor, its actions were too often 'legalistic, corrupt, arbitrary and unfair' (Gilbert/Ward, 1985, p. 254). In Africa high subsidization of urban services and housing provided to high income groups is a characteristic feature of the state, reflecting class power relations (Sanyal, 1981). In Asia it was found that public authorities may be no less aggressive or unfair towards the poor than private land owners (Angel et al., 1983; Bose, 1973). Finally, considering the erratic history of Third World government takeovers and the desultory changes in state policies, more state intervention may also create a critical dependency of low-income dwellers on perhaps unreliable state provisions. Moreover, formal 'integration' tends to deter residents from struggle against inequities. As Harms argues, the incorporation of former squatter populations into urban housing markets and into the legal system inevitably turns them into individualized house consumers. This separates them from one another and impedes solidarity and collective actions (Harms, 1982, p. 49). While some house owners may at least enjoy economic benefits and security from regularization, tenants have little to expect from state interventions: upgrading and legalization usually leads to substantial rent increases not compensated by the introduction of legal protection of the tenancy status.

Thus, in the case of unstable political circumstances or corrupt and preferential states, the expansion of municipal activities in matters of housing and settlement may be a highly ambiguous issue for low-income residents. While the struggle for legalization may sometimes be a strategic objective to protect settlements from haphazard changes in government squatter policies and from impending eviction, an illegal residential status may in other cases be a more effective protection from the intrusion of capitalist land and housing markets or from the clutch of bureaucrats. Here the more pertinent alternative to expanded state action would be its reduction to a regulative minimum with communities having greater responsibility over purely local matters (Gilbert/Ward, 1985, p. 254). But even for the progressive state, more benevolent policies towards squatters and legal low-income communities require more consideration of the negative and divisionary effects of expanded commodification and commercialization on the residential structures of low-income settlements. Housing policies increasingly need to comprehend more than planning and implementing efficient forms of *once only* provisions or improvements. If low-income housing policies are to become more effective and have longevity, they must additionally address the problem of social and spatial urban restructuring and the subsequent redistribution of the existing housing stock by filtering processes.

> Developing countries must thus not simply build, but also anticipate and monitor the redistribution of the older housing stock. An understanding of the process of filtering is one of the basic inputs of coherent housing policy (Ferchiou, 1982, p. 167).

c)   Adapting low-income housing policies to upward filtering of the housing stock

As Baer (1990) has noted, filtering is usually thought to be confined to developed capitalist nations where it figures as a somewhat bashful strategy of low-cost housing provision. Traditionally, filtering indicates a process by which high-cost housing is, in the course of its deterioration, gradually released to lower-income households. This process may be enhanced by governments when subsidies are provided for the construction of new housing for middle- and upper-income groups, allowing lower-income groups to take up the vacated older housing stock. However, there is growing evidence that in many parts of the world socialist or Third World governments have implicitly allowed a traditional filtering-based strategy to dominate their housing policies in 'practice if not in words' (Baer, 1990, p. 69).

A clearer perception of the international dimension of filtering processes and its impact on housing allocation and utilization would require three elements: (1) a more elaborated theoretical framework of filtering to incorporate the Third World situation; (2) a reorientation of research to longitudinal empirical studies of how housing stock and households become reallocated in a chain of moves, or how housing units become restructured according to changing residential preferences and needs; and (3) the recognition by planners, policy-makers and researchers that in many cases de facto filtering processes have a more significant and perhaps countercurrent impact on housing allocation than the official housing policies and, thus, cannot be simply ignored.

In its most general form filtering can be defined as the 'mechanism whereby households adjust their housing to their changing income and preferences' (Baer, 1990, p. 72). In this sense it is an incessant process. By *active* filtering, households adapt housing to their needs by moving, or by improving the existing unit. *Passive* filtering occurs when the household situation remains invariable, but the residential circumstances are changed by either physical or social outside events, leading to a modified equilibrium between housing preferences and the actual standard of housing including the standard of neighbourhood (ibid.).

Since this general definition tends to imply the freedom of households to satisfy their housing preferences on a housing market, the concept will be used in the following to denote the filtering of housing stock, i.e. the mobility of households through an existing housing stock reflecting terms of constrained housing provision (cf. T. Johnson, 1987, p. 174). In the Third World the disparity between desired mobility and the availability of alternative housing greatly modifies the traditional allocation pattern of the filtering process.

Many Third World governments have introduced an institutionalized filtering process through an application system for municipal housing of different standards. Little systematic research has been devoted to this subject. But tentative observations raise doubts as to whether bureaucratic selection practice is always just and in line with nominal criteria for eligibility. In Lusaka, Zambia, registration on the council waiting list for low-cost housing has long been regarded as a waste of registration fees due to the practice of preferential plot or housing allocation to individuals 'out of turn' by corruption, or by arbitrary disregard of the waiting list altogether.

The customary perception that downward filtering of housing stock prevails, reflecting the natural deterioration of aging housing units, is quite inappropriate for Third World housing circumstances. As widely observed, 60-90% of self-help housing will improve within five to fifteen years while most of the public housing will deteriorate (Perlman, 1987). Under conditions of restricted access to legally protected and serviced housing units, upward filtering has become the predominant process when housing of this type becomes available and low-income residents are bought-out or otherwise displaced by higher-income groups. Even where downward filtering of Third World housing stock occurs, evidence shows that the vacancy chain stops before reaching lower-income groups and has little impact on the housing situation of the poor (Baer, 1990, p. 77). This seems to counter expectations raised by Linn and others that an expanded formal housing market will also have a trickle-down effect on low-income housing provision. These findings are however not altogether consistent with other studies indicating that formal and informal housing markets are in fact quite closely interrelated. Housing studies in Mexico, Tunis, and Seoul have shown that varying, but significant degrees of new formal housing-construction (by ownership) extended to units in the informal sector, including subletting arrangements (ibid., 1991, p. 79).

While in First World countries filtering appears as a constant, perpetual process of mobility applying to high- and low-income households alike, Third World housing systems behave significantly differently (T. Johnson, 1987, p. 174). Once ownership of housing can be achieved, mobility stops abruptly both in formal housing and upgraded former squatter settlements. This blocking of the filtering process may have negative effects for land use and for the overall supply of housing. For example it inhibits its transfer to those who could use it more efficiently, or it prevents the realization of its monetary value for other activities that might be economically or socially more useful (Doebele, 1982). On the other hand, upward filtering also provides considerable benefits for middle-class house buyers and the state. As a rule, upward filtering of upgraded former squatter housing is a cheap form of settlement development and includes the capitalist repossession of self-help housing accomplishment at costs below its real market value.

Of course many issues raised by the filtering perspective are not entirely new. In part they have been discussed before in different terms, e.g. as gentrification and commercialization, displacement, preferential and socially biased housing provision, unequal exchange of self-help and petty commodity housing, and so forth. Other research has, following the logic of its study object, implicitly already used a framework comparable to that of the filtering perspective. Nevertheless, the filtering perspective cannot be discarded as the presentation of old facts in new clothes. Importantly it shows that conflicts over housing provisions or certain policy measures cannot be regarded as isolated issues concerning only the settlements or target groups involved. Instead solitary interventions in particular settlements or housing sectors will also create repercussions in the entire urban housing system. These need careful monitoring if posterior reallocation processes are not to counter the intended policies. The same bias may apply to research design. For instance, many critical studies of housing projects have hitherto merely pointed to contradictions between nominal policy intentions and reality. This limited perspective disregards the underlying process of people's changing housing preferences and the inevitable turnover of housing pertaining to life-cycles and the differentiation of household needs. Consequently, the typical effects of commodification and displacement in upgrading cannot be properly judged or anticipated without knowing more about the citywide chain of voluntary and involuntary moves, i.e. who is raiding low-income settlements and where do raiders come from, what has happened to the displaced dwellers and why have they moved. In this way the filtering perspective allows (and compels) disparate findings to be linked together and forces planners or researchers to take a more comprehensive view on housing matters.

Regarding the inevitability of filtering mechanisms and the widespread reinforcement of this process by filtering-based housing policies, the question arises as to what should, and what can be done to control this development in low-income housing schemes. A useful tool for applying the filtering framework to upgrading has been developed by Strassmann (1977). In his 'stock-user matrix' Strassmann assumes the existence of a specific equilibrium between household incomes and value of the occupied dwelling in a particular settlement. As long as there is a correspondence between the type of dwelling and income levels, filtering processes tend to be minimal. But with dwellers' incremental improvements to the house and the settlement conditions, or by upgrading programmes, housing values are bound to increase whereas household incomes usually do not. Subsequently this change in the ratio of household income-to-housing value tends to create a relative disequilibrium, i.e. a 'housing gap'. A first conclusion to be drawn from this model would be that upgrading programmes must carefully analyse the existing equilibrium in order to predict the amount of upward filtering that will be caused by the introduction of new housing and settlement standards. Upgrading is most likely to benefit residents when a negative housing gap prevails (i.e. incomes that are relatively higher than the housing value). Conversely, oversized standards in improvement programmes, or their too rapid implementation, are inclined to result in high post-upgrading displacement if the housing-income equilibrium becomes seriously distorted (Johnson, 1987, p. 190; Kool et al., 1989, p. 191).

While Strassmann's quantitative model may be reasonably reliable in predicting developments in the upgrading of consolidated or matured settlements, the assumptions concerning the ratio between household income-to-housing value seem too linear to comprehend the situation in early stages of informal settlement formation. As observations show, filtering of the housing stock is very distinct in the initial settlement phase and closely related to a consolidation process (Johnson, 1987, p. 190). But longitudinal studies on consolidation from Salvador, Brazil (Engelhardt, 1988), from Mexico City (Ward, 1982), and from Lusaka, Zambia (Schlyter, 1991) make it apparent that housing and land transfers, or the chain of moves, are not always explained by the household-to-housing value ratio as implied in the stock-user matrix. A framework of settlement consolidation must also take into account that internal processes are conditioned by external factors. As Ward points out, comparability of consolidation in different settlements may be problematic for various reasons: topographic or locational aspects directly influence the propensity to squat in a specific area; the accessibility of housing varies greatly between cities; and different political attitudes towards squatters may encourage or deter land invasions and squatter consolidation. The local economic prospects affect income levels and occupational mobility. Finally, the internal organization of dwellers or local leadership structures and their interrelations with the wider polity add another important aspect to the rate of consolidation (Ward, 1982, p. 184). Nevertheless, comparability can be achieved if analysis is directed to the observable spatial, physical, and commercial images of a settlement under consolidation in response to changing external conditions. In reinterpreting the survey data provided by the studies mentioned in terms of the filtering framework, we propose the following model of stages in consolidation of squatter settlement:

- Consolidation is not a linear process, i.e. a function of household incomes and incremental improvement. It is conditioned by four qualitative and partially interferential steps at settlement level. These reflect external constraints and the wider framework of urban development and will at each stage lead to specific typical expressions, e.g. concerning housing and land utilization, patterns of exchange, and mechanisms of value determination.

- These transfer mechanisms and filtering processes are in certain stages of consolidation additionally conditioned by reproductive strategies of households and networking activities and not entirely by the given disequilibrium of income and house value.[26]

In his case study Engelhardt defines settlement consolidation in terms of three factors: (1) the replacement of temporary huts by permanent house constructions of a size meeting the real needs of its dwellers; (2) the introduction of infrastructure (water, electricity, roads, street lighting, social facilities); and (3) a growing feeling of security on the part of squatters after successfully heading off attempts to evict, combined with the de facto official toleration and the mobilization of local political support for legalization (Engelhardt, 1988, p. 18). But in contrast to early assumptions, such as those of J. Turner (1969), that squatter consolidation is a function of dwellers' incremental improvements over time, Engelhardt's findings point to a dual dynamic of consolidation and displacement. Large numbers of invaders and early settlers are, in fact, unable to substantially improve their housing or benefit from settlement improvements. Instead they are forced to sell out to higher income groups who, by their improvement of the housing stock, then become the actual motor of the consolidation process.

126

In reality, therefore, 'consolidation' is quite an ambiguous term as it implies that the stability of the settlement can only be achieved at the cost of destabilization of parts of its population (Engelhardt, 1988, p. 22).

Using the longitudinal data provided by Engelhardt (1985-87) for a favela in Salvador, Brazil founded in 1982, Ward's study of three squatter settlements in Mexico City (1973-74), and Schlyter's account of development in a squatter settlement in Lusaka, Zambia (1965-1989), upgraded in 1978, it is possible to reconstruct four distinct phases in consolidation: these are the *territorial*, the *physical*, the *market*, and the *legal consolidation*, each phase having a specific qualitative impact on populations according to their differentiated housing preferences, needs and income situations.[27] The intervals of consolidation phases are not solely an internal function of the settlement process. They are additionally conditioned by the growth patterns of the wider urban environment. Salvador and Mexico City represent cases of rapid urban expansion with considerable commercial pressures on land and housing development. Their squatter settlements tend to pass through the different stages of consolidation in relatively quick succession. In George settlement in Lusaka the pace has been considerably slower due to a completely different housing market and legal situation. Here land is held in public ownership, and customary land rights exercised by squatters in old, established settlements have usually not been contested by local authorities. Thus, housing values are generally still quite moderate and have only recently moved up due to growing demographic pressure and to low municipal delivery of legal and serviced land. Consolidation phases also need not be consecutive. Overlapping or mutual enhancement may occur, reflecting spatial or income-related heterogeneity in a settlement's development, or external intervention. As in Lusaka, upgrading may, for instance, introduce the legal consolidation at a stage when physical, market, or even territorial consolidation are still pending or ongoing processes.

It would be premature to propose a comprehensive model of the different constituents of displacement from settlements, either illegal or legalized (Kool et al., 1989, p. 197). However, it is thought that the proposed model of 'stages in consolidation' is a contribution to the operational definition of processual developments in the formation of informal settlements. The specific appearances of stages will necessarily differ from country to country and between cities. Indices of consolidation would have to take into account the *relative* local economic, cultural, legal, and urban setting. But once general local patterns have been established, these would allow planners to identify specific phases in the formation of a settlement on account of its characteristic patterns. This would enable the design of more appropriate policies and their implementation with predictable results.

When generalizing on the findings of the three case studies in the following (with additional material from my own studies in Lusaka and in Caracas), the concrete statistical data will be included to illustrate the dimensions of developments. It is understood that the catalogue of indices and tendencies compiled from these cases points to typical consolidation features. The assessment is neither comprehensive nor does it depict absolutely necessary conditions.

The earliest phase of an illegal settlement can best be defined as *territorial consolidation* both with respect to the processes of internal land occupation and development and to the struggle against eviction. In all the case studies, invaders did not make up a homogeneous group. In Mexico City 70% of cases were migrants, but had lived in cities for several years before staking an illegal claim to a plot. While there were only few significant differences between migrant households and city-born households, invaders in Mexico City were not among the poorest urban residents as cheaper accommodation could be found in the inner-city shantytowns. In Salvador invaders were overwhelmingly very poor and came from other informal housing areas in town. A common distinction, however, seems to exist between determined 'early invaders' and groups who will only join the invasion once immediate eviction seems improbable. Like the early invaders, they often retain their old dwellings until the territorial status of the area is reasonably established. According to observations by Gilbert/Ward (1985, p. 100), residents who buy plots after the invasion has become a fait accompli in fact far outnumber the original early invaders. In the incipient settlement phase, self-help and cooperation are the rule in providing the essentials of territorial consolidation, e.g. defining plot sizes, street levelling, making the settlement passable for traffic, or providing facilities for water provision. Another common objective among residents will be action towards defending the territory from repossession by landlords or eviction by municipal authorities.

With the accomplishment of rudimentary territorial consolidation a differentiated informal petty real estate market emerges. Once all vacant land had been taken up, subdivided plots were exchanged at prices in the range of two monthly salaries in Salvador, or at approx. six monthly minimum wages in Mexico City (US$800). Plots on prime sites suitable for commercial use achieved substantially higher prices. Reflecting the insecureness of the settlement, investments in housing were usually kept at a minimum to avoid risks in case of demolition. But as the Salvador case will show, poor housing standards may also be a direct function of very low incomes.

Towards the end of the territorial consolidation phase (in Salvador and Mexico City approximately four years after establishment of the settlement) an accelerated reconstruction of the temporary, mostly single-roomed housing set in. Houses were now rebuilt with more durable building materials on an expanded scale to meet actual space needs. Densities also increased significantly as the area gained attraction for settlers. Even within this relatively short span of time, development was likely to be characterized by a deepened internal differentiation of the population, which became subdivided according to the housing strategies pursued by its residents. At the end of the territorial consolidation (or beginning phase of physical consolidation - see definition below) a considerable portion of original residents (25% in Salvador and Mexico City) had already left the settlement. In Engelhardt's case of Salvador most had moved to a nearby squatter area at a considerably lower level of consolidation (Engelhardt, 1988, p. 21). In Lusaka, where physical consolidation coincided with legalization in 1978, annual changes in housing ownership in the pre-upgrading stage were in the range of 9%. By 1977 61% of dwellings were no longer inhabited by the same household as in 1969, including some cases of vacancies and absentee ownerships (Schlyter, 1990, p. 34).

This typical high fluctuation of squatter populations and the rapid turnover of plots after invasions are considered by many governments as the doings of 'squatter speculators', or 'professional invaders' (Abrams, 1964; Ward, 1982; Gilbert/Ward, 1985). Although professional squatters no doubt exist who invade land for the sole purpose of selling it with profit and not in a strict sense for the satisfaction of housing needs, their significance seems to have been greatly exaggerated for political reasons. Data shows that plots sold during the territorial consolidation generally achieve little more than the capitalization of investments (approx. 2-3 monthly minimum wages) (cf. Gilbert/Ward, 1985, p. 100; Engelhardt, 1988, p. 19). Instead, the high rate of moves before physical consolidation can be taken as an indicator that for many households sale is predominantly a function of subsistence needs, precisely reflecting the invaders' inability to wait for windfall profits obtainable at later stages of consolidation, which then might have rendered substantially higher land values. Any undue prolongation of stay would for them also increase the risks involved in eviction. Contradicting the findings of Linn and Dwyer (see p. 121), high residential mobility appears to be a necessary condition for survival of lowest-income groups. The strategy of perpetual invading minimizes their housing costs and allows them to gain a marginal income from short-term plot transactions. This disposition, it seems, predestines them to spearhead the opening up of cheap residential land needed by substantial numbers of urban low-income groups who are less prepared to shoulder the risks of invading.

The phase of *physical consolidation* comprises both improvements in housing construction and the settlements' gradual expanded provision with basic infrastructure. With investments in housing, the character of the settlement changes visibly. A substantial number of dwellings are now made of permanent building materials with foundations, door frames, windows, and durable roofing (which tends to come last). Larger families will build more than one room; richer households may plaster or paint their houses inside and outside, plots are levelled or secured if on steep terrains, etc. More security of the house will also encourage the development of interior space use, e.g. the acquisition of furniture and household goods. Communal provision systems for water, electricity, and fuel are organized. The commercial infrastructure diversifies with the opening of local markets and/or more shops. Organized informal transport facilities are made available. In this stage land becomes scarce, and territorial formation comes to an end with plot subdivisions down to minimal sizes for the accommodation of a single house (in Salvador average plot sizes declined from 95 m^2 in 1983 to 55 m^2 in 1985). The decrease in public land and higher residential densities also impose a reduction of space available for urban subsistence. For low-income groups this development may deprive them of essential household sustenance, adding to their inclination to move. Physical consolidation in George, Lusaka, reduced the percentage of households with gardens from 61% in 1969 to 42% in 1989 and cut down the average garden size from 34 m² to 12 m² (Schlyter, 1990, p. 22; Rakodi, 1988b). With physical improvements, prices for plots tend to increase further (Salvador: US$120 in 1983 to US$300 in 1985/85), and locational price differences tend to level out between residential prime sites close to roads or on best building grounds and those in formerly more remote parts of the area. This largely reflects the fact that land prices are now related to the amenities of service provisions, growing security and improved access to plots (cf. Tait, 1996 for the Caracas case). Market price ceilings are, however, still restricted by the low attraction for higher income-groups who will wait for a more comprehensive urban infrastructure to appear (e.g. tarred roads, individual water connections, street lighting). The reputation of the settlement, closely related to its probability of surviving, is another important aspect of its final opening up to the urban housing market. As long as the settlement, despite its physical consolidation, is still in a transitory stage with low attraction for households seeking long-term security of tenure, housing turnover tends to remain quite high.

Precise information on the typical movers in this stage is difficult to obtain. However, it must be assumed that upward filtering of the housing stock plays an increasing part in decisions to move. In Mexico City neighbours of movers generally reported that these were amongst the economically worse-off residents. Thus, unable as they were to develop the standard of the house in line with the ongoing physical consolidation, a growing disequilibrium of the household income-to-housing value seems to have occurred for many low-income residents. The observable chain of moves in Salvador at this stage was directed to squatter settlements without infrastructure, often in a two-step fashion: the household obtains a plot in a new squatter area, but secures its dwelling in the old settlement until a minimal security is achieved in the new one. Prices received for the sale of the house in this stage are higher than in the period of territorial consolidation. But again it cannot be considered speculation. Households selling out merely received the market equivalent for land with basic services. Thus, higher prices are simply a compensation for the households' resign of their rights to benefit from the improved urban services they themselves have helped to achieve. Data from Mexico City on the in-migrants at this stage clearly demonstrates the dialectics of consolidation at the cost of destabilization and displacement of original residents: 70% of recent arrivals had achieved a high standard of housing consolidation compared with only 42% on the part of long-term squatter-improvers (Ward, 1982, p. 188). The comparison between consolidators and non-consolidators also began to display a pronounced relevance of occupational and educational categories as the basis for further consolidation. While the income of the head of the household was relatively unimportant for consolidation levels, jobs providing security and socioeconomic mobility ('white-collar' and skilled 'blue-collar' jobs) ranked third amongst the most significant variables for improvements, after household income and education (ibid., p. 190). Thus, Ward concludes that

> ... an inability to improve the physical status of the home was not so much a product of backwardness or indolence but reflected structural barriers which prevented the creation of an investment surplus (ibid., p. 198).

The magnitude of efforts and investments made in the stage of physical consolidation are decisive in determining if and when the settlement reaches the stage of *market consolidation*. With market consolidation the settlement will have established itself as a de facto recognized informal part of the urban system. Housing is now overwhelmingly of permanent character, and residential structures have expanded to allow greater specificity of room functions. Two-storey housing may appear and renting will have become more widespread. The settlement now commands a diversified range of commercial facilities, services, and industrial functions. The bulk of investments in infrastructure, housing, and commerce as well as its improved reputation make it a probable candidate for legalization in the not too distant future. Land and housing values are now oriented *in lieu* towards those on the regular housing market. The settlement's imperfection is, however, its continuing illegal character and the undetermined level of housing-standard at which it will finally stabilize. This situation continues to deter higher income groups from investment as they want to make a long-term housing or commercial decision in an area of predictable standard. At the same time this situation will attract speculation. In lieu market values are substantially higher than those of the previous consolidation phase, but the actual rate of transactions may decrease due to the unresolved legal problem and the unpredictable final character of *residential quality* in the settlement. After market consolidation has taken place, locational aspects and prestige values play an increasing part in defining the living quality that can be offered by a settlement. The rate of transactions and housing prices are determined by a wide range of questions. Is the city moving towards or away from the settlement? Will there be adequate public transport and a convenient road-system to the city's commercial centres, or will there be commuter problems? What is the quality and the reputation of the neighbourhood, will there be safety problems? Will there be urban services adequate to the residential standard? How does the settlement fit into the city's long-term land-use plans, and how will this affect the development of property values? Are there environmental problems?

With *legal consolidation* the area finally becomes an officially recognized freehold land and housing market and is integrated into the municipal administrative and service system. But legally guaranteed safety of tenure may also have considerable drawbacks for those residents who have stood up to the filtering mechanism of the previous consolidation stages. Substantial private and municipal investments may be required to make housing standards comply with building codes and to raise the level of infrastructure provision. Residents may find themselves in a situation where legal consolidation means struggling to pay for services, legal obligations, and for housing credit repayments. Typically the decision to upgrade a settlement will lead to a final peak of transactions before a stabilized residential composition is reached. The incentive for relatively poor residents to sell out and start anew in an illegal settlement may be considerable in highly constrained urban real estate markets. In Mexico City fully legalized plots sold at US$4,500 compared with $800 in illegal, but physically consolidated settlement areas in 1974 (Ward, 1982, p. 185); in Lusaka prices for housing in one settlement in 1989 varied between US$620, if complying with building codes, and US$300 for houses in still unregulated parts of this settlement.

The usefulness of this proposed consolidation model to determine/predict settlement developments and to define improvements capable of retaining the balance of income-to-housing value can be demonstrated by the post-upgrading situation in Lusaka.[28] In particular this case shows that legalization and regularization do not necessarily lead to displacement or filtering-up if they are used as a policy to divert territorial and physical consolidation *away* from middle-class housing standards and preferences.

d) Upgrading in Lusaka: a strategy for consolidation with replicability?

Most of Lusaka's upgrading programmes implemented in the late 1970s were reasonably well adapted to the income situation of dwellers. By and large, project design introduced appropriate standards that helped in avoiding asymmetries between incomes and housing values. Additionally, price escalations were controlled by the citywide implementation of upgrading programmes reaching two-thirds of Lusaka's squatter areas. Despite the provision of basic infrastructure (communal water taps, tarmac main thoroughfares, street lighting, schools and communal facilities) prices for plots with simple adobe housing remained stable in George and in other upgraded settlements (cf. Rakodi, 1988). Some initial undue price differentials between unchanged traditional housing and new housing built with concrete bricks suggested the budding of a speculative market. But this gap closed during the 1980s due to the circumstance that commercialization of housing was slow and displacement by upward filtering of housing was the exception rather then the rule. Registered transfers in the post-upgrading phase have been very low, not exceeding 1-2% annually (Schlyter, 1990, p. 35). This is explained by the fact that physical and market consolidation, although promoted by legalization, were still ongoing processes, advancing only very incrementally. By the end of the 1980s a large part of the old housing stock in upgraded areas had been reconstructed in higher standard building materials. Territorial formation now showed clearer physical demarcations between plots. Nonetheless, in terms of middle-class standards, sites were still erratically disposed and settlement was too dense to allow the kind of territorial demarcation required for middle-class privacy and security (i.e. the inevitable walls around this type of housing). Additionally, plots were for the most part only accessible by unsurfaced footpaths. Thus, the combination of spatial 'disarray', the still low reputation of the settlements, and incomplete physical consolidation seem to have effectively protected most parts of the upgraded areas from becoming eligible for middle-class housing. This was the case although prices for plots and self-construction of a house, or the alternative acquisition of an existing higher standard house in these areas, would have cost only a fraction of the amount demanded for regular middle-class housing on a highly constrained urban market.

Somewhat contrary conclusions on the low post-upgrading displacement rates in Lusaka are drawn by R. Martin (1987). He has argued that this outcome is in part attributable to high default rates in service charges. Due to the support of the ruling party seeking public support, people were openly encouraged to enjoy the benefits from upgrading and servicing without paying for them. But although low or even zero costs for upgrading no doubt support the inclination to stay, it does not make residents immune to the enticements of external market forces. Low-income residents would have been prepared to sell, and middle-class groups would have been prepared to buy-out dwellers, if locations and standards in upgraded areas had met the required standards.

Evidence for these conclusions is supplied by the different upgrading situation in the newly constructed adjacent 'overspill' areas. These were designed to be inhabited by residents whose old houses had to be demolished to make way for roads or infrastructure lines. For these cases, credits, building materials, and technical advice were provided to build a two-roomed house of standard design on an area with orderly terrace-house style ground plan, including tarmac access-roads. In a deliberate effort to 'turn their back' on the village type of development in the old settlement, the vast majority of overspill residents chose high-status materials, like concrete blocks and steel framed windows, and rejected traditional solutions (Martin, 1982, p. 267). The impact of these self-imposed standards has, irrespective of people's reluctance to pay for services, de facto filtered-up the newly constructed housing stock. According to Schlyter (1991, pp. 28-29) this has led to a striking polarization between improvers and non-improvers. In ten years only 50% of housing in George overspill had been expanded beyond the state accomplished with the original loan; 6% had not even been able to finish the two-roomed house. The housing standard of non-improvers seems to have actually decreased. Plastering was not repaired and many broken windows had been blocked up. As overspill areas can easily be transformed into middle-class housing, non-improvers now seem highly susceptible to displacement if pressures on the housing market rise. So far, legal annual transfers have only risen from 0.9% in 1982 to 3.8% in 1988 in George. But selling-out is now well on its way in an upgraded housing scheme with a near identical physical project design in a more sought-after part of Lusaka.

Whereas George is a typical working class housing area close to the town's industrial centre, the former peripheral squatter settlement of Kalingalinga is, due to Lusaka's growth pattern, now surrounded by middle-class council housing. Accordingly market prices offered for housing in Kalingalinga overspill and adjoining areas ($1,150 to $1,875 in 1989) were substantially higher than in the corresponding areas of George (a maximum of $825 in 1988).[29] By 1989, within four years after start of construction, 49% out of a total of 944 households in new extensions of the Kalingalinga overspill area had not been able to resist the enticement and had sold out to middle-class residents.[30] Legal provisions that Kalingalinga residents should have first option to buy any house for sale - as a measure to encourage dedensification - simply could not take effect because market prices were far beyond the financial means of its overwhelmingly low-income population.

A final outcome of legal and physical consolidation in Lusaka (as in most comparable Third World cases) has been a growing rental market. While the earliest data from 1969 shows low rates of subletting and of absentee ownership in the designated upgrading areas, subletting increased substantially during and after upgrading with owners adding rooms to the core house. While subletting is not encouraged by authorities and was not openly admitted by owners, in 1989 29% of houses in a survey of George were in 'multi-family' use, showing a de facto subletting arrangement. In 25% of cases the owners were absent and the house rented (Schlyter, 1990, p. 38). Data presented by Rakodi confirms a similar development in Chawama, another of Lusaka's upgraded settlements, where a high correlation between house improvements and the provision of rental accommodation has been observed (Rakodi, 1988c, p. 316). In general, however, legalization and physical consolidation in Lusaka has not led to market consolidation despite a marked increase in Lusaka's population from 525,830 in 1980 to approx. 1 million in 1989. Supported by land policies revised in 1975 to convert all freehold to leasehold tenure (cf. p. 212), upgrading has overwhelmingly consolidated original ownership. So far, there is only little hint of the development of a capitalist organized rental market with profit-orientation. Instead the provision of rental accommodation has turned into an important source of income for low-income households or, in the case of absentee owners, takes the form of petty landlordism.

It would be an exaggeration to suggest that the terms of upgrading in Lusaka are in toto replicable for other Third World countries. Other implicit and explicit project components (income promotion, cost-recovery, progressive self-help and community self-organization, equality of opportunities, etc.) have been less successful. Poor maintenance of housing and dilapidation of infrastructure is now a chronic problem following Zambia's dramatic economic recession in the last two decades. Nonetheless, the Lusaka project at least exhibits exemplary conditions and insights with respect to the possible control of upward filtering and the containment of commodification in upgraded squatter housing. Regarding the possible transferal of Lusaka's experiences to other upgrading projects, four combined policies - in necessary conjunction with their implementation at specific stages of consolidation - can be identified as promising measures for the avoidance of post-upgrading filtering processes, hitherto usually negatively associated with legalization and land regularization. These are:

(1) anticipatory legalization without comprehensive physical consolidation, (2) appropriate and preventive (low) infrastructure standards, (3) restricted ownership and post-project land control, and (4) widespread implementation.

1. Anticipatory legalization without comprehensive physical consolidation. So far, most planners have come to regard legalization as the crucial mechanism that leads to uncontrolled upward filtering and commodification of housing. However, this analysis overlooks the fact that in practice legalization very rarely reflects explicit planning policies. Mostly decisions to legalize were taken under pressures of de facto physical and market consolidation, often already articulated with potential middle-class or commercial interests in the particular settlements. As the discussion of our case studies indicates, legalization could be a much more powerful planning tool for low-income housing policies if it were not merely used post facto but

- as an anticipatory measure to stabilize settlements that are still in the stage of territorial consolidation, thereby avoiding the displacement mechanisms pertaining to progressive physical and market consolidation when not protected by legal consolidation;

- as an instrument for controlling and enhancing desirable further physical consolidation with sustainability, appropriate to the income situation and the needs of residents.

Judging by the Lusaka case, the most suitable point for legal intervention as a policy of creating sustainable home ownership for low-income settlements would be at the end of territorial consolidation. In this phase the area is mostly inhabited by low-income dwellers with pronounced interests in security of tenure, but with low means of affording quick physical improvement. Here early legalization is capable of freezing up the filtering process and stabilizing the community, which facilitates a controlled, incremental physical consolidation with minimal displacement of residents. In other cases under different residential, spatial, and social circumstances, a later timing of legalization might be more appropriate. If higher settlement standards are aimed at, or seem inevitable due to locational aspects of particular sites, relocation to other sites might be encouraged until an appropriate residential composition is achieved. Planning may also aim at creating a mixed residential composition by enabling a controlled degree of gentrification and upward filtering before legal stabilization is implemented.

2. Appropriate and preventive (low) infrastructure standards. The filtering perspective adds a new important aspect to the discussion of appropriate infrastructure and space-use standards. While the lowering of infrastructure standards with the intent of making upgrading more affordable is regarded as unjust as long as governments continue to subsidize middle and high-cost housing, a positive side-effect should not be overlooked. Overambitious infrastructure standards have consistently violated the planning rule that the determination of technical standards and space-use provisions should not create an asymmetry between the value of housing and the economic status of residents (Strassmann, 1977). Conversely, low initial standards of infrastructure and higher densities have in practice helped maintain the crucial equilibrium of income-to-housing value and effectively protected settlements from filtering-up mechanisms. If preventive low initial standards are introduced for these reasons, provisions should be made for later progressions in accordance with growing income capacities and diversified needs of households. Systematizing these kinds of experiences, the UNCHS now advocates several techniques of appropriate upgrading solutions for low-income groups (cf. T. Johnson, 1987, p. 179). The core intentions of these techniques have been anticipated and verified by the physical project design in Lusaka, with some appropriateness added by later down-scaling owing to financial constraints.

In Lusaka these techniques included introducing infrastructure components at a relatively low standard, and giving priority to communal instead of private utility. Specifically, appropriate preventive solutions in Lusaka comprised the following components: (1) communal water standpipes instead of individual house connections; (2) keeping demolition and essential resettlement for the provision of some all-weather roads with street-lighting at a minimum, thereby retaining a largely pedestrian instead of vehicular circulation; (3) while material infrastructure was designed to satisfy basic needs only, more emphasis was given to social infrastructure, like schools, dispensaries, and community centres; (4) with respect to territorial formation and the existing standard of the housing stock, no compulsory restructuring was imposed on residents. Due to these arrangements, house improvements have been done step-by-step in line with the income capacities of households. Inevitably upgrading has touched off some changes in space use to accommodate the enlargement of many house units and to offer more privacy, e.g. for the increased number of lodger families. However, since the originally planned dedensification measures did not materialize and densities have in fact risen considerably, modified traditional space-use patterns now prevail that necessarily involve a considerable degree of social closeness and mutual acceptance of neighbours. It is owing to these terms of implementation that standards in legalized squatter settlements in Lusaka have largely remained incompatible with middle-class housing preferences. The exceptions to this pattern, as explained, are the newly built-up overspill areas. Due to their adaptation of conventional geometric plot layouts and building standards, these areas are now increasingly becoming subject to upward filtering and displacement of former upgrading participants.

3. Restricted ownership and post-project land control. Land legislation plays a key role in controlling upward filtering of legalized housing. Worldwide, various techniques of post-project control over the property status have been employed in an effort to reduce speculation and cut excessive profits in transfers of legalized land (T. Johnson, 1987, pp. 179-182). But policies of limited or delayed conferral of property rights are not without internal conflicts. On the one hand, it is necessary to grant enough tenure security to encourage private improvements and to confer enough legal rights to make dwellers eligible for official bank credits or mortgages. On the other hand, restrictions on transfers should not prevent house owners from capitalizing the investments in house construction. Delayed freehold and sales restrictions to upgraded or site and service housing have been the most frequently employed policies. In practice, legal time delays for transfers, or the obligatory resale of the plot to the implementing agency, have been effective in curbing speculation and controlling upward filtering. This approach, however, has been less successful in stabilizing upgraded populations since illegal transfers occur anyway if economic pressure is sufficient, or households become unable to afford housing of this type.

Leasehold instead of freehold tenure has been suggested as providing a stronger incentive for residents to remain on the site - provided that residents have an option to buy the lease after 10-15 years (HABITAT, 1982). To avoid speculation, governments and not the residents should receive the main profits from raises in property value. However, contract arrangements should foresee a portion of increased economic land value to be collected by owners at the end of the leasehold period to encourage their investments (T. Johnson, 1987, p. 181). Unfortunately, leasehold or other forms of government control over land usually do not provide the kind of security recognized by private banks, nor will they allow the land to attain its full market value (Wakely, 1989, p. 21). In Lusaka, where leasehold was the sole officially recognized property form, private banks and even the National Building Society denied low-income, 'high-risk households' building credits or mortgage loans (Sanyal, 1981, p. 416).[31] While the leasehold system (with additional government control of rent and house-sale prices) has curbed speculation in Zambia, the drawback of extensive institutional market control and credit restrictions has been a disincentive to home ownership, which has become a privilege of higher-income households.[32]

As a method of avoiding the policy incompatibilities of conventional legal ownership, novel forms of cooperative land ownership have been suggested by Turnbull (1983), Sundra (1976), and Lewin (1981). Cooperative land ownership separates tenure right of land from the dwelling improvements on it. While in the event of sale the improvements may be sold at market value to anyone, the land shares are retrieved at nominal prices to the cooperative that may resell them at market value. Due to this arrangement individual speculation is avoided, while the cooperative may capitalize the increased land values and use the gains for the benefit of communal development.

At the same time, its advantage over leasehold tenure is the ability to mortgage the improvements, since they are owned outright by the household. The household will also solely capture the increase in the dwelling's value as a result of any improvements that they made during their occupancy (T. Johnson, 1987, p. 181).

4. Widespread implementation. Various researchers have suggested that rapid and widespread implementation of upgrading and land regularization would relieve pressures towards upward filtering of newly legalized housing (Schoorl et al., 1983; Linn, 1983). In the first case it would dilute the unsatisfied middle-class housing demand, allowing upgraded communities to cope with the 'isolated' occurrence of intrusions and filtering-up without serious distortions of the settlement's character. Secondly, with more supply of housing and less market pressures on improved and serviced settlements, land and housing prices would be less likely to rise, and residents more likely to maintain the crucial balance between income levels and housing values. The data on two large-scale upgrading schemes, the kampong improvement programme in Djakarta, reaching 70% of eligible squatters (cf. Taylor, 1983), and Lusaka, servicing two-thirds of its squatters at the time of implementation, seem to support these suppositions. In both cases upgrading programmes succeeded in stabilizing settlements, in keeping population turnover low, and in producing only moderate increases in land values. The drawback of widespread implementation may be that it exacerbates the circumstances for follow-up upgrading programmes. In Lusaka the lasting impact of citywide upgrading has been a fundamental transformation of low-income households' housing preferences. In the post-upgrading phase the traditional self-built, mud brick dwellings were gradually replaced by houses now increasingly built by craftsmen with factory-made concrete blocks and roofing materials (corrugated iron or asbestos sheets). The enhanced demand for construction material has considerably added to an over-proportioned price inflation for building materials. The costs of bricks increased by 957% in the decade 1978-1987 while labour-costs had only increased by 279% and consumer prices for low-income households by 672% (NHA, 1989 and GRZ, 1989, p. 19). The disproportion of inflated construction costs and workers' incomes has brought the production of new housing stock by low-income groups (at modern minimal standards) to a near standstill. While vulnerable groups are bought-out of upgraded housing, recent plot extensions in legally declared low-income residential areas were exclusively taken up by lower middle-class builders for financial and not policy reasons. In Lusaka low-income groups simply can no longer afford to build at the officially required minimal standards for newly built-up areas.[33]

e) Some policy conclusions with special reference to lowest-income groups

The global perspectives of Third World countries disclose growing incongruities between capitalist reality and the claims of state authorities to solve the problems inflicted by contemporary growth models. Informalization and de-ruralization are advancing everywhere, confronting cities with the prospects of uncurbed urbanization, economic polarization and an over-proportioned growth of unauthorized settlements. Our analysis of peripheral capitalism and the role of Third World states does not support expectations that the housing situation for low-income groups will be mitigated by future economic development or by enhanced popular state activities. Instead peripheral petty commodity production in the informal sector and collective reproduction are increasingly being stabilized as a regular capitalist relation of production in the peripheral growth model. This leaves little alternative but to view self-help housing as the major future source of housing provision in the Third World. But its potential for satisfying housing needs is not fully used as long as government housing policies, land and building legislation, and local power structures obstruct these activities and do little to appreciate or protect people's accomplishments. New land and housing legislation and revised planning approaches to the squatter problem would substantially improve the housing situation, costing the state little. But class divisions and internationally supported political structures set societal and economic limits to reforms and are the backcloth for the rigidity of many bureaucratic planning dogmas.

The reorientation of the planning role from authoritarian decision-making, often acting on idealistic premises, to participation in planning and more user-orientation has not yet taken place in many Third World countries. Pressures for change are coming from active communities, from NGOs and from outside through international development cooperation. However, the need for changes is not felt only by planners. Individual self-help effort militates against collective action and may be socially divisive in the competition for scarce resources (P. Marcuse, 1989, p. 12). A new understanding of the self-help housing quest must raise social awareness of the unsolved housing problem and the detrimental effects of market-intrusions on its accomplishments. It must get neighbours involved, and it must involve local state and planners for self-help aims. NGOs and bilateral development agencies can be important mediators in this process, in particular with respect to introducing new training concepts for local field staff. Mutual on-site learning by planners and dwellers, as in the concept of 'collaborative discoveries' of new solutions and methods, must replace the technocratic approach based on paternalistic attitudes (Steinberg, 1986, p. 27). New partnership attitudes acquired by field staff may also eventually 'trickle up' to the levels of senior administrative and political decision-makers.

The recent international promotion of 'development from below' as an answer to government and political failure is not without ambiguities. It should not be overlooked that the supposed 'autonomy' of communities is in fact quite often a limited and disguised aspect of cooptative government policies and may not represent a real toleration of community action (Gibert/Ward, 1985, p. 249). A strive for autonomy or empowerment may initially mobilize people, but in the end it cannot avoid the structural problems of the entire economy. As a rule, good projects have not been accomplished against the state but by the cooperation of dwellers, implementing agencies and planners. Ultimately, development requires a synergy between the top and the bottom: a collaborative effort of the actors according to their comparative advantages in contributing to the development process (Sanyal, 1989, p. 7).[34]

In the discussion on housing policies it is virtually impossible to design and propose standardized strategies without providing first a reliable typology of interrelating factors in different national or regional settings. Perhaps already too many precipitate conclusions have been drawn from comparative evaluations, appraising single, isolated components without adequate comprehension of the wider frame of implementation.[35] For example the impacts of the divergent land allocation systems in Africa, Asia, and Latin America or even between different regions and cities have not been systematically scrutinized for project accomplishment or policy formulation (Baross, 1983). The same applies to the state, whose conflicting role in the planning process has hardly been assessed beyond a crude differentiation between authoritarian and progressive regimes. Even this classification may be misleading for the choice of planning approaches or the involvement of intermediate agencies; for example in relation to the question whether to orient people to the state and its possibly unreliable provisions, or to build up and strengthen autonomous community organizations for project implementation. In Africa, apart from its specific cultural setting and still recent colonial experience, most people's political socialization in the postcolonial period was formed by repressive one-party regimes perpetuating many colonial practices for their own good. With little practice in democratic decision-making and self-determined collective actions, even newly emerging progressive governments find it difficult to stimulate people's grassroots development without the state assuming the necessary role as initiator and catalyst for community action. With a few exceptions (e.g. Kenya, Uganda, Malawi), national NGOs have expanded only very slowly in Africa and have not yet established their function as mediators between the state and the people (CDG, 1987; B. Turner, 1988). Their relationship with the state is often more competitive than cooperative, and with respect to dwellers most of the NGOs' operations are still dedicated to getting communities organized instead of being sought and consulted by them.

In its 'Global Strategy for Shelter to the Year 2000', HABITAT has named land, infrastructure, and building materials as the key physical resources for the production and improvement of shelter. The strategy acknowledges that governments are unable to provide housing for all and proposes a division of labour in which governments provide serviced land and infrastructure while it is for the people to produce their own shelter. This approach also recognizes the limits of transplanting strategies from one country to another. Appropriate housing standards and technologies require adaptations according to the specific given needs, resources, and the environmental situation of countries. In the short-term approach, pragmatic expertise, partially acquired by trial and error methods, may help produce locally appropriate solutions if governments comply with this strategy. But in terms of global shelter for all, the problem is not simply one of *providing* but also one of making solutions accessible and maintaining them. Squatter populations are not a homogeneous group, nor

140

can the varied patterns of their housing preferences be reduced to a linear function of income differentials. This applies in particular to the lowest-income urban income groups who predominantly survive in an illegal housing circuit. As housing projects have only very rarely addressed these groups, which also tend to be the first to be displaced by legalization, very little experience is available on appropriate and accessible housing strategies for the urban very poor. Moreover, the little (mainly anthropological) research there is seems to suggest complex, differentiated reproductive patterns in which housing and locational aspects play an imperfectly understood part. On the one hand, some research indicates that poor households tend to be immobile and strongly resist displacement from their socio-spatial network (Kool et al., 1990, p. 193). On the other hand, some of the housing-mobility studies presented earlier, have also shown that poorest households are inclined to move once physical consolidation commences in their settlements. In this case land invasions and temporary dwellings may be used as part of a subsistence-oriented reproductive strategy yielding marginal profits from illegal plot sales. On a more general scale H. D. Evers has characterized the propensity of the poor for constant spatial and economic adaption to urban opportunities in terms of a 'floating mass', i.e. survival by change and mobility (H. D. Evers, 1980, p. 65). Accordingly, attempts to stabilize these groups by tenure arrangements could be self-defeating unless their income situation is first changed, and their mode of housing utilization is dissociated from their present subsistence strategy.

Policies of providing housing and tenure security to lowest income groups require a greatly enlarged data base in order to understand the ambiguous appearance of their housing preferences. Much could be contributed by more knowledge on the citywide chain of moves and their determining factors - data that in Third World countries, due to lack of resident registration, would virtually only become accessible by its incorporation into a population census. Judging by the discussion on the impact of consolidation phases or the logic of the stock-user matrix, it seems highly improbable that housing schemes for lowest-income groups will work solely by market economy without some kind of cross-subsidization and state protection. Considering the vulnerability of poor households to involuntary displacement, a novel approach is required which makes the inevitable process of upward filtering instrumental in improving conditions at the bottom end of the housing scale.

Three approaches might be considered: (1) controlled or selective gentrification, (2) the guiding of households displaced by filtering-up, to planned 'beachhead' areas, and (3) the encouragement of rental unit construction (cf. T. Johnson, 1987, p. 183).

Controlled gentrification with voluntary (and compensated) upward filtering could be introduced in areas with a predictable post-upgrading market value and an effective middle-class demand for the final housing product. Following a proposal made by Strassmann (1982), residents would be given the usual financial and institutional inputs for sites and service or upgrading (but of a standard oriented to the housing preferences of potential buyers) and could live on-site during the improvements. As an incentive, minimal legal and price guarantees would be given for the repossession of the house and plot by the implementing agency. After project completion the filtering-up process would be institutionally stopped at a certain level, offering two options for upgrading programme participants: (1) it would allow part of the former squatter population to stay, exempting them from increases in rent and tax related to the rise in property values. An important concomitant aspect adding to affordability would be that the mixed residential composition offers jobs and income opportunities to the former squatter residents; (2) after project completion, voluntary movers could sell their house product with profit, but they would be bound by a financial arrangement that allows the developing agency to recoup its investments and to collect a portion of the increased property value for the cross-subsidization of the remaining original residents affected by problems of affordability.

Problems with this approach are that it is only justifiable if a near unanimous participation of settlement dwellers can be achieved. Controlled gentrification in a partially upgraded area is bound to introduce uncompensated displacement of those, who, wanting to stay, would opt against participating. Thus, it seems more appropriate as a programme for developing site and service areas, offering lowest income groups temporary homes and substantial profits after completion to improve their living or income situation.

Beachhead areas for squatters would be required in any realistic and socially just assessment of the effects of large-scale upgrading programmes. Residents displaced by upward filtering, or newly arriving low-income migrants, should be guided to low-cost housing areas without, or with only minimal, infrastructure - but with surveyed plots that will allow future upgrading at minimal costs.[36] In the event of considerable pressure towards upward filtering of officially sanctioned settlements, even of lowest standard, it may become necessary to declare certain beachhead areas off-limits for planned interventions until nondiscriminatory improvement schemes can be found.

Finally, the encouragement of *rental housing* has throughout the world not been considered by many governments as an appropriate means of increasing the housing stock at controllable standards (T. Johnson, 1987, p. 186; Gilbert, 1993, p. 1). Preoccupied with partially unrealistic, if not ideological policies of home ownership, municipalities have been deterred from granting credits or subsidies to occupiers for this purpose. Opposition to support for rental housing has mainly been raised on grounds of potential speculative misuse or the fear of uncontrolled densification. However, as practice has shown, expanded unofficial subletting has become a routine aspect of upgrading schemes used by their residents as a means of raising incomes and meeting the risen post-upgrading cost of living. For the poorest community members lacking means to improve their dwellings to meet rising consolidation standards, doubling up and renting out has become one of the last resorts to make staying possible. Thus, an institutional scheme of rental tenancy unit construction at defined minimum standards (water, sanitation, size) financed by a loan programme would make various ends meet if an increase in densification is feasible and local infrastructure

142

capacities are ample. For low-income residents it would provide an income source counteracting the tendency towards displacement and the alienation from valuable locally-established networks. Given the provision of a continuous rental income, risks of defaults in loan repayments seem low and rents could be pledged by the financing agency, if necessary. For urban authorities, rental construction programmes would serve to expand the housing stock of officially desired minimum standard without necessarily counteracting home ownership policies. On the contrary, by collateral legal provisions tied to the loans that stipulate incremental equity transfer of ownership, tenancy under this arrangement could be an important first step towards home ownership for aspiring young households (T. Johnson, 1987, p. 187).[37]

Notes

1   For a critical discussion of the political and economic motivations of the World Bank cf. Tetzlaff (1980, pp. 67-118). According to Tetzlaff, poverty orientation is part of a strategy to stimulate the market economy and commodification on a global scale. In practice the approach was less radical than its rhetoric. As soon realized, real access to programmes on the part of poverty groups required fundamental political reforms. Fearing destabilization by socialist movements as in Vietnam, Cuba, and Chile, the World Bank pragmatically came to terms with most Third World governments that were resistant to reforms. The acknowledged need to press for political and institutional change was, in practice, substituted by appeals for the enlightenment of government elites, or by simply hoping for prudence to prevail in the end (Tetzlaff, 1980, p. 116).

2   As Nientied/Van der Linden (1987) have pointed out, the World Bank's self-help housing policy has omitted vital aspects of the original concept. According to Turner and Abrams the terms of planning and implementation should be left to deci-sion-making of dwellers and their organizations within an appropriate state-provided legal and organizational framework. In the World Bank projects, all major issues are preplanned, leaving only marginal room for dwellers' participation in secondary aspects of implementation such as organizing the self-help labour component and deciding details of essential resettlement, e.g. road lines and locations of water taps or where to build community centres, schools, dispensaries. Details of this type of participation in the Lusaka project are given by Martin, 1981.

3   The general World Bank arrangements are loans repayable within 25 years with 7-8% interest. The recipient country contributes 50% of costs and takes responsibility for cost-recovery. The World Bank also extends managerial and technical expertise for project implementation. For further reading cf. the World Bank sector policy papers on Urbanization (1972), Housing (1975), Urban Transport (1975), Village Water

Supply (1976), Small Scale Enterprise (1978), and the Evaluation of Shelter Programs for the Urban Poor (Keare/Parris, 1982). The evaluation principles of the World Bank are described in Bamberger/Hewitt, 1986.

4   According to Steinberg/Mathéy, upgrading is generally considered the key concept to solving the following urban issues: i) it reduces risks to health through the improvement of housing and living conditions and the provision of social and technical infrastructure; ii) it mobilizes private resources for the housing construction and settlement process by granting legal security of tenure and the utilization of plot and land; iii) the support for and strengthening of illegally developed settlements improves the general tendency of their populations to socially integrate into the urban framework; iv) forms of land utilization and local developments involved in the self-help process can be more easily adapted to the existing spatial town planning; v) by the combination of self-help with various forms of investment and utilization of appropriate building materials, the housing standard can be improved to a level acceptable both to residents and to the municipality; vi) household income is to be improved through vocational training programmes, the provision of credit facilities, and by integrated promotion of local petty business schemes; vii) upgrading can be institutionalized as an extension and complementary field of national and municipal housing policies, thereby offering low and lowest income groups alternative means of housing and housing provision (Steinberg/Mathéy, 1987, p. 4).

5   Based on 1986 prices, Hardoy/Satterthwaite have estimated the comparative costs of housing provision under different options of government spending. In their example, conventional low-cost housing (two rooms) can be provided at US$10,000 per unit; site and service schemes including the necessary land acquisition provide a plot at approx. US$2,000; whereas upgrading of existing housing stock, including the improvement of infrastructure and support for local business, can be achieved at US$150 per unit if residents' organizations are made the responsible implementing agency and local resources are utilized (Hardoy/Satterthwaite, 1989, p. 142). Others are less optimistic about the savings by self-help. For Third World countries in general Burgess (1988) estimates savings by self-help in the range of 20% or less.

6   For World Bank internal evaluations cf. Keare/Jimenez (1983); Keare/Parris (1982). Comprehensive assessments of the World Bank's housing and urbanization policy are given by Grimes (1976) and Linn (1983). Independent, more critical, accounts are given by Bamberger (1981 and 1982); Burgess (1987 and 1988); Burgess/Ramirez (1988); Cabannes (1983); Nientied/van der Linden (1987); Rakodi/Schlyter (1981); Schlyter (1985); Werlin (1988); Williams (1984); Schmetzer (1987). A more detailed coverage of the World Bank housing project in Lusaka, Zambia will be offered in the case-study section of this book.

7   According to the Lusaka Urban District Council, Garden Township (one of the upgrading and site and service areas) has, approx. ten years after project completion, virtually reverted to the state of a squatter settlement (CDG/GRZ, 1989, p. 14).

8   Examples of the change of residents' attitudes and the failure to mobilize post-project self-help in the community will be given in the case study.

9   Exceptions are mostly politically motivated. In Columbia, where approx. half the housing stock produced under the national housing agency has been aided self-help, the nexus with extreme social violence seems obvious. Peru is another case where the legalization of squatter settlements was, under the left-wing government, made a national housing policy. Upgrading programmes at a national level have been implemented by innovative, decentralizing governments in Tanzania (Schmetzer, 1987, p. 21) and Indonesia (Steinberg, 1989, p. 15; Hardoy/Satterthwaite, 1989, p. 121).

10   Following the diversification and specialization of NGOs, the range of their activities is not confined to local community support and consultancy alone. Other typical fields of action are fund raising, public relations, lobbying for change in attitudes at local, national and international levels, and 'alternative' research. They may also act as mediators in conflicts of interests between political groups, industry, and the poor communities. For an informative classification of the various forms and varieties of organizations operating under the NGO label, see White (1989, p. 6).

11   For an overview of current projects cf. B. Turner, 1988; HABITAT FORUM, 1987; CDG, 1988; UNCHS, 1987b; Mathéy/Sampat, 1987, p. 64. Special editions on NGOs & CBOs were presented by *TRIALOG*, No. 22, 1989 and *World Development*, No. 15, 1987.

12   For examples from Zambia cf. chapter X.6.

13   A more explicit discussion of the role of planning transfer in colonial and postcolonial countries, including the mechanisms of its dissemination, will be given in the next chapter on the colonial city.

14   The following suggestions towards alternative planning presuppose the African system of traditional land tenure in which either the state has become the proprietor of urban land, or urban land remains in communal possession with usufruct extended to individuals (Sträb, 1986, pp. 25-26).

15   Alternative planning methods have been proposed by Etzioni (1973) and Koenigsberger (1982). Etzioni's 'mixed scanning' attempts a 'third' approach in planning somewhere between comprehensiveness and incrementalism. Instead of comprehensive planning involving detail-oriented surveying, a photographic 'zoom perspective' would give planners a general overview with enough detail to identify problem zones requiring more detailed strategies and surveying. The limited planning capacities can then be used selectively to attend to areas with demand for immediate action according to developmental priorities. Adopting many aspects of Etzioni's proposal, Koenigsberger

has developed an approach based on 'action planning'. Its methodology is designed to "meet the needs of fast growing cities by a continuous programme of public sector initiatives, conditioned by an overall perspective derived on the one hand from existing national and regional urban policies and on the other from monitoring and feedback procedures tuned to the local scene" (Safier, 1970, p. 11). Planning is oriented to feasible schemes with short intervals between planning and implementation and includes mutual evaluation with the target group (Heinrich, 1987, p. 373).

16 In its compendium of international donor experiences the DAC-OECD reports that practically no post-project evaluation had been done to investigate the sustainability of project measures (DAC-OECD, 1988, p. 12). Awareness of this lack is now growing in the wake of the international discussion on 'sustainable development' following the 1987 'Brundtland Report' (World Commission on Environment and Development, 1987). For a discussion of sustainability of development projects cf. Stockmann, 1989 and 1993; Stockmann/Gaebe, 1993.

17 Simultaneously, the scope for the development of progressive and critical planning approaches seems limited by its predominant character as consignment-research sponsored by administrations and agencies with specific preconceived problem assessments (Häußermann/Siebel, 1978). New impulses for a politicization of planning might be expected from qualitative methods, designed to complement and overcome the status quo orientation of quantitative approaches. Scenario-writing, for instance, has been proposed as a technique of qualitative simulation aiming at greater approximation of reality (Stiens, 1982). It implies a simulation of a hypothetical succession of events with the aim of recognizing causal processes and 'knots' of decision-making, defining their meaning for planning arrangements and incorporating possible alternative developments.

18 For example, in a kampong upgrading programme in Indonesia, Silas (1983) and Taylor (1983) have reported a decline in rental units and a 50-200% increase in rents. Similar post-upgrading results are confirmed for Calcutta (Chakravorty, 1981).

19 Comparative international evidence on factors enhancing involuntary displacement following upgrading is given by Kool/Verboom/Van der Linden (1989).

20 Reviewing works of Saunders (1979), Sandbrook (1982) and Gore (1984) on the local state, Rakodi (1988a, pp. 32-33) has presented the following summary of essential state functions: (1) the provision of productive urban infrastructure, both physical (roads, power, water, sewage, communication, etc.), and social (e.g. education, health systems); (2) assistance for the establishment and accommodation of productive activities by providing financial incentives and by land-use planning. (3) The stimulation of demand, for instance, by the awarding of contracts for infrastructure installation and housing schemes; (4) ensuring the reproduction of labour-power through collective consumption, for example in the form of low-rent housing; (5) official socialization, by which

official and appropriate values and attitudes are diffused, and by which government action is represented as in the common interest; (6) participation in politics and planning, in order to maintain the legitimacy of the state; (7) developmental action, by which the demands of the urban population for land, services and facilities are satisfied to some extent.

21   For a largely corresponding account of state development in Africa cf. Tetzlaff, 1989.

22   In their comprehensive account of community action of the urban poor, Gilbert/Ward came to the following conclusion: "By and large, community participation has been used by governments as a means of legitimizing the political system, either as a structure for garnering votes, or as a means of ensuring compliance with urban political decision-making. Governments have not permitted any extension of power and decision-making to local groups. Indeed, where community participation has led to greater demands for local control over resources and more active involvement in decision-making, governmental enthusiasm has cooled and the proposal dismissed" (Gilbert/Ward, 1984a, p. 780).

23   For a detailed discussion of the filtering concept see next section.

24   "Prices are determined by location, levels of consolidation and servicing and the reputation of the settlement. The illegality of the settlement reduces the price of land but, as most settlers anticipate that regularization of tenure and servicing will eventually be achieved, most illegal settlements survive" (Gilbert/Ward, 1985, p. 128).

25   These features are somewhat in contradiction to other findings (cf. p. 129 and 141) that point to high residential mobility of lowest income groups. It is necessary to distinguish either between consolidated and non-consolidated residential circumstances or between specific fractions of poverty groups pursuing their own reproductive strategies of survival.

26   Factors that have been omitted from this model, but in particular cases will strongly influence decisions to stay or move, stem from the socio-cultural and political setting. Ethnic, religious, linguistic and tribal affiliations may be important aspects encouraging residential clustering, or setting constraints to finding alternative locations (Kool et al., 1989; Doebele, 1983). Access to land or permission to stay in a particular illegal settlement may also depend on the benevolence of local leadership (CDG/GRZ, 1989). In Mexico City intimidation of households by local leaders and their eviction through physical threat were not uncommon if dwellers refused tribute payments (Ward, 1982, p. 186).

27   A somewhat different approach to determining factors in residential consolidation was proposed by Ward (1982). In his case focus was on the consolidation of households and dwellings and not on the spatial consolidation of the settlement. Ward correlated indices of consolidation (services, house standards, inventory of material possessions (ibid., p. 207) with socioeconomic variables (e.g. years of residence in settlement, years

in city, income, household size, education, work type). In the overall analysis, years of settlement residence, income and education contributed most to the statistical explanation of consolidation levels (ibid., p. 190).

28 Similar arguments, referring to the 'maturity' of a settlement as a parameter for an appropriate point of legalization/upgrading, are proposed by T. Johnson (1987, p. 176) and Kool et al. (1989, p. 192).

29 Prices calculated at 1988 rates of exchange: 0.125 Kwacha = US$1.

30 Information provided by council field officers responsible for the area.

31 The state monopoly in land, introduced in the early 1970s under the one-party state, is currently under revision after Zambia's conversion to a multi-party system. Complying with structural adjustment policies, a return to private ownership in land seems likely in 1996.

32 For a comparative approach to land tenure policies in Kenya and Tanzania, with a similar heritage of colonial land legislation to that Zambia, cf. Schmetzer (1987, pp. 18-23).

33 Based on survey observations 1988/89 in Kalingalinga (upgraded) and Kanyama, a still illegal but officially tolerated old squatter settlement. More details of this will be supplied in the case study in the second part of this book.

34 Similar conclusions were drawn in a series of conferences in the 1987 'International Year of Shelter for the Homeless'. cf. CDG, *Workshop 'Participation and Self-help' within HABITAT FORUM BERLIN '87*, Cologne, 1987, and the *Limuru Declaration by the Global IYSH NGO Forum in Nairobi*, April 1987.

35 According to my own observations, following extensive study of the Lusaka situation, not one of the many cross-references found with respect to aspects of its upgrading performance (but excluding those writers who could draw on their own field work in this location) was without serious coercion concerning the conclusions drawn (e.g. on the role of the local NGO, the supposed 'new' attitude of the government towards squatters, the assumed reasons for low displacement rates, and so on).

36 Proposals for the design and step-by-step development of beachhead or reception areas are submitted by Heinrich (1987, p. 376).

37 An annual transfer of equity of the property value from the owner to the tenant until the total ownership is shifted would also safeguard against the problems of absentee landlordship and abuse of the system (T. Johnson, 1987, p. 187).

VI   Colonialism and its legacy for African urban development

1   Introduction: the colonial city in Africa

Much of what was presented in the first part of this book has, no doubt, a certain Latin American focus. This is for three reasons: (1) the phenomenon of hypertrophic growth of squatter settlements in Third World cities first became manifest on this continent, revealing the limitations of conventional planning approaches and the inability of politicians to cope with the urban problems posed by unauthorized settlement; (2) alternative outlooks and concepts on this subject, like those proposed by Mangin and Turner, came out of on-site studies in Latin America; (3) finally, Latin Americans were among the prominent contributors to the debate on the social character of self-help housing provision, considering the issues appropriately in the framework of developmental theory. This necessarily raises some questions as to how far the situation in African cities may be compared to these findings and to what extent the proposed theoretical framework is relevant for the analysis of African urban settings.

Before beginning the discussion of our Lusaka case study on urban planning and the development of squatter settlements, a brief outline of the history of African urbanization will help to clarify the necessary frame of reference for analysis.[1] Implicit comparison of African with Latin American development will show that metropolises on both continents have salient urban features in common that are related to the exposure to contemporary capitalism and the concomitant inequities of global capitalist development. But it will also show that in Africa the socioeconomic structures and determinants of contemporary town planning and housing provision remain far more deeply embedded in recent colonial history than in Latin America.

In the first place, the African urbanization process (perhaps excluding the Arabic part of the continent that has its own specific history) only really started after the departure of colonial powers some 30 years ago. However, within less than 10 years after independence the growth pattern typical of Third World urbanization replicated itself in most of the large African cities - albeit on a smaller absolute population scale. In particular the new capital cities quickly turned into magnets of attraction for migrants from rural areas. By the early 1970s squatter inhabitants already made up the majority of the total urban population in nearly all the major African cities.

Table 6.1
Population developments in selected African cities

	Year	Total urban population	Per cent of population in slums
Addis Ababa	1966	0.7 mil.	85.7%
Nairobi	1971	0.54 mil.	30.5%
Lagos	1973	2.0 mil.	50.0%
Lusaka	1969	0.26 mil.	47.0%

Sources: Bauwelt, No. 13, 1981; Williams, 1986c

The velocity of the incipient African urban formation process is not alone explained by the post-independence expansion of capitalism in these countries, or by their 'catching up' with modern global capitalist urban patterns. African urban growth rates were, and still remain, among the highest in the world because the structure and dynamics of urbanization were to a large extent already predetermined by the contradictions of colonial history. Although colonial capitalist policies nominally followed a dual course of 'native rural' and 'white urban' development, the result of implanted colonial production systems was deruralization and detribalization *without* urbanization. The decomposition of traditional rural modes of production and the recruitment of large numbers of migratory labourers gradually separated the indigenous producers from their means of production and created a latent dependency on urban-based forms of reproduction. This explains the unexpected potentialities for urban development in what on the eve of independence appeared to be rural-based societies but which revealed their true state once the restrictive urban influx policies were abolished by the new African governments.

Variations in the general patterns of African urbanization are found if we consider the specific historical phase and the circumstances of colonial subjugation. Distinct productive functions were assigned to the colonies according to the needs of the 'parent economy' by using various means of penetration and transformation of the indigenous modes of production. In 20th century Africa the main European 'conquistadors', France, Britain, Belgium, Portugal, and Germany, imposed quite different styles of colonial policies. The Portuguese, for example, installed a colonial power structure based on the exportation of their own feudal system; the French almost successfully transformed their colonies into culturally alienated minor replicas of the mother country; whereas British colonists adopted the somewhat more refined policy of indirect rule derived from their Indian experiences. These basic policies were again modified by concrete factors such as the duration of alien rule, the objective and form of production, the cohesion of the traditional society, and local resistance to colonial transformation. However dissimilar the power structures and forms of production may have been, the point is that all colonial policies had a mutual core in the fundamental principles of strict ethnic and racial segregation between the European and the various indigenous population groups.

This segregationist principle was to become the decisive element in colonial town planning, translating the policy of divide and rule into spatial dimensions. In the South African apartheid model the African population was barred from the city altogether, with the labour-force contained in separate townships. Elsewhere in Africa the basic pattern of ethnic zoning was employed, merely modified in detail by the specific planning instruments and residential models adopted by the colonial powers in question. Where traditionally built-up towns existed but were unsuited for the realization of the colonial type of city layout, the European city was built on adjoining sites. Except for western Africa where precolonial urban settlements existed (Ibadan and Oyo in Nigeria, Abome in Benin, Kumasi in Ghana), Sub-Saharan African cities were entirely a colonial creation, built on locations selected exclusively to serve the various colonial interests and to reinforce their power structures. Excepting geophysically determined locations like mining areas, town sites were predominantly set on strategic geographic points suited for military and administrative control of the territory, or along the outward-oriented trunk lines of transport and communication. A suitable climatic environment for European-style habitat also figured as an important selection criterion wherever feasible.

The most prominent and systematic feature of colonial cities was the sharp racial or ethnic demarcation between the European and the native sector, the latter being often ethnically or tribally subdivided. Basic town planning structures and layouts reflected the need for social and military control of the native quarters and hygienic protection of the European residential zones from these areas. The creation of healthy environments with low housing densities and abundant surrounding space became an obsessive concern of planners (King, 1980, p. 210). European quarters were spaciously designed for the residence of the colonial administrators and their families with ample leisure (clubs, parks, sports grounds) and urban service facilities provided. Residential areas consisted of detached housing units in bungalow style with gardens. Major towns would have a government quarter of more or less monumental design. Between these and the African quarters, buffer zones such as native markets, railways, industrial areas, or other geophysical barriers would be disposed. The native quarters needed to house the indigenous labour-force were contained townships built in village style, with provision for control of influx and movement. In the early stages, building was either left

151

to the self-help of inhabitants or was provided for by the individual employers. In the latter employers were also directly responsible for settlement control according to the prevailing town ordinances. Ethnic segregation, as mentioned, was common in these quarters. It to some extent reflected existing rivalries among tribes, but was also frequently externally reinforced by the administration as part of the colonial divide and rule policy. Excepting early industrial mining complexes like those in the Belgian Congo and Rhodesia, municipal housing for Africans did not appear until the final stage of colonial rule when African urbanization, e.g. manifesting itself in the emergence of unauthorized settlements, finally became realized as an irreversible development.

Taking the spatial and physical requirements related to colonial power structures and their ostentatious constructed manifestations for granted, colonial cities were perceived by architects and planners as a unique chance to create 'ideal' urban layouts. Basic planning orientations and objectives were derived from the cultural setting of industrial societies, superimposing them on a completely different indigenous social and economic situation. But it would be wrong to regard the designs and residential standards implemented as simple importations. Instead the specific conditions of colonialism (ample cheap labour, abundant land without property ties, intact natural environments, and omission of low-income working class housing from plans), fostered distinct anti-industrial city planning notions and aesthetic values like those of the 'garden city' movement of E. Howard in Britain. As was the case in Lusaka, these ideas were to become merged with colonial experiences of residence in tropical climates, in particular in India (e.g. the New Delhi model).[2]

In contrast to the carefully planned environments of European residence, the colonial urbanization of Africans was a far less straightforward, even haphazard process. Its development was to become formed by its responses to two sets of contradictions that emerged during colonial domination and the internal proliferation of strategic groups and classes.

- In the *colonial city* itself, contradictions arose between concept and reality due to the increasing number of African residents, on the one hand, and the ostensibly maintained municipal policies and ideologies, on the other. For the most part urban authorities and European residents simply ignored developments in the African part of town, asserting that permanent urban residence and adequate housing provision was strictly for Europeans. But with the advance of de facto African urbanization, conflicts became imminent. Disputes arose between the Colonial Offices, colonial governments, local administrators, resident settlers, and industrial capital with respect to appropriate urban policies for the growing African urban labour-force.

- The *colonial development model* increasingly became entangled in unreconcilable contradictions between the explicit 'native development policies' and the implicit social transformation caused by ongoing capitalist penetration and the creation of prerequisites of the capitalist mode of production - a process that gradually offset the initially planned dualism of segregated European urban and African rural development.

As a rule, colonial development policies for Africans were strictly antiurban. Till the end of their regime in Africa, colonial powers clung to their policy that any kind of development of Africans should be confined to their 'natural rural environment'. In the British colonies any encouragement of African urbanization was considered detrimental to native development, because of the 'detribalizing' effects of long-term exposure to town life. In this sense the African worker in town was seen as an *object* of colonial urbanization and in no way as an *urban subject*. He was merely tolerated as temporary labourer, and was in theory expected (or forced by law) to return to his home area after the termination of his work contract. Never during colonial rule was an enfranchisement of Africans living in towns seriously considered. A single exception concerned a minor number of African leaders who, in the final decade of colonialism, participated in municipal Advisory Councils. The housing conditions of Africans reflected this perception: colonialism was only interested in the mere physical maintenance of its urban labour-power at marginal costs, denying human rights of habitat.

In reality, however, the concentration of African population in cities necessarily grew according to the expanding colonial economy and the diversification of its labour requirements. The officially maintained restrictions to residence were gradually applied less strictly, or could be openly evaded by Africans living in townships under illegal terms. As we shall see in the Northern Rhodesian/Zambian case, this relaxation of existing laws had various practical implications. For example, allowing a certain amount of resident African population proved economically beneficial: an urban surplus population of job seekers kept wages low, and in times of economic crisis workers could be dismissed and rehired afterwards directly from the urban townships, without the need to launch recruitment schemes in the African rural home areas.

A second and much more fundamental contradiction of urbanization under colonial rule was its gradual submission to the socioeconomic transformation that colonial capitalism had imposed through its changing terms of production and the specific forms of labour-power incorporation. In the early phase when the indigenous labour-force was first created, administrative means dominated the system of labourers' allocation to the sites of production. The colonial powers were able to control mobilization, movement, and utilization of workers by sheer political, military, and administrative force. The degree of African involvement in the capitalist sector would be regulated by taxation, resettlement programmes, or by destructive interventions into indigenous subsistence production systems, etc. - all working to create dependency on monetary income. Depending on the varying economic needs, these allocation mechanisms could be manipulated by legal means such as the terms of labour contract imposed, by town ordinances, or by pass laws that would simply force surplus migrant labour to return to the subsistence sector. With the gradual expansion of colonial production and deeper capitalist penetration, countercurrent factors interfered with colonial plans both in the rural and the urban settings:

In the rural areas colonial policies necessarily became self-contradictory. On the one hand, the intention was to maintain the traditional production systems as the reproductive base for the circulatory labour migration to the urban work sites or to agricultural wage-labour. After his temporary contract in the capitalist sector, the worker was expected to return to his family and to derive a living from subsistence production in his home village. On the other hand, the need to create a disposable labour-force inevitably meant introducing destructive elements to traditional production systems. Though women are the main producers in rural Africa, the permanent recruitment of men for work in the monetary sector upset the internal social and economic equilibrium of subsistence production. The long-term absence of men often resulted in a breakdown of traditional modes of production and led to alienation of migrant labourers from village life. A process of de facto proletarianization was introduced by these means, supplying the cities with a job-seeking surplus population.

But in their striving to maintain a dual, ethnically segregated society, spatially divided into white towns and native countrysides, the colonial planners were fighting a losing battle once they employed capitalist means of primary accumulation for the creation of the labour-force (cf. chap. III.2). The generalization of wage-labour, the expansion of monetary relations, the decomposition of subsistence production in rural areas, the commercialization of exchange relations, and the growing industrialization (namely in the mining sectors) were all typical elements of an emerging capitalist mode of production. The self-generative character of the capitalist reproduction process gradually put native development beyond administrative control. Colonial policies increasingly had to defer to the requirements of the more advanced colonial capitalist relations of production. Specifically in the final phase of colonial rule after the Second World War, higher labour productivity was needed in the colonies to feed the capitalist boom in the centres (and to meet the Colonial Offices' demands for increases in colonial government budgets). Despite the higher social costs accruing for African housing and sustenance, the old migratory labour systems had to give way to forms of 'stabilized urban labour-force' that allowed a higher level of job qualification and more specialization. This liberalized mode of labour-incorporation into the colonial economy, demanding some kind of integration into the urban system, was considered highly sensitive to the maintenance of native control as it involved a fundamental breach with customary administrative practices. Reflecting these anxieties, the planning requirements for low-cost worker housing and the experiences with the new model were freely discussed between the different African colonial powers, not excluding the consultancy of private enterprises that had already begun to operate their own workers' housing programmes (King, 1980, pp. 208).

154

In the British colonies, following directives from London's Colonial Office that had expressed growing concern about the social welfare of Africans, development plans were devised by colonial administrations in the late 1940s that acknowledged the need for investment in facilities for African urban residents. New town ordinances were passed in which the African worker was permitted to reunite with his family in urban residence and was granted a permanent stay for the duration of his working life. At the same time the anachronistic tribal forms of urban social control maintained by the British colonial authorities were revised, gradually to become replaced by unionized capital-labour relations and urban Advisory Councils. Importantly, the latter also signified a shift in the say in urban affairs from the colonial central government to the local electorate.

The changes made to the colonial city at this stage were, arguably, the most decisive for postcolonial urbanization and planning concepts. They affected both the European and the African residential situation. Post-war developments in Europe brought an increasing number of settlers and immigrants to the colonies. With the diversification of colonial economies, townships grew into cities that began to base their development on their own urban resources. The domination of residential structures by administrator and settler populations ceased, following a marked internal differentiation of the urban social composition. Urban legislation, formerly designed to administer colonial outposts and rural-based townships, also changed. It now had to comply with the emerging needs of residents for a certain level of participation in local politics and with the new role residents were to play in the post-war colonial policies moving towards self-government. Accordingly, control over urban matters was gradually shifted from the central to local government and to town councils, opening urban development to the influence of the urban electorate. As to African urban affairs, the central government's recognition of the presence of a 'stabilized urban labour-force' reluctantly forced town municipalities into taking some responsibility for their African populations. Minor housing schemes were launched for the elite of African workers, and employers' housing was put under more restrictive control of urban authorities. In the native townships some basic infrastructure was provided to ameliorate the most miserable living conditions. Two established structures, nevertheless, remained unaffected:

1   Legally, Africans remained second class citizens without right of permanent residence or freedom of movement, although they now had the permission to live in towns with their families for the duration of their working life, i.e., they were now expected to leave after retirement.

2   With respect to residential circumstances, the population growth of African dwellers was channelled into the already existing geographical and spatial patterns laid out for native housing. However, new residential categories and housing standards were created for Africans. Settlement areas and housing conditions attained marked internal differentia-

tion according to whether Africans qualified for municipal housing, for employers' housing, or were singled out for unauthorized housing areas. In other words, the urban segregationist policy remained, only now to become moulded around the emerging class differentiation among Africans.

According to all accounts, postcolonial urban developments in the African metropolises have tended to reproduce the original colonial layouts within new master plans - often with the professional backing of First World consultants. Thus, much suggests that the dichotomous, segregationist colonial urban structures were not questioned but in fact functionalized by the new elites, now that the European rulers had left. Habitat, planning, and housing provision in African cities continued to be built around racial, ethnic, and cultural patterns of differentiation and segregation. With some amendments made to the old city layouts to incorporate intermediate housing for middle-class employees, low-income populations tend to find themselves as the successors of what used to be called the 'native population' with respect to their housing standards and residential conditions (cf. Somma, 1990, p. 54).

Undoubtedly the principles of urban segregation, implanted in the African urbanization process by colonial governments and their town municipalities, are an important part of what has come to be termed the 'heritage of the colonial city'. Segregationist notions were to a large extent formative for the newly emerged urban social relationships among Africans to which tribal values did not provide sufficient counterbalancing orientations: the stereotypes of class and social differentiation were learnt from the principles of power imposed by colonial rule, and they were derived from the attitudes of European residents who often adhered to apartheid social perceptions. But the heritage of the 'colonial city' is not the exclusive key to understanding prevailing planning provisions and the uncurbed dynamics of growing urban disparities. The observed failure of sovereign African governments to decolonize the African metropolises and to develop an appropriate concept of an 'African city' in accordance with given needs and cultural traditions, clearly relates to the wider economic and social disparities pertaining to the formation of postcolonial peripheral capitalism and its urban-based power structures.

2 Post-colonial development planning and the transformation of colonial cities

The social and economic decolonization of African countries and of the cities as their political, institutional, and social centres has become virtually impossible for four reasons. *First* and principally, metropolises could not be decolonized due to the failure to decolonize the economic production structures. On the eve of their independence African leaders quite naturally assumed that the nationalization of the centres of colonial production would be the key to economic independence and prosperity. Concomitantly, the export-oriented production sector, as the main contributor to national income and state budgets, received the bulk of investments. Adopting the perspective of given global capitalist divisions of labour into complementary production zones, neither the creation of indigenous industrial production capacities nor the development of rural areas was seen as having any great economic potentiality. Instead, the basic functions of colonial economies were reaffirmed (i.e. the provision of raw materials for the world market, single-crop plantations, cheap labour reserves, etc.), but now run by the Third World countries on 'independent' terms of business. As in Latin America, the post-independence urban growth patterns in Africa can be defined by what Castells has called 'dependent urbanization': urban growth and the contemporary functions of urban formations are responses to the various economic needs of the industrial First World and its modes of exploitation. Most important, Third World cities have become cornerstones in providing the socioeconomic and ideological environment needed to stabilize an indigenous political system and the concomitant class relations that support this power structure. For the ruling elites and intermediate capitalist classes the maintenance of a cosmopolitan lifestyle and Western consumption standards have become inextricably bound up with the development of urban enclave economies with their specific ties to the First World economy.[3]

Second, the colonially founded cities are the 'natural' spine of the established production system. Accordingly, the policy to invest predominantly in the existing growth poles also systematically applied to infrastructure provision and improvement. Aspiring to compete with European models, the existing commercial and administrative centres were over-proportionately equipped with social services and urban infrastructure. This pattern of public spending aggravated rural-urban disparities, with metropolises becoming more and more detached from their rural hinterlands. In the shadow of emerging large cities, regional centres were destined to impede growth, giving no attraction for major commercial enterprises and thus failing to generate job opportunities for rural migrants. Inevitably, mass migration became channelled towards the big cities in the capitalist sectors. These, even if not providing sufficient wage work, would at least offer marginal benefits to squatter populations and allow survival in the growing informal urban economy.

Third, in most parts of Africa dependent development has not allowed the emergence of a strong national bourgeoisie or the formation of influential trade union movements. Economic and political powers are highly centralized on the state that in most of black Africa based its rule on a one-party political system. The state sector (including parastatals) dominates the economy as a whole and, due to lack of private capital, is the major allocator of economic investments and planner of development schemes. The state apparatus and its supportive party system have become the keys to class formation, access to power, and revenue sources. Government elites dominate the class structure and control the national means of production, holding workers and peasants in a subordinated position. Power structures adhere to institutional principles of bureaucratic decision-making modelled during the colonial period. Despite the nominal socialist orientation of many African governments, the state has actively reinforced rural-urban divisions and participated in the creation of segregated provision circuits and of disparities in the access to consumers goods and urban amenities. There is also a considerable state dominance over planned urban development, housing, and residential standards. In the absence of private sector funds and with solvent demand widely lacking, a vast part of the urban housing stock has been built by governments without the intention of satisfying market demand. Instead housing and residential zoning standards, terms of access, and rental rates are defined by socio-political criteria. Government employees, party members or other strategic groups are enjoying privileged access to subsidized, cheap, high-standard housing, or are provided with housing allowances according to their rank and status. Under these terms, postcolonial housing and urbanization have overtly sought to imitate of colonially-introduced social stratification and power relations, the images of which have been translated into differentiated residential circumstances and settlement legislation. Parallel to the government provision of high-standard housing, the growing housing needs of the working class and of job-seeking migrants were left widely uncatered for. On the contrary, self-help housing efforts on the part of these groups merely received token acknowledgement or were confronted with illegalization, eviction, and unrealistic programmes for rural resettlement. More positive attitudes towards squatter settlements, in recognition of their contribution to the urban economy, made some headway during the 1970s following various World Bank sponsored housing programmes in Africa (cf. Obudho/Mhlanga, 1988; Rakodi, 1990). But regularization and legalization of squatter settlements has not become a generally accepted municipal issue and still remains a slow and highly selective process.

Fourth, the rationales of planning provisions and instruments that have led to the building of the colonial city were not questioned by the African successors in planning offices. On the contrary, the transfer of concepts from the industrial nations to the African setting continued or even increased during postcolonial urbanization. The European towns were looked upon by Africans as prototypes for their own urban development. Planning legislation and Housing Statutory Acts of the ex-colonial powers were directly and without amendment made part of African legislation. Western technical expertise and training facilities were made available to African students by the industrial nations in various newly created planning courses, or were disseminated through the various branches of the UN (cf. King, 1980, p. 216). Infrastructure and regional planning were readily provided parts of development aid programmes for Third World countries. Due to this, only very few African nations have their own facilities for professional training of planners. African governments have also made ample use of expatriate planners or have sought the expertise of international consultants for their master plans. But with the unquestioned faith in the 'technical expertise' of Western planning concepts, African nations have also imported the values underpinning them: the notion of uncurbed industrial development based on unlimited availability of natural resources and the belief in the capacity of technology to solve all problems.

The consequences of planning transfer are found in all aspects of the African built environment. Building codes transferred from industrial settings imply high costs and inflexible standards in terms of construction. They also involve a high content of imported building materials and require sophisticated building technology. Elaborate planning legislation is not matched by adequate planning capacities, which makes land surveying, cadastral registry, and plot and title deed allocation a complicated, expensive, and onerous bureaucratic process. Lack of professionals and low managerial competencies are other common constraints in municipal planning offices, resulting from unattractive pay scales in the civil service. Moreover, the highly centralized political system of African states has effectively inhibited the development of appropriate administrative and planning competencies. Urban councils and local governments lack independent funds from taxes and duties and are politically in tutelage of central government powers or ruling parties, leaving very little scope for initiatives or creative change (Bryant/White, 1982). Master plan layouts still follow the fiction of the motorized, industrial society, leading to abundant space use, urban sprawl, extensive motorway networks, and public transport problems. In the end, this means long walks to work for the majority of low-income residents who have been allocated to the urban periphery and are unable to afford public transport to the commercial and industrial centres of towns.

The impact of exported planning and possibly its close association with African and Third World power structures is reflected in the conservatism of indigenous planners with respect to recent developments in the discipline. Following the growing public awareness of the socio-political implications of planning for environmental problems and the abundant use of natural resources and energy during the 1970s and '80s, planners' attitudes are gradually changing in the industrialized First World countries. Issues like appropriate technology, participatory planning methods, environmental protection and sustainable development, use of local resources, energy-saving programmes, and simplified flexible building regulations have been increasingly proposed by Western planners as solutions to the economic and social crisis of Third World cities. In practice, however, this approach is at most a domain of low-profile local NGOs or is incorporated in development aid housing programmes in squatting areas. As a rule their 'experimental' character is tolerated by responsible municipalities, but is discontinued once the aid agency leaves and the settlement becomes a regular part of urban administration. Specifically, these new ideas have not yet seriously entered government planning attitudes or impacted on provisions for the core sectors of municipal administration. Again the point in question is that planning, now with the stance of appropriateness and sustainability, is not simply an unpolitical technical expertise: any introduction of appropriate and sustainable planning procedures would inevitably require devolution of municipal control and decision-making procedures to decentralized institutions, with participative planning by residents or even leading to the empowerment of people's settlement organizations. As illustrated, to politicize planning structures and the prevailing allocation mechanisms in this way, is still in contradiction to the centralized political power structures and the vested interests behind them.

3 Introduction to the Zambian case

The history of Zambia's urbanization process and the study of its capital city Lusaka displays typical features of the colonial city and its postcolonial form of dependent development. There are, however, particular historical and structural circumstances that contribute to its formation and contemporary urban crisis. Zambia is among the countries with the highest rate of urbanization in Africa (approx. 50% of its total population of 8.6 millions in 1990). Between 1963 and 1974 its urban population grew 25 times faster than the rural. In terms of regional allocation, urbanization is highly concentrated on the capitalist sector along the north-south line of rail, linking the mining towns of Kitwe, Ndola, and Kabwe in the north with today's capital city of Lusaka, and with the old capital of Livingstone (1911 to 1931) on the southern border to Zimbabwe.

The fluctuating economic prosperity of the copper mining industry is the unchallenged determinative factor in Zambia's development with regard to every single aspect of its delineation. It was to become the nexus of colonial urban development, emerging in the early 1930s in the Copperbelt (already incorporating illegal forms of settlement) - and became the backbone of post-independence development planning, accelerating the formation of an urban enclave economy at the expense of rural areas. With 80% of productive capital invested in industries and towns along the line of rail (Simons, 1979, p. 14), migration rates into these areas soared to peaks of more than 10% annually (average was 6.8% between 1963 and 1974). With migrants comprising mostly of low-income populations, municipalities were faced with an unprecedented situation when illegal settlements mushroomed everywhere. However, Zambia is one of the few African countries that undertook a substantial effort to integrate its squatter populations. The readily available financial resources provided by the copper boom, lasting till the mid-1970s, inspired Zambia's government to engage in a major upgrading and site and service scheme in Lusaka, serving approximately 60% of the capital's squatter population. Planned follow-up schemes in Lusaka and other major cities, however, did not materialize due to the world market decline in copper prices in the mid 1970s and the failure of the country's import-substitution strategy. Today Zambia, once considered one of the most prosperous African countries, has relapsed into the group of the least developed countries with again gloomy prospects for its still growing squatter populations.

The analysis of this situation, based on an empirical survey of two settlement areas, an investigation of the contemporary state of urban planning, and the municipal policies in

Lusaka, will be the major objective of this study. Various specific features of Lusaka's contemporary development are, however, only adequately understood as responses to extramural historical and structural circumstances:

- As a colonially planned capital to be situated outside the newly prospering industrial centre of the country, the first phases of Lusaka's African urbanization process were determined by developments in the Copperbelt that shaped the country's general policies for urban development.

- Lacking substantial industries and commercial undertakings, Lusaka's urban planning was initially dictated predominantly by the provision of a low-density, garden-city-like environment with government quarters and the railway station as major orientations for spatial layouts. It was assumed that in the course of its 'natural development' the spacious design would be filled in by the expansion of various zones, i.e. for shopping, business, light industry, European residence, and the African market area.

- Although Lusaka grew according to the original plan, the historical terms of concretization during the colonial and the postcolonial period have become the source of serious planning problems. The fate of the colony proved zoning provisions to be over-ambitious: first, the newly developing capital was hit by the economic crisis of 1931-33, that required down-scaling of the original plan; second, aspirations to compete with Southern Rhodesia as a settler colony did not materialize, leaving Lusaka with a much smaller European settler population than expected; third, the Federation with Southern Rhodesia and Nyasaland (1953-63), with Salisbury as the new Capital, deprived Lusaka of its 'capital city' functions and led to stagnation in this period.

- Under the impact of these developments, Lusaka's colonial urban structure remained perforated in the inner city areas (with in-filling partially taking place by low-income African populations encroaching on these areas) and semi-rural on the urban periphery where four-hectare homestead plots had been demarcated for possible country-style settling.

- Postcolonial mass migration to Lusaka was conditioned by these socio-spatial structures at the same time as the continuation of the original development plan was considered appropriate for the new social and political elites. Urban low-density sprawl, allocating squatters to locations distant from the commercial centres, and high densities in inner city squatter settlements (partially regularized) are now the determinative patterns of urban development.

Perhaps more than in other former colonial cities, the contemporary process of urbanization in Lusaka and its administrative framework remains rooted in the structures underpinning its historical expansion. As indicated, these are direct manifestations of colonial policies towards urbanization, or more precisely, they reflect the contradictory and conflicting functions assigned to Lusaka in the varying course of colonial rule in Northern Rhodesia. A brief recapitulation of the emergent capitalist state system in Zambia and its colonial history, therefore, seem an indispensable context for the understanding of urban structures and socio-political processes in Lusaka. This approach will also have the benefit of supplying us with a framework within which to propose possible solutions and policies of urban planning towards squatter settlements.

Notes

1   For a recent, comprehensive bibliography on African urbanization up to independence cf. Coquery-Vidrovitch, 1991.
2   cf. King, A. D., *Colonial Urban Development*, London 1976.
3   The degree of urbanization in Africa and Latin America varies, depending on the advancement of capitalist penetration and the different productive roles assigned to their economies within the international division of labour. In most Latin American metropolises the colonial past has been virtually eradicated from the face of the cities in a succession of urban renewals oriented in style towards European capitals like Paris for the first phase of the 20th century and to the US metropolises since the Second World War. Inner-urban differentiation of architectural design, infrastructure provision, spatial arrangements, housing standards, residential zoning, etc. are undisguised modern manifestations of class divisions and social differentiation in status and power. Colonial-style towns still existing in the hinterland are no exception to this pattern. Like the world cities that are the metropolitan headquarters of transnational capital, they are only another expression of the same development: the mode of integration of Latin American countries and urban formations into the world economy (Friedmann/Wolff, 1982).

VII   Colonial history in Northern Rhodesia

1   The rule of the British South African Company (1888-1924)

The modern geography of Northern Rhodesia/Zambia was shaped by the scramble of European powers at the end of the 19th century to establish their territorial claims and to secure the mineral wealth presumed to exist in central Africa. In this respect, the area was one of the last blank spots on the geopolitical map of Africa but in the centre of potentially overlapping colonial interests. The British claim to the area as an extension of Southern Rhodesia was contested from all sides. In the north were the Belgian rulers of the Congo Free State; looking to the southeast and west the area was a potential axis to uniting the Portuguese possessions of Mozambique and Angola; in the northwest Germany was establishing its colony Tanganyika and in 1884 had annexed South-West Africa; and to the south the Boer Republic raised fears of a possible Boer-German hegemony in the region.

Following the continental division of Africa by the European powers at the Berlin conference 1884-85, separate treaties with Germany (1890), Portugal (1891 and 1905), and Belgium (1894) finally settled the borders of the future colony. Although Britain was able to secure its territorial interests in the region, conquest of Northern Rhodesia was to some extent overshadowed by disappointment. The failure to obtain Katanga and its easily excavatable mineral and copper resources, which fell to Belgium, left a huge sprawling area of 752,614 km² that, in the perception of colonialism, was unable to survive economically on its natural resources. Revenues from a lead and zinc mine, opened 1902 in Broken Hill (Kabwe), proved insufficient to recoup the total expenses of administering the possession. The profitable excavation of the deep lying copper deposits of sulphide ores, known to exist in the Katanga pedicle of Northern Rhodesia, was beyond the technological means of those days (Burdette, 1988, p. 13).

These particular circumstances gave rise to a low-profile, cost-saving course of development on the part of the British Crown. In 1888 the administration and development of the area had been put into the hands of the newly formed British South African Company (BSAC) that maintained responsibility till 1924. According to the analysis of P. Slinn (1972), the BSAC company directors

... wanted to find a way to make the lands pay for themselves, while retaining the company administrative powers and consolidating its mineral rights. The directors resolved first to turn Northern Rhodesia into a reserve of cheap labour serving the white-owned mines and farms of the region. Second, Northern Rhodesia was to be opened up to a limited amount of white settler farming. Last, the territory would be administered as cheaply as possible with a minimal administrative framework made up of a handful of whites, relying on African chiefs to enforce decisions (Burdette, 1988, pp. 13-14).

These pragmatic, businesslike distinctions contain the developmental principles that formed the colony for the next half a century (with more sophistication added to policies by direct British colonial rule from 1924 to 1953). After the forcible subjugation of indigenous tribes had been completed by 1899, the BSAC, faced with limited profitable interests in the area, was hesitant to erect proper administrative structures as it considered Southern Rhodesia its major field of interest. It was not until 1911 that the territories of North-Eastern Rhodesia and Barotseland-North-Western Rhodesia were united into Northern Rhodesia, and Livingstone was made its first capital, replacing the old administrative headquarters in Kalomo.

In sourcing for revenues in its northern territories, the prime interest of the BSAC became directed to mobilizing labour-power as the only visible capital in the region, needed both for the company's mines in Southern Rhodesia and as a means to generate (taxable) monetary income. To this end a recruitment office was set up in Southern Rhodesia in 1903, and officers were sent north of the Zambezi to hire labour. Logistic lines were set up to house and feed the migrant labourers who were in particular contracted from the north-eastern parts of Rhodesia.

At this early stage the company's tribal policies were accordingly dictated by the administrative aims of creating a sufficient disposable and accessible labour reserve at low costs 'slightly above forced servitude' (Burdette, 1988, p. 14). Related to these objectives, differential approaches towards tribes were adopted, depending on their specific proximity to work sites and their propensity to accept and fulfil their role as labour reserve. Although the reproductive base of most tribes had already been seriously impaired by the BSAC during their forceful submission, this did not create an absolute need for wage work.[1] Mobilization of labour additionally required extraeconomic means to enforce participation in the monetary colonial economy. The introduction of hut taxes in Southern (1898), North East (1900), and North West Rhodesia (1904) proved an effective scheme, as it inaugurated a migratory labour system requiring the periodic return of the labourer to his home area where the taxes could be levied by the tribal chiefs. The return of migrant labourers was a particularly important administrative aspect for Northern Rhodesia that till 1920 was an exporter of labour to the Katanga and Transvaal mines and the Wankie Colliery in Southern Rhodesia.

Inevitably, the specific terms of tribal submission to migratory labour schemes began to accentuate regional disparities and differences in the degree of the transformation of the traditional indigenous production systems. Tribal modes of reproduction became decomposed by various colonial-imposed mechanisms. These included the penetration of villages by wage-labour and commodity relations, the drain of young men from rural production by migration, colonial land-allocation schemes interfering with traditional land-use patterns, and finally the impact of colonially installed infrastructure along the line of rail. To a lesser extent this differential process was complemented by tribal idiosyncrasies towards specific forms of wage work. The tribal 'acceptability' of and willingness to perform wage work were determined according to given indigenous modes of production and their prevailing traditional divisions of labour and by other factors like the coherence of tribal organizations, and the varying degrees of preservation/decomposition of rural means of sustenance. By the end of company rule in 1924, regionally differentiated and uneven, irreversible patterns of incorporation into the colonial economy had emerged that are still visible in contemporary Zambia.

-   Following the destruction of their traditional pre-colonial modes of reproduction based on trade, the Bemba and Ngoni in the northwestern and in the eastern parts were struggling hardest for rural sustenance on low-fertility lands. Therefore, they displayed the greatest overall 'propensity' for wage work and migration, specializing in mining where they soon formed the majority of the labour-force in this fast growing industrial sector.

-   The Shona-speaking tribes, living southeast of Lusaka in the border area to Southern Rhodesia, were unwilling to perform mine work and 'preferred' road, railway and land clearing labour activities (cf. Fickert/Wetter, 1981, p. 87)

-   In the western territories, where a pre-colonial, centralized kingship (Litunga) with considerable internal social differentiation existed, colonial penetration took another form. Here the requirements of colonial administration could be grafted onto the given feudal political structure that had developed on a tributary labour system. Barotseland was given a special semi-autonomous status incorporating the chiefs into the colonial political system. As an area in a geographical remote location from the centres of labour recruitment, commodity production of cattle, fish, and grains became the predominant mode of capitalist transformation in this region after the colonial abolition of the old tribute labour system (Cliffe, 1979, p. 161).

165

- When the extension of the railway from Southern Rhodesia to the capital of Katanga, Elizabethville (now Lubumbashi), was completed in 1910, Northern Rhodesia gradually became linked up with the South African economic system. The north-south line of rail turned into the colony's new spatial gravity point, and white settlement was particularly encouraged in the contiguous areas. The best lands were confiscated for settler farming and the indigenous populations resettled on reservations (see Figure 8.1). After 1924 the area along the line of rail was entirely cleared of Africans, converting 23 million acres into Crown Land designated for sale to settlers. Although not more than 1,200 settlers eventually came to Northern Rhodesia, and only 70,000 acres had been effectively turned into farmland by 1958, the lasting effect was a near monopolization of road-accessible central markets by the white settlers. The original African residents of these areas were displaced to less fertile and more densely populated reservations that curbed their agricultural potential and increased their dependency on wage-labour.[2] Nyanya-speaking people (Ngoni and Chewa) of central Northern Rhodesia and the Tonga in the south were the groups most severely affected by this policy (Biermann, 1980, p. 56).

Fortunately, Northern Rhodesia was never to become a typical settler colony as it was unable to compete with the conditions offered to European settlers in Southern Rhodesia. These enjoyed a more developed infrastructure and commodity market, the proximity to world markets, a more suitable climate, more aggressive policies of evicting Africans from the best lands, and cheaper farm labour (Biermann, 1980, p. 50). While newly-arriving settlers in the north were still struggling at near subsistence level, it was the Southern and not the Northern Rhodesian settler farmers who were providing Katanga (and later the Copperbelt) with food via the railway line. Arguably these circumstances saved Northern Rhodesia from becoming an apartheid society. Nevertheless, although white settlement remained marginal in Northern Rhodesia, it would be a mistake to underrate its political influence in terms of absolute numbers. In the eyes of the colonial government the prospects of settlement attained strategic importance: politically a white 'indigenous population' served as legitimization for an alien form of government, and settlers could internally stabilize and disseminate colonial capitalist power structures more effectively than could be done by administrators. Finally, settlers were also inclined to show a particularly acute interest in developing and running the colony; and they were prepared to share administrative tasks by engaging in self-government.

But with regards to any kind of efficient self-government, the colony was by 1921 still grossly underpopulated by white residents. These numbered not more than 3,634 made up of administrators, missionaries, settlers, and a few businessmen - and the colony was still not making any profits for the BSAC. The political developments in Southern Rhodesia, which opted for self-government in 1922 (but decided to exclude Northern Rhodesia), and the eagerness of the BSAC to get rid of its administrative responsibilities (but to maintain its mineral and land rights) finally caused the running of the colony to be retured to the hands of the Colonial Office in 1924.

2   Colonial rule 1924-1952

Nominally Lugard's doctrine of indirect rule was the Colonial Office's official developmental policy for Africa at that time. But the given setting in Northern Rhodesia was far from supportive to policies set to 'guiding Africans to run their own affairs'. The Southern Rhodesia-dictated authoritarian style of imperial government in Northern Rhodesia, under chartered rule, had greatly favoured the settler outlook of political mastery in native policies. Not inappropriately, native commissioners were former policemen or soldiers from South Africa or Southern Rhodesia. It was not until 1927 that the Colonial Office, represented by the second Northern Rhodesian Governor Sir James Maxwell, took more decisive steps towards implementing the official colonial policy in Northern Rhodesia. Nevertheless, to quote Hall, 'implementation was hazardous and difficult' (Hall, 1965, p. 105).

- Settlers believed that powers should be handed over to them, keeping Africans in subordinate positions. Politically important, they could look to Southern Rhodesia and South Africa for political backing in this matter (a policy finally to prevail in the 1953-63 Federation with Southern Rhodesia and Nyasaland).

- The authority of tribal chiefs had already been seriously undermined by direct rule, obliterating an important precondition for their designated role in local administration. Moreover, the migratory labour system had already led to a massive exodus of men from tribal areas, leaving most of the tribal organizations weak and impoverished. The rapid expansion of the copper industries in Northern Rhodesia in the late 1920s only aggravated this state of affairs. On the part of the educated Africans, suspicion was roused that indirect rule would simply mean a 'reversion to tribal rule' instead of participation of Africans in the beginning industrialization process (Hall, 1965, p. 105).

- A technical breakthrough in the early 1920s that made the sulphide copper ores in the Copperbelt exploitable and highly profitable, changed the colony's economic and administrative situation overnight. By the end of the decade the BSAC and a few mining enterprises had become the true runners of the country. Since the mineral and land rights had been retained by the BSAC, colonial capital was able to erect an oligopolist enclave economy drawing heavily on the natural and human resources of the country, but giving back almost nothing. By special arrangements with the Crown, the bulk of royalties and taxes went to the BSAC and to the British Treasury with not more than 12.5% of total taxes levied between 1930-40 returned to the Northern Rhodesian Government in the form of grants for development (Burdette, 1988, pp. 20-21). The weak revenue situation of government was complemented by administrative and political contradictions in devising policies for Africans and settlers adequate to the economic and social development. This was increasingly spurred by the dominant mining industry with its necessary growing tendencies towards urbanization and proletarianization.

Faced with very much the same administrative problems as the BSAC, the British Government introduced indirect rule as a practical instrument for delegating administrative functions to native authorities and to maintain the status quo of the labour reserves. The Native Authority Ordinances and the Native Courts Ordinance came into force on 1 April 1930.[3] As Burdette states, indirect rule was in many ways

> ... simply a recognition of the limitations of British authority and was based on traditions of obedience and respect for the existing local political leaders. Furthermore it helped the colonial authorities preserve the rural areas as reservoirs of labour and saved money by having the existing political authorities collect taxes and extract that labour (Burdette, 1988, p. 15).

During the entire period of colonial rule, developmental policies towards Africans were for Northern Rhodesia's government a matter of constant negotiation between the directives from Colonial Office and the local pressures of mining industry and settlers. According to Berger's account, Northern Rhodesia was by 'custom and practice a colour-bar country in the tradition of its southern neighbours' (Berger, 1974, p. 42). Directives from London to open job opportunities and support the Africanisation of the colony were met with the firm resistance of settlers (who were the electorate of Legislative Council), the mining sector, and most low ranking administrators. Struggling to reconcile these conflicting pressures, the Northern Rhodesian government adopted a multitude of tactics to dilute and sidestep directions from London regarding any change in the existing racial relations whenever they conflicted with the interests of mining industry and roused the fears of settlers. The outcome of this predicament was in many cases a *de jure* implementation of official London policies and the *de facto* continuation of racial discrimination against Africans (cf. Berger, 1974, p. 43).

The first official policy of 'African Paramountcy' declared in 1930, stipulated that in cases of conflict between settlers and Africans the colonial power would intervene in favour of the Africans in order to maintain and to preserve the rural-based tribal society. This policy was abandoned two years later, now making the 1931 endorsed policy of 'complementary development' the official position.[4] In this version it was emphasized that both races, African and European, needed each other in contrast to the racial concept of dual or parallel development expressed by African Paramountcy (cf. Heisler, 1971, p. 132).

Arguably, therefore, indirect rule was never implemented in Northern Rhodesia to its full effect as defined or intended by the official policies of the Colonial Office. This is documented by the reports of two commissions sent from London to evaluate policy progress in Northern Rhodesia. The comments of the Blendisloe Commission in 1939, investigating the implementation of 'complementary development' are indicative for the state of African affairs under the ideological cover of indirect rule. It found the implementation 'still awaiting' mainly due to the backwardness of Northern Rhodesia in promoting the well-being and cooperation of the Europeans who mistrusted the official government policy. A similar verdict had already been given by the Pim Commission in 1938, concluding that the provincial administration had hardly done anything in the way of developing the rural areas and that they had ignored their duties to provide a proper system of welfare and education for the de facto permanent urban workforce.

However significant the disagreements between the Colonial Office and the Northern Rhodesian administration may have been, there can be no doubt that the administrative standing in Northern Rhodesia was highly submissive to the economic needs of the mining industry and that it grossly privileged the social and economic position of the white European residents and settlers. Until 1946 the situation of African workers in towns was widely regarded as a private matter between the employer and the worker, i.e. beyond the immediate responsibility of the colonial authorities. Despite the fact that by the mid-1930s approx. 90,000 young men out of a total population of 1.3 million were working outside their villages, the official policies unabashedly legitimized the well-maintained administrators' fiction that African development should be rural based and its tribal organizations be protected at all costs. The functionality of this dual concept for the colonial production system will become evident once we come to discuss the colonial policies towards the urbanization of Africans, and once we have analysed the colonial political economy and its disastrous effects on rural areas under the ideological shield of indirect rule.

3 Mining industry and the migratory labour system

The industrial boom in Northern Rhodesia was initiated by coinciding world market developments and technical innovations allowing the excavation of sulphide ores and the extraction of metals by a flotation process. Driven by Britain's dependency on the USA for copper - coming amidst high demand for the newly flourishing automobile and electrical industry - intensive mineral prospecting began in 1923, financially supported by the British government. To avoid fragmentation of claims and to fend off any North American speculation, the allocation of prospecting rights was restricted to syndicates capable of constructing large-scale copper mines and running refinery plants for the expensive flotation process. After a series of takeovers and financial manoeuvres the copper industry was by 1928 dominated by two companies: the Anglo American Corporation of South Africa (AAC) and the American Roan Selection Trust (RST). The BSAC was a substantial shareholder in both of these companies. Large-scale production, however, did not begin until the economic depression of 1931/32 was overcome. Demand for copper was enhanced by the rearmament programmes of Germany and Britain and by the termination of the USA-dominated Copper Exporters' Incorporated Trust in 1932 (cf. Burdette, 1988, pp. 16-20; Biermann, 1980, p. 70).

The impact of mining industry on the social and economic development of the colony was unprecedented. By 1934 Northern Rhodesia was providing 13% of world market copper and had become the most important copper producer in the Commonwealth and was the fourth largest in the world. Foreign trade increased fivefold between 1930 and 1933 with copper making a 90% contribution to the colony's export values. The already existing colonial migratory labour system was a paramount condition in maintaining low production costs and ensuing a stable world market position somewhat independent from international price fluctuations. Due to cheap colonial labour, Northern Rhodesian production costs in 1932 were less than £16 per ton, compared with £38-46 per ton of the major competitor USA (Heisler, 1971, p. 16).

Table 7.1
Migratory African labour in sectors and in per cent of total labour

Year	Total	Abroad		Copper Mines		Agriculture	
		N	%	N	%	N	%
1928	87,851	36,873	(41.9)	10,700	(12.2)	15,600	(17.0)
1929	99,600	42,900	(43.0)	16,000	(16.7)	-	-
1930	109,900	39,400	(35.8)	21,900	(20.0)	10,885	(10.0)
1932	79,500	30,900	(38.7)	5,500	(6.9)	6,530	(8.0)
1936	104,700	51,000	(48.6)	15,100	(14.3)	9,155	(8.8)
1946	186,100	45,400	(24.4)	31,000	(16.7)	-	-
1951	277,200	48,500	(17.5)	-	-	-	-
1956	302,700	39,580	(13.1)	46,000	(15.2)	-	-

Note: missing percentages to total are attributable to non-copper mining, domestic work, and a small fraction of urban artisans

Source: *Biermann, 1980, p. 64 and 93* (compiled from various sources, mainly from the report of the Pim Commission, 1938).

As shown in Table 7.1, the major effect of emerging copper mining in Northern Rhodesia was not an increase in wage-labour, but the redistribution of the colony's existing labour reserve. Northern Rhodesians working as far abroad as Kenya and South Africa were now attracted to the Copperbelt that also became a major competitor for agricultural labour. Mining wages were slightly higher, explaining the absolute decrease of labour in the agricultural sector (Average wages in 1930: mining 10s. - £1 / agriculture 7 - 12s.; cf. Pim Report, 1938, p. 52).

The mechanisms applied to keep wage costs in Northern Rhodesia at a low level were hardly unique. All over Africa, colonial systems had succeeded in depressing wages in the colonial capitalist sector by enforcing terms of labour contract and wage remuneration that effectively burdened large parts of necessary reproduction costs of workers on rural domestic production. In the usual arrangement those family members forced to enter the cash economy were only paid an amount sufficient to meet tax obligations and to sustain themselves at pre-capitalist living standards for the duration of their contract only. Typically, wage rates would not allow any substantial transfers to their families or enable savings. With respect to the Northern Rhodesian case, Cliffe has described the logic of the migratory labour system as follows:

> The responsibility for providing for the long-term reproduction of the labour-force - the social security, retirement provision, the bringing up of the next generation and meeting the subsistence needs of the workers' families - did not fall on the employer nor on the settler state, but was borne by domestic production. The continuation of this pattern typically required further conditions. It required mechanisms, political and/or economic (the poll tax was the favourite), to force certain members of the family to enter the cash economy but at the same time had to limit possibilities for acquiring cash through independent commodity production ... More generally, it required the penetration of the pre-capitalist social formations to make them accept their role but it also had to maintain elements of the preexisting relationships in order to preserve their ability to reproduce the labour-force. One concomitant was therefore varying measures to slow down the proletarianization of the labour-force (Cliffe, 1979, p. 151).[5]

For colonial administrators and employers, the mutual interests in this system are obvious. The official assumption was that rural areas were the centres of African livelihood. Migration was considered a temporary incident in the life of workers who would return to their home villages after termination of contract and take up their old life as agriculturalists. The experiences in the 1931/32 crisis, when 75% of mine workers were laid off, reinforced the practical side of this arrangement. It was felt that any encouragement of permanent urban settlement by social service provisions would inevitably result in an uncontrollable influx from villages, aggragating unemployment and detribalization, and bringing on an undesirable competition between white and black over jobs (cf. Berger, 1974, p. 68). The position of black miners was further weakened by the unionized formation of skilled miners from Europe and South Africa, who imposed an agreement on mine management to block African progress in labour arrangements. The privileged position of white urban workers was entrenched by a dual wage scale for Europeans and Africans and by an unofficial racial industrial colour bar imposed in the tradition of its southern neighbours: the black labourer was welcomed, but the understanding was that he should assist and not compete with white workers who were to hold the more qualified jobs.[6]

African workers' strikes and riots in 1935 and the formation of an African miners' trade union in 1936 that demanded 'equal pay for equal work' did not meet with the solidarity of European workers. Despite a considerable rise in African skills, the bargaining power of the socially isolated African miners was insufficient to improve wages for various reasons. Since the world economic crisis of 1931/32, mines could rely on a substantial reserve army of indigenous job seekers. The nearby Katanga mines across the border were only 'second choice' because wages paid there, due to the Belgian stabilization policy, were even lower than in Northern Rhodesia. Moreover, due to labour-substituting mechanization in the Copperbelt, increases in mining production were not accompanied by a proportionally higher demand for African labour (see Table 7.1). The continuing high rate of Northern Rhodesians forced to work abroad emphasizes the proposition of a surplus labour supply in Northern Rhodesia and of a strong competition amongst indigenous labourers over jobs.

Administrative policies in this period were in complete support of colonial industry's dual wage scale. Authorities adhered to a theory that saw low wages as an appropriate means to avoid urban unemployment and detribalization, and to encourage Africans to stay in and to develop their poverty-stricken home areas. Ordinances adopting the South African forms of racial labour control like the 'Employment of Natives' (1926), the 'Native Registration' (1929), and the 'Township Ordinance' (1929), were designed to reinforce the intended return to home areas. Legal urban stay in a company's labour compound or in other townships was tied to a work contract, and in general did not include the right to bring wife or family. Some mining companies in the Copperbelt and Kabwe were exceptions, realizing the non-monetary inducement to work for low wages if families were allowed (cf. Hansen, 1984, p. 223). After the end of his contract (maximum two years), a worker lost his accommodation in the company compound and was only allowed to stay a further 30 days in town to search for work - if he were able to pay rent and found new vacant accommodation. In theory, population influx was controlled by obligatory police registration within 24 hours after arrival and eviction in case of illegal stay. Repatriation to home areas after termination of the work contract was at one time considered by the government. But as with most of the regulations devised to control the movement of Africans, the government lacked the personnel and financial means, and the tribal authorities lacked the determination, to effectively impose them - both being simply overwhelmed by the vast number of populations deserting their rural homesteads.

While government held on to its official position that the migratory labour system and influx control would not lead to African urban residence, and that rural systems could adapt to requirements of labour provision without impairing their traditional organization, the first anthropological studies by the Rhodes Livingstone Institute clearly disclosed the spurious character of these assumptions.

Wilson's 1940 study of mining labour in Broken Hill (Kabwe) showed that 75% of workers had permanently stayed in towns for nearly seven years. Usually leaving the village at 16 years of age, they had continually moved from one job to another (with an average of 7.5 jobs in 10 years). Home villages were not visited more than three times in 10 years. Savings amounted to an average of 17.7% of earnings, declining to 13.7% when higher transport costs accrued for long-distant travel to home areas (Wilson, 1947, p. 43). Official estimates at the end of the 1930s suggest 65% of all male taxpayers fit for work were absent from their villages, with peak rates rising up to 90%, e.g. in the case of the Bemba mine workers. The early form of migration to and from the villages had steadily turned into circular migration between the capitalist centres. Thus, instead of repatriation after the work period, migration effectively entailed growing absence and alienation from villages.

The early anthropological studies of tribal areas found the villages not only depopulated and lacking manpower but already in a state of social disruption. This was parallelled by the emergence of a degenerative agricultural production cycle following the breakdown of traditional, ecologically balanced methods of cultivation. Necessary switches in basic food crops from maize back to cassava or millet sometimes resulted in malnutrition and starvation of old people and children (Burdette, 1988, p. 21). Although it is true that women traditionally perform a large part of manual labour on the fields - estimates at that time suggested that a rate of 60 to 75% of absent young men would be tolerable to maintain cultivation standards (Fickert/Wetter, 1981, p. 95) - closer study showed that men were in fact indispensable for maintaining the more complex indigenous modes of production of which methods of cultivation are only one aspect.

The social reproductive system of the village was based on a close network of cooperation and reciprocal personal responsibilities and dependencies among its members. Skills and knowledge vital to social cohesion and material reproduction were handed on and reinforced by close contact among the villagers. The permanent absence of young men led to the breakdown of this social system as a vital link was now missing in the line of transmission, specifically with respect to the long-term preservation of values and traditions. Long-term absence from the home village and exposure to town life also added to the alienation from tribal values.

With the Bemba, the long-term fertility of land was based on a shifting cultivation method called 'citemene', only effectively performed by young men. By this method large trees are periodically cut down, burnt, and the ashes applied to the fields, leaving the old areas to regenerate in long periods of fallow. Neglect of this important part of environmental adaptation to low-fertility land, when the latter was left to women or the older men, inevitably set off the degenerative cycle of decline in yields, overtilling, and finally erosion (cf. Cliffe, 1979, p. 155). This situation was aggravated by the constrained time budget of women who were now burdened with the entire task of crop production and had to take on a number of other activities usually done by men.[7]

Despite the nominal efforts of administration to preserve the tribal character of rural areas, incipient capitalism crept into village life, gradually transforming and commercializing traditional social relations. Cash exchanges for marriage payments, property transactions based on monetary terms of valuation, and hired labour began to displace the traditional forms of exchange and mutual reciprocity in all parts of the colony (Cliffe, 1979, p. 156). As early as 1930 missionaries had pointed to what they observed as the 'debilitating effect of labour migration on family life and the breakdown of traditional society and its values'. Refuting the government's effort to confine unmarried women to the villages with the help of tribal authorities, increasing numbers of women left the villages to join their husbands in town, or single women established cohabitational relations with single men to whom they provided personal services in exchange for food, shelter, and clothing (Hansen, 1987, p. 12 and 1984, p. 223). With authorities unable to police the legal restrictions on family life in towns, Africans showed themselves quick in adapting to the new urban conditions, living semi-legally with women in some of the company compounds or illegally in adjoining townships. According to Heisler's study of the mining town of Broken Hill (Kabwe), by 1940 40% of mine workers were married and already living with their wives. Only 14.4% of married men had left their wives in the village (Heisler, 1971, p. 132).

Notes

1   Resistance was particularly fierce in the northern Bemba-land warrior kingdom, finally broken by military force in 1899. Submission involved the destruction of their economic base of long-distance trade to Zanzibar and to the coast with salt, ivory and slaves. Similarly, the defeat of the Ngoni in the western region involved the crucial loss of cattle herds, crippling their traditional reproductive base.

2   Often land alienation directly and indirectly resulted in ecological problems. Some of the depopulated lands became infested with tsetse fly and are now unsuited for agriculture, in others the return of the bush now requires considerable inputs to reopen them for agricultural cultivation. With growing population in the poorer lands of former native reserves, overtilling and overgrazing has become frequent with fertility decreasing even further.

3   As stated by M. Thomsen, the Secretary for Native Affairs, "The new Bill introduces a more advanced form of native administration, which gives to the chiefs the management of their own affairs within their tribal areas, and it is hoped it will preserve and maintain all that is good in native custom and tribal organization" (Thomsen addressing the Legislative Council in 1929; quoted by Hall, 1965, p. 103).

4   According to Heisler, African Paramountcy remained the underlying policy till 1945-46 despite the official attitudes of the administrative Service, meaning the preservation of the rural based tribal society. After 1945 and the decision to make positive provisions for urban growth, African Paramountcy survived in the formula of 'balanced growth' redressing the imbalances realized in the rural areas (Heisler, 1971, p. 128).

5   For a more detailed treatment of this subject cf. Meillassoux (1980). It should be noted that the principal mechanisms are still very much alive in the peripheral economies of today. The element of colonial force in maintaining the tributary relations between the capitalist and a non-capitalist sector can be replaced by economic or socio-political means of creating the necessary disparities in the workforce. For a contemporary case in the Sudan, applying socio-political segregation, cf. Tait (1979 and 1983).

6   The politics of the BSAC had to balance the interests of the settlers on the railway line and in the Copperbelt (who were even more radical supporters of the colour bar theory than the government of Southern Rhodesia) and the directives of the Colonial Office in London demanding unlimited opportunities for Africans. Moreover, the settlers, as the electorate for the legislative Council, were also in favour of the Union with Southern Rhodesia, the underlying impetus of which was to safeguard the system of race relations. The loophole for the private sector enabling it to maintain its restrictive colour bar policy was provided by the Colonial Office itself, which in 1935 asserted that employers in the private sector were indeed free to give preference to any race or colour they preferred. The opening of government services for Africans did not materialize until 1939 when training of Africans as clerks, telegraphists and post office workers began (cf. Berger, 1974, p. 43 and 47).

7   Richards (1951) reports that amongst the duties of Bemba men were tree-cutting, sowing, hoeing, hunting and fishing, collecting of honey, building of huts and granaries, the making of furniture, baskets, mats and musical instruments (cf. Fickert/Wetter, 1981, p. 126).

VIII African urbanization and proletarianization

1 Colonial urbanization policies

After the consolidation of the mining industry in 1933, three sets of events put the social and economic structures of Northern Rhodesia onto a new trajectory:

- Following the economic crisis of 1931/32, the European population declined from a peak of 14,000 in 1931 to 10,000 in 1936. Between 1931 and 1946, 27,000 Europeans immigrated into the country, with almost as many leaving. Thus, hopes of demographic support for the claim of white dominance rested on a solution of the urban problem in terms considered adequate by the European population, 95% of which lived in or close to urban areas (Heisler, 1971, p. 141).

- By 1940 the policy of parallel development, aligned into a European urban and a native rural sector, was evidently incompatible with the demands of the mining industry and the debilitation of rural areas. With the return of many African labourers from abroad (particularly from the Katanga mines in the Belgian Congo), the de facto urbanization in Northern Rhodesia proceeded. By 1944 it was estimated that 94,000 Africans populated the labour camps and locations, including a growing portion of women (23%) and children (27%) (Heisler, 1974, p. 92).

- The 1935 spontaneous riots in the Copperbelt on tax increases, the budding union movement of Africans, and the growing problems with 'detribalized' African town dwellers precipitately aborted further discussions on African urbanization. The government urged mines to stick to the migratory labour system. But with the consolidation of the copper industry in the mid-1930s government slowly had to face the fact of an irreversible movement towards a permanent industrialized African urban community.

Despite the apparent immediate need for government action towards urban development, policy solutions were very slow to mature and were implemented hesitantly. Influenced by British town planning legislation, a Town Planning Ordinance was introduced in 1929 followed by the Public Health Ordinance of 1930. The Town Planning Boards created out of this legislation were exclusively concerned with the health and welfare of the European populations and dealt with means of protecting them from the hazards arising from the living conditions in the native areas. But while British building regulations were applied in the expatriate housing areas, local authorities simply ignored conditions in the African housing and settlement areas (Rakodi, 1986b, p. 198). It was not until 1946 that legal and infrastructural provisions were resolved to create a 'stabilized urban society' to include the African population of Northern Rhodesia.

H. Heisler, a former member of Northern Rhodesia's civil service, presents in his various writings the most profound analysis of this transition process (cf. Heisler, 1971 and 1974). However, the perspective is somewhat narrowed as the study is established on the historical facts provided in statements, memorandums, and reports of the Colonial Office and the Northern Rhodesian government. According to Heisler's reading, the very reluctant inclination to promote proper African urbanization was attributable both to the traditional antiurban stance of colonial administration and to the pressures applied to authorities by the various local European residential groups. Although these groups were by no means homogeneous, the vast majority of Europeans were united in their strive to secure white dominance in urban affairs and, if possible, to translate racial segregation into spatial urban-rural segregation.

Heisler identified four 'categories of interest' that were concerned with an urban future for Zambia (cf. Heisler, 1971, p 126):

- First was the *metropolitan government* of the UK as the nominally most powerful interest group - although its impact on Northern Rhodesian affairs was at times 'more apparent than real'.

- Second were *Africans* by their de facto migration to towns, although they remained unenfranchised till 1963 and could take no active part in the decisions that finally led to the Ten Year Plan of 1946 to create a stabilized urban society.

- Third were *ruling elites* composed of the colonial administrative service, the chief executives of mining companies, and the missionaries - all mostly of UK origin. This group, although not in accord on all issues, constituted the most important internal set of interests in the country. According to their viewpoint, modernization was to be for the benefit of Africans without denying the legitimate claims of the locally settled Europeans.

- The fourth group were the *locally settled Europeans* who until 1941 were politically led by mercantile and farming fractions. Through their spatial concentration along the line of rail, most settler farmers lived within one hour's drive from urban centres. Thus, with other urban residents (miners, public employees, construction workers, traders) they shared the interest of forming a civilized urban society in which they conceived their role as indispensable and dominant, deserving a larger reward than Africans in the urban society (Heisler, 1971, p. 127).

Two alliances between these strategic interest groups were formative for policy discussions and delimited progression in urban development. In the *first alliance*, the ruling elites shared the attitude of the Colonial Office that the role of Africans in mining industry could not be ignored and that their de facto urbanization required a revision of African Affairs along the lines of the 1931 officially endorsed policy of complementarity of African and European interests. In the course of this policy, unlimited job opportunities should be opened to Africans including the civil service, and the colour bar was to be removed in the private sector.

In the *second alliance*, the position of the locally settled Europeans (in reality mostly composed of immigrants from South Africa) was backed and reinforced by the 'rank and file members' of the provincial administration. In Heisler's verdict, the official policy of complementary development was simply disregarded by civil servants mistrustful of any government policy deviating from the traditional colonial approach of a rurally-confined native development. In their view, support for African urbanization would make rural areas less attractive, hinder development there, and lead to rural exodus. For the provincial governments, urbanization and its job attractions were a cancer to tribal life and would destroy the changes of Africans of finding their own way into modern life (Heisler, 1971, pp. 133-134).

Lack of cooperation on the part of its own civil service and of the indigenous Europeans, thus, required prudent government approaches to urban matters. Since economic development depended on the capital and activities of Europeans, their cooperation in native development was considered indispensable and would be deterred by open competition between races and undue aspirations of Africans if their urbanization was pushed too fast by government (Berger, 1974, pp. 52-53). Adding to this, the transiency of European settlers in the 1930s interlaced with the issues of African urbanization in the need to stabilize the European population first before advances towards self-government could be made.

Irrespective of the government's growing awareness that by 1940 the segregated urban-rural development had gone a long way in turning Northern Rhodesia into a racist society, provisions for African urbanization remained in a political impasse till 1946 (Heisler, 1971, p. 133). The only exception was the decision to establish African townships for the elite of African artisans and clerks following the 1935 Copperbelt riots. While definite administrative action remained blocked by the disagreements between the rural biased provincial administration

178

and the more urban orientation at secretary level of central government, it was an unexpected shift in alliances that finally brought the breakthrough. During the 1940s the British government developed a new policy to disengage from responsibilities towards its colonies and to encourage their self-government and financial autonomy. Implementation of such policies in Northern Rhodesia necessarily entailed a revaluation of the Legislative Council and the local European electorate. Heisler comments:

> Britain's attitude towards the Europeans and complementary development arose from two considerations. The most explicit was the long-term policy to devolve power piece by piece to the colonial dependencies. The second, unavowed but more decisive in fact, was the growing strength of the Northern Rhodesian economy, making for a large measure of financial autonomy (Heisler, 1971, p. 135).

This shift in colonial policies coincided with a growing awareness on the part of European residents (and administrators) in Northern Rhodesia that independence from Britain hinged on efforts towards an economically self-sustaining development that could pay for its own infrastructure and social services. It was realized that funds of this order could only come from a substantial improvement in the urban sector. This revised point of view also shed new light on the role Africans could play in urban development. Any continuation of the implicit policy of African paramountcy and migratory labour meant that the contributions of Africans - after all the great majority of the de facto urban work force - were partially 'lost' to the rural areas. Thus, African stabilization and complementary development gradually became acceptable propositions for the urban Europeans under the implicit perspective that racial relationships could be preserved under their own independent regime.

Once encouraged by the new policy of the Colonial Office to find domestic sources of finance, the European residents of Northern Rhodesia came to realize that these resources already existed. However, these funds were lost to the British government due to its tax arrangements with the BSAC and the mining companies. Under constant pressure from the European community, the ruling British Labour Party, unable to deny that it was exploiting Northern Rhodesia, amended these tax inequities during the 1940s. Though the colony was then supplied with sufficient budget resources to attempt a policy of urban stabilization, hesitation and internal policy dispute continued on the part of the Northern Rhodesian government. The matter was only finally settled by firm directives from the Colonial Office in 1944 to incorporate a stabilization policy into the Ten-Year Territorial Development Plan (Heisler, 1971, p. 131).

The newly devised policy of 'balanced stabilization' declared in 1945 now legalized the permanent residence of Africans with their families in towns for the duration of their active working life. But it did not at first remove the rural bias of African development. It was not until 1947, with the implementation of the Ten-Year Plan, that priorities were finally set on urban investment and that local municipalities became responsible for African housing and settlements. According to Heisler's estimates, by 1952 £9.6 million out of a total of £12.5 million allocated to community, social, and economic services were spent on urban development at the expense of the rural areas (Heisler, 1971, p. 144; cf. Table 8.1).

Table 8.1
Recurrent and capital expenditure of the Northern
Rhodesia government 1938 to 1954 in £ million

Year	General services	Community services	Social services	Economic services	Not allocable	Total
1938	0.4	0.0	0.1	0.1	0.3	0.9
1942	0.6	0.2	0.2	0.2	0.6	1.8
1947	1.4	0.5	0.7	0.9	1.3	4.9
1948	1.7	0.6	1.0	2.1	1.7	7.1
1949	1.6	0.6	1.8	2.8	3.7	10.6
1950	2.3	1.1	2.3	3.6	4.8	14.1
1951	3.2	1.4	2.9	4.1	7.5	19.1
1952	4.4	2.1	4.0	6.4	13.0	29.9
1953/54	8.0	3.7	8.2	11.5	17.2	48.5

Source: Financial Reports, Lusaka, Government Printer. Compiled by Heisler, 1971, p. 143)

Quite rightly, Heisler considered the new legal and financial framework for a stabilized urbanization of Africans as a 'turning point in the development of Northern Rhodesia':

> During the next fifteen years there followed a fivefold multiplication of the population concerned. At the same time the camps were transformed into mosquito-free towns with water-borne sanitation, tarmac roads, street lighting, overcrowded but well-built houses, clean open spaces, public transport for Africans and civil administration modelled on Britain and South Africa (Heisler, 1971, p. 125).

2   The political economy of the colonial urban labour-force

Undoubtedly Heisler gave an important insight into the political evolution of urban policies in a racially divided colonial society. His account also clarified the limitations and biases of the colonial administration in adapting to socioeconomic changes by making them politically compatible with the terms of governing a racially segregated society. However, the conclusions omit the limit functions within which administration and central colonial power had to act. These can be defined as the vital process of transforming the colonial political economy and its old mode of labour-power exploitation into appropriate urban-based forms. This incorporated the change from administrative control of African labour reserves to the management of a self-regulative reproduction under colonial capitalist market mechanisms. The solution to this problem in Northern Rhodesia fell far short of an open urban society moving towards partnership of races and enfranchisement of Africans. Instead the outcome was a modified colonial city that could act as labour reserve and increase internal social differentiation of Africans, enabling more variety in the urban forms of their reproduction.

As Berger remarks, British colonial administrators in their traditionally hostile attitude towards urbanization were ill-equipped to deal with the problems that arose when a sprawling copper industry developed in their protectorate (Berger, 1974). However, the policy of stalling any determinate action towards African urbanization for nearly two decades was possibly a quite functional approach considering the rapid and unpredictable developments related to managing the urban situation with inadequate financial means and backward-looking policy instruments. Central aspects of potential administrative and legislative action in urban areas rested heavily on the dynamics of the proliferating and expanding mining industry. Therefore no partial solution was possible until definite structures concerning the following interrelated issues had been established:

- In order to stabilize the uncompetitive settler farmers and to secure the provision of urban and mining areas with cheap food, marketing control boards were introduced for maize and cattle in 1936.[1] By unevenly dividing the internal market pool between Africans (25%) and settlers (75%), and by granting state price subsidies to the internal market and selling below world market prices to the mines, the intention was to supply mines with cheap food and at the same time to fend off the strong competition of African producers (cf. Biermann, 1980, pp. 45-65; Seidman, 1979a, pp. 37-41; Simons, 1979, p. 6).

- In the course of technological advances and growing integration into the world copper market, the specific capital-labour relations and forms of work force sustainment employed by the mining companies were subject to variance. Short-term labour contracts and migration gradually became a constraint to necessary higher job qualifications. Various mines in Northern Rhodesia began to experiment with stabilization models to increase the efficiency of labour management and to raise work productivity. But any abolition of the migratory labour system required definite policy decisions and provisions towards urban African housing and settlement, welfare, social control, education, etc.

- By simply ignoring that by the end of the 1930s a large part of the African population was living outside the native authority, administrators could cling to their perception that the social order of Africans was naturally based on tribal values. Any detribalization in the urban environment due to permanent residence was equated with loss of social orientation, alienation from tribal society, sure delinquency, and social disruption. Although reports proved the contrary, showing that Africans assimilated readily to urban life, administration necessarily steered clear of any encouragement of African urban stabilization until agreement could be reached with the mines on how to organize the urban work force.

- Most importantly, the shift from short-term utilization of migratory labour to long-term urban reproduction of stabilized labour-power signified a major breach with established colonial modes of labour exploitation that dislocated large parts of reproduction costs to rural areas. For mining companies the contradiction emerged that a high turnover of Africans workers was considered uneconomic at the same time as costly provisions for permanent settlement in compounds were considered unwise, excepting a small fraction of skilled senior men (Berger, 1974, p. 70). Thus, mines and administration readily adopted a laissez-faire attitude to solutions offered by Africans that, with minimal official involvement, would enable a semi-permanent urban labour-force to be houses and fed in townships outside of mine compounds.

From various vantage points the growth of an informal urban sector in townships proved an indispensable key element in the reconciliation of the opposing policy demands attached to urbanization of Africans: (1) the growing relocation of labour to townships allowed the dual policy of restricting the growth of properly serviced (expensive) labour camps without curbing the industrial demand for stabilized local labour; (2) the minimization of properly serviced urban areas for Africans (at least in theory) worked towards lowering the attractiveness of towns for rural residents; (3) this pattern of African urban growth also had the positive aspect of appeasing the European community concerned about a too rapid expansion of African urbanization and growing job competition; (4) the internal differentiation of the African urban structure into compounds and townships (the nucleus for adjoining illegal squatting areas) was also highly functional in running the growing urban-based (i.e. stabilized) labour market at wage scale levels originally modelled for the minimal sustainment of unmarried migratory labourers.

3 African urbanization in Northern Rhodesia

The Copperbelt case is very probably one of the earliest examples of explicit capitalist utilization of informal housing and urban subsistence production as a means to reduce the necessary reproduction costs of the urban work force in and out of employment. Estimations of the part of the labour force living informally are difficult as mine statistics of labour turnover took no account of the total number of engagements or the whereabouts of labour in the periods before or between contracts (cf. Berger, 1974, p. 71). However individual studies in the town of Ndola (Davis, 1933) and general reports on the Copperbelt (Safferey, 1943 and Heisler, 1974) illustrate the living conditions, though they may not explicitly distinguish between the miners in company compounds and the legal and illegal residential groups falling under other occupational categories living in municipal townships.

Till the final decision was taken in 1948 to embark on proper urbanization and proletarianization of Africans, the mining industry was divided on how to reorganize the labour-force under its own regime without losing its highly competitive advantage of low labour-costs. According to various sources, two mine companies (Roan Antelope and Mufulira), accounting for roughly 50% of total production, were strongly inclined to encourage a longer-term stay of married labourers who were found more disciplined and productive than bachelors.[2] But with the other mining companies they shared uncertainties about the work potential of Africans and doubted if the wage increases necessary to sustain a family would pay off. Some mine officials feared exhaustion of African labour after a work period of 18 months; others felt that it would become uneconomic to keep workers longer than 5 years (Berger, 1974, p. 70). The data presentation with respect to the actual labour costs in question is somewhat disparate depending on sources. According to Safferey, an investigation in 1943 showed that an average family would require £6.11.s.7d. per month for a reasonable living standard. In the same year one mining company estimated the cost of feeding and housing a worker's wife at 12s.8d. per month (Berger, 1974, p. 70). At the same time mine earnings ranged from £2.5s.10d. to £4.14s.7d. (Safferey, 1943; quoted by Simons, 1979, pp. 8-9). Another source puts the average 'real' African mining wage rate in the 1940s at slightly below £2 per month (Baldwin, 1966, p. 87; quoted by Biermann, 1980, p. 98).[3]

Whatever the real economic costs of labour might have been, the fact is that by 1946 none of the mines had launched any programmes to provide housing for married labour or found it necessary to grant family allowances. This underscores the important function performed by informal urban structures in transforming and supporting the colonial labour system without intervening in the dual urban wage system. The need to house the various groups of African labour outside the European residential areas gave rise to diversification in the forms of native compounds. The municipal townships run under the authority of the District Commissioner were only one of the nexuses for informal housing activities. Semilegal housing areas also emerged from the labour camps of private contractors or grew on unused peri-urban farm lands rented to Africans by private landlords. True forms of illegal squatting occurred on lands held vacant by the British Crown for later use. In the official terminology of Northern Rhodesia, later adapted by the Zambian government, little distinction was made between these various residential circumstances. The term 'squatter compound' came to be used indifferently for all forms of African dwelling areas outside company or municipal control (Hansen, 1982, p. 119).

Unable to control African residence or provide properly administered housing areas even for African contract labour (i.e. with legal residence), local authorities turned 'a blind eye to conditions in compounds and locations' (Simons, 1979, p. 9). Under these terms, the costs and the infrastructural provisions for the de facto stabilization could be kept minimal. Vast parts of reproduction of the African work-force were simply aligned to the informal urban sector and the self-help housing production of Africans who were left with no other option but to come to towns for survival under whatever conditions:

> Single urban Zambians lived in bachelor quarters in barracks, compounds or locations. Others who had their families with them were expected to build their own houses. They could not afford to build or pay an economic rent for a decent dwelling, nor would the government, or employers generally, subsidize one for a man supposed to be a temporary and family-less worker. For these reasons the 'shanty town', and 'squatters camp' emerged in the early days of urban growth. Urban workers erected pole and dagga shelters[4] and sun-baked brick houses, drew water from nearby streams, wells and the occasional stand-pipe, and for sanitation used pit latrines and the surrounding bush (Simons, 1979, p. 9).

In the municipal location of Ndola, said to be typical of the situation in the 1930s, 90% of houses consisted of mud-built single rooms in rural style, spaced 12 feet apart and accommodating an average of 7.3 persons per room (Davis, 1933, p. 80). With populations living under high density conditions with only marginal incomes and practically no hygiene control on the part of local authorities, malnutrition diseases were common and tuberculosis was spreading (Safferey, 1933; quoted by Simons, 1979, pp. 8-9).

The internally differentiated residential structure of Africans into camps, townships, and semilegal locations not only solved the housing problem; it also proved functional for the operations of the labour market and for the maintenance of native control. In the mine compounds life was strictly regulated by autonomous company rule. The worker was not allowed to leave the compound between 9 pm and 5 am or without permission from the compound manager. Cohabitation with women was prohibited, and discipline was enforced by mine police, later to be replaced by a proper police post. Since workers were still considered tribal members, social control was to some extent exerted by the social authority of elders, practised in a similar fashion to that in the villages. This officially supported system seems to have been generally respected by African workers till the early 1950s when its functions were replaced by the Urban Advisory Council.

In contrast to this, living in townships and squatter areas had numerous advantages, despite the lack of urban amenities like water and sanitation. Families could live together and engage in growing subsistence crops (maize or bananas) to subsidize low wages - activities that were prohibited in mine compounds due to the threat to public health by mosquito infestations.

Not bound by zoning laws or building codes, houses could be built according to needs, and people could move more freely than in employer-controlled dwelling areas. Social and commercial life in which women played a great part thrived in these areas:

> Living in a dwelling built by his own hands, a squatter could freely choose his own male and female companions and have privacy unlike the joint quarters of compounds. Markets also developed in these townships providing goods and services legally unavailable in the employer-controlled native compounds. Chief among them were the sale of prepared foods, home-brewed beer and sex which found a ready clientele, given the unbalanced male-female ratio that resulted from influx control and employment ordinance. Since women found few wage-labour opportunities in the colonial town, the beer and sex nexus provided some with a livelihood (Hansen, 1984, p. 119).

With the strict police regulations towards illegal stay in towns without a work contract, townships and squatter areas functioned as a refuge for the urban unemployed and job seekers from rural areas. Chiefs often ran a guest house to accommodate tribal members in this situation. Cheap accommodation was also provided by resident artisans and construction workers who adopted subletting as an additional source of income. Given the fact that the urban unemployment ratio of men in the 1940s was reported to be 8% (Simons, 1979, p. 9), we can conclude that townships obviously performed the vital function of sustaining an urban-based surplus labour reserve at low costs. By this, employers could save costs for recruitment in rural areas and use the standby urban labour reserve as a lever to reduce the bargaining power of the active work force and keep wages low.

During this interim period of 'stabilization without urbanization', the African's capacity for self-organization in townships and locations was undeniable and laid the foundations for the rapid postwar African urbanization. In particular it confuted the colonial concept of 'detribalization' that in a racist and paternalistic way assumed that Africans, removed from their natural social environment, would be dependent on the guidance and mastery of Europeans in an urban situation alien to them. Although tribal associations and tribal values remained dominant patterns in residential clustering, or in neighbourhood networks of reciprocity (particularly among women), their contents gradually changed in response to the new urban and industrial relationships and to class differentiation amongst Africans (Epstein, 1969, p. 116). In this process some of the traditional relationships played a part in urban contexts as long as no altogether new terms of interaction developed. The Bemba, Ngoni, and the Ndebele as warrior tribes enjoyed high esteem amongst all and became a point of orientation in the general structuring of formal native relationships in town. Other intertribal relationships were already pre-shaped by the colonial and missionary impact. Africans from Barotseland and Nyasaland were predestined for white-collar work through the early educational efforts made by missionaries in these regions. The predominance of specific languages was another important factor. Town Bemba became the lingua franca in the Copperbelt and extended to Lusaka, reflecting the cultural position of this tribe. Thus, in towns, tribalism attained a new meaning, not as the specific decent from a tribe but the affiliation to a major ethnic group that determined the informal day-to-day interaction and cultural orientation between urban dwellers. Although traditions were continued, the specific new aspect in their custom was the absence of the hierarchical tribal order in towns, since only very few of the elders were present and the urban mode of reproduction was different from that on which the old authorities were based (cf. Fickert/Wetter, 1979, pp. 153-165).

Whereas tribal relations remained relatively important in the informal organization of townships and tentatively supported the colonial efforts to maintain tribal self-control, industrialization gave considerable impetus to the transformation towards a modern social differentiation among Africans. The colonial administration had in 1935 already taken the first step in this direction by providing African clerks, supervisors, and artisans with separate compounds and giving them other privileges, like the right to rent garden plots. In the devolution of relations between capital and labour, tribal leaders soon proved unable to maintain their leadership position. In the case of strikes their attitudes identified them as allies of mine management. With the strikes of the 1940s, ethnic background no longer played a part in workers' organizations. Rather, individual determination to struggle for rights and higher wages became the nexus for African workers' affiliations. What sometimes (e.g. in the combat between the Lozi and the Bemba on the question as to who should represent the workers in the unions) may have looked like tribal rivalries inside the unions, in fact reflected the differently emerging class positions: Bemba were the mine labourers; Lozi were office workers (Fickert/Wetter, 1979, p. 155).

The role of the colonial administration in promoting the development of Northern Rhodesia towards an urban society was certainly neither very prudent nor just towards Africans, nor even explicit in terms of planning. Laissez-faire and drastic regulatory interventions towards Africans were the two sides of the coin of colonial rule - overwhelmed by the developments it had touched off and was unable to control. Convictions under the various influx control and tax laws averaged nearly 10,000 a year (Simons, 1979, p. 12). But under the surface of two decades of urban policy abstention, the British colonial administration haphazardly introduced vital elements of peripheral capitalism, anticipating contemporary Third World urban formation in its interlocking of formal and informal structures in urban reproduction.

When a sharp swing in developments during the Second World War finally made the reconsideration of urban policies inevitable, it did not hit the colony or its African population unprepared in adapting to new developments: The copper industry boomed, providing substantial revenues that gave rise to a prosperous urban development. Labour shortages induced by army drafting of Africans continued in all occupational categories during the postwar years, instigating the proletarianization of a larger segment of the African labour-force. With the declaration of the 1948 'African Housing Ordinance', the matter of native settlement was handed over to the responsibility of urban authorities, enabling them to build suburbs for the Africans using government funds. Employers were now legally bound to house their employees, and in the case of large enterprises with more than 25 employees they could be obliged to build their own workers living quarters. At the request of Africans, accommodation would be provided for one wife. Alternatively, employees could be housed in municipal African housing areas erected exclusively for their residence. Rents in this case were payable to the local management boards. Local authorities were also required to build hostels for single and married job seekers (Collins, 1986, p. 122). These developments, originating from labour market exigence, coincided with necessary requirements in managing growing colonial cities whose populations were no longer composed of bachelor administrators and workers but increasingly made up of families. Accordingly the standards of African residential areas were raised to comply with the minimal hygiene requirements to maintaining a healthy work-force under densely populated conditions. These measures served to protect the growing European quarters from health hazards and mitigated the dissatisfaction of Africans who might violate the zoning arrangements.

Importantly for the operations of the reformed colonial labour market, the informal sector and the toleration of squatter settlements remained an integral part of urban structures - despite officially voiced disapproval. Unauthorized settlements not only retained their function to absorb and house migrants and unemployed job seekers - with the new developments they even grew over-proportionately: migration to towns multiplied in the prosperous postwar decade, driven by new job attractions, higher wages, and expanded urban services. Lacking comprehensive agrarian development programmes, ongoing capitalist expansion in rural areas accentuated class divisions among Africans into a small group of emergent commercial farmers and a growing mass of impoverished small peasants (Seidman, 1979, p. 44). Accordingly, neither employment nor the provision of municipal and employer housing could keep pace with the rural exodus. Concentrated on six towns holding 69.9% of urban dwellers, more and more newcomers were canalized into squatter areas for their settlement and survival (Kay, 1967).

Momentum was added to this development by the political and socioeconomic decline of Northern Rhodesia in the 1953-63 Federation with Southern Rhodesia and Nyasaland. The preeminence of Southern Rhodesia in this Federation reinforced racial discrimination against africans and generally impaired Northern Rhodesian development under the federal taxation system (Burdette, 1984, p. 26). In the division of powers between the federal and territorial governments, the latter became responsible for African Affairs, entailing a gradual reversing of priorities on African urbanization. With low copper prices in 1954-55 and 1957-58 giving rise to unemployment, housing subsidies for Africans were withdrawn in 1958 and plans postponed to increase the municipal housing stock for Africans (Rothman, 1972, p. 90).

The economic and political impact of the copper industry and its exigencies on the final shaping of disparate national sociospatial structures was immense. In the 1950s and 1960s copper mining accounted for more than 90% of export earnings, between 60 and 90% of gross domestic product (depending on copper prices), and for more than 50% of government revenues (cf. Biermann, 1980, p. 89; Burdette, 1984, p. 80). In 1963, 47% of Northern Rhodesia's wage-employment was in the comparatively small Copperbelt Province encompassing only 15.6% of total population (Tetzlaff, 1975, p. 107 and Ohadike, 1981, p. 13). The existing structural deficiencies were deepened in the Federation period due to Salisbury's policy of internal colonization towards Northern Rhodesia. At the end of the colonial regime the country was socially and spatially divided into three production zones:

(1) An *urbanized capitalist core* area that, except for Lusaka, was economically based on mining and associated servicing industries (timber, cement, electrical power, repair, and distributive services). This area was populated by 20% of a total population of 3.49 million in 1963. (2) A *European farm area* on Crown land along the line of rail that, together with its African labour stock, made up 5% of the total population. (3) *African rural areas* that were inhabited by 75% of the total population, divided into native reserves, native trust areas, and the Barotseland Protectorate (see Figure 8.1). These areas were practically cut off from development, forcing their populations to survive at subsistence level in dilapidated rural production systems.

Outside the line of rail and the Copperbelt towns, virtually no physical or social infrastructure existed. The national energy, communication, and transport lines were primarily laid out to service the mining industry, linking the Copperbelt with seaports (Bulawayo, Lourenço Marques), the Kariba hydroelectric power plant, and the Wankie coal mines in Southern Rhodesia, and finally with South Africa. This decisive southward orientation underscores the dependency of Northern Rhodesia on its economic alignment with the southern African region: in terms of communication and infrastructure, the central spine of Northern Rhodesia was practically a protuberance of this system. This made the centre of Northern Rhodesia internally isolated from its western and northeastern parts and externally

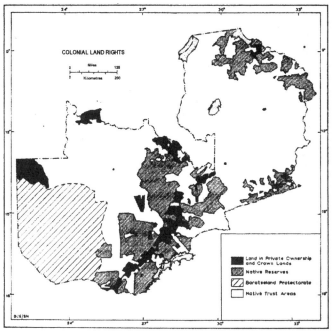

Figure 8.1   Colonial land rights
Source: Davis, 1971

isolated from the rest of Africa.

Lusaka, made the new capital of Northern Rhodesia in 1935, was to become the only major urban growth pole outside the mining areas. Ranked eighth amongst the Northern Rhodesian towns in 1931 with 1,750 inhabitants, Lusaka had by 1946 become the fourth largest town (9,215), growing to a population of 110,000 in 1963 and thereby equalling Kitwe as the largest city in Northern Rhodesia (Collins, 1986, p. 110; Simons, 1979, p. 12). With respect to the employment structure and ethnic composition of its population, Lusaka displays a marked difference from the Copperbelt towns. As mining jobs were traditionally a domain of the Bemba tribes from Northern and Luapula Province (and of foreigners), the liberalization of African urbanization by town ordinances and Lusaka's gradual economic growth made the capital the most important destination for migrants from the Eastern, Central, Southern, Northern, and the Copperbelt Provinces in that order (ranking weighted according to the relative population of province - see Table 8.2).

Although data on exact migration to Lusaka by Provinces is not available prior to the 1968-69 study of Ohadike (Ohadike, 1981), the survey of languages spoken incorporated in this study confirms an apparent long-term predominance of migrants from eastern, Copperbelt, central and southern regions. The eastern Nyanya had virtually become the lingua-franca in Lusaka and was spoken by 41% of residents as their mother tongue. Northern Bemba was spoken by 23% of survey respondents, and Tonga-Ila from the south, spoken by 14.1%, was the third most common language, (Ohadike, 1981, pp. 68-69; see also Wood, 1986, p. 170).

189

Table 8.2
Proportion of Lusaka migrants from various provinces
by last place of residence

Province of last residence	Per cent of migrants in Lusaka	Provincial population in % of total population
Eastern	29.5%	12.5%
Central	14.3%	17.6%
Copperbelt	12.6%	20.1%
Northern	11.8%	13.4%
Southern	9.3%	12.2%
Western	4.5%	10.1%
Luapula	2.1%	8.3%
North-Western	1.7%	5.7%
Outside Zambia	14.2%	-

Source: Compiled from Ohadike, 1981, p. 67 and 13-14

Notes

1   To a large extent the high fluctuation in the numbers of settlers in Northern Rhodesia was due to unproductive farming and shortages of African labour prepared to work for the low wages offered. Despite a rapidly growing internal demand from the mining industry for maize and meat and the favourable locations created by displacement of Africans from the zones along the line of rail, settlers were unable to keep pace with world market prices and productivity. Moreover, African competition began to grow in the early 1930s. To protect settler farming, the Maize Control Board offered subsidized prices above world market level and acted as monopolistic buyer to operate the quotation system. Surplus production of maize was sold on the world market at dumping prices. As only the internal market, widely reserved for European farmers, offered price guarantees, African producers were discriminated as they had to face the risks of export production. The productivity of settlers in cattle rearing was even lower. By 1936 Africans were supplying 67% of total production in this field. The Cattle Control Board adopted a policy of quality restriction to market sale that disqualified African products, which then could only be sold at low prices to the mines (cf. Biermann, 1980, pp. 62-63).

2   In the Belgian Congo mining region of Katanga, a permanently stabilized labour-force with family housing and urban services was introduced in the 1920s. Being able to draw on successive generations of wage workers, qualification standards of Africans were

considerably higher than in Northern Rhodesia or in South Africa and could be shaped to employers' specifications. The arrangement also had economic advantages: (i) the expensive skilled European labour could be substituted by Africans whose low wage rate could be maintained by authoritarian state control; (ii) in the absence of migratory labour systems, the situation in rural areas could be kept more stable, avoiding the problems associated with urban influx (cf. Simons, 1980, p. 10). The first companies to adopt this model in Northern Rhodesia were the lead and zinc mines in Broken Hill (Kabwe) who, in order to compete with the higher wages paid in the Copperbelt, improved the residential circumstances for their African labour. In addition to rented housing, a separate plot scheme was started in 1925 where employees could build houses according to their own requirements and could have gardens. These areas were supplied with water, sewerage and refuse disposal systems and had primary schools and clinics (Rakodi, 1986b, p. 199).

3   Some of these divergences may be accounted for by the difficulties in estimating the cost of 'real' wages. A major part of wages was paid in kind: the employer usually paid for food, housing, fuel, and travel expenses for visits to the home areas.

4   Pole and dagga is a traditional rural adobe building technique. The basic form is made from poles and wickerwork and then plastered with adobe (cf. Schmetzer, 1989).

IX   Colonial planning and African urbanization in Lusaka

1   The early settlement years of Lusaka 1905-1931

Lusaka came into existence in 1905 when the railway construction work on the single-track line connecting Livingstone and Broken Hill (Kabwe) reached the area. The location was selected for a railway siding and was named after the Lenje headman (Lusaakas) of an existing small village on the site. Adverse climatic conditions made the township a less than ideal settlement area. Situated on a plateau at an altitude of approx. 1,100 to 1,400m and with (at that time) only sparse tree vegetation, Lusaka was exposed to cold winds and dust storms in the dry season. But lacking exploitable mineral deposits, the land was sold off cheap by the Northern Copper Company, and plots had the advantage of being easy to clear for farm use. Incipient migration to Lusaka was in particular encouraged by the disruption in South Africa following the Boer War. Substantial numbers of Dutch (Afrikaner) settlers moved to the new township and still outnumbered the British community by 2:1 in the 1917-25 period. By 1908 commercial developments began when the first shops were opened. The first school serving the Dutch community was to follow in the next year. A hotel was built in 1912. In the same year the township's development had reached such a point that a residents' meeting resolved to form a Village Management Board. One of its first decisions was the allocation of a site for an African compound. It was built 1914 in the west of the township where it stayed till its removal to Chibolya in 1931. The first township regulations were passed in 1913, laying out a half a mile area either side of the railway for orderly development with special concern given to communal organization of sanitation and health.

Lacking vital commercial or administrative interests, Lusaka's early development until 1931 was spontaneous in character, predominantly serving local needs. Similarly, Lusaka's role as the geographic turntable in the country's north-south/east-west traffic routes is a modern, acquired function, emanating from the needs of the established town; but it did not add, as might be presumed, to its early growth (Williams, 1986b, pp. 71-72). Lusaka gradually attained some administrative functions and was to become the service centre for the region (government station, school and hospital). Nonetheless, developments were minor compared to the old capital of Livingstone, or compared to the more rapid urban growth of Broken Hill and of the Copperbelt towns in the late 1920s. The first enlargement of the administrative area to the north (Villa Elisabetta, Emmasdale), enacted in 1916, already anticipated what was to become a characteristic feature of Lusaka's urban growth: it was the result not of an expanding core-settlement area, but of an amalgamation of the centre with suburban areas following population and land-ownership developments that took place by the subdivision of farm areas on the outskirts of town. At the same time, plots demarcated in the centre of the township were not entirely taken up until 1922 (Williams, 1986b, p. 77).

The particular course of Lusaka's urban expansion is to a considerable extent determined by obstructive geophysical structures. Its topographical locality, partially on a watershed limestone surface with frequent rock outcrops and solution hollows and partially on a schist bedrock, posed various problems of servicing and developing the area (Turner/Turner, 1986 and Williams, 1986b, p. 75). In particular the limestone terrains made the township prone to flooding when the ground water table rose to the surface after heavy rains. Lack of natural surface drainage was the source of serious health hazards like typhoid fever or malaria. This had two aspects: latrines would become flooded, while pit latrines and septic tanks could not be used due to the difficulty of sinking pits through the rocks under the surface and the danger of polluting the high ground water table. On the other hand, stagnant surface water turned various parts of the town into notorious breeding grounds for mosquitoes. With the economic depression after the First World War, little was done to solve these problems, excepting the ditch finally built in 1927 to drain the main (Cairo) Road in the central commercial area. Up to the eve of its selection as capital city Lusaka was considered an unhealthy place to live. In fact, various initiatives were made to relocate the township to a more favourable area, e.g. Chilanga 10 miles south. As late as 1928 the local government doctor concluded that Lusaka should be evacuated as the present site was 'totally unsuited for a township' (quoted by Sampson, 1971, p. 51). In the end the weight of investments made by plot holders in Lusaka prevented any move. However, the geophysically-based problems of finding good settlement sites and maintaining hygiene standards predetermined the main course of European settlement expansions directed to the more elevated terrains in the north and east of the town centre.

The economic base of Lusaka was mainly agricultural. Its trades and crafts served as a centre for the substantial hinterland of settler farms around Lusaka that extended some 50km to the south along the line of rail. A bank opened in 1918, and in terms of social infrastructure the town had at the end of the 1920s a police station, a post office, a hospital, a marketplace and a market hall (also used for social functions), hotels, a school, and various sports facilities. Two limestone quarries were to become the first industries and the largest

193

employers in town, attracting migrant labour (with some 150 native workers reported in 1920). After a peak of production in 1915, based on some export successes, business became uncompetitive and declined, thereby releasing most of its African labour.

In general the observation of regulations regarding the administration of circulatory labour migration was less strict in Lusaka than elsewhere in the colony. Settlement of jobless Africans was tolerated instead of their immediate repatriation according to the official ordinances. The wish to avoid losing a standby labour-force in times of economic recession, especially in competition with higher wage rates in the Copperbelt and Broken Hill, is an important reason for this practice. Even more important, Lusaka's land-owning residents discovered that a sizable African population was also a potential source of revenue. For example, the African workers laid off in the quarries could rent the now unused mining land that was particularly attractive for informal settlement due to the nearby supply of firewood and water. This practice of making an additional income through renting out land to individual Africans, or to employers as private compounds, became quite common in the Lusaka area and was referred to as 'Kaffir farming'. While the official compound was overcrowded and liable to payment of fees to the Management Board, private compounds had the advantage that only a nominal monthly fee was due for the land and that workers could be accommodated closer to their work site. Under this system housing was provided by the contracted workers who were given a few days off work to build grass huts. Although these huts were to be demolished after the end of the work contract, this usually did not happen, and they remained to become illegal settlements (Hansen, 1982, p. 119). The general abundance of land also seems to have encouraged squatter settlement on private plots adjoining the huts of domestic servants who were allowed to build on the plots of their employers. Futile efforts were made by the Management Board to prevent the creation of private compounds within 2 miles of the railway station. The failure to implement this policy is most probably due to the importance of income derived by landowners from renting out sections of their spacious estates as private compounds (Williams, 1986b, p. 79).

In considering the early settlement patterns of European and African populations in Lusaka, two formative factors stand out from others. Excepting the grid-style central commercial area, the inner-town compounds laid out for Africans, and the small Asian community, Lusaka grew without any plan guidance concerning land use in its surrounding areas. Regarding future developments it was thought that growth potentials were limited, and with abundant land appropriate sites would be found easily if required. Under this approach, land use became valuated under the specific circumstances of that time leading to a generous residential spreading. This means that land was valorized and dispersed according to its organic physical or use-value in relation to the immediate preferences of its residents. This form of land utilization largely omitted all aspects of urban differential land value and sequel servicing costs in the land dispersion process:

Lusaka was characterized by that 'spread' which characterized most of other Rhodesian settlements; land was cheap; time was no object; people liked privacy and built their houses far away from each other, a practice encouraged by poor families for sanitation, the administration itself usually making a point of building their offices in a separate area. This 'spread' gave Rhodesians plenty of elbow room but made the subsequent provision of municipal services more difficult than it might have been (Gann, 1964 quoted by Williams, 1986b, p. 79).

Another factor said to have added to the spread was speculation with urban land, already realized in the 1920s by some farmers to be more profitable than farming (Rakodi, 1986b, p. 197). However, this assumption is not confirmed with the lands selected by the central government for the site of its administrative capital. Largely unsuited for farming, this area was in 1931 still nearly vacant Crown Land, only in public use as grounds for sports facilities.

Lusaka's high content of African population that generated income directly or indirectly for landowners seems to have supported the development of a more relaxed attitude on the part of authorities and European residents towards squatter settlements. With people's appreciation of low density residence, a rural oriented colonial lifestyle, ample space, and a corresponding valuation of land, this seems to have implanted an untypical structure of African settlement for a colonial town. Although the conventional colonial pattern of segregated housing for Europeans and Africans was maintained in principal, the town's specific historic development and its land use practice have led to an unconventional scattering of small African settlements nearly all over town. African and European residential groups came to live divided but spatially overlapping according to the different topographical alignments that divided high from low value land. *High value* lands were those with the best physical suitability for residential use on easy to service, elevated grounds, or the soils on the schist bedrock that were best suited for commercial farming. *Low value* lands were those on limestone terrain, frequently with rock outcrops, or were to be found in the surface-water collecting depression areas like Kalingalinga. Both types of low-value land pose hazardous hygiene conditions for residential use due to perennial flooding and ground water pollution and are physically obstructive and expensive to service land forms (cf. Figure 9.1).

With two exceptions this nexus between geophysical substructures and land value/ utilization also applies to the development of the immediate surrounding of the town centre, making it ineligible for proper residential use. Most of this area is inside (i.e. south) of the NW-SE running dividing line between inimical land on limestone/dolomite surfaces and the more favourable land forms for urban development to the north (van den Berg, 1986, p. 298). The validity of this argument can best be exemplified by looking at the contemporary development of this part of town. The first of the exceptions indicated was the Fairview area contiguous to the southeastern part of town centre, that became earmarked for commercial development in the 1933 non-statutory plan in order to fill the emerging gap between the old (commercial) and the new (administrative) centre. Although this part of town only finally began to be developed in the 1980s, land-use control was applied in

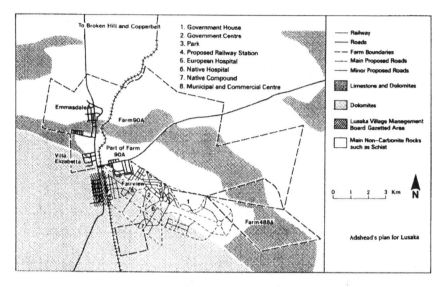

Figure 9.1   Ashead's plan for Lusaka with superimposed geophysical features
Source: Rakodi, 1986b

the interim period to keep the area open for its designated purpose. The second exception concerns the two industrial zones, most of which developed in the postwar period. Today's light industry zone takes up the small remaining limestone/dolomite corner in the northeast of the town centre, whereas the heavy industry zone extends some 2 km northwest, closely following the boundary between the limestone/dolomite and schist terrains, only recently moving down to the west of the town centre. But regarding the southwest and southern surrounding area, there is a near absence of a differential land value despite its relative closeness to the commercial and industrial centres. This valuation is also reflected in the fact that while boundary expansions constantly moved to the north and east (e.g. 1928, 1936 and 1951), it took nearly 50 years for the eastern and southern administrative boundaries to move more than 2 km from the old town centre. Only since 1970 has the urban centre also become the geographical centre of Lusaka. This central area incorporates the now considerable population living on the town's geologically most problematic land: the landscape to the south that has been devastated by dolomite quarrying going on since the 1940s, with no attempts made to restore the surface. The area, pitted with holes, now resembles a lunar landscape beyond rehabilitation (Kay, 1967). To the southwest lies,

196

undoubtedly, the most hostile limestone surface of Lusaka, frequently flooded and most difficult to service due to large rock outcrops. Nevertheless, in accordance with prevailing land valuation and with growing population pressure on lands, vast parts of these areas have gradually become occupied by large unauthorized and low-income settlements (Kanyama, Chibolya, Misisi, Chawama, etc.).

An analogous variation in this land valuation mechanism can be observed in the official low-cost housing belt planned in the 1930s to serve the new capital. This area, beginning at a short distance from the southeastern corner of the town centre (Kamwala), extends along the limestone terrain south of the ridge that was to become the site of the second (administrative) centre of Lusaka. Further (unauthorized) extension of low-income housing to the south of this area has been curbed by the declaration of this fertile land as a forest reserve and water protection zone.

Coming back to the early history, it was no coincidence that Lusaka, owing to its extensive spatial growth, became known as the 'motor town'. The internal road system proliferated at an early stage and was extended along the Great East Road to Fort Jameson (Chipata) and to the west in 1928, and to Mazabuka and Broken Hill (Kabwe) by the Great North Road in 1924.

Overall estimates of Lusaka's urban progress by 1928 are somewhat divided. R. Sampson, the mayor of Lusaka in 1961-63, in his history of the capital of Zambia describes the state of the town in the late 1920s as 'extremely dull and parochial' (Sampson, 1971, p. 53). Although Williams considers this an exaggeration (Williams, 1986b, p. 90), there can be no doubt that Lusaka was largely unaffected by the budding economic developments of the colony that were taking place in the Copperbelt. In 1928 Lusaka was still an outsized village inhabited by not more than 282 Europeans and 1,596 Africans but spread over an area of 36.25 km^2. In terms of urban achievement there was little to predestine the township to become the future capital - with one possible exception: the abundant use of space had given rise to extravagant facilities for sporting activities such as a race-course and a golf course on a 44.5 ha area less than 2 km east of the town centre on elevated, well-drained grounds.

2   The planning of the colonial city 1931-1945

The 1924 division of the colony into 'two Rhodesias' and the emergent Copperbelt industrialization in the north had put the old capital of Livingstone on the southern border in a remote position to govern the vast country. In 1929/30 it was decided to move the capital, and eight possible locations, including four Copperbelt towns, Broken Hill (Kabwe), and Chilanga, were considered. But it seems that the mining towns were ruled out from the very beginning by the Governor due to possible domination by the corporations. A committee appointed by the governor proposed the Lilayi-Lusaka area that met the defined selection criteria of centrality, access to communications, and avoidance of the copper mining district. Moreover, it was found that the proposed area fulfilled the essential requirements for adequate health standards and displayed favourable soil and water conditions (Lilly, 1982, p. 69). As there was some doubt about the last point, it was decided to bring in some external expertise. S. D. Adshead, a consultant and professor of town planning at London University, was brought to the country in 1930 to advise on the selection of the final site and to prepare a plan. Lusaka was finally proposed by Adshead in 1931, explaining

... that if it were not important that the site be a great city, but only a government centre, Lusaka offered all the facilities, but that in my opinion it would never become an important city, and for economic reasons it could only be a Government and Health Centre (Adshead, 1931, as quoted in Sampson, 1971, p. 55).

The land allocations and the layouts of the government quarter in Adshead's plan neatly fitted into the prevailing growth patterns described earlier. The selected location on Crown Land between 1 and 4 km east and southeast of the railway posed no serious problems in terms of physical development or land ownership. Situated on a sandstone ridge above flooding level in wooded surrounding, the area was attractive and made a good building ground. Due to its limited suitability as farmland, most of the area had not yet been sold and required little repossession. The major administrative and service buildings (Government House, the Government Centre, European Hospital, and army barracks) were planned along the ridge with designated native areas adjoining to the south on the lower-lying limestone susceptible to flooding (cf. Figure 9.2). Influenced by E. Howard's garden city movement in the UK, Adshead was anxious to avoid the grid-pattern layouts of other African colonial cities like Salisbury or Bulawayo but seems to have readily adopted the colonial perception of white urban supremacy. Working with unrealistic population projections of 8,000 Europeans and only 5,000 Africans, spatial layouts and densities of the planned capital were designed to spaciously accommodate a privileged European class in a garden-like surrounding, completely ignoring the needs of its grossly underestimated future African population (cf. Collins, 1969 and 1980). Although the garden city concept was no breach with the de facto prevailing space use in Lusaka, it nonetheless figures as a case of planning export in which colonial segregationist policies were ideologically palliated by European planning expertise. As Rakodi notes:

The original concept of a 'garden city' envisaged the creation of a balanced community, providing jobs, houses and facilities for the whole population within walking or cycling distance. In the case of Lusaka (Zambia), one or two components of Howard's idea (generous planting, organic rather than grid layouts) were lifted out of one context and utilized in another, to influence the planning of residential areas for only one section of the urban population: the Europeans (Rakodi, 1986b, p. 213).

Adshead's report, submitted in 1931, coincided with the economic depression, entailing uncertain prospects for the mining industry. With dwindling government funds the project had to be scaled down and was revised by the government town planner P. J. Bowling. In 1933 seven main land use zones were declared in a plan that never attained statutory force but was finally approved in 1938 by the governor as a 'Non-Statutory Development Plan'. Still only half complete, the capital was inaugurated in 1935. Various components remained in a state of partial implementation due to lack of revenue sources and governmental urban priorities. In particular the grossly overestimated growth of the European population confounded expectations that costs could be recouped from the sale of leases. According to estimates by Collins, by 1946 only 34 households were owner-occupiers. Consequently, most of the European housing area had to be developed at government cost with two-thirds of occupiers (mostly civil servants) living rent free or paying only nominal rents (Rakodi, 1986b, p. 207). Fulfilling Adshead's prophesy, the prewar commercial base of Lusaka proved too weak to make any substantial contribution to the capital's development (Rakodi, 1986b, p. 205). However, most of the plan's substance eventually did materialize, even if delayed to postcolonial times as the comparison between designated land use in 1933 and today's physical structures in Lusaka on the next page demonstrates (cf. also Figure 9.2 'The Bowling plan for the new capital').

Major infrastructural schemes built under the Bowling plan were the pump station and the water protection area south of the African housing area in Old Kabwata, the city airport, the Lusaka Club, a second golf club, the European hospital, and a technical school. To judge from his various planning proposals, Bowling was well aware that Adshead's garden city concept for the government quarter was imposing a space use on the town not in line with vital urban requirements and detrimental to the economic maintenance of urban services. The failure to relocate the commercial centres closer to the government area (i.e. the proposed business zones and the special shopping zone) and the abandoned plan to build a new railway line and station - which was obviously also to function as a 'contamination belt' between the African housing area in the south and the European residential and government areas - has created lasting problems of spatially disintegrated development between two physically separated centres. Designed to accommodate a population of not more than 125,000 in the 1952 town boundary (or 500,000 within today's boundaries), Lusaka's urban growth to a population of more than 1.2 million in 1995 has exceeded all foreseeable dimensions but has continued to expand along the original planning guidelines. Vast commuter problems and the need to 'weld together the present scattered development into a town with an urban character' (as stated in the 1952 Statutory

Plan) still stand out as the major challenges to contemporary urban planning. In particular, more appropriate urban planning would involve a reversal of the prevailing paradigm of space use (cf. Schmetzer, 1990, p. 2).

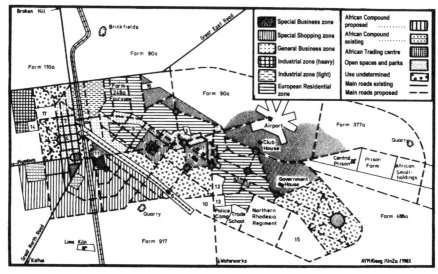

1. Central Government Offices; 2. Municipal Buildings Site 3. Car Park; 4. Post Office; 5. Existing Railway Station; 6. Proposed Railway Station; 7. Existing Market Square; 8. Water Tower; 9. European School Site; 10. Civil Training; 11. African Playing Fields; 12. European Hospital; 13. European Cemetery; 14. Abattoir; 15. Government Nursery; 16. Existing Cemetery; 17. Outspan

Figure 9.2   **The Bowling plan for the new capital (1933)**
Source: Williams, 1986

The history of the planning of Lusaka shows ... a recurring trend, namely that proposals which might have reduced the sprawl and increased the overall density always tend to be the ones deliberately omitted or quietly forgotten (Collins, 1986, p. 104).

There are three obvious sources of this planning legacy: the division of planning competencies and competition between urban authorities responsible, an inappropriate legal framework for urban development, and unrealistic settlement policies in the first 20 years of Lusaka's development as a capital town. In the first place, the government area was built on Crown Land under the direct disposal of central government for whatever use considered appropriate, and was, thus, for some years put beyond the control of the authorities of the old township. The government area, ostensibly named 'New Lusaka Township' (but called 'Snobs Hill' by Lusaka's established residents), came under the control of the Provincial Governor who was free to enact bye-laws and regulations regarding siting, zoning, and building codes.The non-statutory status of the plan added to the freedom to amend space use whenever necessary - as happened with designated residential areas later transformed into schools and a police camp, which enlarged even more the area with low density space use (Collins, 1986, p. 104).

Main character zones of the Bowling plan

Designated zones in 1933	Today's use
1. Special business zone, i.e. offices but no shops	Embassies, High Court, hotels, schools, offices, ministries
2. Special shopping zone to which commerce was to be moved from the old town centre closer to government quarters	Residential area built up after 1950. (Original plan abandoned due to lack of funds to compensate shop-owners)
3. Two general business zones including the old town and an extension to the east	Eastern part not developed; partially vacant/partially used as prime centre sites for parastatals, UNIP headquarters, and for inter-city bus terminal
4. A light industrial zone east of the railway	Utilized according to plan (i.e. government printers, mills, garages, bakeries)
5. A heavy industrial zone west of the old town	The nucleus of today's industrial area now expanded to the north and NW
6. European residential zones of three types	First and second class housing built for civil service. Third class housing not implemented and reassigned for public use
7. African government housing in Old Kabwata and Kamwala and small self-help site and service schemes in Maploto (Old Chilenje) and Chinika west of town centre. Chibolya was designated as reserve area.	Old Kabwata, Kamwala and Old and New Chilenje are low/ medium cost council housing areas; most of Chinika was transformed into an industrial zone, whereas Chibolya still remains an unauthorized housing area

Source: Compiled from Collins (1986, p. 102); Rakodi (1986b, p. 206), and author's observations 1988/89 and 1995

At the same time the old part of Lusaka fell under the 1929 Township Ordinance originally designed to manage the development of small rural-based communities. It gave only landowners franchise and the right to vote in the Board in accordance with the proportions of the land owned. Consequently, Lusaka's urban development became partially dictated by settler policies and their specific interests, and partially by the interests of the government civil service. An example of settler-dictated urban politics was the decision in 1935 to subdivide parcels of four hectare land and set them aside within the modern town boundaries (e.g. Kabulonga) for the expected settlers preferring the semi-rural type of homestead. This means that the old colonial space-use concept was extended to areas earmarked for future urban residence. But whatever interest dominated in the town's Management Board, it excluded its European and African urban residents (the latter being 'represented' by the District Commissioner). It was not until 1943 that the old township and the government areas were de facto amalgamated, and the capital put under the central administration of the Lusaka Management Board, thereby regaining some of its relative autonomy from central government (Sampson, 1971, p. 65).

3 Lusaka's postwar development and African urbanization under the stabilization policy 1946-1963

a) Town planning and economic development

Lacking a proper economic base, the 1931-46 phase of Lusaka's urban development as a colonial capital was dominated by government service and government housing, leading to neglect of the old part of the township. Its African population was dependent on the European demand for domestic service and for the most part resided on the employers' premises. However, the prosperous postwar period of 1946-56 occasioned economic growth and diversification, adding manufacturing and commerce to the government-service dominated occupational structure. In 1954 the town finally attained municipal status. The growth of Lusaka's European population (from 1,640 to 5,121 in 1946-1951 and to 13,300 in 1961), nonetheless, fell far behind projections of the 1952 development Plan that aspired to form Lusaka into a settler city on the Southern Rhodesian model. Instead it was the growth of the African population and its residential circumstances that were to make the most significant impact on the development of Lusaka in the pre-independence era (Collins, 1986, p. 133).

Although the colonial authorities placed Lusaka's postwar development on a new town planning scheme that was to incorporate African urbanization, the proposals put forward in the 1952 Statutory Development Plan were strangely out of tune with realized space needs. Assuming a near realistic ratio of 1:6 between Europeans and Africans, 22,000 Europeans were to be housed on 2,842 ha, including 11,184 on 1,333 ha low-density areas, 4,859 on 70 ha for multi-storey flats, and 5,876 on 1,439 ha outside the city boundary. Only 692 ha were designated for African housing that, at a density between 49 and 74 persons per ha, was to provide accommodation for 52,640. The recognized additional need of 1,446 ha to meet the full size of the African population-projection was in fact not allocated, thus practically *creating* the problem of unauthorized settlements at town planning level. As

Collins notes: '.. in short, the Europeans were to have their garden suburbs by simply ignoring 60% of the estimated future African population' (Collins, 1986, p. 113).

It seems that colonial town planners of this period were largely preoccupied with the revised completion of the original Adshead garden city plan and conceitedly considered the European sector as their core interest. Their failure to understand the implications of the ongoing African urbanization process for urban growth quickly resulted in conflicts between de facto African settlement and formal town planning provisions. Moreover, the garden city concept, entailing low-density residence in central urban areas and considerable urban sprawl, made Lusaka very vulnerable to unplanned, illegal settling as most 'vacant' property was government owned. In the course of these contradictions between planned and unplanned developments, town planning was in practice reduced to a series of ad hoc decisions - leaving the virtual physical and spatial formation of Lusaka to be determined by external factors and by the informal planning of African settlers. In particular Lusaka's urban structure was, thus, to become shaped by three factors:

1   The new legal status of Africans as urban residents, following the introduction of the Urban African Housing Ordinance in 1948 and its modifications made in 1957-63 to fit the new economic and labour market requirements of Lusaka.

2   The sheer magnitude of demographic growth and changes in the internal composition of its population by gender and race, adding a growing proportion of African women to Lusaka's population without access to formal job opportunities.

3   Growing economic and occupational disparities
     a) leading to a departure from the legal nexus between employment and housing, as municipal and employers' housing provision failed to keep pace with the demand of African residents in employment;
     b) leading to unemployment and income decline that enhanced demand for cheap housing and informal job opportunities in squatter areas.

Following the decisions to stabilize an African labour-force, major employment of Africans in Lusaka was in 1956/61 found in the occupational sectors shown in the table below. Census data from 1946-1961 did not record African unemployment or self-employment. Generally, however, the expansion of employment in the first postwar decade 1946-56 seems to have kept pace with demographic development. As economic recession came in the late 1950s, sample surveys in 1957 put self-employment at 8%, with the unemployment rate moving up to 7.5% (Collins, 1986, p. 119 and 124). The slump in construction work from 1956 to 1961 also reflects the loss of capital city functions to

Salisbury during the Federation period and the uncertain political future of Northern Rhodesia.

Table 9.1
African occupational structure in 1956 and 1961[*]

Main occupational fields	1956		1961	
	No.	Per cent	No.	Per cent
Services (including administ.)	3,919	17.5%	6,393	25.6%
Private domestic services	5,073	22.6%	5,450	21.9%
Construction	5,708	25.4%	3,681	14.7%
Manufacturing	2,985	13.3%	2,957	11.9%
Commerce & finance	2,088	9.3%	2,423	9.7 %
Agriculture & forestry	423	1.9%	1,890	7.6 %
Transport & communications	1,272	5.7%	1,564	6.3 %
Total (including mis.)	22,444		24,942	

[*] Data refers to the African population within the city boundary of 1970
Source: Collins, 1986, p. 119

b) African housing, unauthorized settlement, and labour relations

The first census of Lusaka's African population in 1946 counted 7,485 men and 59 women in wage-employment, not accounting for the approx. 19% unemployed. African population figures rose to totals of 77,328 in 1957 and to 114,672 in 1963 with employment of women remaining negligible (Collins, 1986, p. 107 and Williams, 1986c, p. 150). By 1963 the ratio of Africans to Europeans had increased to 8:1. Most of the newly built African housing of this period introduced the classical principles of the colonial city to Lusaka, now situating the newly planned native residential areas in clear separation from the European quarters. Complying with the Town Planning Scheme of 1952, major new municipal African residential areas were provided at the northeastern (Matero) and southwestern (Chilenje) ends of the town's already sprawling main urban axis. Minor municipal housing was built in Old Kabwata, Chibolya, and Kamwala, expanding the existing, more central African housing areas provided under the 1933 plan. In 1963 47% of Lusaka's African population was living in municipal townships, 22% in domestic quarters of employers, 10% in government or private compounds, and 21% in unauthorized settlements (Simons, 1979, p. 12).

Considering the allocation deficits of the 1952 Statutory Development Plan towards African residential areas, it is no surprise that squatter settlements remained a permanent feature in Lusaka's residential pattern. In 1957 the squatter population was estimated at 22,000, approximately 22% of the city's population (Martin, 1974, p. 74). It is noteworthy that this data does not signify a major change in the relative proportions of authorized and unauthorized housing compared to the situation in the final stage of circulatory labour migration: the earliest available systematic survey of 1944 stated that 19% of adult males (632) were already living unauthorized on Crown Land in the vicinity of municipalities or townships. Unfortunately no specific settlement names were given. This report also showed that 23% of the workforce were either self- or unemployed - once more conveying that loopholes in the nominally strict Ordinances concerning employment and housing of Africans were the rule in Lusaka (Eccles, 1944, quoted by Collins, 1986, p. 108).

Certainly amongst unauthorized settlements referred to in the 1944 report were Kalingalinga, and probably Kanyama (both chosen for our sample survey). In 1963 these two settlements had grown into the largest squatting areas in town with populations of 3,033 and 2,961 respectively. At that time both areas were situated just beyond the inner city boundary but had managed to evade the newly enforced pattern of allocating larger African settlements to even more remote peri-urban areas. This exception is explained by their specific topographic situation on a surfacing limestone plane with perennial waterlogging, officially considered ineligible for the regular planned town expansion. Other large unauthorized settlements of more than 2,000 inhabitants emerged in Marrapodi-Mandevu, adjoining the large peri-urban municipal housing area of Matero (Collins, 1986, p. 125).

Although efforts were made to house the entire African workforce according to the requirements of the Housing Ordinance, the provision of municipal housing fell far behind demand. Since housing legislation had been designed with the big mining companies in mind, deficits were particularly pronounced in employers' housing. Only a few of Lusaka's private employers had more than 25 employees, making them compulsorily required to build company housing for their employees. The housing requirements of the now stabilized African workforce also no longer fitted into the old concept that had provided them with cheap accommodation in single-roomed bachelors' quarters. From the very beginning of the migration wave to Lusaka in the 1950s the sex ratio of the African population was fairly balanced (1950: 1.35 men to 1 woman, 1963: 1.27 to 1). Family accommodation, coming in high demand (52% of Lusaka's African population in 1963 were 21 and younger), was largely left unserviced by official housing provision. Under these pressures and as a means to relax the obligatory housing provision for employees, an amendment to the Housing Ordinance in 1957 approved the payment of a housing allowance by the employer as an alternative to the old arrangement.

> This enabled an employer to opt out of his obligation to provide rent-free housing or pay their Council rents for them. Instead, subject to the approval of the Commissioner for Labour, he was now allowed to pay a cash allowance in addition to the nominal wage, leaving his employee the responsibility for housing himself. In

the long run this tended to increase the number of people looking for a type of housing available only in unauthorized compounds (Collins, 1986, p. 124).

Inevitably, housing allowances became a major incentive for the development of a low-cost housing market in unauthorized housing areas. In particular, newly growing squatter areas of the late 1950s, like Old Kanyama, are known to have specialized in the provision of cheap rental accommodation. The concomitant of this policy would be that established house owners in squatter areas would not encourage the erection of new dwellings by newcomers in their settlement. Instead they would channel housing demand into existing accommodation or that provided by enlargements of existing houses. Although only very little data is available showing the extent of rental arrangements in other squatter settlements in these years, there are some general indications to support the proposition of a growing unauthorized housing market in the form of expanded subletting and not of new house building. The total housing stock of unauthorized housing areas in the 1957-63 period declined from 4,821 to 4,486, whereas its population increased from 16,381 to 18,731 (Rakodi, 1986b, p. 209 and 211). Assuming that the statistical data is correct, this leaves two conclusions. Despite a growing demand for unauthorized housing, no new dwelling units were built while the occupancy rates per dwelling increased from 3.4 in 1957 to 4.2 in 1963 (+23.5%). Even taking the natural birth rate into consideration, this data probably signifies a growing propensity of house owners to rent out parts of their dwellings to service the demand fuelled by housing allowances. However, a similar densification effect was also observable in the official low-cost rented housing where the deficits in new housing provision and the policy of infilling led to an increase in occupancy rates from 4.26 to 5.29 (+24.1%) in the same period.

In conclusion, the expansion of unauthorized housing areas in the late 1950s cannot be explained as a mistake of planning. As in the 1930 Copperbelt case, the official laissez faire attitude towards squatter development met the various changing needs of the growing colonial urban economy. It also reflected the inability of the colonial administration to either control the African urbanization process or provide adequate means of sustenance in rural areas in order to slow down migration. This kind of housing and settlement policy had direct economic benefits. For *employers*, wage levels could be maintained at bachelors' rates, forcing families to live at income levels below the poverty line (Bettison, 1959). Under these terms an urban standby labour reserve could only be sustained through the existence and official toleration of squatter settlements rendering informal work opportunities.

For the *urban administration*, the toleration of these settlements was a cost-saving exercise as no urban infrastructure was built and housing was provided by the self-help of residents. With the permission of the landowners and paying rent, dwellers could build rural style housing according to their needs on vacant, unserviced land (van den Berg, 1986, p. 303). This solution to the housing problem proved particularly indispensable in the late 1950s when, with the relaxation of influx control, migration rates moved up from 6.8% in 1957 to 14.0% in 1963 - but was confronted with near stagnation in the employment situation and the suspension of African housing provision (Williams, 1986b, p. 150 and Collins, 1986, p. 119). While the population increased from 1957 to 1963 by 48%, the number of dwelling units only grew by 29%, raising the average occupancy rates from 3.8 persons per dwelling to 5.7 (Rakodi, 1986b, p. 211). With growing organized opposition to the colonial regime and the Federation, political control of Africans was also becoming difficult. Lusaka had been the site of various strikes and demonstrations against the colour bar and other forms of discrimination. In this sense the official attitude of disregarding squatter populations was a loophole to the enforcement of colonial laws requiring the repatriation of unemployed men to their rural homes. The division of responsibilities in the greater Lusaka area between the urban council and rural authorities worked in the same way, as most of the peri-urban squatter settlements were outside the town boundaries and beyond the jurisdiction of the Lusaka authorities. Vagrancy laws, however, were imposed to some extent on 'solitary' children and 'unattached' women, particularly if illegal beer brewing was involved with the latter (Hansen, 1982, p. 123). Pass laws and other restrictions on freedom of movement and of residence (e.g. the prevention of ethnic clustering) were nonetheless in full effect in the official African residential areas, adding to the attraction of illegal settlements.

Picture 9.1   **Rural-style housing from Eastern Province typical for Lusaka townships in the 1950s**

For the *Africans,* unauthorized settlement areas performed versatile functions for urbanization outside the restrictive formal structures. For the newly arriving migrants they were the entry gate to town; a place where accommodation could be found with the help of tribal relations, and where houses could be built quickly in traditional rural style (cf. Picture 9.1). For those laid off work - meaning loss of accommodation - illegal housing and settlement were a refuge that also provided access to informal work opportunities for survival. For the retired, living in a township was the only alternative to the return to rural home areas as stipulated by the Town Ordinance. In 1963 this group accounted for 1%

of Lusaka's African urban population. But for many impoverished families, residence in these areas became a permanent arrangement, as surveys conducted in the late 1960s and early 1970s have shown. On average, squatter residents had spent one-fifth of their life in town (Martin, 1974, p. 74).

Except for African markets, information about the dimensions and circumstances of informal activities pursued during the 1950s and '60s is vague. Marketeering was performed predominantly by men, but considered by them as a transitory activity between periods of wage-employment. A survey in 1954 recorded two recognized markets in Luburma and Matero with 143 and 130 traders respectively. 'Bush markets' existed in Matero, Mandevu and near Kamala. Fish was the most important trade article, followed by bread and vegetables (the latter bought from nearby farms). Informal activities quickly diversified as service and crafts entered the markets by 1959 (Todd/Mulenga/Mupimpila, 1979, p. 49). As a study of the case of religious groups rejecting wage-labour exemplifies, in Marrapodi/ Mandevu tin-smithing, basketmaking and carpentry works were self-sustaining activities providing livelihood outside formal labour relations (Hansen, 1982, p. 124).

Under the official toleration of women's presence by urban authorities, but without giving them access to jobs in the formal sector, it would have seemed a natural development that women would gradually replace men as domestic servants. However, despite official encouragement, women were reluctant to accept this role as it meant absence from home and children and loss of their traditionally esteemed autonomy. Instead women, aspiring to have their own income and to make an independent contribution to family sustainment, readily engaged in the informal trading sector as a permanent occupation. The proportion of women traders, mostly starting in their husbands' business, increased from 20% in 1954 to 29% in 1959 (to become the majority in post-independence days). Activities were mainly the sale of cooked food, fruit and vegetables on local markets and road stands. Illegal beer brewing became a domain of the much-pursued single women who violated the beer monopoly held by local authorities in legal townships. Prostitution is another source of income for single women who are widely excluded from work opportunities by a gender-biased economic system (Hansen, 1987, p. 13 and 1982, p. 124). In utilizing abundant open spaces provided by the garden city concept of Lusaka, house plot gardening (mainly maize, sweet potatoes, pumpkins, and groundnuts) was another frequently employed women's practice to secure urban subsistence, particularly with low-income families. Illegal distant gardening on vacant land was also practised but was constantly in jeopardy as authorities razed maize cultivations then incorrectly regarded as a breeding place for mosquitoes (Jaeger/Huckabay, 1986, p. 269).

X The political and economic determinants of housing provision in post-independence Zambia

Bearing in mind that under the colonial regime the residential circumstances of Africans were perceived as an integral part of the racist and segregationist system, it was inevitable that high expectations were raised by the housing policies of the independent national government. But the abolition of colonial restrictions on freedom of movement and place of residence by the new Zambian constitution was not complemented by indiscriminate provision or access to housing. Contrary to the promises of the ruling United National Independence Party (UNIP) to provide housing for everybody, the inequalities of state housing provision in fact quickly became one of the most pronounced manifestations of emerging class divisions among Zambians.

In contrast to theoretical postulations regarding the production, consumption and exchange of housing entirely through the mechanisms of the market, capitalist principles have not played a decisive role in the Zambian system of state-dominated housing provision.[1] Instead, the issue of housing became part of the complex process of postcolonial class formation, largely replicating or imitating colonial patterns of social differentiation. The inevitable result was to revive the colonial institutionalized social and political means to reproduce these structures. The close ties between the emerging mechanisms of social differentiation and the formation of power elites within the state apparatus will be one strand in explaining low political commitment to the declared housing policy aims. The second no less important strand will be to show how colonial urban policies could survive due to the failure of decolonizing administrative structures and institutions. To a large extent colonial planning offices were simply instrumentalized by their Zambian appointees according to the new political directives.

Much also suggests that Zambian politicians and administrators shared the social perception of their colonial predecessors in office. An example is given by Simons (1979) with reference to the Chona Commission's Report of 1972 on the Constitution. Various Zambian experts giving evidence in the hearings openly adhered to the former colonial perception of rural migrants. These were claimed to represent an unstable element in urban settlement and were held responsible for high crime rates and unemployment. Looking for remedies, the Commission even seem to have considered the reinstallation of 'native influx control' policies. Opinions were voiced that unemployed urban residents should be repatriated to their home areas and migration be forestalled through move-permits required from the local chiefs. Although in the end it was felt that outright restriction of movement would infringe constitutional rights, the Commission approved of measures to repatriate 'illegal' immigrants and to abolish 'illegal' settlements in squatter compounds (Simons, 1979, p. 14).

These are clear indications that after the breach with colonialism Zambia's reputed antisegregationist foreign policy was not complemented by a movement towards an egalitarian society, as proposed by the official philosophy of Zambian Humanism by President Kaunda (cf. Kaunda, 1974, p. xiii). Instead, colonially established social structures were used by the new ruling elites as reinforcement of their own political and socioeconomic interests. As Zambian observers noted in the early 1970s, segregation continued between races and among Zambians and was encouraged rather than counteracted by government town planning and housing policies. The pattern of residential zoning was found to be reproduced all over the country in newly built, ill-serviced compounds, juxtaposed with privileged housing provision for top civil servants and political elites (Knauder, 1982, p. 2). Thus, as Simons concludes:

> Colonial capitalism became Zambian capitalism; racial inequalities became class inequalities; and segregatory arrangements persisted in the distinction between high and low density residential areas (Simons, 1979, p. 14).

In the initial design of this study my intention was to concentrate on local aspects of squatter settlement, i.e. on policies of the Lusaka Urban District Council (LUDC) and on the situation at settlement level itself. My post festum impression is that an analysis of the devolution of municipal policies and the approaches to squatter settlement would be inadequate without a detailed assessment of the part played by central government and its associated political structures in local policy decisions. The main thesis is that all major urban developments in Lusaka (or rejection of 'necessary' developments) were not the outcome of professional planning decisions, tempered by the restrictions of available resources. Instead they directly or indirectly reflected vested political and economic interests on the part of central government, UNIP, or the local political system.[2] Accordingly, part of this chapter will address the national alignment of state and party powers and the related political decision-making structures under conditions of dependent capitalist development in Zambia.

Although postcolonial housing policies and planning practices in Zambia tend to be predetermined by the biases of the socio-political system, the devolution of concrete policies would only be inadequately understood without an account of the restrictions imposed by the *physical and statutory side* of the colonial legacy. The 'inherited' ensemble of infrastructure, urban facility provisions, land-use and legal tenure arrangements, planning legislation, manpower resources, etc. are all vital antecedents to the formation of national urban development policies. An assessment of the situation in the first decade after independence will be given in the first part of this chapter, providing the necessary background information required to understand incipient urban politics.

1   The colonial legacy in planning and urban development

The impact of the colonial legacy largely predetermines the first decade of postcolonial housing and town planning and imposed considerable restrictions to policy options. The situation in 1965 was such that there was arguably no other initial choice but to go on with the established colonial approaches and adapt them to the immediate requirements of nationalization. The relevant professional staff in councils were exclusively expatriates. Out of 135 architects and planners in Zambia only 2 were Zambians; only 1 out of 277 civil engineers was a national. The construction sector was monopolized by non-Zambians with only one Zambian-owned firm eligible for contracts registered with the Public Works Department. In the field of artisans, the colour bar had effectively ruled out Zambians from attaining qualified skills under apprenticeship schemes (Rakodi, 1986b, p. 215).

The transformation of colonial legislation and structures of possession became a particularly intricate aspect of town planning and planning legislation. The country largely adopted the British legal system, but various provisions proved misplaced in the Zambian context, creating overlapping or even contradictory jurisdiction (Rakodi, 1988a, p. 33). For example, most of the squatters considered 'illegal' under the 1974 Statutory and Improvement Areas Act have attained outright residence according to the provisions of the Town and Country Planning Act Cap. 475.[3] Since the change in the voters' constituency from the place of origin to the place of residence in 1975, they also reside in legally recognized constituencies under the Electoral Act (CDG/GRZ, 1989, p. 12).

The 1965 Local Government Act imposed ill-defined legislative, administrative, and functional divisions between councils and the provincial governments. The perhaps most striking case applies to the administration of the peri-urban areas. These areas had attained a specific status coming neither under the jurisdiction of the municipal councils nor under that of the adjoining rural councils. Due to this anomaly in the Local Government Act, the status of peri-urban areas - accommodating most squatters - remained undefined and fell under the direct administration of provincial governments. Although these were entitled to collect levy, by legal provisions they did not render any kind of service. In greater Lusaka this situation was the source of considerable conflicts between the Urban Council and the Provincial Government over squatter policies. Whereas the Lusaka Council was mildly sympathetic towards squatters, the District Commissioner became notorious for the repressive actions of his Squatting Control Unit. This dispute was finally resolved in 1970 by the decision to extend all city boundaries to include peri-urban areas (Rakodi, 1988a, p. 33).

The new constitutional provisions towards land ownership also proved incompatible with fundamental requirements of local urban development planning and land use. In the balance of interests between the constitutional recognition of private property rights and the legal requirements of town planning, preeminence was given in 1965 to the interests of landowners who had acquired their property titles under the colonial freehold or tenure system. Under these legal provisions, vast parts of Lusaka's urban space remained under the control of European and Asian landowners - quite often in the form of absentee landlordism. This situation encouraged excessive land speculation, including by Zambian businessmen. The definition of landed property as a freely transferable market commodity also became a major constraint to urban planning, confronting councils with prohibitive price increases on prime sites and in prospective development areas (Kajoba, 1986, p. 310). The only exception from this land ownership structure applied to areas that were former Crown Land (e.g. the government district in Lusaka), which were put under direct government control.

Transformation of colonial law into appropriate legislation not only involved dealings with inherited formal property rights. It also had to address the problem of traditional legal systems. Under the town and country planning legislation, not more than 78 nationals in Zambia were in 1964 the legal proprietors of their houses (Simons, 1980, p. 16). However, many urban settlers claimed right of residence and right to land under the traditional system of usufruct. This customary law gives a person the right to occupy and to use land in the home area of his mother, father or more remote ancestors. Outside home areas, the right to use communally held land can be conferred by local headmen or other responsible authorities (Simons, 1979, p. 16). Accordingly, squatting was generally not considered by dwellers to be an illegal practice. Conflicts between claims to land under the customary tenure system and claims of private landowners to their unutilized land under the modern Zambian legislation were common and added to the mounting problems of early postcolonial urban development.

A principal solution to these opposing interests finally came with the 1970 Land Acquisition and the 1975 Land Conversion Acts. Both were designed to combat land speculation and to redefine land legislation according to the requirements of town planning: the provisions of the Act included the compulsory state acquisition of any land of public interest, the general prohibition of real estate, the abolition of freeholds, and the appropriation of vacant or unutilized land by the state or the local authorities.[4] Nevertheless, legal procedures of land acquisition and land-delivery by the council remained an intricate and time-consuming process, particularly when mixed forms of state- and privately-owned land occurred, involving compensation for the former private owners (Pasteur, 1979, p. 78). This situation applied to most of the squatting areas in Lusaka. For example, a large number of plots allocated in the World Bank's major upgrading and resettlement project in the 1970s were still overdue for legalization in the mid-1980s (LUDC, 1987).

Under revised land-use and planning legislation, policies towards squatters gradually began to diversify in line with the new national priorities formulated in the Second National Development Plan (SNDP) of 1972. The plan recognized that squatting areas represented assets in both social and financial terms and required planning and services. It also noted that the demolition of 'good and bad houses alike' was not a practical solution (GRZ, 1972, p. 148). Under these new political directives, land claims under the customary law were, as a rule, acknowledged in areas controlled by the Lusaka Urban Council. Whereas evictions were a regular policy in the peri-urban areas under the jurisdiction of the Provincial Government until 1970, settlement clearances by the Lusaka Council stopped by 1972 (Van Velsen, 1972). For the next 20 years the Lusaka authorities tended to tolerate settlement under the customary law if it did not conflict with public interests and land-use plans. The first breach with this policy appeared with the new government of 1991 taking action to stop the encroachment of squatter settlement on Lusaka's central business area. In Kanyama 100 dwellings were demolished, but planned further proceedings were stopped by the President after massive political protest. However, with squatter areas developed under the Housing and Statutory Act of 1974, the Lusaka Council has been prepared to transform usufruct into occupancy rights. But as the frequent and continuing evictions in other towns in Zambia show, there is still a considerable amount of political arbitrariness whenever conflicts arise over illegal settlement.[5] This in effect shows that residence founded on customary law has not received an official legal status within Zambian jurisdiction.

2 Development planning and housing provision

Most fundamentally for the urban space use and housing provision system in Lusaka, the major town planning guidelines from colonial times were not revised but instead adopted by the Zambian authorities in satisfying the growing demand for housing. With the exodus of colonial civil servants, vacant high-cost, spacious housing with garden surrounding was allocated to politicians and Zambian civil servants. Accordingly, this type of accommodation came to be regarded as appropriate by the new national elites. These housing standards, involving a high content of imported building materials and sophisticated building techniques, were also adopted for the high and medium-cost housing programmes for the growing numbers of employees in government and councils. This housing stock was financed by grants from the central government. Following the colonial tradition of 'tied' housing, provision at subsidized rent rates was retained as part of the job arrangement by government and councils (Sanyal, 1981, p. 414). Rents were fixed at rates in the range of 6 to 10% of basic salaries, i.e. well below economic costs. This practice also applied to the staff members of the growing parastatal sector, whereas private employers, excepting the mining companies, discontinued housing provision for their low-income workers by the early 1970s (Collins, 1970).

Despite the officially heralded policy of general housing provision for all enfranchised urban residents, political commitment to the housing needs of low-income groups remained low, even at times of large budgets fuelled by copper exports. Although these favourable conditions applied at least until the early 1970s for the first and second development plans, target investments in low-cost housing not only failed to keep step with the unprecedented migration rates from rural areas. The performance of the first 1965 Transitional Development Plan, which allocated more than 50% of the government's housing budget to civil service housing, already displayed a distinct bias against the provision of low-income housing.

This characterization became a permanent feature in Zambian development planning in this specific sector (Sanyal, 1981, p. 415; Kasongo/Tipple, 1990, p. 157). Although development plans regularly assigned nominal priority to low-cost housing, de facto budget expenditures have invariably privileged the provision of high- and medium-cost housing through state budgets. In order to serve the housing demands of civil servants and government employees, overspending on institutional housing and substantial deductions from the nominal plan allocations to low-income housing have become the routine. Obviously complying with the political significance attached to discriminatory housing provision, disproportions have steadily increased despite the awareness of growing problems with unauthorized urban settlements. In its appraisal of the Second and Third National Development Plans (SNDP and TNDP), the ILO Basic Needs Mission to Zambia found a 'disconcerting' performance with respect to the basic needs provision of low-cost housing in the SNDP-period:

> During the SNDP and in spite of the priority accorded to squatter upgrading, two-thirds of housing investment went to the development of formal sector dwellings - largely medium-and high-cost houses (ILO, 1981, p. 107).

According to the latest figures made available by the Fourth National Development Plan (FNDP), the declining economic situation of the country seems to have further increased the discrepancy between target budgets and actual achievements in low-cost housing. Government sectoral performance of housing was such that the envisaged 90.3% of expenditure dedicated to low- and very low-cost housing in the 1985-86 plan period (including institutional costs) was in reality downgraded to a mere 25.3%. Using the income categories proposed by this plan, this implies that 74.7% of government's housing finance went into medium- and high-cost housing, serving only the 3.6% of the total population that make up the country's middle and high income groups (cf. GRZ (FNDP), 1989, p. 287 and 293).

These outlined political priorities in national housing provision are reflected in Lusaka's urban development in the first development decade: Table 10.1 shows a near 500% increase in the high- and medium-cost housing stock from 1964 to 1973 while official low-cost housing provision became near stagnant. Site and service schemes were introduced by the city council as a cheaper alternative in various smaller squatter settlement areas of Lusaka. Following problems of residents' acceptance and debates on the appropriateness of standards (deemed too low by central government), these schemes did not mature into a generally accepted solution to the housing problem (Rakodi, 1986c, p. 192). Thus, implementation remained half-hearted and did not contribute substantially to satisfying the growing housing demand. With annual migration rates soaring up to 13.4% in the 1963-69 period and only slackening to a rate of 9.9% from 1969 to 1974 (Rakodi, 1981, p. 58), Lusaka's population increased from 149,628 in 1965 to 429,569 in 1975 (Williams, 1986c, p. 150).

Table 10.1
Development of the housing stock in Lusaka 1964/1973

Type of housing	1964		1973		1964-73
	Number	%	Number	%	Increase
High and medium cost	2.215	10.4%	11.019	16.6%	+497%
Official low-cost	10.347	48.5%	16.938	25.6%	+63%
Squatting	7.500	41.1%	26.322	39.7%	+351%
Site and service	-	-	5.400	8.1%	-
Self-help plots	-	-	1.265	1.9%	-
Servants' quarters	n.a.	-	5.350	8.1%	-
Total		100%		100%	

Data compiled from Rakodi, 1986a, p. 196

According to a study by Ohadike, approximately 80% of migrants surveyed in 1968-69 were absorbed by the official high density and unauthorized housing areas (Ohadike, 1981, p. 61). With council low-cost housing capacities depleted by the end of the decade, squatting increasingly became the primary means of access to affordable housing. By 1974 squatter housing accounted for 61% of all new urban dwellings (Knauder, 1982, p. 16). It is important to note that these divisions between formal and informal housing only marginally reflect the occupational division between formal and informal workers. Squatter settlements did not only house the newly arriving, temporary unemployed rural migrants: these settlements overwhelmingly housed the city's formal labour-force of skilled and unskilled manual workers. Moreover, as Ohadike's sample survey of more than 20,000 Lusaka residents revealed for the first time, the residents in unauthorized housing areas also comprised 4.9% of technical and administrative professionals, 3.8% of clerical workers and teachers, and 4.6% of residents occupied in trading (Ohadike, 1981, p. 78). Various township case studies carried out in the early and mid-1970s confirmed these general residential and occupational patterns as typical features of unauthorized housing (cf. summary of findings in Todd/Shaw, undated).

By the end of the 1960s, the municipal authorities realized that Lusaka's urban structures needed reconsideration to solve basic planning problems. With the extension of the city boundaries enacted in 1970, the peri-urban belt was incorporated into the Lusaka municipal area. In conjunction with other expansions, this increased Lusaka's built-up area from 32.63 km^2 in 1965 to 72.63 km^2 in 1975. Despite considerable population growth, predominantly in high density housing areas, urban densities had only risen modestly from 4,586 to 5,914 pop/km^2. This is explained by the counterbalancing effect of the colonial-style space use maintained in new high- and medium cost housing areas. As a side effect of this development pattern, a growing accentuation of spatial division became apparent between the highly centralized commercial and the industrial areas, on the one hand, and the sprawling residential areas on the other hand. In the late 1960s this problem came to be regarded as the most pressing for Lusaka's future urban development (Williams, 1986c, p. 150). Considerable resources of the SNDP housing budget, which might have been better used to build up indigenous planning capacities, were used by the Ministry of Local Government and Housing to commission the international consultancy *Doxiadis Associates* to draw up a comprehensive master plan for Lusaka. The proposals that came out of a ten-year study of Lusaka in 1968-78 are a classical example of First World-biased planning export.

The Doxiadis plan assumptions were moulded around the perspectives of an industrialized type of development based on ample financial resources from copper exports. In disregard of cost factors (that give Lusaka its present topography developing *away* from the difficult to service geological terrains), the plan conversely proposed a north-south linear growth pattern following the railway line. Main new extensions were to be directed southwards as far as Chilanga and some 10 km westwards. The proposed compact urbanization belt was intended to give Lusaka a 'shape and form suited to dynamic growth' and to bring new residential areas closer to the commercial and industrial centre. Under the projection that by the year 2000 nearly every second resident of Lusaka would have a car (!), a gridiron network of high-speed roads was proposed, giving provision for private vehicles priority over public transport (Williams, 1986c, p. 150). This plan was, however, never officially enacted and has become obsolete since the country's financial resources declined dramatically in the late 1970s. Informally it still seems to serve as a space use plan insofar as it coincides with the prevailing growth pattern that continues to expand in eastern and northern directions (cf. Schmetzer, 1990).

Another obstacle preventing the implementation of the Doxiadis plan came out of the experiences of an early attempt to relocate squatter populations in accordance with the proposed new urban structure. The failure of this reallocation scheme seems to have had a considerable impact on the government's perception of feasible squatter policies: to enable the proposed developments to the south and to the west, which would have given Lusaka a more symmetrically-disposed urban centre, it was understood that substantial resettlement of squatters living in these areas (e.g. Kanyama, Chawama) was required. In line with policies of central government to resettle all of Lusaka's squatters on serviced plots, it was agreed to select four sites, all outside the 1963 city boundary - then still coming under the jurisdiction of the Ministry of Local Government. 16,000 squatter families were to be relocated within one year.

Implementation began in 1970 at Kaunda Square, approx. 9 km northwest of the city centre and 11 km from the industrial area. But events soon exposed the inappropriateness of the Doxiadis concept. For cost reasons the plot size (9 x 18.3 m) was considerably smaller than the council standard of 12 x 27 m that complied with desired residents' space-use. Only 15% of houses were to have road access. Apart from these space-related problems of acceptability, the scheme was mainly rejected by its potential target group due to its remoteness from employment and reasonable markets - both exclusively to be found in Lusaka's centre. Lack of adequate public transportation and rising costs aggravated the problem of acceptance by low-income groups (Rakodi, 1986a, p. 194). Despite a waiting list of more than 28,000 applicants for low-cost council housing, by 1973 only 57% of plots had been allocated and 753 out of 1,977 planned houses had been built. After responsibility for the area was transferred to the Lusaka Urban Council in late 1970, Kaunda Square Stage II was implemented with standards revised to council specifications concerning plot size and improved road access. But these improved standards seem to have only insignificantly raised the acceptability of the scheme, with remoteness of location remaining the main problem. Following very similar discouraging experiences in Mutendere, the second of the selected relocation sites, the remaining resettlement schemes devised under the Doxiadis concept were never implemented.

By then the government was coming under growing pressure to find a solution to the problem of unauthorized settlements. Authorities began to realize that high growth rates were a permanent and irreversible feature of urban development. Migration could neither be deterred through repressive influx control measures, nor were migrants discouraged by the poor living conditions offered in Lusaka's illegal settlements. With the authorities' recognition of the political and social infeasibility of the Doxiadis plan to *export* Lusaka's squatters to locations on the urban periphery, policy became paralysed in the early 1970s. Opinions on the course of action were divided between different ministries, high and low rank party levels, consultants, and professionals. An interim solution was the establishment of the National Housing Authority (NHA) by an Act of Parliament in 1971, intended to 'spearhead a rethinking of housing policy' (Martin, 1982, p. 255). Still, no decisive action was taken until the end of 1972. The fact that in 1973/74 the Zambian Government finally came forward with a plan to legalize and service two-thirds of Lusaka's squatter populations with the help of the World Bank should not lead to precipitate conclusions (1) concerning the nature of the intermediate political developments in which the pro-squatter lobby appeared to have come out triumphant and (2) with respect to the seemingly fundamental change in attitudes towards a positive recognition of squatters' dwelling rights on the part of municipal and national planning authorities.

Richard Martin, an architect actively involved in the decision-making process (and later deputy director of the World Bank Housing Project Unit), has given a detailed account of the debate between the pro- and the anti-squatter lobbies (cf. Martin, 1982, p. 254): public opinion, shared by many politicians and civil servants, saw squatter settlements as refuges of foreigners, criminals, and unemployed layabouts who were parasites on society and ought best to be repatriated to their home areas. Expatriate experts like the Doxiadis consultants continued to advocate the necessity of resettlement and strongly advised against providing facilities to squatter areas that would mean holding on to 'bad organization' and surely end in 'chaos and anarchy'. A similar verdict was given by the UN Senior Local Government Advisor in his 1967 report on the national housing policy in Zambia. To provide services to existing squatter areas would be 'costly, and indeed impracticable' (Rowland, 1967, p. 41). Moreover, it was feared that squatter programmes would inevitably lower the prevailing housing standards and perpetuate their slum character. However substantial these arguments might have appeared, related policies had a serious imperfection: with squatters simply refusing to move to alternative sites, these solutions would have meant demolition and eviction by force - an option feared by city councillors due to the political repercussions involved (Seymour, 1975, p. 73).

The pro-squatting lobby had gradually formed in Lusaka at the end of the 1960s, spurred by various feasibility studies on site and service schemes sponsored by the Department of Community Development and the Ministry of Local Government and Housing. The official character of these studies seems to have greatly supported policy-making and caused a gradual change in attitudes towards squatters. Empirical investigations by Rakodi in Mwaziona (now George) revealed that 90% of its inhabitants were in employment, overwhelmingly (i.e. 83%) in the formal sector (GRZ, 1973). These findings were confirmed for most other unauthorized areas, e.g. for Chawama by the various influential writings of R. Martin (cf. Martin, 1969; 1974 and 1976; also Boswell, 1969; 1975a, b and c), for Kalingalinga (Zelter/Witola, 1967), and for George (Ludgren/T. Schlyter, 1969). The picture established showed that, contrary to prejudiced belief, these settlements were neither provisional nor unplanned, nor did their populations lack the will to improve their living and housing conditions. Spatial arrangements and building procedures in the settlements were highly organized, reflecting people's needs and priorities in the given situation. They included locational aspects such as proximity to work and the building up of local self-help and solidarity networks. Besides, most of the population participated in the UNIP local party structure established in their settlements.

Even in poverty areas such as Kalingalinga with a lower rate of formal labour, people were found to contribute to Lusaka's informal economy by utilizing vacant plots around town for 'distant gardening' (Schlyter/Schlyter, 1979). Products (maize, vegetables, fruits, etc.) were partially self-consumed or were offered on street-markets (Martin, 1972; van den Berg, 1982; Jaeger/Huckabay, 1986).

Importantly, these studies ascertained that incomes were high enough to sustain improvements in housing and to pay for municipal services if the Council decided to provide them. All this led to the conclusion that low standards of housing in unauthorized settlements reflected an *insecure tenement situation* and given disparities in state housing and infrastructural provision at that time, rather than lack of will to integrate socially and economically on the part of their inhabitants. The question was, therefore, not one of necessary resettlement, but of finding adequate forms and policies for integrating the existing sites into the framework of Lusaka's town planning, and of devising ways of making use of dwellers' self-help potentials and resources in the improvement of services and living conditions. Consequently, it was suggested that upgrading, possibly with a self-help component, was a feasible and much cheaper alternative to the officially favoured site and service concept.

In 1970 a non-governmental pressure group called SAIL (Social Action in Lusaka) engaged in various activities (cf. Gumede/Shumba, 1976): a press campaign was staged, and various responsible authorities were lobbied in support of upgrading; a 'house building advice office' was opened for dwellers in George, and the group aimed to establish a demonstration project. This scheme was, however, only partially realized due to the reluctance of the urban council to cooperate in 'illegal' settlement affairs (Martin, 1982, p. 257).

The breakthrough came with the SNDP recognition of squatter settlements as 'social and financial assets' and the government's granting of funds for a limited squatter upgrading programme (K7.5 million out of a total allocation of K150 million for housing). But as shown earlier, budget plan allocations are only very unreliable indicators of the real political intentions and priorities. And without disregarding the combined efforts of the pro-squatter lobby to persuade government into an upgrading project, much indicates that it would not have been decided or accomplished in the way it was without considerable extra-functional significance attached to the various aspects involved in its realization. These extra-functional aspects are to be found in the exigencies of the following:

- In an economy moving towards a system of state capitalism, national development planning required an amendment of housing policies that were no longer to rest alone on provision by the government. The new policies were to include the promotion of home ownership, modifications of the housing allowance system, the introduction of cost-recovery principles, and the abolition of subsidies for low-cost housing.

- With the Party crisis at that time and UNIP's strive to rouse popular support for its single-party political system, the squatter areas were still largely controlled by the ANC opposition. This was parallelled by the formation of local interests in squatter settlements with respect to land tenure and the new significance of squatters for the electoral system (i.e. for councillors, members of parliament and Party representatives) after the enfranchisement of peri-urban settlements in 1970.

- The requirements of stabilizing Lusaka's urban development had become pressing after the failure of squatter containment policies, and there was a need to extend the control over these areas with respect to building and health regulations.

- There was an emerging influence of the IMF and World Bank on Zambian fiscal policies that coincided with specific interests of the Bank in implementing a large low-cost housing project designed to fulfil specific experimental requirements with model character for its replication in other Third World countries (e.g. affordable and acceptable standards, cost-recovery, and participation).

A deeper exploration of each set of interests involved in the Lusaka project will show that the joint action failed to come together into a stable policy framework for future squatter development. In fact many of the actors involved represented de facto countercurrent interests to such an extent that the accomplishment of the project comes close to being a 'historical coincidence' born out of a short-term convergence of interests - but without the chance of ever repeating itself to solve the contemporary squatter situation. Under these conditions the reasonably successful accomplishment of the upgrading project must be credited to the World Bank whose implementing momentum (and financial resources) simply supplanted crumbling national support. As to the terms of implementation, Martin's competent verdict is illuminating:

> In this process it is possible to state with hindsight that the intervention of the World Bank facilitated the adoption of a solution far more radical than would have been likely with normal government and local authority mechanisms. In addition the Bank's insistence upon the establishment of strict time schedules and on solutions that the residents could afford ... introduced a rationale in policy-making and standard-setting that had not featured strongly in government thinking before (Martin, 1982, p. 258).

3 The political and economic background to revised squatter policies in the 1970s

Drawing on the abundant revenues from its copper mining industry, Zambia undertook considerable efforts to reconstruct its postcolonial economy into an independent, modern industrial society. But from the outset, national policies to this end were seriously impaired by intricate structures of dependency and international pressures deeply penetrating the process of internal state class formation. In particular, the country's landlocked geopolitical situation, its regional dependency on the South African economy, extensive foreign investments, and its continuous reliance on export production for the world market, proved insuperable barriers to policy readjustment. Zambia's explicit anti-imperialist foreign policy and its support for liberation movements in Mozambique and Angola added to the accentuation of regional conflicts with its southern African neighbours. Southern Rhodesia's unilateral declaration of independence in 1965 and Zambia's impositions of sanctions on the racist Smith regime entailed heavy investments (hydroelectric power, rail and road transport, a pipeline to Dar es Salaam) to create an independent physical infrastructure and to avoid becoming cut off from world market access routes (Tetzlaff, 1975, p. 109). These geopolitical realities strongly influenced the design of the First National Development Plan. While mining was to remain the backbone of the economy, rapid industrial diversification was to be achieved by import substitution. While early growth rates were impressive with the GDP increasing by 83% from 1965 to 1970 and average earnings of workers rising by 97%, structural problems of distorted growth soon began to emerge (Burdette, 1988, p. 91): domestic production could supply more than a third of the local demand for manufactured goods and thus failed to remove the dependency on imports for consumer goods (Turok, 1979, p. 73). The concentration of import substitution on high quality consumer goods for the well-paid elites and not on mass production in turn created an additional dependency on imported materials, technology, machinery, spare parts, and skilled expatriate manpower (Seidman, 1979b, p. 101). This led to a lopsided economy in which

> ... the composition of consumer imports is almost entirely shaped by the demands for luxury items of the 10% of the population which accumulates over half, and perhaps as much as three-fourths, of Zambia's national income in the form of high salaries, profits, interest and rent. The remaining 90% of the inhabitants ... earn little more than bare subsistence wages ... (ibid., p. 103).

In the context of an urban-biased economic development, regional inequities featured strongly in all major economic and social indicators (D.H. Davies, 1971). In particular little effort was made to rehabilitate the rural subsistence sector suffering from colonial decomposition. Typically not more than 3% of government budget allocations were granted for the rural production sector that in 1964 encompassed 80% of the total population. Compared to the annual growth rates of 10.6% in the urban economy in the late 1960s, those of the agricultural sector stagnated at a mere 3.3%. Additionally, agricultural growth was largely attributable to a small fraction of commercial farmers and not to the peasantry who received no more than 5% of government investments in this sector (Mezger, 1989, p. 37). In the verdict of the ILO, the low levels of government service provision, arbitrary price control of agricultural products, and disadvantageous urban-rural terms of trade have given rise to a 'multiple deprivation' of rural populations (ILO, 1981, pp. 22-27). All this explains the inevitability of an uncurbed rural exodus and the lasting hypertrophic growth rates of Zambian cities as the direct impact of urban-based national development policies (Mezger, 1989, p. 30). The country's substantial improvements in social infrastructure and welfare programmes have tended to reinforce this tendency as the provision of new health facilities and educational institutions followed the colonial allocation pattern concentrating on urban growth poles along the line of rail.

The failure of Zambia's economy to attract foreign investments (even from its foreign-owned mining industries) and to reduce the dependency on copper exports as single foreign currency earner gradually encouraged the state to take a stronger control over the economy. Following the 1968 Mulungushi reforms, policies were redirected to nationalizing key industries held by foreign capital and to creating a large parastatal network with direct state participation (Burdette, 1988, p. 85). By the early 1970s parastatals had become preponderant in the entire economy, numbering well over 100 enterprises that provided employment for over a third of the formal sector work-force and contributed about half the GDP (Turok, 1979b, p. 75). However, the Zambian Government, despite its nominal socialist orientation, held back from policies leading to outright nationalization. Its control over parastatals was only ensured by majority holdings of shares and was curbed by the low ability of the state bureaucracy to devise appropriate industrial policies. The standing of the state has been even more timid with respect to foreign capital that strategically links Zambia's economy with the world market. Under strong domestic pressures for Zambianization, mining industries were nominally transformed into joint ventures in 1969-70, with the government holding 51% of shares. But in the de facto realignment of the Zambian state towards foreign capital the status of mines remained widely 'extraterritorial', that is, autonomous enclaves under the effective control of the South African and Southern Rhodesian parent companies. Contrary to the government's anti-imperialist and anti-apartheid rhetoric, the disengagement from the regional economy dominated by South Africa has, too, been only partial, due to the continuing reliance on industrial production factors of that origin (Burdette, 1984, p. 199).

These cleavages and contradictions between nationally proclaimed policies of socialism and anti-imperialism, on the one hand, and the political reality of growing proto-capitalist value orientations (Ollowa, 1979, p. 465) in a world-market-dependent system of state capitalism, on the other, were only reconciled by the paramount and uncontested status of President Kaunda as a national integrator. Nonetheless, subliminally strong frictions between the different emerging fractions of the ruling class became inevitable, making permanent crisis management a routine operation of Kaunda's government (Tetzlaff, 1975, p. 112; Adam, 1977). In Zambia the ruling class, in its core made up of freedom fighters, remained weak in a society consisting of a large peasantry, a strong, organized African miner working class, and a small but powerful category of white settlers and foreign capitalists. Also it was not in control of the major surplus-generating sectors, i.e. the mines. In this sense the political class was not a ruling class but a governing state class (Burdette, 1984, p. 203).[6]

As Tetzlaff (1975, p. 111) has underscored, the source of the structural weakness of the state and UNIP as the ruling party of President Kaunda is to be found in the heritage of the colonial production system. The new ruling class neither came out of class conflicts nor did it have experience in running modern enterprises. Instead it merely inherited the colonial administration and survived on the royalties from foreign exploitation of the country's mineral resources. The scope for structural adjustments of the economy was further impaired by the circumstance that UNIP did not receive the backing of the strong and well-organized proletariat in the Copperbelt. While the miners, for their union goals, eagerly engaged in action against mine capital perceived as the former imperialists, they were widely alienated from the national goals imposed on them by the government. Wage-freezes, strike bans and appeals for more productivity in the 'national interest' were met with rejection, as were plans to put the mining communities under proper Zambian jurisdiction (cf. note 5).

The inevitable countermovement to factional and regional political dissipation and national disunity was the illegalization of opposition and the centralization of power in a one-party system in 1972. Although this measure seemed to be legitimized by the growing hostility of surrounding regimes and the need to unify the nation in its struggle for freedom, authoritarian and repressive elements have been present in government from the beginning of the First Republic. As Sichone argues

> ... the idea of UNIP supremacy, of subordinating parliament, government, even the judiciary to the party programme was operating long before the one-party state came into being (Sichone, 1989, p. 140).

Threats to UNIP's hegemony arose in the late 1960s with the revival of the major opposition party ANC and the emergence of other sectionally based parties. The economic decline of the mining industry in the minor crisis of 1971-72, following nationalization policies, disclosed the fiscal vulnerability of the ruling powers when state revenues declined by almost a third. Thus, the declaration of the one-party system, which finally achieved the 'centralization of power in Lusaka' and the 'personalization of power by the President' (Chikulo, 1981), did not reflect the strength of the party but the decline in UNIP power and the attempt to retain its command by authoritarian means.[7]

A concomitant aspect of power centralization has been its democratic legitimization by the nominal decentralization of power and the introduction of so-called 'participatory democracy' in UNIP committees at places of work, village or ward. While people's real participation in certain aspects of community affairs cannot be denied entirely (even if in part due to discrepancies between local-based UNIP representatives and top-level party members), there is little doubt that the main intention of the system introduced was expanded *control* and not *devolution* of power to the grassroots. With respect to the later fully developed official policy of decentralization that fused party and government structures at District Council level in 1980, Chikulo notes that the

> ... intention is to make the state bureaucracy into a structural extension of UNIP and thus enhance the 'leading role' of the party. The centre is to devolve power to the district level albeit through party officials and political appointees; the latter are subject to tight central political control (Chikulo, 1981, p. 81).

Coming back to policies of urban development, the decision taken in 1971 to rehabilitate housing and to legalize settlement in three of Lusaka's squatter compounds can now be seen in the light of two political intentions: (1) to express the needs of the newly constructed power structure and its revised approach to development planning in the SNDP and (2) as an attempt by UNIP to achieve broader popular legitimacy and to tighten its political control over the urban masses.

Electoral support for UNIP had declined continuously and was at its lowest in 1973. Although most of the opposition leaders had been coopted by UNIP after the banning of their parties, the realignment of their followers to UNIP was far from unanimous. Although Kaunda, as sole contender for presidency, was reelected uncontested, voter turnout was a mere 39%. In particular the situation in various squatter areas in Lusaka known as strongholds of the ANC indicated that acceptance of local UNIP leadership had yet to be established in these areas. The implementation of upgrading and site and service schemes in unauthorized settlements would therefore not only raise public support for UNIP and government; an active role for local party members in this process would also give them a unique opportunity of establishing a sound leadership position based on merit.

Strong pressures towards finding a solution to the squatter problem were also put forward by the local political setting. Following the extension of city boundaries in 1970, a large number of squatter settlements were released from the responsibility of the Ministry of Local Government and now came under the jurisdiction of the Lusaka Council. According to Seymour (1975, p. 73) the council had from 1971 onwards urged government to adopt an upgrading policy. These changes also affected the electoral significance of squatters. Those candidates for office as city councillors who were deemed eligible by the Party for these constituencies, were typically petty businessmen or were members of the bureaucracy (Pasteur, 1974). As these groups, as a rule, neither came from a squatter background nor resided in their constituency, problems of electoral support and political legitimization emerged. These problems were aggravated after the 1975 revision of electoral constituencies when the place of residence replaced the place of origin as the voter's constituency (Kasongo/Tipple, 1990, p. 153). Accordingly councillors, who for obvious reasons feared the political repercussions of eviction or resettlement attached to the previous policy of squatter containment, became strong advocates for upgrading.

Vested interests in squatter policies also typically arise from the spoils system when politicians use their position to gain access to local material resources or use their office either to reward supporters or to discriminate against political opponents. This system, quite common in Africa as a way for officials in insecure jobs to secure material benefits (cf. Tetzlaff, 1989; Szeftel, 1982), is also present in Zambia. The 1969 Presidential inquiry into the affairs of the Lusaka City Council revealed frequent irregularities in the administration of markets, awarding of building contracts, and granting of planning permission. Political influence in the allocation of plots in high density housing areas was also evident (Rakodi, 1988a, p. 31). Vested political and economic interests were also articulated with respect to land regularization. As Seymour notes:

> ... close to the levers of state power are a number of Zambians who have bought large farms around Lusaka and have special interest in the restoration of legality in the field of land tenure. It is significant that, during upgrading, squatters will be expected to contribute towards the purchase of their land from private owners, even though they would have been legally entitled (under surviving English common law) to claim ownership after 12 years settlement (Seymour, 1975, p. 76).[8]

Under the Housing (Statutory and Improvement Areas) Act introduced in 1974, site and service plots in Statutory Housing Areas received a 99-year leasehold title while upgraded plots in the Improvement Areas became entitled to a 30-year occupancy licence. Conforming with legal provisos imposed by the World Bank for its engagement, specifically in view of cost-recovery, both these forms of tenure have created individualized legal accountancy of rights and duties in housing project areas. While the Housing Act empowered government to acquire and develop land in squatter areas, Pasteur reports fierce resistance on the part of landowners to sell at valuation prices in two of Lusaka's former privately owned upgrading areas. Considerable delays in land transfers were therefore not only associated with bureaucratic and legal constraints but also arose from 'social and political forces' in terms of compensation for expropriation (Pasteur, 1979, p. 82).

Thus, in contrast to the semblance of converted squatter policies, upgrading in Lusaka did not signify a fundamental change in attitudes towards unauthorized housing. As Seymour suggests, the rapid growth of squatting areas and the need to make them conform to urban building and health regulations (in particular with respect to cholera prevention), on the one hand, and the failure of squatter containment policies and the weight of local political interests, on the other, simply left no alternative but to abandon the favoured, but now unrealistic, comprehensive site and service approach and to try out an upgrading programme (Seymour, 1975, p. 73). The top-level political decision was taken in 1971. However, the implementation of plans prepared by the Lusaka Council was postponed due to fiscal crisis. The matter was then handed on to the newly operating NHA that, following interest expressed by the World Bank, submitted an application to the Bank in June 1973. Negotiations took place in 1974 resulting in a US$41.2 million project. Financing was shared by the World Bank (47%) and the Zambian Government (48%). The World Bank provided all foreign exchange costs (approx. 33% of total costs).[9] An additional 5% of local costs were contributed by other international donating agencies (UNICEF and the American Friends Service Committee).

Components of the Lusaka Project included the following: the provision of services to 17,000 upgraded dwellings and the preparation of 7,600 plots in adjacent overspill areas for those affected by essential resettlement; the servicing of 3,200 full site and service plots (with individual water and sewer connections) to extend five existing schemes of this type, and the provision of communal water supply and pit latrines to another 1,200 site and service plots of basic standard. Upgrading of infrastructure comprised water supply, improved sanitation, refuse disposal, street lighting, road access, and drainage. Community facilities funded by the project from the portfolios of responsible ministries were primary schools, community centres, clinics, and markets. Additionally sites were provided for small-scale industrial and commercial use.

The technical and political terms of the project expressed a convergence of interests between the World Bank and the Government of Zambia (GRZ) at various levels. In its most general dimension the housing project was to become the precursor of a growing influence of international agencies and banks on the foreign and domestic policies of the GRZ.[10] At that time the interest of the World Bank in implementing a large-scale upgrading programme in Lusaka corresponded with its need to establish reliable policy criteria to support the Bank's recent engagement in urban development and stabilization. As documented in Keare/Parris (1982), Lusaka was, with three other Third World cities, chosen as pilot scheme for the evaluation of upgrading project components designed to replace the Bank's earlier site and service approach. Associated with upgrading policies were criteria for eligible settlements. According to Fickert/Wetter (1981, p. 201) the priorities of the World Bank were put on proximity to places of work and to urban provision systems, suitable geological terrains for infrastructure lines (pipes and trenches), and conformity of site locations to the general plans for urban development and land-use.

In accordance with these principles, three major working class squatting areas (George, Chaisa/Chipata, Chawama) were selected for upgrading (see Figure 10.1). Land use in these areas also conformed to residential allocations in the Doxiadis master plan (although originally not laid out for high-density housing). Squatter areas omitted and indefinitely destined for eviction were (1) Chibolya and the adjoining Misisi and John Laing compounds (all on the potential development axis of the commercial centre), (2) Kalingalinga, in the vicinity of a site and service housing area and of the university (destined for institutional use but later upgraded by German Aid), and finally (3) Old Kanyama that was considered ineligible due to its difficult to service geological formation. Other peripheral squatting areas like Bauleni or Chainda do not seem to have been seriously considered for selection at that time.

The terms of participation agreed upon between the World Bank and the GRZ for project implementation expressis verbis made stipulations intended to make the respective concepts and aims of participation compatible. For practical and political reasons the World Bank opted not to create new CBOs but to use the existing system of local representative democracy as mediator between residents and the implementing agency. In the official setup the Housing Project Unit (HPU) was established as an independent body within the Lusaka City Council and was supposed to cooperate with the Ward Development Committees organized by the Ward Councillors, Party officials, and Council officers. This institutional arrangement, however, proved inefficient as it did not represent the de facto political power in the settlements that rested with the annually elected local Branch leaders (a Branch represents approx. 500 houses).

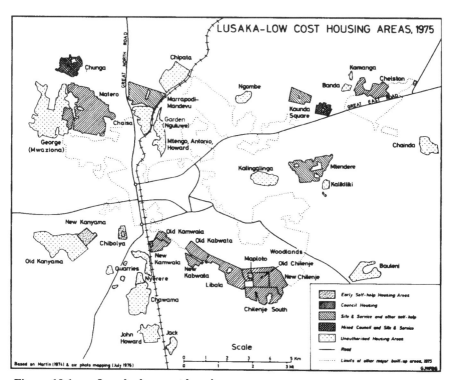

Figure 10.1   Lusaka low-cost housing areas
Source: Rakodi, 1986

227

Accordingly, implementation came to rely heavily on the hierarchical local Party system at Section, Branch, and Constituency level. While the aim of speedy and conflict-free implementation was achieved by this decision, other wider ranging aspects of participation like the promotion of community self-reliance and progressive self-help development tended to be impeded by party activities. *First*, as various writers have pointed out, participation in the context of the Zambian state philosophy of 'Humanism' excluded criticism of party and state or the formation of particularist group interests deviant from the officially declared national developmental goals (Rakodi, 1981, p. 65; Pasteur, 1979; Ollowa, 1979; Tordoff, 1974). Ollowa concluded that despite the official commitment to participation, it was, in practice, an instrument for promoting ideological and developmental goals and legitimizing political control, especially over local areas (Ollowa, 1979). *Second*, the World Bank's 'ostentatious aim of strengthening self-reliance and to provide a basis for continued upgrading based on community initiative' was not backed by real participation of residents' in decision-making or accomplishment.[11] Due to the need to preplan most project components with a view to obtain World Bank approval, this left little more than token areas of decision-making during implementation. With participation widely channelled through the Party and reduced to auxiliary works, enthusiasm for self-help was limited and called for pressures of leaders towards its provision. *Third*, as a result of the monopolization of settlement activities by local party members, UNIP had largely substituted the functions of local government (including police authority exerted by party vigilantes). Community issues became tightly interwoven with party reasoning and were politicized by local leaders' aspirations to political office. Thus, the scope for local mobilization of self-help and community activities was diverted from the settlement process and from people's possible self-organization. Instead it came to rest exclusively on the degree of popular legitimization of the party-dominated system of representative democracy.[12]

With respect to development planning, the economic terms of squatter policies advocated by the World Bank largely conformed to the newly proclaimed Zambian policies of reducing welfare programmes and introducing economic costs in the government provision of housing. The SNDP (1972-76) recognized that the state could not provide housing for all. Instead private home ownership was to be encouraged and government subsidization of housing removed, including that for site and service and squatter upgrading. Local authorities were instructed to achieve full cost-recovery from their housing activities. To facilitate these policies the Zambian National Building Society (ZNBS) and the NHA were founded. The ZNBS was to provide loans for house construction while the NHA was to build and sell housing for low- and middle-income groups at economic costs. Additionally a monthly housing allowance was provided for registered home owners according to the house value (Sanyal, 1981, p. 415). However, by 1979 home ownership in the housing stock had only increased to a total of 5% and remained a privilege of urban high-income households. The major cause for this outcome was the socially and politically biased implementation of new policies that have acted as a disincentive to home ownership in general and as a discrimination against low-income groups in particular (GRZ, 1989, p. 783): While low-income groups were cut off from subsidies, all government authorities, parastatals, and many large private companies continued to provide heavily subsidized housing for their employees at rental rates ranging from 6% of basic salaries for low-cost housing to 10% for high-cost housing. A similar bias is observable in the operations of the NHA and the ZNBS. Contrary to their designated aim, the profit-orientation of both organizations has led to the exclusive servicing of high- and middle-income groups as low-income households are considered by them a 'high risk' and inclined to default on loan repayments. Even the cheapest housing offered by the NHA exceeds by far the paying capacities of the working class while in 1980 the ZNBS did not offer loans below US$6,200, requiring a monthly repayment of at least US$250. In comparison, the monthly rent for one room with a pit latrine in an upgraded settlement was approx. US$15.

4 The legacy of upgrading experiences in Lusaka: the squatter situation in the 1980s

The combination of World-Bank-organized expert action and rigid community mobilization by UNIP has made the Lusaka project a reasonable success. This applies both to the physical accomplishment and, as shown in chapter V, to the social consolidation of affected residents.[13] By 1980, 19,911 plots were provided with basic infrastructure and within a short time 5,494 households were resettled with provision to build new core houses at adequate standards. In particular the sceptically viewed upgrading component has demonstrated its remedial potential of improving housing conditions at lower costs than the site and service schemes. According to 1981 estimates, the 3,666 new site and service plots, accounting for only 13% of total serviced plots, devoured approx. 48% of total project costs (Rakodi, 1986c, p. 199). Explicit political commitments to adopt the approach for future housing policies were made at the National Housing Policy Conference in 1978. In the appraisal of project achievements, the potential of upgrading in conjunction with site and service in 'overspill' areas was stressed as a model for future policies. The new spirit of pro-squatter policies was also evident in the provisions of the Third National Development Plan (TNDP). In accordance with the goals of the HABITAT declaration on the provision of minimum shelter standards, 'highest priority' was to be given to low-income groups through the promotion of home ownership, credit facilities, self-reliance through community participation, and demonstration projects (GRZ, 1989, pp. 285-286). Finally, these aims were to receive institutional support by the creation of a Housing Bank for the purpose of assisting low-income earners.

In the light of these propositions, the reviews of the performance of the TNDP (1978-84) and of the Interim National Development Plan (1987-88) are disillusioning. While total housing provisions exceeded planned estimates, allocation patterns continued the previous bias towards high- and medium-cost housing and paid particular attention to the rising demand for accommodation of civil service employees (see Table 10.2).

Table 10.2
Investments in government and institutional housing 1978-1987
at current prices in Kwacha millions and per cent of total

	Planned K mil.	Actual K mil.	Actual per cent
Housing schemes			
Conventional housing	20.3	10.6	4.3%
Site & service/upgrading	40.5	19.5	8.0%
Institutional finance			
Low-cost housing	5.1	42.4	17.3%
Medium and high cost housing	24.6	172.5	70.4%
Total	90.5	245.0	100%

Source: GRZ, 1989, p. 287

The 13,162 squatter upgrading units (out of a target of 110,900) completed in 1980-87 comprised entirely (1) final components of the World Bank project; (2) the Kalingalinga upgrading implemented in 1980 by German development aid (GTZ), which involved only an 11% funding by the Zambian government; and finally (3) a rural site and service core housing programme financed by the European Development Fund (EDF).[14] As with other Zambian councils formerly engaged in upgrading, liberal attitudes on the part of local government in Lusaka towards squatters were only short-lived (cf. Kasongo/Tipple (1989) for parallels in the unfolding of upgrading policies in Kitwe). Since 1980 attitudes have again become more hostile, and assistance to squatters has been coupled with demands for their resettlement and conformation to higher standards. After completion of the World Bank and GTZ projects, the Lusaka Council has exclusively concentrated on high-standard site and service and low-cost council housing.[15] But even in this field provision was far below the actual housing demand. No provision was made to improve or authorize habitat in the remaining illegal squatter areas, nor was adequate action taken to accommodate the demographic growth of low-income households. Lusaka's population continued to grow at a rate of 6.7% p.a., increasing from a total of 528,469 in 1980 to approx. 972,101 in 1990 (GRZ, 1989, p. 655). Rakodi estimates that annually more than 5,000 households from the low-income bracket enter the housing market (Rakodi, 1986c, p. 206).

Due to substantial rises in construction costs, market prices for council self-help and low-cost housing have in the 1980s moved even further beyond the paying capacities of lower-income households. In the early 1980s the LUDC was selling houses in the statutory area of Libala for K11,000. At the end of the 1980s the council was offering site and service plots on newly acquired farm land in the south of Lusaka for US$2,200, equivalent to five average annual incomes (Schmetzer, 1989). According to council information, 'low-cost housing' offered in 1989 in Old Chilenje was to be sold at K350-400,000 for a four-unit plot (two rooms each with individual water connections). Very much the same middle-class bias in housing provision applies in the case of the NHA activities. Since its participation in the World Bank project, the NHA has failed to take any further substantial initiative in the urban low-income housing problem. Minor exceptions were its consultancy to the EDF-financed rural housing programme mentioned and a urban low-cost building research programme financed by the UNDP. It has also produced two low-cost demonstration houses, like the one on exhibition at the Lusaka showgrounds in 1989 and a revised model presented at the recent Kamanga housing project. Both are, however, clearly beyond the paying capacities of low-income groups. Otherwise NHA housing redevelopment schemes in Lusaka have rather

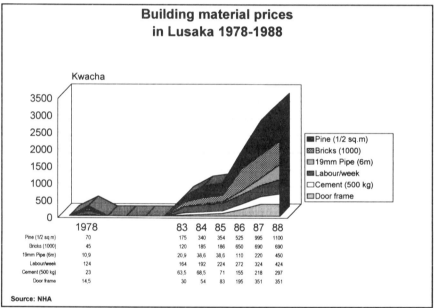

Figure 10.2   **Approximate (selected) material inputs for a low-cost core house**
Source: NHA, 1989

serviced middle- and high-income groups, not excluding resettlement of the original lower-income residents, e.g. in Old Kabwata (Rakodi, 1986c, p. 205).

The general failure of home ownership policies has also made the planned Housing Bank obsolete. During the FNDP it was instead decided to modify the conditions of the ZNBS to reduce statutory restrictions on housing developed under the Land Improvements Act.

Nonetheless, the accordingly revised mortgage terms still effectively exclude low-income groups. Like private banks, the ZNBS does not recognize the 30-year occupancy licenses issued for sites in upgrading areas; even the 99-year leasehold titles issued for site and service areas only qualify for loans if housing standards fully comply with building regulations. Other factors have added to the low impact of institutional financing for statutory housing: (1) even under these restricted lending conditions, the operations of the ZNBS have been limited by shortages of capital (Rakodi, 1986c, p. 205); (2) due to considerable delays in the conferral of leasehold titles in newly authorized housing areas, ZNBS loans have virtually been unavailable in the initial construction phase when needed most; (3) even after the completion of legal procedures not many residents seem inclined to legally register their plots; very many in fact are disqualified from registration due to arrears in service charges.

Another potential credit facility is provided by the right to withdraw five years' contributions from the Zambia National Provident Fund. As these savings are only available to employees in the formal sector, this gave little incentive for home ownership by private resources since government and private employers continued their subsidized housing provisions for these occupational groups (GRZ, 1989, p. 783). Thus, the only evident form of housing finance made available to low-income groups was a council programme to provide small building loans for house improvements in upgrading areas during the implementation phase (US$155 in the World Bank project and K650 in 1985 for Kalingalinga upgrading). These now terminated programmes were not, however, even during project implementation, topped up to meet with the high inflation of building costs (compare Figure 10.2). A new initiative to provide housing finance to private low-income households was under discussion in 1989. A Housing Fund is to be created and plans were underway to make a budget allocation to the Zambian National Building Society. These funds are to be made available to District Councils for distribution as loans to low-income groups (CDG/GRZ, 1989).

As indicated, the post-project change in attitudes towards squatters was not so much explained by actual developments in the 1980s but by the re-emergence of old squatter prejudices and inappropriate urban development models after the projects had performed vital political functions and had mitigated some of the most pressing urban development problems. Rakodi comments in retrospect:

> ... although the political/administrative elite accepted upgrading, ... because of the availability of World Bank funds, fear of cholera and a vested interest in retaining the regressive subsidy distribution, the upgraded areas were of too low a standard to be viewed as the hoped for once and for all solution and to yield political capital except for the Party leaders within them (Rakodi, 1989, p. 24).

Political reasoning devoid of any realistic assessment of what is feasible for councils and squatters, and the obstinacy of political leadership in adhering to inappropriate urban development concepts, figure as the key elements in the contemporary impasse in squatter policies. But policy readjustment in this field does not only rest on a revised top level political decision-making. A more favourable climate for appropriate low-cost housing provision would also require major changes in the entire framework of planning legislation, administration and professional planning as well as new approaches to the management of local affairs. More appropriate techniques of self-help housing provision, adapted to local circumstances and resources, would be a concomitant aspect of any new approach. The experiences with the Lusaka projects have disclosed various problems with administration and implementation that have played a strategic role in reinforcing the negative image of upgrading. A review of these experiences will point to aspects that have allowed administrators to view squatter policies as 'impracticable' when they are implemented with special provisions deviating from those of conventional housing.

In the first place, the World Bank project lacked an adequate integration into the ongoing Lusaka Council operations with respect to both the organizational setup and professional cooperation. Irrespective of whether the bank assumed that the Zambian project-initiative signified a positive change in attitudes towards squatters, or was indeed aware of the need for further persuasion at administrative level to this end, it chose to opt for a demonstration of Western planning efficiency and not for professional collaboration. Many of the World Bank's project operations displayed tendencies towards expert paternalism in respect to the Zambian professional counterparts when their advice was ignored. Although the measures and standards proposed by international experts were probably more realistically adapted to the local situation, they de facto imposed planning export on local planning authorities instead of disseminating innovative ideas. This has led to the paradoxical result that one of the largest, most internationally reputed upgrading projects has given its objective a negative political feedback at national and local level.

While the detailed proposal for the project had been formulated in all aspects by an interdisciplinary team of the Council and the NHA, the World Bank insisted on the HPU as a separate semi-autonomous implementing agency under the umbrella of the Lusaka Council. As the rationale given for this setup was the avoidance of the council's inefficient bureaucracy, and the bias of the Department of Housing and Social Services towards conventional housing solutions, the decision was naturally strongly opposed by the council (Bamberger et al., 1982, p. 75). According to Sanyal, this implicit implication of the council's incompetence resulted in an atmosphere of 'general hostility' between the two authorities, fostered by higher pay scales in the HPU (Sanyal, 1987, p. 289). Under these conditions, professional cooperation, an essential prerequisite for post-project handover and maintenance, was seriously impaired. Instead of acknowledging and addressing the problem of administrative deficits and low planning competencies as an integral part of the project, constraints on timely project implementation were simply overcome by autonomous actions of the planning unit. Instead of, as intended, liaising with those council departments responsible for cost-recovery, service charges, maintenance of infrastructure, issuing of title certificates and licences, etc. the HPU has done most of this itself. As a result, a chance was missed to enhance professional competencies of council staff and to lobby for a stronger pro-squatting attitude. Moreover, the lack of coordination has led to a misjudgment of the council's financial and manpower capacities to operate and maintain services like the refuse disposal, the water supply system, arterial roads or to effectively administer the system of service repayment collection (Rakodi, 1989, p. 13). In turn, residents' disappointment over low service standards and the rapid deterioration of infrastructure when coming under council administration had adverse effects on the performance of the repayment scheme (Martin, 1982, p. 269). In view of Zambia's general policy under the SNDP of abolishing housing subsidies and having councils recoup their expenses from service charges and rents, the failure of the cost recovery system in the Lusaka project has added to the lasting impairment of squatter policies in the post-project phase.

According to the detailed national financial setup, 87% of housing project costs were met by a loan from the GRZ to be recovered from individual project beneficiaries and general revenues of the Lusaka Council. The remaining costs for land acquisition, training and social infrastructure were absorbed by the GRZ (Sanyal, 1987, p. 288). Participating households were liable to service charges comprising costs for plot development, recurrent charges for water, sewerage, property taxes, and management costs. A second payment was due for households that had received a building material loan. With the World Bank pressing for low, affordable standards, the initial estimate was that most households could afford to spend 25% of incomes on cost repayment. Contrary to these assumptions, cost-recovery in Lusaka has remained one of the lowest among the Bank's 62 urban projects worldwide. From the outset, overall default rates were in the range of 75%, with a peak of 99% reported in one particular settlement in 1982 (Rakodi, 1989, p. 13). Although assumptions on affordability proved too optimistic for the lowest 20-30% of households, this did not seem to be the major cause of defaults. An HPU evaluation on cost-recovery in 1978 disclosed no significant correlation between payment rates and incomes or occupational status (Sanyal, 1987, p. 291). According to supplementary information from detailed income surveys, only approx. 10-15% of households in upgraded areas, and 5-10% of households in site and service areas, could claim real problems in meeting their financial obligations.

A retrospective analysis of the institutionalized cost-recovery system conveys various shortcomings in its adaptation to the local social and political environment. Despite the circumstance that squatters were accustomed to the natural right of usufruct of land but were unfamiliar with institutional obligations and financial liabilities, no efforts were made to find a system of legal arrangements corresponding to those in the traditional systems. There was also a potential contradiction between the *individual* accountability for charges, and the *collective* character of provisions and sanctions. On the assumption that a social pressure system could be used, individual defaults were penalized by disconnection of standpipes

234

affecting all residents in a section of 25 houses. Similarly a certain rate of defaults in a community served as justification for the Council to cut off sections, or the entire settlement from service provision and maintenance.[16] This design of sanctions seems to have overestimated communal coherence, and unjustly shifted council duties of collection to individual residents. The background to all this is that unlike land invasions in other countries, squatting in Zambia did not result from collective actions that tend to enhance communal coherence and participation. Usually settlement in a particular place comes out of individual negotiations with local leaders. Settlement is also not particularly associated with ethnic clustering that was, in fact, opposed by authorities in colonial times (Epstein, 1969, p. 95). In the African tradition, communal affairs are delegated to leaders. In this respect it was significant that this system was impaired by the replacement of traditional leadership by the new local party structure. At the time of implementation the party leaders in the arbitrarily fixed housing sections had not attained popular credibility, nor did the demarcations between house groups (adopted by the council as their core administrative unit) necessarily reflect actually existing neighbourhood relationships. Thus, the decision to apply sanctions in the sensitive area of water supply proved an ambiguous measure. The failure of residents or leaders to apply social pressures on defaulting neighbours in turn acted as a disincentive to those willing to pay for services. No alternative provisions were made to reduce the size of units to comply with effective mutual neighbourhood systems or to individualize utility systems, which, following a suggestion by Rakodi, would have allowed solvent residents to sell water (cf. Rakodi, 1989, p. 13)

These administrative deficits were by no means on the part of the Lusaka Council alone. Even under HPU management, the bureaucratic cost-recovery system implemented was poorly explained, inefficiently managed, and tended to strongly interlace with the local political leadership system.

- Surveys of information levels showed that only half the participants had attended meetings called to explain repayment procedures; 75% of people were unaware of negative consequences of defaulting, and nobody knew the correct breakdown of service charges (Sanyal, 1987, p. 292). As these information gaps could not be closed by the few community development officers, service charges in the perception of residents appeared to be payable for tangible provisions like water, roads and refuse, making the entire cost-recovery system crucially dependent on the maintenance standard of these items.

- The propensity to delay or default on charges was further reinforced by poor accounting systems and lack of coordination between the HPU and the Council. At the designated point of handover, the City Treasurer's Department was not prepared to handle the large addition of newly serviced households. An understaffed interim HPU Collection Unit struggled to keep accounts, but in some cases notifications of arrears were overdue for more than a year. All this did not support impressions that the council itself was seriously dedicated to its proclaimed collection principles or was inclined to impose sanctions.[17]

- Finally, the decision to make UNIP section leaders (each heading 25 houses) responsible for collection resulted in 'potentially contradicting roles of party officials as vote-catchers, advocates and debt-collectors' (Rakodi, 1981, p. 77). Various cases of personal misappropriation of monthly payments were reported with the consequence that dwellers later refused payments even to new section chairmen. The unjustified water disconnection as a sanction towards defaulting sections additionally roused mistrust of the council (Sanyal, 1987, p. 292). The council's authority to enforce charges, and if necessary to take legal action against defaulters, finally crumbled altogether when it became apparent that it was refraining for political and juridical reasons from using its last forceful sanction - that of eviction.[18] Finally, defaulting residents also received strong backing from local politicians. With the implicit support of UNIP, the undecided attitude of the council encouraged councillors and local leaders for electoral reasons to openly oppose the introduction of sanctions (ibid., p. 294).

Finding a solution to the cost-recovery problem has now been recognized by the council as a priority issue in view of future low-cost housing programmes. In the absence of any such programmes in the 1980s, new collection systems had not been decided upon by 1989. However, the FNDP made an allocation of K0.5 million towards an evaluation of alternative methods of cost-recovery. A first study commissioned by the LUDC was completed in 1989. It proposes community work programmes as an alternative means of repayment (Osei-Hwedie/Mijere, 1989). Local authorities represented at a Lusaka conference on legal aspects of self-help housing provision in 1989 acknowledged the need to impose effective sanction systems, but also pointed out that administrative capacities for collecting and accountancy are still very limited (CDG/GRZ, 1989).[19] As Sanyal suggests, a new organizational setup would have to avoid making collection systems rely on individuals who depend on popular support. Private collection agencies may be more effective in keeping accounts and imposing sanctions with the necessary backing of the council. But no such reputable organizations exist in Zambia while their creation may again be resisted by local politicians as a threat to the existing patronage system. Finally the efficiency of any collection system would also heavily depend on firm general attitudes towards cost-recovery and unambiguous political support for this aim (Sanyal, 1987, p. 294). As experiences with other institutional loan programmes in Zambia have shown, the nature of credit systems is generally not well established. In particular when international agencies are involved, even businessmen tend to view loans as a gift, entailing tight controls on the part of the lending agency towards repayment schemes and the appropriate use of loans (Kurbjuweit, 1989).[20]

Thus, it seems doubtful whether the cost-recovery issue can be solved by alternative techniques for administering collection alone. In view of factors like the inertia of public service, prevailing socioeconomic disparities, the de facto state subsidization of higher-income groups, and the abuse of revenues by the political spoils system, it will be difficult to restore popular credibility in Zambian institutions for new programmes with cost-recovery. Although service charges demanded by the LUDC are not unfair considering the real investments in low-cost housing, a lasting problem is that the reputation and authority of the council have suffered since services and maintenance systems have deteriorated in authorized former squatter areas. Therefore indirect methods of collection, such as by self-administration involving trusted local leaders, may not lead to better results if people suspect that their financial contributions will be 'misused' for other purposes, and they will not benefit from them. This conclusion is supported by the observations of field officers in George during the early phase of the World Bank/GRZ upgrading programme. Here cost-recovery seems to have worked as long as residents were under the (wrong) impression that their service charge payments remained in a special settlement account and were not absorbed by the LUDC coffers.

The only ray of hope in the impasse of the cost-recovery problem has been the experiences in Kalingalinga with the two non-government revolving funds schemes set up by the GTZ for cost-recovery from housing loans, and to provide petty business loans. According to Oestereich, the revolving housing loan scheme, in the 1980s repaid with 12% interest to make up for inflation and a few defaults, has worked without any problems (Oestereich, 1986, p. 27). This is in striking contrast to attitudes of Kalingalinga residents towards the parallel payments to the council. A study of service charge arrears has confirmed that the conventional council collection system is not operating significantly better in Kalingalinga than in the World Bank/GRZ upgraded areas (Osei-Hwedie/Mijere, 1989). In particular rising defaults in the late 1980s can be attributed to severe declines in real income.[21]

The revolving fund business-loan scheme under the management of an Economic Promotion Unit (EPU) was perhaps an even bigger success than the one for housing (cf. Goethert/Oestereich, 1987, pp. 16-17).[22] Based on a seed fund provided by the GTZ, this scheme had been running effectively since 1985 with virtually no defaults or misuse occurring (Maembe/Tomecko, 1987). Due to loan profits, the fund pool initially expanded and was providing the community with means for continuous economic promotion. In 1989 the ready acceptance and appreciation of this scheme by Kalingalinga residents had encouraged the council to consider its extension as a semi-public corporation to other areas in Lusaka. An LUDC-commissioned study on the market potentials in Chawama, George, Garden and Chipata recommended the introduction of an EPU-programme in these areas where it would have provided the first source of credits for informal petty business. The first EPU office was to be established in George with a seed fund of K35,000 (Maembe, 1989a, p. 38). The council was in 1989 also studying the possibilities of creating a revolving low-cost housing fund as an alternative to the customary repayment scheme. However, as the restudy of Lusaka in 1995 showed, neither of these schemes had been implemented and the projects had already been dismissed by the council before the shift in government. The EPU in Kalingalinga was still in operation but had been seriously affected by the dramatic inflation of the Zambian Kwacha in the early 1990s. Despite high interest rates for loans, the working capital of the fund declined in 1995 to US$1,000 and, contrary to agreements, has not been replenished by the Council.

5   Initiatives to solve the problem of unauthorized urban development in Zambia in the late 1980s [23)]

Parallel to the discussion on ways of implementing more successful squatter projects, the unabated and uncontrolled growth of squatter settlements in Zambia had also received revived political attention. Following considerable damage to squatter housing by torrential rains in 1989, President Kaunda in a speech attacked the 'chaotic town and country planning' responsible for allowing substandard townships to mushroom all over Zambia. Instead settlements should be approved and properly planned to required standards by the councils (*Times of Zambia*, 20.6.89). Earlier the Local Government Association of Zambia (LGAZ) had already held councils responsible for flood damage to housing on account of 'doing little' to implement the 1986 presidential directive to demolish illegal settlements and to resettle the affected people elsewhere (*Times of Zambia*, 19.2.89).[24)]

First action was taken in a meeting of town planning authorities and professionals on the squatter problem, summoned by Pres. Kaunda in 1989. An outcome was a memorandum from the Commissioner for Town and Country Planning on 'Problems and opportunities of unauthorized developments in urban areas'. It stated the following priorities in resolving problems (cf. Maimbolwa, 1990, pp. 4-5):

(1) The creation of a Ministry of Housing, Physical Planning and Urban Development that was to provide a coordinated institutional framework for the planning and implementation of rural and urban settlement development programmes.

(2) Prioritizing of the housing, planning and urban development sectors by the Ministry of Finance and National Commission for Development Planning. Due to the classification of 1989, investments in these sectors did not qualify for foreign aid or assistance from donor agencies. Needs stated in this field were: (i) educational expertise for project implementation; (ii) technical expertise to train local staff; (iii) technical equipment; (iv) funding.

(3) Strengthening of the Department of Town and Country Planning in order to enable this Office of the Prime Minister to carry out urban planning and development projects.

(4) In order to control unauthorized development, the Town and Country Planning Act Cap. 475 should be applied to all urban areas, and the 1963/64 Cabinet decision to exempt squatter settlements from this Act be revoked. Under the provisions of the Act, all development and subdivisions including those in squatter areas were subject to planning permission. This Act would also empower planning authorities to serve an Enforcement Notice in respect of an illegal development and to impose fines in case of violations.

Commenting on these proposals, it is realized that they foremost reflected the urgent need to give town planning authorities in Zambia a more appropriate role in development and physical planning and endow them with real implementing powers. In particular this would require a reversal of the precedence of particularist political decision-making over professional planning in three interrelated aspects:

1   Because of prevailing political priorities, the professional, technical and manpower capacities of town planning have not been developed according to the growing problems of urban growth, which has given rise to a situation then recognized as 'chaotic development in towns and cities' (Maimbolwa, 1990, p. 2).

2   This state of affairs has been aggravated by a strong politicization of the Zambian civil service in particular with respect to the levels of responsible Permanent Secretaries and Ministers. The political remedy applied to mitigate competing political interests, enmeshed in personal and sectional disputes, has been a spontaneous Presidential 'reshuffling' of officeholders, and frequent realignments of responsibilities between ministries. To combat the spoils system, senior politicians and civil servants could not expect to serve longer than 18 months in any particular post (Burdette, 1988, pp. 69-70). While the aim of preventing particularistic power bases in the bureaucracy may have been achieved by these measures, they have been detrimental to rational administrative functions in fields requiring long-term planning continuity and professionalism. Instead decision-making in planning has become highly susceptible to short-term political opportunism rather than being guided by long-term problem assessments.

3   While the practice of filling seniors posts according to political instead of professional criteria is not confined to Third World countries, 'reshuffling' has, however, created a system that rewards loyalty to the President more than meritorious service. These political structures have depreciated the role of planners as professional guidance to political decision-making, and they have generally acted as a disincentive to the professional

dedication of civil servants in planning offices. More efficiency and job dedication might be expected if the status and pay scales of planners were more appropriately adjusted to their important role in the development process.[25] A revision would also have to bring town planning authorities closer to the levers of political implementing powers and, related to this, closer to the effective budget allocating mechanisms.

While the proposals of the Commissioner for Town and Country Planning for institutional restructuring appropriately address some of the most obvious constraints to more effective planning, some of his solutions, however, require additional comments.

Concerning *point (1)*, i.e. the creation of a Ministry of Planning, there are arguments for and against. In the first place the functions of this new institution would necessarily be subject to the entire set of political and bureaucratic constraints outlined above. A ministry might be too aloof of local and regional problems, or too politicized to promote the urgently required rationalization of national planning procedures. On the other hand, considering Zambia's highly centralized political decision-making structure, it might be expected that a planning authority with its own portfolio and ample planning capacities could voice the requirements of planning and its necessary financial commitments at national level more effectively than is currently possible by decentralized planning authorities. Much seems to depend on finding an appropriate division of responsibilities between the proposed ministry and the district councils, releasing the latter from some of the excessive planning competencies bestowed on them by the 1980 decentralization policies.

In line with national decentralization policies implemented in 1980, aimed at creating a greater degree of self-sufficiency and self-reliance, the 1965 Local Government Act was revised to replace the old structure of City, Municipal, Township and Rural Councils by District and Provincial Councils. According to the 1980 Local Administration Act (Cap. 480) District Councils were in addition to the range of duties hitherto imposed on local authorities (town planning, building control, water, roads, electricity, sanitation, fire protection, etc.), requested to perform a wide range of additional duties. These comprehended: (1) the formulation of long and short-term district development programmes (including political, economic, social and cultural, scientific and technological, defence and security programmes); (2) the preparation of annual estimates, accounts, and reports for publication; (3) ensuring the efficient operation of all public institutions and parastatal organizations in the district (Rakodi, 1988a, p. 40).[26] In practice the implementation of the 1980 Act has been slow and erratic. As Lungu has pointed out, the Act in the first place seriously lacked provisions as to how the greater degree of integration between local and central government was to be achieved (Lungu, 1986). According to a Committee of the National Assembly, the Act failed to define a 'working relationship of central and line ministries in accordance with decentralization' and has instead led to a lack of coordination of development efforts at district level (GRZ, 1985, p. 7).

The aim of providing simplified administrative hierarchy and an 'integrated local administration system' was also counteracted by lack of adequate provision to councils to allow them cope with their expanded responsibilities. As the report of the Committee on Local Administration also states, the enlargement of district council functions was not complemented with appropriate financial arrangements or manpower allocations to deal with the transfer of powers (GRZ, 1985, p. 3). Since 1980 most district councils (including Lusaka) have, due to this lack of manpower, been unable to provide reports or audits of account. With respect to the division of revenue between central government and councils, the Committee has noted that 'Central Government is taking a large slice of the revenue while at the same time delegating more and more financial responsibilities to district councils' (ibid., p. 5). Thus, working with an insufficient revenue base comprising rates, licence fees, user charges, local sales taxes, and profits from commercial ventures, councils have become unable even to maintain the most vital of their urban functions (cf. Chioshi, 1984).[27]

According to this brief problem assessment, it seems evident that decentralization under the single-party system had led to a striking contradiction between legislation and the institutional setup that retained its top-down hierarchical arrangement with central political powers in the dominant position. While central government has intermittently accused district councils of failing to cope with unauthorized developments, these councils had in fact neither the financial and planning capacities, nor the legislative powers to appropriately address the problems coming under their responsibility. For example, annual estimates of council revenues and expenditures are subject to central government and parliamentary approval; at the same time recommendations of councils to increase service charges and rents to meet real economic costs have, for political reasons, not been approved by the Ministry of Decentralization (GRZ, 1985, p. 65). While under-funded by the central government, councils are lawfully authorized to raise alternative funds by loans, mortgage of council property, and by issuing stocks and bonds. In practice however, following press reports of cases of rampant mismanagement, misappropriation of funds, and disregard of financial regulations on the part of councils, financial institutions from the national commercial sector became reluctant to cooperate with them (ibid.). The same reluctance was observable on the part of foreign sponsors and international banks towards financing council-controlled new urban projects for low-income groups.

Proposal (3) concerning the strengthening of the Department of Town and Country Planning in order to allow it to carry out urban planning and development projects has now been realized by the new government. As a result of its conversion to a Ministry of Local Government and Housing it now performs a key role in the newly defined decentralization process that, ultimately, is to give financial and political autonomy to urban and rural districts in deciding local affairs.

To control unauthorized development, *proposal (4)* suggests that the Town and Country Planning Act Cap. 475 should apply to squatting areas, subjecting all developments to the requirements for planning permission. This proposal is perhaps the most controversial, considering the current deficits in administrative capacities of councils, and the inappropriateness of many legal provisions with respect to self-help housing and informal planning. Before planning capacities, in particular those concerning surveying and land delivery, have been brought up to standards allowing *forward* planning, any precipitate enactment of Cap. 475 in unauthorized housing areas might simply mean going back to repressive squatter control. Instead of rejecting unauthorized developments, councils should make greater efforts to guide the existing informal planning at settlement level to conform with town planning requirements, and should more flexibly adapt town planning to actual needs. A leverage to this aim is provided by the retained traditional system of land allocation in unauthorized housing areas: in contrast to the impression of a haphazard, spontaneously disposed settlement sprawl, squatting is a highly regulated process. In most cases permission to reside or build in a particular site is granted by local leaders according to customary law. Also UNIP leaders, opposing resettlement policies, have used their political function in local administration to assign building plots to newly arriving migrants (Waldeck, 1986, p. 161).

In the past the LUDC has intermittently made efforts to train leaders and acquaint them with building regulations. But dedication to the aim of LUDC cooperation with local leaders has been low, since residential allocations by them have frequently violated existing land-use plans. The council has also argued that resistance to cooperation also occurs due to vested interests in preventing the legalization of settlements, as the illegal status can be an important factor in preserving incumbencies for local leaders (CDG/GRZ, 1989, p. 13). Non-governmental professionals in Lusaka have, however, questioned the validity of these arguments in view of the council's failure to allocate residential land and its inability to revise the now 20-year old land-use plan to reflect real social and economic developments (cf. Nienhuys, 1989; Schmetzer, 1990).

Examples of fictitious 'threats' to designated land-use by informal allocations concern both industrial vs. residential use and the residential use of land in the hypothetical growth direction of the city centre. Even if Lusaka's industrial development is stagnant and areas earmarked for this use are still vacant, the council is reluctant to recognize existing settlements in the vicinity of such areas (e.g. Chinika and Chibolya). The same applies to a settlement on the extended axis of the commercial centre. The commercial centre is already considered overstretched lengthwise and should more appropriately be widened to the abundant vacant areas to the east and west as suggested in the Bowling Plan as far back as 1933. However, according to the Commissioner of Lands, the land to the west on prime sites is legally not available, being held in direct lease by parastatal organizations for future developments (Schmetzer, 1990). Thus, Misisi, situated more than 1 km to the south of the commercial centre, remains under the permanent threat of eviction, even if only due to highly improbable developments. The UNCHS/DANIDA consultant in Lusaka has aptly characterized the general problem behind this piece of bureaucratic planning dogma (and more realistic approaches to solving it) in Lusaka:

> One can reserve extensive areas for commercial facilities, etc., but if the economy does not bring forth those developments to justify the facilities, then it is not surprising that the real priorities are taking charge. If the economy will become strong, then all sorts of substandard housing will automatically make room for economically stronger commercial activities and existing holes in the town will be filled in (Nienhuys, 1989, p. 5).

Growth patterns in high density housing areas (both legal and unauthorized) in the 1980s did not give indications of infringement on valuable lands or arouse concern about hypertrophic growth. Compared to the town's overall growth rate of 6.7% p.a., only two areas (Garden with 11.7% and George 8.7%) displayed more than average population growth from 1969 to 1980 (Williams, 1986c, p. 179; Wood, 1986). Instead the general pattern of spatial and demographic growth in squatter and in upgraded areas displays a tendency to evenly affect areas all over town, including a substantial shift of population growth to the urban periphery such as to Kaunda Sq. and Bauleni (cf. Waldeck, 1986, p. 362). At the same time growth in sensitive areas like Chibolya and Misisi has been near stagnant in the same period (1.1%), indicating that mechanisms of self-containment in communal expansion exist in these areas. Thus, while squatter and site and service areas with residential densities/ha of 120 to 230 are absorbing most of Lusaka's population growth, high cost housing areas are making excessive use of valuable urban space with densities in the range of only 14 to 27 persons/ha (Williams, 1986c, p. 178).

These conclusions concerning inappropriate space-use have received strong support from an international consultancy that has investigated the comprehensive growth problems of Lusaka. At the request of the LUDC, channelled through UNCHS, the consultancy Peat Marwick McLintock was in 1988 brought in to review the old Doxiadis master plan in view of growth management and improved land use control. Funds to implement the proposed development of a new comprehensive physical plan, referred to as 'Structure Plan', have not yet become available. However, the preliminary report suggests that prevailing space use plans have tended to create a faulty polarization between presumptive needs and unauthorized misuse of land by squatters. Stated differently, the ongoing conflict over space use is founded on premises of the old plan that would no longer be valid according to the requirements of the new Structure Plan. Based on observations and proposals of H. Schmetzer, one of the consultants commissioned to investigate the situation, various revisions of space use seem appropriate to solve both the problems of inner city development, and residential space use for growing squatter settlements (cf. Schmetzer, 1990):

- While the Land Department's annual report for 1985 states 'that there is an acute shortage of land for residential development particularly in the Lusaka Urban District', the consultancy has noted the self-made character of this constraint. At an average of 73 persons/ha the city of Lusaka has one of the lowest urban population densities in the world, incurring costly servicing and commuter problems. A more appropriate growth pattern would have to consider more intensive utilization of land by the re-zoning of sites designated for residential use, subdivisions of larger plots, and a change in the building clause to allow high rise development.

- The study also points to restrictions to urban restructuring due to the leasehold system. While the abolition of freeholds has effectively curbed private speculation, a drawback has been that potentially valuable land has been withheld from adequate use. For instance, many government owned inner city buildings with spacious gardens are now visibly dilapidated due to loss of their original function. These lands also have considerable value for potential commercial use. Thus, in the absence of a self-regulating land market, redevelopment on prime sites according to prevailing needs should either receive the special attention of planners to monitor and speed up developments, or be encouraged by inviting commercial developers to submit proposals. A necessary vital aspect of redevelopment would be the conservation of historic buildings and the preservation of their natural surroundings of avenues and gardens, especially in the Ridgeway area. With still relative abundance of space, appropriately guided redevelopment schemes, perhaps even essential to saving these historic buildings of the 1930s, could incorporate existing structures without violating Lusaka's characteristic feature of a 'garden city'.

- Following the opening of the international airport in 1972, the old Lusaka City Airport is now used exclusively for small aircraft. This traffic could be redirected to the third airport 9 km south of Lusaka, thereby releasing 200 ha of land for other use on prime sites ideally suited for decentralization measures. This area, not more than 5 km from the city centre, is also the exclusive site of a golf club that might be relocated, especially as a second golf course within the city area already exists. On the same perimeter a considerable area is also in use for military purposes. A perhaps misguided impression on my own part is that a spacious vacant area also surrounds the University of Zambia that seems over-dimensional to be kept exclusively in reserve for future extensions. Finally, even if the inner city land currently retained by parastatals for indefinite future development cannot be repossessed for political reasons, the LUDC should press for a substantially increased land-withholding tax both as an incentive to comply with intended land use and as a cross-subsidization for necessary alternative developments to make up for unutilized lands.

- Pertinent measures to revise space use would also have to curtail the problems of Lusaka's urban sprawl involving enormous relative per capita investments for infrastructure in low density housing areas. While it might be politically difficult to scale-down established standards, this type of development is characterized by Schmetzer as 'anachronistic and no longer feasible'. In terms of aggregate costs it might be more economic to level and drain central areas on difficult terrains than to open new residential areas on the outskirts of town as is the present practice.

In view of these findings on the inevitability of a comprehensive revision of physical planning and space use, it seems inappropriate, as suggested by the former Commissioner of Town and Country Planning, to insist on the rigid observation of outdated planning regulations that might only unnecessarily rouse conflicts between planners and squatters. Instead, planners should seek cooperation with local leaders and use their informal planning authority to solve acute problems. In this way, at least, extensions and subdivisions in unauthorized areas could be coordinated with basic requirements of town planning - in particular with a view to a rational process of upgrading in the future. A training programme for leaders to this end would be essential. Experiences in this direction were made available through the 1984-1994 UNCHS/DANIDA Community Participation Programme that, among other things, aimed at teaching basic leadership skills.[28] The physical and educational facilities developed by this programme are available to the Ministry of Housing and Local Government at its Chalimbana training institute. In view of the common perception of leaders in unauthorized areas who see their relationship with the council in terms of a potential threat to their own territorial authority, it is significant that one of the main objectives of the UNCHS/DANIDA leadership training was to 'establish a dialogue between the established organizational structure or governmental officials and the community' (Zambia UNCHS/DANIDA, 1988). A further incentive to mutual cooperation could be given if the council gave priorities to upgrading or other service improvements to communities which cooperated accordingly. Given farsighted leaders, a growing awareness of the need to structure informal residential developments in their areas might be achieved: for example leaders could on their own account adopt council space-use standards and plot allocation patterns in extensions to squatter areas. These spatial provisions would allow room for roads and infrastructure lines that will facilitate future upgrading without essential resettlement.

While further developments on the squatter issue in Lusaka are compounded with new approaches to physical planning, various authors have drawn attention to the various impediments to effective administration imposed through current land legislation (Schmetzer, 1990; Nienhuys, 1989; Todd/Mulimbwa, 1979; Mulenga, 1989). Zambia's adaptation of British Town and Country Planning laws has imposed sophisticated legislation not matched by the country's administrative capacities nor modelled to the specific circumstances of a Third World country. Complicated legal procedures, lack of qualified land surveyors, and a bureaucratic administration make surveying, cadastral registry, plot and title deed allocation a complicated, expensive and lengthy process. With an estimated need of 7-8,000 new dwellings every year, only 842 direct leases were issued by the Lands Department for Lusaka in 1985 (Schmetzer, 1990).

The constraints to speedy implementation of housing projects have been described in full detail by Nienhuys/Matibini (1990). According to their account, from the point of first proposal of a Statutory Housing or Improvement Area until its final declaration, no less than 11 major administrative steps of action are required involving permission/registration by seven different Ministries and Departments (i.e. the Council, the Provincial Planning Authority, the Ministry of Lands, Water and Natural Resources, the Registrar of Lands and Deeds, the Commissioner of Lands, the Surveyor General, and finally the Decentralisation Division under the Office of the Prime Minister). The simplification of these legal procedures seems a priority issue in order to streamline administration and land allocation. Under the current legislation, surveying itself may not necessarily be a constraint as the procedure adopted in upgrading areas shows. Here planning approval can be given by the Commissioner of Lands to unsurveyed land, or he can accept a sketch plan based on available aerial photographs (scale 1:1,000) for cadastral purposes. In this case a 30-year occupancy licence may be issued. To obtain a 99-year title deed for Statutory Housing Areas, however, a full ground survey is still required. This provision seems exaggerated considering the backlog in surveying. Intermediate solutions like the use of aerial photos in upgrading areas should be considered for Statutory Housing as well, to speed up surveying and land delivery to meet actual demands.

Other parts of legislation that seem inappropriate in informal housing areas concern restrictions on subletting and the imposition of partially inappropriate building regulations. (1) An occupant in an Improvement Area is required by law to use the premises entirely for himself and his 'immediate family'. Even granting that little effort is made to enforce this regulation in Lusaka, it would be more appropriate to amend the Act, and recognize the valuable function of subletting to reduce the housing demand and to provide an additional source of income for poor households. As argued earlier, tenancy is not an alternative to home ownership but, in view of long waiting lists, usually the first step towards its achievement. The present illegal status of tenancy arrangements impairs any kind of official support or programmes to help house owners to create new legal housing facilities by subdivisions. (2) The enforcement of building regulations is somewhat inconsistent and biased against low-income households. While old structures in Development Areas qualify for an occupancy licence, all newly built houses in these areas are required to comply with one of the four offered standard (site and service) council house plans, or alternatively builders are required to submit a plan to the council for approval (cf. Figure 10.3). The provisions of the building code require first the construction of a pit latrine 3-5m deep if no main sewage is available, then the completion of the core house (minimum of two rooms with foundation fitted with

246

permanent roofing sheets and all external doors) within six months. Failure to comply with this time schedule, with a possible six-month grace period, results in repossession of the plot. The use of building materials is prescribed as follows: foundations are to be made from concrete; the main walls are to be made of either concrete, soil-cement or burnt bricks; the use of sun-dried bricks is prohibited if not plastered with a 20mm cement/sand plaster. The minimum size of habitable rooms is to be 8.4m^2. Roofing sheets are to be of either corrugated iron or asbestos cement or concrete. Earth rammed floors can be permitted. Minimum window size is not to be less than 10% of the room area. Second-hand materials may be used but require permission from the Development Secretary Construction Staff (cf. LUDC, undated).

While the technical intention of these regulations may be to produce durable and waterproof new building structures, its middle-class bias practically spells out an anti-improvement programme for low-income households. In view of the enormous costs of a completed core house and the absence of credit programmes, the very tight time schedule effectively prohibits any form of progressive, incremental building adapted to the income situation of poor families. It also openly encourages gentrification and lends itself to corruption when decisions as to whether a building complies with regulations or not are taken by local inspectors. Building activities observed in 1989 on new extension plots of declared Development Areas (e.g. Kalingalinga) are exclusively conducted by middle-class households or by private firms to provide housing for their employees. In view of the dramatic decline in real incomes, site and service building regulations are prohibitive to residents in upgrading areas. Regulations should be confined to necessary requirements of space use and plot layouts and more appropriate approaches to durable - but affordable - housing urgently considered.[29]

A further piece of contradictory legislation exists in the *exemption* of squatting areas and old structures in upgraded squatter areas from building regulations, but their *inclusion* by the Public Health Act Cap. 535. According to the far-reaching provisions of this Act, the promotion of public health requires that all buildings conform to regulations and have building permission (Todd/Mulimbwa, 1979, p. 32). Again, most of this legislation is in practice ignored with respect to squatting areas. However, as all unauthorized housing is potentially unhygienic, the Act may be used at any time to legitimize evictions and has in fact been applied to this end in other towns in Zambia, albeit not in Lusaka in the 1972-1990 period. To legally protect all unauthorized housing from possible arbitrary political evictions based on the Public Health Act, special provisions should be made in the Act for adequate health promotion in this type of housing and settlement environment.

Concerning the important role of the informal sector in economically sustaining the inhabitants of squatter and Improvement Areas, more support for their economic activities could be given by a relaxation of the Local Authority Bye-Law, Regulation 5. This prohibits the sale of any 'goods' within a radius of two miles from a market in any public place except a market (Todd/Mulimbwa, 1979, p. 35). As happens with the above-mentioned housing regulations, the existence of petty trading on street stands is tolerated in upgraded settlements

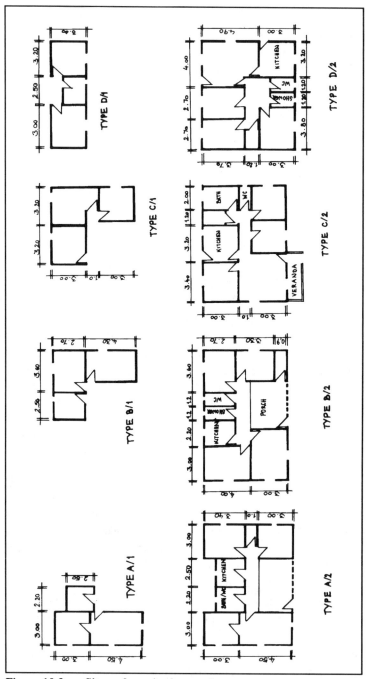

Figure 10.3   Site and service house plans
Source: Redrawn from Lusaka Urban District Council

248

and on main roads. But this does not exempt vendors from occasional harassment, e.g. during raids on black marketeers. Selling or producing marketable goods is also not permissible under the Town and Country Planning Act in areas zoned for dwelling. Regarding the stronger promotion of the informal sector, both these legal provisions should be more realistically adapted to the struggle for survival of the poorer urban population. In Lusaka the urban informal sector is still comparatively small (approx. 20% of working population), but is growing faster than the wage employment sector (Todd/Shaw, undated, p. 31). However, its absorptive capacities for the growing labour-force are limited as present informal activities are dominated by marketing, food processing, and selling on now saturated markets. In contrast to official proclamations, the informal sector has not yet been linked with the country's overall economic framework and informal activities are mostly, but not exclusively, confined to local networks (ILO, 1981, p. 181; Todd/Shaw, ibid.). Thus, the removal of territorial restrictions would be part of a policy to encourage and diversify informal activities that could then cater for higher income groups all over town. Bringing these activities closer to residential areas instead of barring them out, could in some fields act as a corrective to the over-centralized commercial structure of Lusaka. This kind of policy would perhaps even remove some strain from the public transport situation.

6 The urban situation under the multi-party system 1991-1995

The final descent of Kaunda's single-party system began with the 1987 decision to unilaterally suspend the IMF/World Bank structural adjustment programme (SAP) and to limit the international debt serving to 10% of export earnings. Oriented to IMF policies, the 'home grown' New Economic Recovery Programme (NERP) of 1987-88 was introduced as an attempt to reconcile domestic and international interests in the economic reform process. NERP, however, failed to receive the approval of the IMF, leading to Zambia's isolation within the international donor community. The loss of credibility also brought a serious decline in bilateral aid, with even reliable donors like the Nordic countries freezing up their programmes and pressing for a return to IMF conditions. With continuing economic decay and uncontrolled inflation, Zambia agreed in 1989 to fulfil key elements of SAP. But in the course of a 15-year economic crisis the powers of UNIP had finally eroded and public support for programme implementation diminished. The abolition of maize meal subsidies in 1990 and an announced doubling of prices for this commodity led to food riots in various cities in which 26 civilians were killed and about 1,000 demonstrators arrested. On the eve of political transformation in 1991, Zambian observers of the impact of SAP on Zambia gave the following verdict:

The events of June 1990 have had a tremendous impact on Zambia. The political drama that is now unfolding is, in fact, a manifestation of the resistance of the mainly urban population to the further erosion in living standards. Large numbers of the urban population, especially the workers and the intelligentsia, have withdrawn their support from the ruling party (UNIP) and agitated for political change along the lines of multi-party democracy. The divorce of UNIP has destroyed the social consensus achieved during the late 1960s and 1970s which was based on a symbiotic relationship involving the party, the Zambian Congress of Trade Union (ZCTU) and other interest groups (Mwanza/Mwamba/Kakuwa, 1992, p. 149).

The multi-party system was introduced in 1990, and in the 1991 elections President Kaunda was clearly defeated, with 76% of votes going to the newly formed party Movement for Multi-Party Democracy (MMD) under Mr Chiluba, a former ZCTU leader. Since then Zambia has adapted to the IMF/World Bank SAP and has now retained its international credibility. Importantly, new national policies have fully opened themselves to the key components of the structural adjustment package including, among others, the privatization of state enterprises, of which 113 were to be sold by the end of 1995, a substantial reduction in government spending including the dismissal of 10,000 civil servants, deregulation of all markets, and decentralization of state powers. This conversion to democracy and the carrying out of demanded policy reforms have been 'rewarded' by the international community in various ways. In 1994 part of Zambia's foreign debt was cancelled and new credits negotiated to repay old ones (Dallas, 1995, p. 229). A coming joint major programme of the World Bank, UNDP, AfDB, the British ODA and the Norwegian Government will rehabilitate public facilities and utilities in nine major cities in Zambia (but will exclude Lusaka)[30]. Meanwhile resurrected bilateral aid, formerly concentrating on rural areas, now includes urban development programmes made possible through policies that allow direct participation of communities in projects without council control. In the African country ranking, Zambia has with US$105 per head become the fifth largest aid receiving country. Finally, democratization has also encouraged various internationally operating NGOs to become active in the field of community development in Zambian cities.

These achievements in international relations have been overshadowed by domestic policy constraints. Economic targets have been negatively affected by a now four-year drought, rising costs of copper due to extraction from deep-lying reserves, an average GDP decline of 4% in 1990-94, and the only recently controlled inflation. The exchange rate of the Zambian Kwacha, now internationally convertible, has fallen from 16.1 Kwacha per US$ in 1989 to 925 in 1995. The new government has also been affected by various accusations of corruption, union strikes, a planned military coup alleged to some members of UNIP, and deflections of prominent MMD Ministers and MPs who formed their own National Party. The weakness of the new government and the turmoil caused by democratization have slowed the pace of structural reforms in the political system and in local government. However, some incipient steps have been taken at national policy level. Councils have been advised to enter public-private partnerships in infrastructure provision. To ensure that public interests are safeguarded with the privatization of water and sanitation, the Programme Coordinating Unit (PCU), established by the Cabinet in 1993, has proposed the creation of council-owned regional companies. These are to replace the inefficiently operating Zambian national water and sanitation parastatal. The regional companies are to come under the supervision of the Ministry of Local Government and Housing and to receive government financial support for investments in peri-urban and rural areas. It is expected that in these areas sufficient revenues will be raised to sustain operations and maintenance by tariffs and internal cross-subsidies (PCU, 1994, p. 20). The councils have also been advised to privatize all other functions. Formerly highly subsidized council housing is now being sold. The old system of employers' housing allowances is still in operation but is under revision according to the national housing policy. It is also planned to deregulate housing finance and to end the monopoly of the Zambian National Building Society (ZNBS), which in the past has imposed excessive interest rates. Public transport has been privatized since the financial breakdown of the national bus company UBZ in 1994, and as a measure to reduce traffic congestion the government now encourages the importation of buses with a seating capacity of more than 14 by tax and tariff exemptions. The government openly acknowledges that urban development in Zambia is highly disorganized due to lack of planning capacities (only 20 planners available nationwide) and to poor urban management. The country still lacks national institutions to train its own planners and is additionally suffering from a considerable drain of planners to other countries in Southern Africa (e.g. Botswana) where they enjoy favourable expatriate pay scales. Both available master plans and the Town and Country planning legislation are considered outdated by national planners and require revision. As a first step to address these problems, the government in late 1995 drafted its first national housing policy that is intended to enable appropriate and affordable housing production for all income groups, and to improve housing finance and land delivery. The government in 1991 also passed legislation to implement a more effective form of decentralization and strengthening of local government as part of the Public Service Reform Programme. Comments on these proposals will be given below and in the final chapter.

Lusaka's urban situation in 1995 remains characterized by the familiar disparities of the 1980s. Compared to the national growth rate of 2.7%, migration to Lusaka has remained high in the '90s, leading to an average total urban growth rate of 6.1% annually. According to council information, the city's population is now estimated at 1.2 million, and the proportion of people living in poorly serviced high density housing areas (upgraded and squatter areas) has risen to 70%. Council or local government provisions to service the demographic growth have been near absent due to lack of funds and planning capacities. In particular water provision is struggling to cope with the growing demand. A project by the

Japanese International Cooperation Agency (JICA) to rehabilitate the water network will not start before 1996. The number of LUDC town planners has been reduced to two, with various posts currently vacant; for the peri-urban area there is no planner. Land delivery has remained at a fraction of actual demand and even then has been susceptible to invasions on demarcated sites due to delays in infrastructural development.[31] A single exception to this paralysis is the council's participation in an upgrading project of Irish Aid and the international NGO CARE Canada in Kamanga Township, some 12 km to the north-east of the city centre. This programme, basically following the model of Kalingalinga in terms of components provided and its participative approach, started in 1991 and serves a population of 9,000 in 1,043 housing units. In view of limitations on manpower and financial capacities, functions of the Lusaka Council are to be restored by the encouragement of private-public partnerships in the provision of infrastructure and services. The decision was taken to contract out solid waste management to a private company, but so far no organization has come forward. The council will also sell its commercial activities and fully privatize its operations run by parastatals (i.e. telephone, post-office, electricity, water and sewerage). For road maintenance a newly founded Roads Board has introduced a levy of US$0.30 per litre on petrol to finance repairs. This matter will also receive attention from a JICA road rehabilitation project in the coming year.

Fortunately, the liberalization of political structures has removed the former monopoly of the council and the local UNIP party representatives in dealing with community development. This political standpoint had evolved into an unacceptable position for international NGOs, and increasingly also for bilateral aid organizations, who would no longer engage in urban projects without adequate participation of residents. In the new communal structure, Resident Development Committees (RDCs) are elected independently of political party membership. As part of the new decentralization policy that aims at creating politically and financially autonomous Local Authorities (starting with city and municipal councils) RDCs will participate with the councils and with the District Development Co-ordinating Committees (DDCCs) in the preparation of district plans. The Ministry of Local Government and Housing (MLGH) will only provide guidelines and necessary support to Local Authorities besides monitoring their performance and coordinating their activities (MLGH, 1995). Following these revisions, various international NGOs and bilateral aid agencies have become active in Lusaka, attending to the infrastructure provision in squatter settlements or in upgraded areas where provision standards have deteriorated. All these programmes have been implemented in close cooperation with community organizations and incorporated community development and self-help components. Various examples of this new type of community development approach have now been implemented in Lusaka:

- As a forerunner to current developments, the local NGO HUZA had already under the old regime established a borehole-provided water network in Kanyama that was built in self-help by residents in 1987 with financial grants from the NGO UK Water Aid (cf. page 324). After some administrative and technical difficulties, the scheme went into operation in 1990.

- In George Township, upgraded by the World Bank/GRZ in the 1970s, growing water shortages have been addressed by JICA with the technique successfully adapted in Kanyama. The JICA project has provided boreholes in order to tap the lower, unpolluted reserves of ground water, and has installed tanks, pipes and communal water taps. The necessary excavation works for the pipe network were done in community self-help.

- In the squatter settlement of Bauleni a similar borehole scheme for water provision has been introduced by the local NGO Human Settlements of Zambia (HUZA) with sponsoring by EZE, a German church-related NGO and DANIDA. As this programme also included additional elements of upgrading (improvement of drainage and pit latrines) and used alternative building materials, it was the first case of an extensive settlement development in Lusaka done entirely by NGOs with community participation.

- In Kamanga, a peripheral squatter settlement of 9,000 inhabitants, Irish Aid is currently implementing a comprehensive upgrading scheme, which also uses this alternative technique of water supply. This project, carried out in cooperation with the council, will attain full legal recognition under the Development Areas Act. It includes facilities like schools, a dispensary, and a community centre. Part of the community will be resettled on an adjoining site in houses conforming to site and service building regulations.

- The NGO CARE Canada has become active in community development and in the improvement of infrastructure. In its food-for-work programme PUSH (Peri-Urban Self-Help) residents are mobilized for road improvement, unblocking of storm drainage, refuse collection, etc. Places of action are Kalingalinga (the GTZ upgrading project of the early 1980s), and the above-mentioned settlements of Bauleni and Kamanga.

NGO initiatives have received tentative recognition by the government, which, for instance, has committed itself to a 10% contribution to the running costs of PUSH operations. But these improvements cannot conceal the fact that the government and councils have so far failed to come forward with a comprehensive concept of how to integrate unauthorized housing areas in planned urban growth. On the contrary, policies towards squatter communities have remained erratic and rigid. One of the first actions under the new government was a repeal of the previous 'non-interference' policy towards squatters. As a demonstration of the new 'orderly and not haphazard development', the Minister of Housing and Local Government ordered without notice the bulldozing of 100 illegal dwellings in

Kanyama to stop the encroachment on the city's central business areas. The complete loss of dwellers' possessions and the drastic form of action, hardly conducive to the establishment of democratic relations between authorities and citizens, produced a unanimous public outcry forcing the president to intervene (cf. *Southern African Economist*, 1992, p. 12). Action may, however, be resumed as a study is planned for 1996 to assess the benefits and disadvantages of upgrading inner city settlements or relocating them to the urban periphery to make way for commercial developments. Another piece of erratic action was the temporary dissolving of the peri-urban section in the Lusaka Council and the withdrawal of field staff from upgraded areas for some time in 1991. With the later replacement of the minister responsible, approaches have become more liberal, but are still undecided in moving towards an enabling policy that supports the NGO initiatives.

While NGOs are mitigating the most serious deficits in provisions of low-income settlements, there are signs of potential disconcertion within this new type of public-private partnership. This, in part, appears to arise from the policies of international NGOs of not restricting themselves to complementary service provisions but of enhancing mobilization, and finally achieving self-sustainability in community participation. With NGOs pressing forward and acting independently of hesitant councils and politicians, a lack of real cooperation and coordination with authorities is now appearing (cf. UNCHS, 1993, p. 44). The government responded to these problems in 1995 by establishing Development Co-ordinating Committees at national, provincial and district levels that involve all actors with the aim of providing a 'forum for dialogue and co-ordination on development issues between the local authority, line departments, Donors and NGOs in the Districts' (GRZ, 1995a). Nonetheless, political conflicts apparently continue over the role of NGOs in the urban development process. The Zambian government decided in 1995 to temporarily freeze its support for CARE programmes.[32] According to the Ministry of Local Government and Housing, the independent action of this organization without coordination with responsible authorities was in contradiction to the aims of decentralization. The complaint was also made that its 'not properly operating' food-for-work approach was destroying local self-help capacities. Finally, this programme was also claimed not to be working with an acceptable cost-benefit relation to justify its public support.

The issue of official support for NGOs is also linked to the legal reconstitution of community organizations into RDCs, which contrasts with the only minor success in real devolution of powers by authorities to the local level and the slow adaptation of planning to requirements of enabling policies. Although RDCs are generally the weakest part of decentralization, active RDCs assuming their designated role according to the Decentraliza-tion Act are a potential challenge to the prevailing local power structures. The mobilization and strengthening of communities through NGO programmes may for local leaders and politicians mean loss of control over local resources. An example of this type of conflict is the Kamanga upgrading project in Lusaka where Irish Aid reported serious interventions by local politicians in decisions of the RDCs. In the course of this controversy over resources put at the disposal of the RDC, the project had to be suspended for half a year. Enabling policies also represent a considerable break with the traditional professional role of planners who are now expected to adopt participatory planning with communities according to needs and priorities defined by them. To build up capacities for this aim, the MLGH is jointly with British ODA conducting a programme to sensitize councils on strategic planning involving all their professional departments and locally active private organizations. But at present councils are still ill-equipped with planning capacities, viable concepts and financial resources, and for political reasons may fear the expectations raised in communities receiving active support by NGOs. The de facto planning encouraged by the direct involvement of NGOs in infrastructure provision may also be regarded as being in potential contradiction to requirements of sustainable planning when unauthorized areas gain demographic attraction through the improvement of their infrastructure standards. As coordination with NGOs currently comes under the responsibility of the Ministry of Community Development, a possible improvement might be achieved by transferring responsibility to the MLGH for activities in the field of infrastructure provision. Finally, since planning has in the past been strongly contained by interventions and political interests of local councillors, a politically undesirable side effect of NGO activities could also be the strengthening of local councillors in the affected areas that make spatial and physical developments even more difficult to reverse for alternative land use. A case in point is the above-mentioned conflict over demolitions in Kanyama where planners are at odds with local councillors and public opinion.

An entirely new dimension to these problems will be added with the planned constitutional revisions concerning land ownership. In accordance with deregulation policies, the 1970 and 1975 abolishment of private land ownership under the old government is currently being reconsidered. Although no details have been settled, the privatization of state and council-owned land and the probable reprivatization of freeholds converted by the 1975 Act may pose serious problems for unauthorized housing areas not protected by the Development Area Act. The illegal settlements of Chibolya, Misisi and the northern parts of Kanyama, closest to the central business area, would have the greatest potential for future development by private investors. However, solutions to convert squatter settlements for alternative land use need not be sought exclusively by imposing land rights in advance of actual developments on the land market. The enactment of rights to private property will also reintroduce differential land values depending on market demand and location. Even on a deregulated real estate market, interests are likely to concentrate first on the old western parts of the business area where developed infrastructure on prime sites already exists, but is still only under extensive use by old one- or two-storey commercial buildings. If Lusaka's urban growth eventually moves in the direction of squatter settlements, conflicts over resettlement could be avoided by then introducing market solutions instead of political or judicial coercion. As land coming under demand will also become valuable, profits realized from its sale would be substantial enough for the council (or private owners) to offer compensation to illegal dwellers for moving and their rebuilding of houses on alternative sites. For this 'market solution' of the squatter problem to work it would, however, be necessary not only to have private property rights but also to acknowledge occupiers' traditional right to land by and make them entitled to compensation for the loss of physical values of housing in case of resettlement. Also, acceptable alternative building sites would have to be provided so as not to perpetuate illegal squatting.

Arguably the pattern of squatter expansion in inner-city areas has changed in the last years. The city's continuing demographic growth combined with the council's failure to provide new serviced housing areas within a reasonable distance of the commercial centre has led to the breakdown of the previous self-containment of squatter expansion in areas of sensitive space use. This applies particularly to Kanyama where the former 1.5 km of free space between the city and the north east limit of the settlement is now being rapidly taken up by new squatter developments (cf. Figure 12.1 p. 318). Whatever planning action is finally taken, both upgrading or partial resettlement are highly sensitive issues in achieving sustainable solutions. Without a careful assessment of the prevailing situation, new housing regulations or policies are likely to impose incalculable and undesirable effects on the housing situation. Comprehensive solutions to the squatter problem should also pay particular attention to the situation of the lowest 20-30% of income earners who seem unable to make any kind of substantial improvement to their housing situation. At present these groups seem fairly well integrated into the existing low-income settlements, but they might be highly vulnerable to changes inflicted by new regulations or resettlement however appropriately designed. Changes in residential preferences also seem inevitable due to necessary adaptations of household reproduction to the new economic realities of impoverishment. Still little is known about the social and economic consequences in terms of residential composition, processes of filtering the housing stock, and the further course of settlement consolidation in all the aspects outlined earlier.

The field study presented here on the residential circumstances of high density housing areas in Lusaka, conducted in 1988 and 1989, gives an indication of the tendencies in question. Both selected areas, Kalingalinga and Kanyama, belong to the oldest and poorest low-income settlements in town. Additionally the study allows a comparison between developments under authorized and illegal settlement conditions: Kalingalinga is Lusaka's most recent completely upgraded squatter settlement while Kanyama is the town's largest consolidated but unauthorized squatter settlement. As to the validity of the 1989 field results for the contemporary situation, visits to the sites and interviews with the housing officers responsible in 1995 showed that physical standards in housing and the situation of low-income households have basically remained unchanged since they were analysed last. Displacements of vulnerable residents through the housing market and expansions of informal settlements have clearly grown in dimension but continue along the trajectory already laid out and predicted in 1989.

Notes

1   The conversion to market principles in housing provision is a very recent development initiated under the new multi-party government. For details cf. chapter X.6.

2   These statements are not affected by the introduction of a multi-party system and the election of a new government in 1991. New policies on urban development and major shifts in the power structures were still forthcoming in 1995 and administrative reforms have not yet taken full effect.

3   Settlements existing for more than four years without councils taking action towards eviction attain outright planning permission as housing areas (CDG, 1989, p. 13). According to the Housing Act, residents who have attained this outright planning permission would in case of eviction also be entitled to compensation. However a Cabinet decision in 1963/64 viewed squatting as a political problem, instructing that the powers of the Act CAP 475 in question should not be used in these settlements (Maimbolwa, 1990, p. 1).

4   In more detail the Land Conversion of Titles Act of 1975 included the following major provisions: (i) all freehold titles, including those held by commercial farmers, were abolished and replaced by 100-year leases. Unutilized farm land was taken over by the state; (ii) no land in urban areas was to be sold, though development on the land could be sold; (iii) all vacant plots and undeveloped land in and around the towns were to be taken over by local authorities; iv) real estate agencies were closed down immediately. All land administered by real estate agencies, banks, and law firms were to be taken over by local authorities or by central government; v) blocks and flats owned by non-Zambians were to be taken over by local authorities. Individuals owning property for renting were to cease this activity by 1978 (Kajoba, 1986, p. 312).

5   With the retainment of local government functions by the mining corporations (now parastatals) for their housing areas, the situation for squatters is worse in the six Copperbelt towns. Evictions in line with the traditional containment policy of the mining corporations were frequent. Although the handover to local authorities was agreed in 1976 to comply with the Local Government Act, the process is still incomplete with resistance coming from the approx. 200,000 who are effectively disenfranchised: miners still enjoy preferential housing terms compared to those provided by local authorities and are for political reasons not eager to come under governmental control (Rakodi, 1988a, p. 34).

6   In contrast to the definition by Turok (1979) who sees the ruling class in Zambia as an 'emergent quasi-bourgeoisie which straddles the public and private sectors of the economy', following Burdette (and Cohen) the term 'political class' is preferable in the context of Zambian class formation. Cohen (1972) defines the political class as a class in transition 'whose relations to the means of production are mediated through the control of political power rather than its members' direct ownership of production, property or employment of labour' (Burdette, 1984, p. 203). For more reading on Zambian class formation cf. Baylies/Szeftel (1982); Eriksen (1977); Southall (1980).

7   For a further discussion cf. Tordoff (1974); Ollowa (1979). For background information on the emergence of single-party systems in Africa see Nuscheler/Ziemer (1980).

8   Contrary to Seymour's assumptions, however, costs for land acquisition were borne by the government and did not accrue in service charges (Sanyal, 1987, p. 288).

9   The World Bank loan is repayable in 25 years with 7-8% interest. The capital cost of utilities is repayable by participants in 30 years with 7.5% interest, whereas housing loans are repayable in 15 years with 7.5% interest.

10   With the beginning of economic decline in 1975, borrowing has become a permanent feature in Zambia's economic survival. It has resulted in an ever increasing indebtedness and growing interventions by the IMF in domestic policies, deepening Zambia's integration into the global capitalist economy (cf. Good, 1988; Wulf, 1988; Sano, 1988).

11   For example, initially projected building standards for community facilities that would have enabled self-help construction by residents with the help of local informal contractors were rejected by the ministries responsible. The subsequent contracting of building firms for the achievement of more elaborate standards has, in turn, reduced participation to the contribution of menial labour for ready-planned civil works activities (Rakodi, 1981, p. 74). Most other cases of necessary local decision-making (e.g. planning road routes with implicit decisions on who should be resettled) were taken entirely by the leadership. Their decisions were, however, usually accepted by residents affected (Martin, 1982, p. 268).

12   A full account of participation in the Lusaka project is given by Rakodi (1981), Pasteur (1979) and Jere (1984). As R. Martin has emphasized, any critique of the limited scope for participation should also consider the 'enormous degree of delegation implicit throughout African tradition in decision-making and politics', giving leaders almost dictatorial powers (Martin, 1986, p. 268).

13   For comprehensive evaluations see Bamberger et al., 1982; Keare/Parris, 1982; Rakodi/ Schlyter, 1981; Rakodi, 1989; Martin, 1986; Turok/Sanyal, 1978; Pasteur, 1979.

14   In this site and service project an EEC loan of K2.5 million (at 1979 prices) was provided for 1,005 serviced plots in six rural areas (NHA, 1988, p. 3).

15   The theoretical exception was a proposal to upgrade Bauleni with the help of the GTZ in 1987 (LUDC, 1987). Following political pressure from UNIP, councillors, and local leadership, a resolution was passed by the council that this settlement was the next to be upgraded subject to the availability of funds (LUDC, 1987, p. 2). However, no further action has been taken on the part of the GTZ or the LUDC towards concretizing the project. Alternative financing was eventually found in the early 1990s from a German NGO for HUZA to make infrastructure improvements.

16   According to an analysis by Todd/Mulimbwa on the effects of this sanction practice in Chawama, 92% of residents felt that collective sanctioning by water disconnection was a bad and unfair system (Todd/Mulimbwa, 1979, p. 58). As Todd/Mulimbwa also point out, these measures forced residents, at least temporarily, to draw drinking water from wells contaminated by nearby pit latrines, thereby contradicting initial policies of removing a major health hazard by the provision of piped water. However, as observations in the late 1980s show, the LUDC seems to have generally stopped water sanctions (cf. Osei-Hwedie/Mijere, 1989).

17   Until 1980 the council itself had in fact not, as required by the special arrangement for formal sector employers, deducted charges from the salaries of its employees who had participated in the housing project (Sanyal, 1987, p. 292).

18   Concerning defaults, the legal provisions in the Statutory Housing Act state that "A family which has defaulted for 3 months and has not shown any interest to remedy the breach, shall immediately vacate the land upon which such buildings are situated and shall remove such buildings from such land and shall reinstate, level off, and restore such land to its former state and condition" (GRZ, 1974, p. 47). The council has claimed that such action could not be taken due to ambiguities of the Act in stating whether the council or courts were empowered to take action. Also eviction and demolishing of housing would be contrary to the policy of increasing housing stock and would not lead to recovery of debts (Sanyal, 1987, p. 293).

19   This conference held in Lusaka 13.- 15.4. 1989 was jointly organized by the German Carl Duisberg Gesellschaft (CDG) and the Decentralisation Division, Office of the Prime Minister of Zambia. Organizations represented besides the initiators were the Lusaka Urban District Council (Peri-Urban Division), NHA, HUZA, and the Zambian Cooperatives Federation.

20   These observations are based on the experiences of the German Ebert Foundation with its 'Small Scale Enterprises Promotion Limited' in Lusaka, a programme started in 1982.

21   In comparing indices of consumer prices and real wages (1977=100), prices in 1983 had risen to 211 while real incomes declined to 69 (Mwenda/Nyirongo, 1988, p. 22). Although no newer aggregate data is available on wages, the gap between price inflation and incomes increased significantly after 1985: the indices of consumer prices (1975=100) had risen to 513 in 1985, but jumped up to 1731 in 1988 (CSO, 1989).

22   Services of the EPU include small loans, bookkeeping lessons, the procurement of materials, advice on technical and commercial skills, assistance in marketing and the organization of production and shelter in an economic promotion yard (Oestereich, 1986, p. 22). More details about the operations of EPU are provided in the next chapter.

23   For the reasons stated in the introduction, this chapter is largely retained in its original 1994 form. Although it focuses on proposals for institutional reform made by the former Commissioner for Town and Country Planning, the issues raised remain topical. The actual changes to the institutional and administrative structures introduced by the MMD-government by 1995 will be indicated in the final chapter.

24   According to the LZAG Chairman P. Lishika, the issue was not the total elimination of squatter townships, but "to ensure that their existence is made permanent and this calls for affected people to adhere to certain acceptable building regulations so that their houses can stand fast in the face of floods and other ravages of nature." (As quoted by *Times of Zambia*, 19.2.89)

25   In the 1989 pay scale, monthly salaries of a council architect were not more than K1000, which was approx. only double the amount earned by an unskilled labourer. Not surprisingly, council professionals are devoting a large part of their work time to private assignments. By 1995 various planning posts were vacant due to a growing tendency of Zambian planners to seek better pay and work conditions abroad in the Southern African region.

26   The concurrence of interests behind the decision to decentralize may not be explained solely by the aim of rationalizing administration. It is perhaps significant that elected mayors were replaced under the new Act by appointed governors and political secretaries. Rakodi, presenting one of the most detailed accounts of decentralization in Zambia, therefore speculates that the Act " ... stemmed from a Presidential and/or Party initiative, aimed at consolidating power in the provinces and supporting the Party's political mobilization efforts, perhaps to counteract the growing power of bureaucratic, parastatal and bourgeois interests in the centre, and perhaps also genuinely to promote more effective achievement of development goals" (Rakodi, 1988a, p. 39).

27   For example the annual deficit of the LUDC was estimated to be K2,831,350 in 1984, leading to an accumulated deficit of K22,256,584 in that year (GRZ, 1985, p. 70).

28   Stage one of this project (1984-87) was directed to developing training courses for mid-level government officials responsible for low-income housing. In stage two (1988-91) the target group was expanded to include section leaders in the communities in a formal one-year course at Chalimbana Training Institute. The final 1992-94 stage concentrated on 'situation-centred' workshops at local councils or in the settlements with the aim of involving communities in the development process and enhancing participation in decision-making. For a general overview of experiences and achievements of the project cf. Davidson, 1994 and UNCHS, 1993.

29 Concrete suggestions for more appropriate building regulations and housing technologies for low-income groups will be discussed in the concluding chapter.

30 This project will also identify lowest-income areas and promote public-private participation in water supply, sewerage and sanitation. It further supports government reform programmes by building up capacities in infrastructure, accounting, physical planning and administration.

31 Provision of high and medium cost housing has been retained entirely by the NHA that in its commercial housing schemes includes a complete package of infrastructure (i.e. roads, water, electricity, refuse collection points), the costs of which are borne by the purchasers. The NHA has also been advised to sell its rental property, for which 'Second Title' legislation was passed in 1994 to enable private ownership of flats.

32 In an interview in October 1995 the organization was not prepared to comment on this politically sensitive issue.

XI Kalingalinga: settlement history, upgrading and consolidation of a former squatter area

1   The history of settlement and consolidation

The settlement history of Kalingalinga dates back to the early 1940s when the Indian property owners of two abandoned farms allowed Africans to build huts in the area. Because of its geomorphologic situation the 60 ha area was predestined to become a squatter settlement. Sharing the fate of most of the other African townships on limestone terrain, Kalingalinga was highly susceptible to water-logging and made neither good farmland, nor was it suitable for a municipal housing area. Renting out low-value land of this kind to Africans was quite a common income-generating practice for Lusaka's landowners - though a formal violation of the Township Ordinance. The area was less centrally located than other squatter areas and cut off from the central parts of Lusaka by a surrounding marsh and the city airport. But Kalingalinga was within reasonable walking distance (5 km) of the town centre and the industrial area (6 km). Also very much in contrast to the barren appearance of most of the other squatting areas in town, it had the advantage of having lots of trees and shrubs, giving the place a rural touch. Nevertheless, Kalingalinga only became a 'second choice' squatting area: it was cheaper and less crowded than other unauthorized housing areas, but its drawback was that it quickly became known for its poor health and living conditions. As Kalingalinga is located in a geomorphologic depression area, the high water table and the underlying limestone make flooding and water-logging severe in the rainy season. Pit latrines contaminated ground water, and the pollution of wells caused a shortage of potable water in the dry season. In its incipient stage in the 1940s it also had the reputation of being a violent place, causing many residents to move to the adjacent area of Mutendere.

Fortunately the township's development was intermittently surveyed (1967, 1979, and 1988), allowing a good review of its demographic development and consolidation process. With a view to estimating its economic potentiality for resettlement, the first 1967

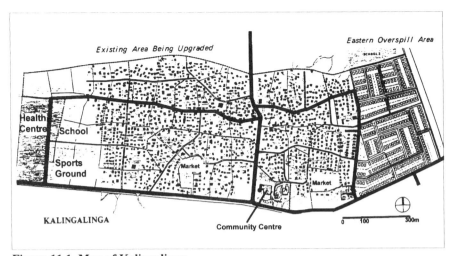

Figure 11.1 Map of Kalingalinga

Source: GRZ Survey Department and Goethert/Oestereich, 1987

socioeconomic study of Kalingalinga was conducted by the Research Unit of the Dept. of Community Development. This study also gives some information on the early demographic development of the settlement (cf. Zelter/Witola, 1967). With a steady population influx in the range of 4.6% in the years between 1957 and 1963, Kalingalinga until 1964 mainly served as an overflow from Lusaka and not as a reception area for newcomers to town. Of the movers from other parts of Lusaka, 44.2% had lived there for 10 years or more before coming to the area (ibid., p. 20).

A change in this influx pattern appeared after Zambia's independence when migrants from rural areas, finding living in Lusaka too crowded and expensive, discovered Kalingalinga as a cheaper alternative with still ample space to settle. Generous space use was in particular an attractive aspect for extended families. As Zelter/Witola note, 26% of households had relatives living with them who did not belong to the nuclear family - a much higher rate than in the other Lusaka townships. For the 1964-67 period Zelter/Witola report a peak annual growth rate of 18.1%, nearly double Lusaka's average in those years. By 1967 Kalingalinga had reached a population of 5,806 living in 1,268 houses. This added up to an occupancy rate of 4.6 persons per house. Although a majority of 56.9% of the housing stock was self-built and owner-occupied, Kalingalinga also had a higher proportion of shifting population and of housing turnover compared to the other townships in Lusaka: 23.5% of the housing stock had been bought, and 13.7% of houses were rented (ibid., p. 9). According to Zelter/Witola's observations on building materials, the thatched village-style housing typical of Lusaka's squatter areas in the 1950s had already disappeared by 1967.[1] Most housing had two to four rooms, built with mud-brick, and had corrugated iron or tin roofing.

263

Reported communal and private facilities were 85 shallow water wells (some already polluted), 465 latrines, 9 shops (3 Indian, 6 African), and 1 marketplace (ibid., p. 3 and 7).

The occupational situation of 1967 already showed a distinctive feature in that workers in Kalingalinga, unlike those in other squatter areas, were more oriented towards local job opportunities than to the main employment areas in central Lusaka. 77% of heads of household were employees, 17.25% were self-employed and 5.75% were unemployed. While the rate of 8.9% employed in services (watchmen, waiters, office orderlies, etc.) was typical of squatter communities, other occupational categories were clearly affected by the vicinity of low-density housing areas (Kabulonga, Twin Palms, Woodlands) for *domestic work* (17.2% of total occupations) or by the nearby university and hospital both then under construction for *building trades* (50%). Conversely, there were relatively few local job opportunities (23.9%) for skilled or unskilled *non-building trades* (ibid., p. 21).

Looking at the early settlement consolidation process, J. Oestereich's claim that in-migration to Kalingalinga nearly came to a standstill after reaching a population of 5,000 (Oestereich, 1986, p. 5) is not supported by statistical data. As Figure 11.2 shows, whether the place was unhealthy or not (like most of the other Lusaka squatter areas), population growth and urbanization in Kalingalinga advanced steadily. As shown by Waldeck (1986) and Wood (1986) the NHA's 1973 classification of Kalingalinga as a 'rural type informal settlement', characterized by low densities (less than 30 houses per ha), was a rather perplexing assessment perhaps serving to justify its exclusion from the World Bank/GRZ Housing project. According to the 1969 population census, residential density per ha in Kalingalinga was 228.3, which in fact made it the most densely populated area in town (cf. Wood, 1986, p. 178). As Waldeck had inferred from 1978 aerial photos, densities in Kalingalinga were in the range of 27 houses/ha in the old core area and 41 houses/ha on the fringe. Considering the near stagnant development of the housing stock, this means that even in 1973 densities in Kalingalinga were well above the level defined by the NHA to qualify for a rural type housing area (Waldeck, 1986, p. 161). Territorial consolidation was characterized by a rising density but an only marginal increase in the housing stock. Although some expansion of the residential area to a total of approx. 66 ha had taken place, constraints to finding new housing sites were both physical and legal: extensions to the north would have moved into the marsh, to the south was the city airport, and to have expanded to the vacant areas in the east or west would have meant encroaching on the council housing area of Mutendere (east) or onto the area reserved for the mass-media complex (west). In both cases this would have involved a considerable risk of being evicted even if Kalingalinga was within the old city boundary and therefore not subject to the rigid squatter control of peri-urban areas.[2]

With territorial consolidation advancing gradually, efforts towards physical consolidation met with various restrictions. *First*, it could not start until the private property impositions from colonial times were removed. On Zambia's independence in 1964, Kalingalinga residents denounced the rights of the Indian landowners and abolished the old restrictions on erecting solid building structures (Oestereich, 1986, p. 5). By community self-help, 22 stand-pipes were installed either in 1972 (GTZ, 1987, p. 4) or in 1976 (Oestereich, 1986, p. 6). *Second*, further development quickly began to be obstructed by the conviction of the Lusaka Council that for health reasons demolition and resettlement were inevitable, and that Kalingalinga could not be included in the World Bank/GRZ upgrading programme. A parcel of nearby land set aside by the council for resettlement in 1976 was, however, quickly taken up by invaders. An alternative council plan to rebuild the area in geometrized terrace-style housing was rejected by residents as far too expensive. This left Kalingalinga's fate undecided until 1979 when at the request of the Government the West German development agency GTZ made a proposal to assist in upgrading the area.

A 'baseline survey' conducted by the GTZ preparatory mission in 1979 disclosed no great difference in the housing or infrastructure situation compared to 1967. The population had grown to 13,000 living in a housing stock of 1,460 units, of which approx. 1,000 were owner-occupied with the rest sublet to tenants. But Kalingalinga still lacked essential facilities like adequate water provision, proper sanitation, schools, security lighting or a dispensary. 40 wells were in operation containing polluted water. But some amount of commercial diversification had taken place. The local commercial situation was summarized by the GTZ as follows.

> There were very few small-scale producers, tinsmiths, tailors, basket-makers, carpenters, and the like. They had a shortage of tools and raw materials (or transport to collect them) and lacked regular market outlet, since the purchasing power of their neighbours was low and areas with higher demand were not readily accessible. A few general retailers were scattered throughout the compound. About 40 grocers and vegetable sellers had organized a cooperative market while other groups of sellers were smaller and less organized. In addition there was a large number of 'front door' stands where the women of the community offered cooking oil, tomatoes or vegetables in season (GTZ, 1986, pp. 4-5).

Although not many details were disclosed, the GTZ account of the occupational situation in 1979 seems to show a decline in work opportunities since 1967 after construction-works in the vicinity had terminated. Unemployment of heads of household was around 10%, and 30% of households had at least one unemployed member of working age (Oestereich, 1987, p. 31). In terms of income distribution, most households were in the official Zambian 'very low' (US$32-48) or, having more than one income-earner, in the 'low-income' (US$64-80) brackets (Oestereich, 1986, p. 7).

With rising unemployment and stagnating incomes, urban subsistence gardening played a major role in making ends meet for Kalingalinga residents. 20% of households had their own small house plot gardens, but according to GTZ (1986, p. 4) and Bowa et al. (1979) as many as 70% of Kalingalinga residents cultivated distant gardens at the end of the 1970s - the highest rate of Lusaka's townships. This includes elevated 'termitaria gardening' in the rainy season (on eroded termite mounds) that is extensively used by Kalingalinga residents on nearby land.

Thanks to Lusaka's 'garden city' image, distant urban gardening (90% of which is however within walking distance) is a common practice of township populations. Suitable areas for gardens are found on vacant land on the urban fringe allowing quite sizable plots for rainy-season cultivation. A study by Sanyal in 1980 of various townships estimated a median size of 864m^2 (Sanyal, 1984, p. 94). Judging by comparative data from George Township, the significance of urban subsistence seems to have increased considerably during the 1970s parallel to the economic decline of Zambia that brought soaring food prices, a fall in wages, and a decline in formal employment opportunities: in George the rate of households with distant gardens rose from 24% in 1969 to 54% in 1977 (Schlyter/Schlyter, 1979, p. 108). By tradition, cultivating is mainly a woman's duty irrespective of whether she has other employment. The crops, mostly maize as the main staple food, are predominantly used for immediate consumption and not for sale on the market (Jaeger/Huckabay, 1986, p. 268).[3]

2   The integrated upgrading project

In designing the Kalingalinga upgrading programme, planners had the obvious advantage of being able to draw both on the experiences of the recent World Bank/GRZ project and on international housing schemes. In the first place it was recognized that projects of the magnitude of the HPU programme would not be replicable, and that the terms of the project had not matured into a politically accepted housing policy to cope with unauthorized developments. In particular the citywide upgrading had grossly overstretched the administrative capacities of the council. It was also recognized that the malfunctioning of infrastructure maintenance on the part of municipal authorities was one of the key problems leading to the near complete failure of cost-recovery. The novel approach proposed by the GTZ was therefore a strategy of *decentralization*. This put priority on the strengthening of the local problem-solving capacities and delegating decision-making and implementation powers as far as possible to the community itself. In this vein, participation was not only to be self-help contributions in installing infrastructure and building the communal facilities, but also giving the community responsibility for running and maintaining these facilities (cf. Oestereich, 1986, p. 15). Thus, according to the GTZ, the overriding objective of the project was to 'improve the living conditions of the families in Kalingalinga while at the same time testing a model that is replicable throughout the unauthorized settlements in Lusaka' (GTZ, 1986, p. 10).[4] The components of the project were (ibid.):

266

(1) the provision of community facilities, i.e. school, clinic and a community centre; (2)water standpipes and refuse bins for each section (25 houses), tarmac arterial roads, and street lighting; (3) housing improvement loans through a community-based revolving fund; (4) the promotion of economic activities and income generation measures also using a revolving fund loan scheme (but not addressing subsistence gardening); (5) experimentation with lower cost construction materials and techniques as well as alternative sanitation methods.

Agreement on these terms was reached both with the LUDC and with the active involvement of Kalingalinga leaders. Two-thirds of the total funding (K3.1 million) came from GTZ in the form of grants for infrastructure, personnel, equipment, and seed money for

Picture 11.1   Communal water taps

the revolving funds.[5] Zambian contributions came from the LUDC and the Ministries of Health and Education as directly involved authorities. It was estimated that total private building investments of residents were equivalent to those of the Zambian authorities (GTZ, 1986, p. 13). The legal arrangements were the same as with the World Bank/GRZ project: the area was declared under the Statutory Housing and Improvement Areas Act that entitles residents to a 30-year occupancy right. With a view to designated self-administration in Kalingalinga, service charge rates (initially K2, in 1989 K3 per house and month) were considerably lower than in the HPU project (K5) and better adjusted to the paying capacities of residents. In order to prevent the revolving funds from drying up from devaluation and defaults in repayments, optional loans for housing and economic promotion (EPU) included a 12% interest rate.

For residents affected by essential resettlement on new plots in the 'overspill' area, special loan terms were introduced. These households were supplied with building material loans to build a one or two-roomed house according to standards laid down by the site and service building regulations (cf. page 246). The building credit is repayable at 2% interest p.a., a rate set well below the rent for one room (Oestereich, 1987, p. 32). Implementation began in 1980. By 1983 the new water network was installed and physical improvements were completed by 1986 including the physical development of a 31 ha 'overspill' area for resettlement in the eastern part of Kalingalinga.

In view of the many problems of the old upgrading schemes stemming from the overlapping of project implementation with political and party interests, it was fortunate that Kalingalinga was less subject to vested UNIP interests. Kalingalinga was a former stronghold of the ANC opposition. But after the conversion to a single-party system in 1972 the ANC's political authority gradually dwindled in the area. However, the old ANC leadership was replaced by UNIP party members of 'inferior stature' in both of its constituent Branches (Oestereich, 1987, p. 32). A remedial attempt by UNIP to strengthen its local standing by changing the boundaries of another ward so as to include Kalingalinga and have it represented by a Party veteran was not successful. The new leader was unpopular and showed little interest in Kalingalinga affairs.

> As a consequence of this, a sort of informal leadership had evolved. The more active officers of the two party branches and certain prominent section leaders, many of them former opposition partisans, gathered in the so-called 'Residents' Committee'. It was this committee which negotiated for the project and was engaged in its preparation (Oestereich, 1987, p. 32).

According to Oestereich, leadership under this committee, which stayed in office until 1983, ensured a large degree of residents' participation in deciding the particular details of physical planning (the road and water network, essential resettlement, the sites of the communal facilities, etc.).[6] It was also effective in mobilizing collective self-help, supervising the resettlement process, and in disseminating the terms of project to residents. Labour-saving self-help efforts of residents (trenches for water pipes and drainage, land clearing for community facilities, a wall around the marketplace) saved more than K200,000. Close social control by the leaders was also conducive to keeping dropout rates low and avoiding property specu-

Picture 11.2   **Tarred access road**

lation (ibid.). Even under these favourable conditions, which perhaps came as close to a real CBO as was possible in Zambia's political system of that time, various cultural and social limitations of self-help and community self-management became apparent.

In the first place, menial work like digging trenches and clearing land is of low esteem with all squatter residents and will only be performed if leaders 'command' this. Moreover, the general propensity of urban residents to organize mutual self-help is quite low. According to observations by various planners in Zambia the traditional practice of mutual help has disappeared in rural and urban areas alike and is now widely supplanted by monetary relations. Free collaborations of urban residents have only appeared in the form of producer or retailer cooperatives and have not spread to housing or settlement affairs. As a result, the provision of self-help labour proved difficult to organize in Kalingalinga. Various components of the project that were supposed to have been done in self-help were actually built by wage-labour in order to meet project time schedules (e.g. the community centre). Even in the case of other work components intended to be done by recruitment of local wage-labour, the response from residents was very low and in the end required the hiring of outside labour. But the reason for this was cultural and not economic. In fact Kalingalinga residents were at the same time doing the same kind of wage-labour they rejected in Kalingalinga in another part of Lusaka; only the difference was that 'their friends could not see them' (Oestereich, 1987, p. 32).

Other general aspects detrimental to the expansion of a communal self-help spirit are to be found in the prevalence of ethnocentrism in personal networks and in the established urban leadership structure. The decline of the tribal elder system (abakumwesu) in the 1950s, led to its being replaced by the political organization of dwellers by the ANC in order to involve the people in African townships in the struggle for independence. The 'section' as the smallest territorial unit was (secretly) introduced in 1961. Besides their political function, these sections quickly attained the role of a formal organization of urban neighbourhood relationships:

> Section committees by 1964 had under their control a whole body of formal and semi-formal procedures of social control from settling marital disputes to arranging burials and the repatriation of widows. Thus the freedom of choice an individual had as to whether he should remain a section attender was limited, as he was unable to opt out entirely from the section's influence (Harries-Jones, 1969, p. 311).

But unlike the situation in rural villages, the urban sectional relationships did not monopolize rights and duties among members. The cohesiveness of sectional organization is mediated by a second, tribal-based social network for mutual aid and services that has been retained in the urban environment. In the language of ethnology this second network is called 'home-boy' ties, meaning the tribal affiliation of those 'that are from my home', which in

269

Zambia may also include different tribes coming from the same administrative district (cf. Harries-Jones, 1969, p. 299).[7] With respect to creating the social prerequisites for a community-based organization enabling participation of all its members, neither of the two

Picture 11.3　Community centre

existing social networks seemed entirely supportive. The sectional organization has the advantage that it is less inclined to have an ethnic base. Its drawback is that it orients and delegates the responsibilities for communal affairs quite exclusively to leaders, who - due to divided interests or their lending themselves to clientelism - may not pursue the real interests of the community. In the hierarchical party system local leadership was often the entry ticket to a wide range of privileges that UNIP bestowed on its activists if they served to party interests. Even if this established leadership structure is in decline now that UNIP no longer monopolizes politics, a communal organization according to kinship and tribal ties may not be a better alternative. It might very well tend to be socially selective and fail to incorporate all members of the multiethnic townships in Lusaka. True egalitarian terms of dwellers' territorial organization and new forms of community-based associations may perhaps only be possible after the democratization of Zambian society and a further reduction of ethnic ties in social and political processes.

From this it follows that the potential for importing successful participatory self-help models to Zambia from the Latin American or Asian settings still seems limited and requires adapting the approach to the specific cultural and political situation. Both the residents' delegation of responsibilities to leadership and the cooption of local leaders into a party-dominated hierarchical leadership system appeared as invariant factors in the political culture of Zambia until the introduction of the multi-party system. Against this background the new potentials of elected RDCs will take time to develop and to become emancipated from political tutelage. It would appear that the enhancement of devolution and communal self-reliance would best be promoted by training programmes for administrators and leaders, thereby (1) developing local leadership competencies and (2) achieving a more cooperative attitude on the part of the council and its local representatives towards community participation. Housing authorities like the LUDC and the NHA have so far only conducted

270

a few ad hoc training courses to this end. However, a more promising approach has been developed by the Ministry of Decentralisation in conjunction with the UNCHS and DANIDA, the Danish Development Agency. In a Community Participation Training Programme launched in 1988, District Council staff, local leaders and training staff can take part in courses at the Chalimbana Training Institute. The aims of this programme are threefold:

1 "To create a pool of effective implementors, policymakers and promoters of community participation in low-income housing in specific among District Council staff ...

2 To create a pool of effective trainers and resource persons for the continuation of similar future training courses ...

3 The training of community leaders such as Branch, Ward and Section leaders to enable them to better deal with problems in their communities in order to improve their settlements" (Zambia UNCHS/DANIDA, 1989(b), p. 1).

Similar community development programmes are also a standard approach of international NGOs that have become active in Zambia since the conversion to a multi-party system. But in the absence of such programmes in the early 1980s, the evidence from the Kalingalinga devolution experiment was indicative of problems with importing programmes without the provision of long-term political, administrative and financial support after the withdrawal of the implementing agency. During the implementation phase the community of Kalingalinga demonstrated its ability to reorganize the community structures in compliance with the necessary division of responsibilities and tasks allocated to the Ward, Branch, and Section levels respectively.[8] The new Ward Committee had also taken decisive steps towards formulating its own independent community policies, for example towards restricted in-migration and plot allocation or defining the terms of the local economic promotion scheme (a separate account of this successful part of the project will be given later).

The study of the 1989 state of consolidation showed that the communal planning capacities developed during implementation had largely been retained. According to interviews with Kalingalinga leaders, the LUDC had also accepted its part of the arrangement that the community is responsible for decisions concerning local town planning and the economic promotion scheme. Leaders also showed themselves satisfied with the way communication was working between the community and the LUDC via the local council field office. But as with the HPU-scheme there is no indication that the aim of creating community self-reliance has been achieved. Instead various parallels to HPU experiences have appeared, as well as additional problems. A problem assessment of the Kalingalinga devolution model can be summarized in 4 points.

First, despite the moderate service charges that in 1983 were equivalent to approx. 1% of total income for most households (and in 1989 were well below this rate), low commitment to paying for services has been replicated in Kalingalinga. Only 59% of residents had up to 1988 made some payments for service charges. In a study of Kalingalinga service charge arrears conducted by Osei-Hwedie/Mijere (1989) only two major reasons for defaults were stated: most residents (63%) claimed financial reasons for not being able to pay, followed by 22% who stated that they were 'not asked by the LUDC' (ibid., p. 12).[9] As with the HPU project, the high rate of arrears has led to the disengagement of the council from some of its responsibilities. While no sanctions like water cuts were imposed, refuse collection has ceased since 1988 and the maintenance of roads, street lighting and water standpipes is no longer ensured. But it should be noted that in a setting where the community used to be suffering from lack of urban amenities, the housing project has restored the residents' general confidence in the council. Although its standing had suffered somewhat due to the decline in service provisions, most Kalingalinga residents still looked to the council more than to their leaders for further development (see below). Even if the aim of developing a devolution model replicable in Lusaka's other townships has not been completely successful, the council has importantly retained its interest in this experiment and sponsored various studies to follow-up specific areas of constraint.[10] The council's planned adaptation of the EPU programme would have been the first innovation transferred from Kalingalinga to other low-income areas in town (cf. page 237). Following the positive experiences in Kalingalinga with the revolving funds for housing, this approach was in 1989 under discussion as an appropriate method of financing low-income housing in other townships. If other proposals were implemented that researchers had derived from Kalingalinga experiences, it would have been the site of further experiments aimed at finding novel approaches to the still unsolved problems of service charge recoupment and the mobilization of self-help labour. For example, a community works programme was proposed as an alternative means of service charge redemption for households with arrears. Unfortunately, none of these proposals had been realized by 1995, and policy directives of the new government on low-income housing areas, which may take up some of the ideas, have yet to appear.

Second, the council had also infringed the sovereignty of the community over its own land policies. Despite the considerable reduction in residential density/ha from the former peak of 228 (1969) down to 155 (1983) through upgrading, the community has stuck to its policy of restricting in-migration to Kalingalinga. Moreover, to cope with future developments, the original project design comprehended community land control and dedensification measures. New plots were to be reserved exclusively for resettlement of Kalingalinga residents. In spite of renewed increases in density (see Figure 11.2), this programme was aborted by the council in 1987 in favour of new plot allocations to outside developers who, in contrast to Kalingalinga residents, could finance construction in compliance with the legally required building standard for new structures. This decision effectively destroys the long-term prospects of a community-controlled dedensification. Affected areas were extensions to the north (moving into the old area) but also plot allocations in the northwestern and western parts within the administrative boundary where various companies were discreetly constructing large employees' housing with the help of nominal 'resident builders'.[11] To serve its own residents on waiting lists for plots, the community must now search for new land. An application was submitted to the Lusaka District Governor to give a piece of land behind the clinic in the direction of the mass media complex. In 1989 the application was under

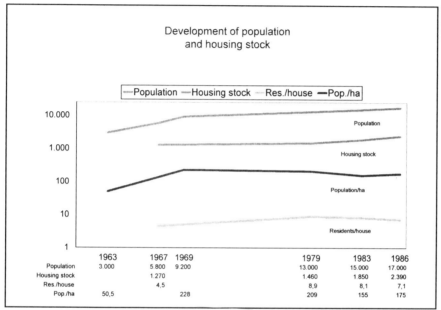

Figure 11.2   Development of population and housing stock in Kalingalinga

consideration with the Prime Minister's Office for approval but seems to have been rejected as no new developments in this area were visible in 1995.

Third, the administrative and planning sides of local self-management were working - mainly due to the commitment of Party activists - and gave considerable scope for participation. In 1989 only 27% of households were not involved in some kind of communal organization or activity: in 56% of households at least one member took part in meetings of UNIP, 8.1% had a Party 'activist', 5.4% were in the Party Youth Organization, and 2.7% of households had a member of a cooperative. Nevertheless, local leadership had been unable to sustain the self-help potentials developed during project times, nor had it made much progress towards achieving self-reliance on the part of the community. In this respect, perhaps the most crucial problem has been the failure of the council to establish the separate community budget envisaged. Without means to implement its own decisions, this had left the Ward Committee suspended between a council with a severely constrained budget and insufficient administrative capacities, on the one hand, and problems of raising residents' self-help activities, on the other. Typical examples were the inability of leaders to solve two problems that seem well within the reach of self-help solving capacities. The accumulated solid waste in and around the no longer emptied refuse bins could be removed by handcarts - possibly to a nearby unused quarry. But aversion amongst residents to any dealing with refuse is considerable, and leaders had not been able to mobilize any action. The same applies to trench-digging for improved drainage or the maintenance of old trenches.[12] In both cases the self-help issue was a divided one among dwellers. Many denied any responsibility as in their view they had made their self-help contribution during project implementation and held the council responsible for maintenance. In considering this attitude we should bear in mind the political background of highly subsidized middle- and high-cost housing. Residents were aware of the fact that they were being requested to pay for services or expected to contribute labour for the provision of urban amenities that were being given to others free of charge. However, the notion of self-help was not rejected completely. In my household survey 81.8% agreed that more could be done by self-help. Fields of action suggested were *individual self-help*, like marketeering (13.8%) and income raising (17.2%); but a total of 58.2% of respondents made specific suggestions towards a wide range of *communal self-help* works. Subtotals for specific activities were 20.5% for communal facilities, like schools and the clinic, 13.8% for digging trenches for drainage. Other items mentioned were road repair, land clearing, refuse collection, security, and raising money from outside. Only 10.3% had no suggestions or foresaw difficulties due to lack of people's cooperation.

Fourth, in view of the project's priority aim of enhancing devolution, the confidence of dwellers in the problem-solving capacity of local leadership was disappointing. In response to the question 'who can solve community problems', 32.3% of Kalingalinga residents named the LUDC, 19.4% thought assistance from outside was needed, 12.9% named self-help, but only 9.7% mentioned local leadership, with UNIP coming last with 6.5% of responses (35.5% of answers were 'don't know' or 'none of these'). Perhaps even more disillusioning results for leadership have been presented in the study of Kalingalinga service charge arrears by Osei-Hwedie/Mijere (1989). While 86% of respondents favoured the idea of making a cooperative society responsible for services and the collection of charges, only 1% thought the society should be headed by local leaders, and only 3% thought that leaders should even take part in the selection process for membership (ibid., p. 23).

The conclusion to be drawn from this problem assessment is obviously not that devolution cannot work in Lusaka's political and social environment. At all levels we find constraints and untapped potentials counterpoised. In the end devolution is not simply an administrative act but a dual and dynamic process in which the various actors must find their roles, and an appropriate organizational structure must be found that provides the conditions to enable participation. Changes to the old model that envisaged only the council and local leadership as the key actors were inevitable. The creation of elected RDCs as intermediate bodies between the council and communities is an important new development. The legally institutionalized RDC structure has the advantage that these organizations have contractual capacities. But mandatory institutions do not automatically guarantee participation and mobilization of communities. As there are strong indications that leadership may not be the appropriate catalyst for the unblocking of self-help potentials, direct forms of residents' involvement should be considered, introducing dwellers' associations as third party counterparts of the council besides formal leadership and RDCs.

An appropriate field in which residents may cooperate and participate directly with the council in managing community affairs is the unsolved problem of reliable service provision and payment of service charges. In an LUDC-sponsored survey based on 500 respondents from Kalingalinga, Osei-Hwedie/Mijere proposed the idea of introducing a community works programme for those having service charge arrears.[13] Considering the presumed negative attitude towards service charges - as expressed by the high default rate - responses were surprisingly positive: 65% argued against writing off the defaults and 68% favoured the idea that residents with arrears should do community works as an alternative (Osei-Hwedie/Mijere, 1989, p. 21). 86% of respondents agreed that a cooperative society should become responsible for delivering services and collecting charges. People not only expected that this arrangement would solve the cost-recovery problem; many also thought that this would 'bring people together again' and give new perspectives to the solution of community problems.

If the proposed cooperative is not to become a field for token participation, or worse, simply a new sanction instrument, it is essential that it fulfils the expectations placed in it by residents. The expressed readiness to perform community works or to pay for services necessarily hinges on an increased reliability of service provisions. The present form of self-management of services merely concerns supervision at the various levels. For example, the responsibility of section leaders (or the equivalent under the RDC) for the technical maintenance of water taps only requires that they report malfunctions to branch leaders and to the local council staff. There are no funds or competencies of the community to take repairs into their own hands. To reduce dependency on the council and its engineering Dept. and to speed up urgent repairs it might, therefore, be expedient to allow a responsible cooperative to commission its own repairs and maintenance. Funds might be provided through putting a portion of service charges into a revolving fund. This approach would also enhance communal responsibility for the utilities installed and exert social control over service charge payments. Once the level of services in a defined unit, such as the Branch, depends on the propensity of its members to contribute to the fund and to properly maintain the facilities (or protect them from misuse and vandalism), they themselves are liable for its operation or failure. As a further incentive, 'saved' funds could be used to finance improvements in standards agreed upon by the unit. Residents have also expressed their willingness to pay more if standards of service improved. Thus, a special fund might be established within the cooperative to finance improvements in infrastructure.

To promote local responsibility the cooperatives should be decentralized as far as possible. Osei-Hwedie/Mijere have suggested that each Branch should have its own cooperative (ibid., p. 28). This is supported by Oestereich's observation that the old Branches representing approx. 250 houses or 2,000 inhabitants have shown the greatest potential for self-management and might be assigned more tasks than initially thought (Oestereich, 1987, p. 35). The running of service cooperatives should be put on a strictly professional base. They should operate in close collaboration with the council and be liable to financial control not only by residents and local leadership but also by legally recognized authorities. The Zambian Cooperatives Union that has its own training facilities in Lusaka might conjointly with the LUDC organize training courses in accountancy and management and help in selecting qualified persons from Kalingalinga as prospective managers for this organization. To integrate the cooperatives into the local political structure, the organization of community works and the decisions concerning activities to be performed should involve the active participation of the existing organizations of self-government and should be coordinated with the developmental goals of the community.

3   The 1989 survey of housing and socioeconomic development

The information presented in this section is based on two household surveys conducted in May/June 1989. The first questionnaire investigates intensively the housing and household situation of 37 families (referred to in the following as *'household sample'*) while the second, more basic questionnaire (called *'housing sample'*) involved 133 households in separate houses in order to obtain a representative picture of housing standards and forms of tenure. Occasional minor differences in percentages may occur, depending on which sample was used. In both cases random sampling procedures were designed to assure representativeness of all housing sections ('blocks'). The selection of blocks and houses was done according to the Statutory Housing Sketch Plan provided by the LUDC survey section. In view of divergent housing standards in the newly developed overspill area (required to meet housing regulations) and in the old settlement area, the sample was weighted in proportion to the total number of housing units in each area respectively (i.e. 65% Old Kalingalinga and 35% overspill). Supplementary information was acquired from interviews with local leaders, informal sector artisans and marketeers, and residents engaged in house construction at the time of survey.

a) Demographic information

Of the households interviewed 83.8% consisted of families headed by both parents, 8.1% were headed by a single woman parent, and 2.7% each fell into the categories 'male bachelor', 'male widow' and 'several families living together'. The average size of households was 7.84, with 3.3 children under 12 years old. To an average of 1.35 working members there were 6.43 economically dependant family members. Average per capita costs of living for adults amounted to K1,116.22 (or K147.34 including children under 12). The difference in living costs is quite considerable between large and small families. As may be seen from Table 11.1 below, lower living costs and employment rates per head for large families were not alone accounted for by a greater number of children. A more substantial impact on large families' budgets is made by the relative weight of the economically dependent members, i.e. those without employment, retired, etc.

Table 11.1
Employment, living costs and number of children by size of family

Size of family	Children under 12	Employment rate per capita	Dependent family members	Living costs per capita
	Mean	Mean	Mean	Mean K
1 to 7	2.10	0.41	4.25	165.85
8 and more	4.71	0.27	9.00	125.56

In a small preview survey it became apparent that in estimating household budgets the inquiry into 'living costs' was preferable to one into 'income' for two reasons: (1) while incomes of heads of household would have been readily disclosed by most respondents, this was found not to be the case for further members in employment. Their incomes were frequently not known by the interviewed heads of household, or the latter did not feel authorized to supply this information. Adding to this it would have been difficult to quantify the amounts made available from these incomes to household budgets; (2) contributions of women to household budgets were quite significant, but these subsidiary, often irregular economic activities were not perceived by them as employment. Related to this, women were often not able to assess their average contribution to household income in monetary terms. Thus, the inquiry into total 'living costs' of the family simply sidestepped both these problems and provided a reliable aggregate parameter that could be controlled by cross-checking with a detailed assessment of household items bought, the prices of which were gathered from the local markets. The information on household goods bought was provided by a separate interview with women if they were not the head of household.

The occupational diversity in 1989 is not dramatically different from that in 1967 but shows some significant adaptations to changes in contemporary local job opportunities (see below for a table adopting the same occupational categories as Zelter/Witola in 1968). Importantly the informal sector has grown from 17% in 1967 to 28% in 1989 with a notable

Table 11.2
Occupational categories by sector in 1989 and 1967[14]

	1989		1967[*]	
	Formal sector	Informal sector	Formal sector	Informal sector
Retailing	-	5.1%	-	8.0%
Building crafts	5.1%	2.6%	25.3%	0.6%
Services	28.2%	2.6%	5.5%	0.6%
Technicians	2.6%	2.6%	-	-
Other crafts	5.1%	10.3%	6.8%	4.3%
Qualified office jobs	2.6%	-	1.8%	-
Labourer, unqualified	7.7%	-	16.0%	-
Domestic servants	2.6%	-	14.2%	-
Worker, non-building	15.4%	2.6%	13.0%	2.5%
Others (soldier, herbalist)	2.6%	2.6%	-	-
Totals by sector	71.9%	28.4%	82.6%	17.2%

*) Compiled from Zelter/Witola, 1968, p. 21

expansion of non-building crafts and minor developments in services and technical occupations (e.g. repair workshops). The growth in informal building crafts is mainly explained by the informalization of this type of activity following the slump in formal sector construction. Perhaps surprisingly, retailing was not found to be an informal growth pole. With regard to the categories of formal occupations, major changes are observable in the sharp decline in craftsmen in construction (-20%) that also affected the rate of formal/ informal building labour (-10%). While building used to be a major activity of Kalingalinga's workforce, providing work for 41% in 1967, this rate has gone down to a total of 15% for both sectors. Instead, services in the formal sector (e.g. watchmen, waiters) have developed into the major single income-earning bracket, giving sustenance to a total of 28%. If servants and informal sector services are included in this category, approx. one-third of the population in Kalingalinga now work in the tertiary sector (but not 65% as the local council officers have claimed). Simultaneously, domestic service - which used to be quite a common activity in 1967 - has now become near insignificant as a main occupational field.

The occupational situation of women in Kalingalinga reflects the general vast gap between men and women in access to wage employment that assigns to women the role of finding income generating activities in the informal sector (Hansen, 1987). Approx. 40% of wives

278

in Kalingalinga were economically active. Of their total activities 46.2% were marketeering, 23% were home producers of food, 7.7% home producers of clothing, and 7.7% each were in the categories of 'employment', 'farming during the rainy season' and 'unspecific activities' (due to the limited sample size of valid cases, frequencies below 10% should, here, only be considered approximations). It was beyond the scope of this study to undertake the difficult task of estimating contributions of women to household budgets. Nevertheless, their evident economic impact on household sustenance in filling the 'margin between survival and starvation' (Hansen, 1987, p. 10) can be seen in the next table.

Table 11.3
Economic activities of women and living costs in Kwacha

	Living costs per capita				
	Women economically active				
	No		Yes		Row total
Job sector of husband	Mean K	Per cent	Mean K	Per cent	Per cent
Employed by government	130.5	60.0%	144.6	40.0%	100%
Employed by a company	92.9	40.0%	149.1	60.0%	100%
Employed privately	191.6	66.7%	128.5	33.3%	100%
Pieceworker	183.3	100%	-	-	100%
Self-employed business	203.5	100%	-	-	100%
Retired	125.0	100%	-	-	100%

The results are also indicative of what kind of household situation determines whether women work or not. In the group of 'husbands employed by the government', 40% of wives were working, which manifests itself in a higher per capita family budget (K144) compared to those cases where women did not work (K130). The effect of bridging the income gap is even more noticeable in the next group of heads of household 'employed by a company'. Here average incomes from employment tend to be much lower and economic activities of women much higher. The 60% of working wives in this group again result in quite a substantial increase in household income compared to cases of non-working wives. Zero rates of wives' economic activity in the remaining cases (excepting the retired) are explained by the fact that per capita household budgets are above the grand average in Kalingalinga of K147. This might be interpreted in that a certain income threshold is necessary to provide an adequate sustenance level. Only if regular incomes of husbands and other income earners do not provide this level, will it become probable that women will take on subsidiary work.

Another assumption tested was that the number of children under 12 and the aspect of child-care might negatively affect the inclination of women to work. However, findings were quite to the contrary. Economically active women had a *higher* average of 3.8 children and

279

came from larger households (9.4 members) while the equivalent data for non-working women was 2.9 children and 7.2 household members. This supports the proposition of an economically induced obligation of women to work: that is, the more children to feed and the bigger the family, the higher the tendency of wives to take on subsidiary activities.

Gardening, the traditional subsistence activity of women, was found at a much lower frequency than expected. Only 21.9% of households claimed to have a garden; only two cases (6.3% of total) had sizable distant gardens of seven ha or more (that indicate cases of proper commercial farming). The remaining households merely had house gardens of less than 10m². I am not aware of any legal restrictions enforced since 1980 concerning the utilization of vacant land. Thus, in view of the earlier mentioned surveys showing a rate of 70% of low-income Kalingalinga households cultivating distant gardens, one possible explanation for the vast discrepancy might be that reference was only made to gardens under cultivation at the time of interview in June. Another explanation might be that the 1988/89 rainy season produced torrential rains destroying many crops. On the other hand, the 15.6% that reported having gardens near the house are in a range comparable to the 1979 GTZ data where approx. 20% of cases with house gardens were reported. Consequently, the survey results denoting a substantial reduction of distant gardening should be treated with caution. 18% of households also reported animal husbandry, made up of 12% who had a small number of poultry while the other 6% of cases were holding cattle on their commercial farm areas.

Another important aspect of household budgeting concerns the various networking activities and systems of mutual support used by residents in times of crisis (cf. Schlyter, 1988; Hansen, 1985). A comprehensive coverage of this aspect would again have required separate anthropological research efforts. However, the empirical survey of lending and borrowing practice was considered a pertinent indicator for the significance and functioning of reciprocal networks. In total 78% of households borrowed and 71.4% lent money. Nearby friends were by far the most important lending and borrowing group (53.1%), followed by relatives in Kalingalinga and in town (25%), workmates of husband (9.4%), friends in another part of Kalingalinga (6.3%), and finally employers and churches (3.1% each). Interesting aspects appeared in the closer analysis of (1) who would borrow or lend or not and (2) if the resettlement of residents to the overspill with a new neighbourhood had any effect on networks.

The common assumption might be that the extent of networks is closely related to the duration of residence and collaterally to the necessary time of building up relationships with neighbours. This was found not to be true. In fact the borrowing rate of the group that had come to Kalingalinga most recently (after 1986) was 100%. From the perspective of total average years of residence there is in fact no difference between borrowing and non-borrowing groups. Also no particular, either high or low, income-group is principally excluded from borrowing. But in examining mean values in Table 11.4 below, some differential tendencies appear. For example, differences became more pronounced when considering the size of

Table 11.4
Socioeconomic circumstances of borrowing groups

Borrowing money	Living costs per head	Size of household	Years in Kalinga-linga	Employment rate	Children under 12	Dependent family members
	Mean K	Mean	Mean	Mean	Mean	Mean
Yes	156.1	8	12	0.33	4	7
No	118.3	7	12	0.32	1	5

family and most importantly the number of young children and living costs. According to this, the inclination to borrow from neighbours is not particularly related to absolute economic needs in terms of low living costs. Generally, those who borrow will also have living costs in the range of the overall Kalingalinga per capita average of K147 whereas poorer families, despite their potential greater need, are more likely to belong to those who will not borrow. Their relative exclusion is perhaps explained by their lower ability to repay. Judging by the fact that the number of children is the most decisive single factor for borrowing, we can conclude that networking is promoted most by the needs of young families in sustaining children under 12 years of age.

The data from the overspill subsample shows a generally slightly lower level of network participation and a stronger confinement of network ties to friends in the immediate neighbourhood that alone made up 66.7% of all borrowing cases. While 25% of network ties in the old area were established with relatives in Lusaka and with friends in other parts of Kalingalinga, none of these ties occurred in the overspill. On the other hand, the tendency of younger families with small children to lend and borrow was even more pronounced in the overspill. Non-borrowing cases had lived in Kalingalinga much longer (17 years) than borrowers (10 years). They were also composed of smaller households (4 compared to 7 of borrowers), and they had quite a high employment rate (0.50 compared to 0.28). With respect to lending, those that would not lend were also long-term residents. They had a distinctly higher income level than the average. From this we can deduce that resettlement within the same neighbourhood does not involve uprooting from established network relations. Also, the residential circumstances of living in the overspill did not seem to impair networking activities of young families with children. With respect to an observable stronger lend-ing/borrowing polarization between younger and older households in the overspill, this might be explained by a somewhat stronger social isolation of the older residential group, not excluding tendencies towards social aspirations on their part. In this respect the clustering of an older residential group in the overspill after resettlement is not coincidental. The terms of essential resettlement with its concurrent provision of a solid house by the project management also provided an outlet for residential aspirations. As Oestereich reports, it was quite frequent that residents whose houses had to be removed, but chose to stay in the old part, could swap their houses with those willing to move (Oestereich, 1987, p. 32).

b) The Kalingalinga informal sector and economic promotion

According to estimates by the ILO, the proportion of formal sector wage earning in Zambia declined steadily from 27% in 1969 to 21% in 1979, and if current trends continue it will probably drop to 13% in the year 2000 (ILO, 1981, p. 39). Considering the country's high and still growing urbanization rate, the importance of the urban informal sector in absorbing job seekers and providing urban sustenance is paramount. While decentralization and self-reliance are the officially proclaimed developmental strategy, the informal sector still does not receive adequate political and institutional support. Its needs and priorities are also not addressed by physical town planning. A case in point are the previously mentioned legal restriction on deploying informal sector activities in towns, i.e. on bringing markets closer to residential areas, as well as running businesses or providing premises for production in Statutory Housing Areas. Indeed, a fundamental self-contradiction of contemporary urban policies is the attempt to implement decentralization by a highly centralized master planning without local participation in decision-making. In a study of policies and programmes for the urban informal sector Maembe/Sibbuku (1987) have explained that although jurisdiction for council plans lies with the ward councillors, their actual role in the planning process can be characterized as a *fait accompli* with regard to council intensions (ibid., p. 14). The siting of markets by the council is an example of the lack of awareness of the specific needs of informal sector operations. While the council undertakes considerable efforts to assist informal retailing (and to curb street vending) by the provision of marketplaces, work sites, and services, it has continued to select market locations according to principles of centrality and not of commercial suitability.[15] Various of these centrally disposed markets in Lusaka (e.g. in Garden Township) were abandoned by marketeers who moved business to new illegal and unserviced sites in more affluent nearby areas (ibid., p. 15).

The Kalingalinga integrated upgrading project has supplied most valuable information which can be used to develop more appropriate decentralization policies. This, notably concerns (1) the delegation of responsibilities by the council to local leadership, in particular for the allocation of markets and commercial plots, and (2) the development of intermediate and unconventional measures of economic promotion of informal sector workers and businesses. In the course of these experiences perhaps the most important discovery was the greater economic potential released by supporting *individual* entrepreneurship compared to the traditionally highly-favoured cooperatives approach. For the early project stage the LUDC had contracted HUZA, a local NGO, to implement a programme of economic promotion. During 1980-84 HUZA concentrated on training informal workers in crafts like candle and soap making, carpentry, smithery, dressmaking, and oil extraction, and it experimented with the production of innovative building materials introduced by the housing project (laterite cement bricks, fibre-cement roofing sheets). To initiate business, HUZA also established a revolving loan system. However, the aim of creating cooperatives with its trainees was, in the end, unsuccessful for three reasons:[16]

1   The approach of first creating technical skills and then looking for prospective markets overestimated the local market demand and underestimated the difficulties of establishing business in competitive informal sector markets. With the new building materials, the production schemes additionally struggled with problems of local acceptability of laterite cement building blocks. In the case of sisal cement roofing sheets, they were not able to overcome problems of sisal supply and encountered technical difficulties in maintaining adequate production standards.

2   Basic technical skills that are taught in training courses are prerequisites but no substitutes for the astute knowledge needed to start independent business in a specific occupational field. In particular the understanding of marketing linkages with the formal sector and building-up connections with the local environment are keys to commercial success in the urban informal sector. Thus, as a rule, the required business competence for craftsmen may only be acquired in the formal sector from apprenticeship and on-the-job experience or locally from informal practitioners. The same applies to retailing where learning from somebody who is successfully running an informal business seems a more effective way of becoming acquainted with the specific rules of the trade.

3   Finally, HUZA was not in a position to play the role of a business consultant. It also proved inexperienced and overtasked in handling the managerial and administrative aspects of forming cooperatives and guiding them to successful business. As most business newcomers were unable to takeoff commercially, loan defaults were very high and the costs involved in the administration of funds proved out of proportion to the very limited commercial benefits.

Accordingly, this programme was considered a failure, and HUZA withdrew at the end of 1984. Alternative approaches were sought, and in 1985 the GTZ came up with a solution to implement a new type of programme successfully tried out in the Sudan. The core components of the new EPU were based on extending short-term loans to small-scale businesses with interest rates that allow the establishment of an independent, self-sustaining funding organization. Loans are provided from a revolving fund. Therefore availability of these funds becomes directly dependent on repayment, and to this end social control is exerted by those waiting for loans. To receive loans, applicants must be of Zambian nationality and have resided in Kalingalinga for the past 3 years. Before disbursement, the integrity of the applicant is reviewed by EPU field staff by home and business visits and inquiries are made with neighbours.

In detail the EPU provides 3 types of loans: (loans and interest rates of 1995 in brackets) (1) micro loans of a maximum of K200 (5,000) repayable within 9 days with 1% (20%) interest per day and daily instalments; (2) working capital loans with a provision ceiling of K1,000 (30,000) repayable within 5 weeks at an interest rate of 2% (25%) per week and weekly instalments; (3) hire purchase of tools and equipment at a maximum of K1,000 (30,000) and a maturity of up to 20 months with 4% (30%) interest and monthly instalments. All loans require a guarantor with steady income on the official minimal wage level of K500 (50,000). Another integral service component of the EPU is the supplying of business advise to all applicants on matters like accountancy, marketing, and general management. For this (if required by applicants) additional commission fees are payable and a non-refundable minor registration fee is obligatory.

By the end of 1985 the EPU had served 130 businesses (approx. 30% of the total in Kalingalinga). Defaults in repayment have been very low in spite of the relatively high interest rates. Moreover, the EPU can claim that the loan scheme has had an educational effect on its clients. In order to meet obligations more attention was paid to business discipline and people began to take a more realistic view of profit expectations.

According to observations by Mr Chiila, the local EPU officer responsible in 1989, the smooth functioning of the scheme does not conceal that it is not yet living up to its Zambian name 'Yambani Pang' Ono - Ndikukula Kwambili' (start small - grow big). Although taking out loans has become a regular practice for many petty businesses (95% of clients come back for a further loan), for most it has not stimulated a dynamic growth, nor have most of the clients been able to enter new markets outside Kalingalinga. Taking up the argument that loans are too small to expand business properly, the Ward Committee was in 1989 discussing with the EPU whether loan ceilings should be raised to K1,000-5,000. But considering the 1986 EPU funding volume of just over K12,000 (US$1,920) that allowed annual disbursements of K34,000, higher loans with longer maturity dates would evidently be impractical without finding a sponsor to substantially stock up funds. According to expert assessment, precipitate expansion of the EPU loan volume beyond K50,000 may also overstretch the handling capacity of the EPU (Maembe/Tomecko, 1987, p. 26). Therefore another approach might be for the EPU to help Kalingalinga entrepreneurs to participate in other business promotion programmes like the Small-Scale Enterprises Promotion Ltd. (SEP) that provides overseas-financed soft loans, or the ILO sponsored 'Improve Your Business' programme. The situation in 1995 was that no raising of the loan ceiling had been negotiated. On the contrary, despite high interest rates, soaring inflation of above 100% during 1990-94 has reduced the seed fund by nearly 50% to K1,000,000 - equivalent to US$1,000. An EPU application for a new grant has been forwarded to the Lusaka Council, which is responsible for any necessary replenishing of funds. But, as yet, no decisions have been taken to revive this most sustainable component of the Kalingalinga project.

However, giving higher loans to reliable clients may only be part of the remedy. According to an overview of EPU disbursements in 1985, the distribution sector is the main beneficiary of the scheme, reflecting the local dominance of this type of activity (cf. Table 11.5). According to an EPU census in 1985, covering all small business activities, 80% of operators are in distribution, 12% in manufacturing, and 6% in repairs and services.[17] Since 80% of small businesses are run by women who on average achieve a turnover that is only 20% the

Table 11.5
EPU loans by economic sector in 1985

Food marketeering	58.3%
Other shops	2.8%
Producer/retailer (baking)	16.7%
Crafts	13.9%
Taverns	8.3%

rate of their male counterparts, it seems obvious that the bulk of EPU funds is not extended to potential growth activities. While serving the aim of strengthening the local economic network, most activities of women are directed to achieving subsidiary income with no aim of expanding business beyond the local network. Therefore the promotion of this type of activity is already to some extent merely redistributive as it can achieve little more than enhancing internal competition within a delimited market.

Instead, the promotion of manufacturing and crafts seems to have a greater potential for expanding markets beyond the confined frame of Kalingalinga. As interviews with seven informal sector businesses illustrate, lack of market outlet still appears a crucial bottleneck of the entire local economic network (see Table 11.6). In spite of the general economic decline, business prospects of the surveyed craftsmen were generally quite good, especially if they had established an outside market and had good qualifications. This contrasted with low EPU-servicing of this group who have quite a substantial need for starting capital.

The three resident producers who had taken up business more recently had not even heard about the EPU, while two other craftsmen were unable to obtain loans due to depletion of EPU-funds. Thus, to promote a potential growth sector, policies of the EPU might be redirected towards giving funding priorities to craftsmen and towards more dissemination of information to business newcomers in this field. The EPU might also take steps to improve the local transport situation that is a major undue cost factor hampering both local business and supplies for house construction. Commercial rates for truck transportation were K350 per haul in 1989, devouring 70% of a monthly minimal wage. Local demand for transport seems to be of a magnitude that would easily sustain a transport cooperative with trucks and

Table 11.6

Survey of informal business in Kalingalinga

	Tinsmith #1	Carpenter #1	Painter	Bricklayer
When did business start?	1987	1989	1978	1986
Where did you learn this craft?	From friend in Kalingalinga	Learnt with company in Lusaka	In Kabwe Trade Institute	Learnt with company
Did you have a shop before this?	No	No, worked for company 10 years before	No, was domestic servant before	Worked for company for 25 years
Market outlet	Only Kalingalinga	Local orders and selling on premises	Main work is in town	Kabulonga, Northmead, Kaunda Sq. and Kalingalinga
Has business expanded in past years?	Yes, but needs funds to employ helpers	Business is slack because he makes expensive things	Yes, is now known by companies and offices	Yes, people are building wall-fences in these areas
How does economic recession affect business?	More negotiation on prices	Same as above	---	No negotiations - gets fixed prices
Do you have helpers?	No	No	Sometimes, depends on job	No employees, but some pieceworkers
Is there an advantage to having a shop in Kalingalinga?	Yes, people know you	Can be self-reliant	No, has plot and house here	No, has house and plot here only. Outside markets are more important
Are you thinking of moving the business?	No, too much competition and better products in Lusaka	Perhaps later when business is established	---	---
Have you taken a loan from EPU?	No, has not heard about EPU	No, has not heard about EPU	No, because no money available this year	---
What do you think about EPU?	Would help a lot	Would be good idea	Would help a lot to get loan	---
How did you get starting capital?	From friend who taught him	Had tools already	From UN development programme	Savings
How much capital is needed to start?	Only K200, but bought tools one-by-one for K500	Approx. K7,000	K5,000 because paint is very expensive	K5,000 for tools and transport
Where do you get your materials from?	Some from town, some offered on location	From Matero market; no scraps	From shops; needs to make capital advances for jobs	From quarry in Misisi; is considering buying his own car
Have you any advice to business starters?	Save money and invest	Craft training not so important, learn from friends	Get training; buy tools and paint	Start with shareholder; get independent when experienced
What qualifications do you have?	Good teaching and on-the-job training	Carpentry training	Painting-course certificate	---
What are your products?	Pots, tubs, charcoal stove	Doors, beds, chairs, wardrobes, tables	----	Makes bricks on order

... continued

	Tinsmith #2	Carpenter #2	Market shopkeeper
When did business start?	1989	1975	1984
Where did you learn this craft?	From brother in Kalingalinga	Learnt with company in Lusaka	No training required
Did you have a shop before this?	No, was painter at airport	No, worked for contractor before	No, was tinsmith at Co-op market before
Market outlet	Only Kalingalinga; sells from workshop only	Only local orders and selling on site	Local only
Has business expanded in past years?	Yes, a lot	Yes, has expanded	No, is the same as before
How does economic recession affect business?	More negotiation on prices, makes cheaper prices for poor	Is not affected; lots of customers; can live on his job	Was difficult to repay EPU loan as business was slack
Do you have helpers?	Started alone, but brother now helps	No, they are unreliable	No
Is there an advantage to having a shop in Kalingalinga?	Can live on the premises	---	Difficult to find a place for shop, but better than labouring
Are you thinking of moving the business?	No, but would sell on other markets if given a chance	---	Would need a lot of money to start outside market
Have you taken a loan from EPU?	No, has not heard about EPU	Knows about it, but was told that there was no money	Yes, but short-term repayment is difficult
What do you think about EPU?	Would be good	Would help with transport problem getting materials from town	More important now due to shortage of money
How did you get starting capital?	Savings for buying tools	Savings	EPU loan scheme
How much capital is needed to start?	---	Approx. K900 in 1975. Would need K2,500 today	K200-300 in 1984. Would now need K7,000-8,000
Where do you get your materials from?	Industrial area; buys scraps, oil drums, metal sheets	In Matero; requires transport of approx. K300 per trip	From wholesaler in town; uses own transport for jobs
Have you any advice to business starters?	Someone has to keep budget in mind, save money	Needs capital and buying of tools. Would be prepared to teach them	Get capital
What qualifications do you have?	---	Certificate from Lusaka Trade Inst.	Nothing special
What are your products?	Pots, tubs, charcoal stoves, buckets	Doors, windows, cupboards, chairs	Soap, biscuits, batteries, medicines ..

and drivers. Improved and cheaper transportation would also help in overcoming the relative locational disadvantage of Kalingalinga with its greater distances to central markets in town.

Unemployment amongst school-leavers is a growing problem for the community and has received attention from the political leadership. A tutorial system provided by the Village

Industries Service and SIDO is to be arranged. In June 1989 there were 106 applicants, but the number was expected to go up to 500 once the scheme is inaugurated. Support will be given to course graduates to form their own business and make them eligible for EPU credits. However the professional reputation of these training organizations is not particularly good and may reproduce the above mentioned limitations and biases of training focusing on technical aspects. With the difficulties of finding access to formal jobs and training, more use could be made of locally available abilities. For example, a scheme might be considered to arrange and financially support apprenticeships with successfully established Kalingalinga craftsmen.

c) Marketeering and street vending

Kalingalinga has two officially recognized markets both emanating from self-help efforts of marketeers. The main market of Kalingalinga in the eastern part started on an individual basis in the 1960s and was reorganized in 1973 by UNIP leadership with the aim of establishing its official recognition. This was finally achieved in 1979 when the market was transformed into a cooperative society. Market facilities like shelters, sheds and toilets were provided by its members in self-help. These efforts were supported by the GTZ during upgrading. In 1984 a loan of K3,000 was granted to improve security conditions by building a wall around the marketplace. Construction work was done by self-help, and the loan has now been repaid. In 1988 this cooperative had 49 members whose contribution of shares (K20) and daily fees (K0.75) allowed it to employ seven workers for market administration and servicing as well as the provision of small loans to its members. On a daily fee base of K1 non-members are welcome to use the facilities. According to a survey by LUDC, the main problem of the market in the view of its members is the lack of electricity. Its provision would reduce security problems (mainly theft) and allow more diversification and expansion of economic activities (LUDC, 1988, p. 15). A feasibility study by the Zambian national electricity company was completed in 1988. But the estimated costs of K88,500 for connecting the market to the main electricity supply line 300 metres away are considerable and no decision had been taken by 1989 (ibid., p. 42). There was also no change to this state of affairs in 1995.

The opening of the second Chifundo Market in the western part of Kalingalinga in 1985 goes back to an initiative by ward officials to accommodate the large number of street vendors and to protect then from harassment by police. This market has been recognized by the Lusaka Council and UNIP, and it is planned to register it as a cooperative. Despite much lower service standards (no water, no toilets, no wall fence) and greater security problems, Chifundo market has expanded rapidly. Due to lower fees (K0.30) and its less formal character it has become particularly suitable for women petty-marketeers and business newcomers who have used EPU loans to set up businesses. The market now has 87 shops and is used by 164 marketeers. Although the marketplace was expanded in 1987, it does not provide enough room to allow all applicants to be considered. With insufficient absorption capacity of markets, selling along the main roads is, therefore, still a common practice. Moreover, the local competition of markets does not seem to have affected the selling of goods as an odd job for women in front

Picture 11.4   Informal production and selling of building materials

of house plots. An entirely new line of business to be observed in 1995 outside of markets was the extensive selling of self-produced building materials (crushed stones, sand, bricks) offered alongside the main road leading to town (Alick Nkhata Ave).

Table 11.7
Prices of selected commodities on central
(Soveto and Kamwala) and in Kalingalinga markets in K

| | Soveto / Kamwala | | Kalingalinga | | | |
| | Wholesale prices | | Market | | Street/house vending | |
	price	units	price	units	price	units
Cooking oil	97	5 l	5 (3.2)*	cup	5 (3.2)*	cup
Beans	60	4 kg	7 (3.75)	plate	7 (3.75)	plate
Sugar	8	packet	5 (1.3)	bag	5 (1.3)	bag
Salt	5	2.5 kg	3 (3.0)	plate	5 (3.0)	plate
Peanuts	60	4 kg	5 (3.0)	plate	5 (3.0)	plate
Okra	50	1.5 kg	2 (1.25)	heap	2-4 (1.25)	heap
Onions	180	10 kg			3 (2.2)	2 small ones
Cabbage	65	25 kg	5 (4.3)	med.size		
Karpentra+)	900	21 kg	5 (1.25)	heap		
Charcoal	80	90 kg	10 (1.7)	2 kg	8 (0.9)	1 kg
Paraffin	5	750 ml	5 (-)	750 ml	2.5 (1.2)	bottle

*) Values in brackets are wholesale prices converted to the equivalent petty-unit prices of local quantity relations of cups, plates, heaps etc.
+) Dried fish

289

Most of the commodities offered on Kalingalinga markets and by street vendors are acquired from central markets in town excepting a few items like drinks, buns, salt, and sugar bought locally in shops. A principal structural limitation to marketeering is that there is no wholesale market, i.e. marketeers and private households can procure goods at the same markets for the same prices.

For marketeers this reduces the sources of profit to the breaking of bulk and using the locational advantage of offering everyday goods on-site while the procurement of the same commodity on more reasonable priced markets in town would involve transport costs for customers. The price differentials which may be derived from these retailing strategies are presented in Table 11.7 above, showing the comparative prices and commodity units in the central markets in town and in Kalingalinga respectively for June 1989.

As the household survey has shown, individual households will, whenever possible, take advantage of bulk buying of durable goods on central markets in town. This applies to items like charcoal,[18] cooking oil, and paraffin that make up more than 60% of total household expenditure of poorer families.

Table 11.8
Main items of expenditure in per cent of total cost of living

Total family expenditure	Expenditure on oil	Expenditure on charcoal	Expenditure on paraffin
	Mean	Mean	Mean
Less than K1,000	25.96%	25.48%	11.60%
More than K1,000	6.87%	14.36%	6.41%

Purchasing of these items in small quantities on local markets is therefore the exception, explaining the extraordinarily high prices demanded for them in Kalingalinga markets. Mealie meal, the main staple food, on the other hand, at that time played no great part as a market commodity as it was mainly distributed through a statutory rationing system under the auspices of UNIP.

Breaking bulk is also the main strategy in market or street vending of products available in local shops (e.g. sugar, salt). Looking at prices, perishable goods like vegetables seem most reasonably priced in comparison to central markets. This helps to explain why products from local gardens are mainly self-consumed and not sold on markets. A final good demonstration of marketeers' inventiveness in sourcing for even the most marginal benefits is the idea of buying a large quantity of standard-price buns from a bakery and reselling the larger ones at an extra price.

4 The settlement and housing process

In the following section Kalingalinga's demographic development will be analysed in two aspects: first with respect to the province of birth, indicating the ethnic origin and composition of residents, and second with respect to the last place of residence before coming to the specific house or plot. The latter will suggest the demographic function of Kalingalinga within Lusaka's growth pattern. In the next table comparisons are possible between our own 1989 sample data and Ohadike's 1968/69 study of migration (see page 189).

Table 11.9

Province of birth and periods of arrival in Kalingalinga

(heads of households in the 'household sample' N=37)

Province or country of birth	Periods of arrival				
	Before 1969	1972-1978	1979-1983	After 1986	Row total
Lusaka	5.4%	-	5.4%	2.7%	13.5%
Luapula	-	2.7%	-	-	2.7%
Southern	2.7%	-	2.7%	2.7%	8.1%
Copperbelt	-	-	-	2.7%	2.7%
Malawi	2.7%	2.7%	-	-	5.4%
Botswana	-	2.7%	-	-	2.7%
Central	2.7%	5.4%	8.1%	2.7%	18.9%
Western	2.7%	2.7%	-	-	5.4%
Northern	-	2.7%	2.7%	-	5.4%
Eastern	5.4%	8.1%	13.5%	8.1%	35.1%
Total	21.6 %	27.0 %	32.4 %	18.9 %	100 %

Two major tendencies are apparent. First, the residential distribution in Kalingalinga by province of birth is fairly typical of Lusaka's general residential composition (cf. Ohadike, 1981, p. 67). Accordingly, there are residential distribution peaks of people coming from Eastern and Central Provinces and a growing proportion of locally-born people. Additionally, the general demographic pattern of Kalingalinga shows a good residential mix of people from all parts of Zambia. Only the proportion of foreigners is slightly lower than the Lusaka average. Second, with the proviso that the sample size may set limits to generalizations, there does not appear to have been a significant change in the distribution of in-migrants by origin in the last 20 years. Thus, the relative proportionate intake from the major provinces has been maintained throughout all periods. The population totals by periods, however, show some discrimination. In particular there was a peak rate of in-migration in the comparatively short time span of 1979-83 that can probably be attributed to the attraction provided by the upgrading project and the prospects of getting a serviced plot (cf. Table 11.10). Details to substantiate this supposition are given later in the section on housing allocation in the overspill resettlement area. On the other hand, Kalingalinga's general demographic growth-decline after 1986 is explained by the local policy of stopping in-migration - in fact the vast majority of cases occurring after 1986 are renters.

Table 11.10
Former residential area and period of arrival (N=60)

| Former place of residence | Periods of arrival | | | | |
	Before 1969	1972-1978	1979-1983	After 1986	Row total
Lusaka site&service	1.7%	5.0%	8.3%	13.3%	28.3%
Lusaka upgraded	-	5.0%	-	-	5.0%
Lusaka unauthorized	-	3.3%	5.0%	1.7%	10.0%
Kalingalinga	10.0%	1.7%	5.0%	-	16.7%
Other town	6.7%	3.3%	3.3%	5.0%	18.3%
Rural area	1.7%	1.7%	5.0%	3.3%	11.7%
Foreign country	3.3%	-	1.7%	-	5.0%
Employers' housing	-	3.3%	1.7%	-	5.0%
Total					100 %

According to our housing survey (with 60 households responding to the question of 'last place of residence'), Kalingalinga has retained in a modified form its function of being an 'overflow' for other residential areas in Lusaka. Only 35% of Kalingalinga's growth is accounted for by in-migration from outside Lusaka, of this group the largest part (18.3%) had come from other towns, 11.7% had come directly from rural areas, and 5% had come from a foreign country. Of Kalingalinga's households 43.3% are recruited from other parts of Lusaka while 16.7% of growth is accounted for by internal population increase.

A closer look at the specific last place of residence within Lusaka is indicative for the various filtering-up and filtering-down processes that correspond to specific housing and settlement policies. The most striking fact is that Kalingalinga is a major absorbing area for residents coming from site and service and authorized high density housing areas. As much as 15% of Kalingalinga's population has come from nearby Mutendere (an early site and service scheme started in 1967) and a further 13.3% from various other site and service schemes. These movers encompass residential fractions displaced for three reasons: (1) people who were unable to meet the financial obligations of site and service projects and, for example, were forced to move during the implementation phase of the HPU project (i.e. in 1972-78); (2) active participants of site and service schemes who were affected by the consecutive upward filtering of housing in these areas and, as the victims of advancing gentrification, had to move after 1979; and (3) newly established younger families and a minority of single persons whose housing demand was not served in their original place of residence and have come to Kalingalinga as renters. As 90% of renters claim to be looking for a plot of their own, their decision to come to Kalingalinga is either an interim solution or is motivated by the hope of eventually qualifying for local plots.

The growing pressures on the Lusaka housing market and Kalingalinga's role as an 'overflow area' are also clearly reflected in the reasons stated for coming to the area. In particular there has been a shift in housing preferences between the early pre-upgrading periods, when employment or joining relatives were named as major reasons for coming, and all the following periods where the satisfaction of housing demand has taken top priority.

Table 11.11
Specific reasons for coming to house and plot by period

Reasons for coming	Periods of arrival			
	Before 1969	1972-1978	1979-1983	After 1986
From childhood	16.7%	-	-	-
Employment	33.3%	-	-	-
Marriage	16.7%	-	-	-
Unspecific	-	16.7%	-	16.7%
Join relatives	16.7%	33.3%	12.5%	
Be independent from parents	-	-	-	16.7%
Education for children	-	-	12.5%	-
House and plot	16.7%	50.0%	75.0%	66.7%
Total	100 %	100 %	100 %	100 %

But difficulties in accommodating its own population growth are becoming acute in Kalingalinga. As Table 11.10 has shown, the bulk of locally satisfied housing demand dates back to the 1960s, with a second peak occurring during the upgrading phase. The absence of new plot allocations to local residents after 1986 already shows the impact of the aborted dedensification policy and the council's intervention in local land policies by allocating new plots to solvent outside developers. The 6.5% of home ownership cases after 1986 are, thus, attributable either to these direct council allocations or to residents' individual sales of housing to outside buyers.

The next table, portraying the income situation of in-migrants, points out considerable differences between various population segments depending on when they came to Kalingalinga. Assuming that 1989 living standards reflect not just the contemporary occupational situation but to some extent also the long-term structural economic dispositions of households, this allowed interesting retrospection of probable reasons for their moving to Kalingalinga. For example, the income situation of house owners who came from site and service areas before 1985 is very poor. This underscores the proposition that the main reason for their displacement was probably failure in meeting the rising economic demands of housing areas susceptible to processes of upward filtering. In fact, their income situation very much resembles that of the fraction of poor residents who came to Kalingalinga from unauthorized housing areas. Differentiation also seems to have taken place among migrants coming from outside Lusaka. With groups who proceeded directly to Kalingalinga, there is

Table 11.12
Former place of residence by time of arrival in Kalingalinga (or present plot) and 1989 living costs in Kwacha

	Periods of arrival			
	Before 1969	1972-1978	1979-1983	After 1986
Former place of residence	Living costs per capita	Living costs per capita	Living costs per capita	Living costs per capita
	Mean K	Mean K	Mean K	Mean K
Lusaka site&service	-	79.17	108.33	200.00
Lusaka upgraded	-	202.65	-	-
Lusaka unauthorized	-	75.00	115.00	-
Kalingalinga	95.83	-	183.33	-
Other town	139.58	75.00	66.67	191.67
Rural area	85.71	114.29	169.84	250.00
Foreign country	250.00	-	142.86	-
Employers' housing	-	138.89	166.67	-

a significant income discrepancy between movers from other towns and movers from rural areas. Whereas former town dwellers have remained among the poorest, those who moved directly from the countryside to the capital city after 1980 - i.e. without the usual intermediate step via a smaller town - are in the top income categories. This points to the emergence of a relative threshold for rural dwellers who will only venture a direct move to Lusaka if they have good confidence in their own ability to make a reasonable living in a new socioeconomic environment. It is also interesting to note that foreigners, whose capacity to integrate economically and socially has often been questioned, are the most prosperous of Kalingalinga's residents, especially if they have resided there for a longer period.

As in other upgraded housing areas (cf. Rakodi, 1988c, p. 309), a major effect of regularization in Kalingalinga has been an expansion of the local rental housing market. From a former rate of less than 10% tenant households, rented accommodation has risen to a total of 32.2% households after upgrading (or 33% if employers' housing is included). There can be no doubt that the surge of renters to Kalingalinga during and in particular after upgrading (i.e. after 1986) is a welcome addition to the local economy (cf. Table 11.13). The residential fraction of renters that came after 1979, alone making up 24% of total households, had notably higher average living costs per head of K205 compared to K130 of house owners. Moreover, the total employment rate of tenants (0.41) is higher than that of the house owners (0.32), which emphasizes their importance for local markets as a new consumer group with stable incomes.

Table 11.13
Ownership status in housing and period of arrival (N=133)

Period of arrival	Ownership status		
	Landlord	Resident owners	Employers' house
After 1986	15.3%	6.5%	-
1979-85	9.7%	23.4%	-
1972-78	2.4%	14.5%	-
Before 1969	4.8%	22.6%	0.8%

In the sample distribution of households in the two areas, we find a slight over-proportion of tenant housing stock in the overspill: it comprehends 44.2% of total rental cases (but only 39.8% of total households) whereas 55.8% of total rentals are in the old area (but 60.2% of total households). In tenancy arrangements for all Kalingalinga, 19.1% are subletting cases with the landlords living in the same house, 23.4% cases of landlords who were living elsewhere in Kalingalinga, and 57.4% of cases with landlords living outside the area. The impression that a genuine commercial rental housing market has emerged is underscored by the fact that 81.8% of tenancy arrangements were agreed between legal parties of no kinship relation, with only 9.1% each of tenants belonging to the categories of 'friends' or people from the 'same home area'. In view of the nominal upgrading policy of promoting home ownership and the official ban on absentee landlordism, the local council housing officers, when confronted with this data, proposed that most cases of tenancies were explained by temporary absence of the owners or as reservations for future family extensions.[19] To clarify this issue, tenant households were re-interviewed inquiring into reasons on whether they believed landlords were going to come back to their house. According to this supplementary survey, 28.6% of respondents were sure of a permanent tenancy status in the house - particularly in the old area. However, the specific reasons given in the second part of the following table make it probable that as many as 38% of cases qualify as absentee landlordism.

Even disregarding landlords 'absent for work' that are certain to comprise further cases of absentee landlordism, we can conclude that approx. as much as 38% of Kalingalinga's rental housing stock is rented out permanently. In figures for the entire housing stock of Kalingalinga this adds up to a total of about 16% absentee landlordism - a rate that puts it

Table 11.14
Potential absentee landlordism in tenancy arrangements

	Old area	Overspill	Total
Landlord is coming back?			
Yes	19.0%	33.3%	52.4%
No	19.0%	9.5%	28.6%
Don't know	14.3%	4.8%	19.0%
Total			100.0%
Reason for landlord coming back?			
Owns house	4.8%	-	4.8%
Has family need	4.8%	-	4.8%
Absent for work	23.8%	19.0%	42.9%
Claim was reaffirmed	-	9.5%	9.5%
Subtotal: probable future requirement of house by owner			62.0%
No claim	4.8%	-	4.8%
Lodger house	9.5%	4.8%	14.3%
Married away	-	4.8%	4.8%
Owns farm	4.8%	4.8%	9.5%
Runs business in the area	-	4.8%	4.8%
Subtotal: probable absentee landlordism			38.2%

in the range of other upgraded areas in Lusaka (cf. Schlyter, 1988 for George; and Rakodi, 1988c for Chawama). While the discrepancy between the reality of growing absentee landlordism and its legal and political condemnation remains unreconciled, new developments require the problem to be reconsidered from a different vantage point as there is no doubt that absentee landlordism is introducing operations of rental capital and housing speculation to areas designated for home ownership of low-income populations.

A fraction of about 10% of Kalingalinga households (i.e. the new cases of absentee landlordism after 1980) have apparently not used the upgrading programme for their own housing benefit but for speculation with housing. With the current economic crisis and the absence of subsidized housing programmes in Zambia, new house construction by low-income owner-occupiers has become practically impossible, even if the constraints on the delivery of suitable sites were to be overcome by the council. Thus, absentee landlordism should be considered a *solution* rather than a housing problem under two conditions: (1) that it provides new housing stock through vacancies; (2) that for low-income tenants already residing in this type of housing, the growing rental market should not lead to their displacement by more affluent renters. The newly developed rental market in Kalingalinga seems to meet both these provisos. The main form of absentee landlordism has occurred by vacancies of proprietors owing to settlement regularization and the opening of an economic rental market. There is,

296

however, also a fraction of landlordism that has come about by manipulating the resettlement programme (cf. the section on housing in the overspill). While it is true that the new rental groups who have moved into these vacancies are somewhat more affluent than the average original residents, Table 11.15 shows that the diversity of building standards in Kalingalinga also provides a differentiated rental market with rent rates that serve various income groups.

Table 11.15
Basic household data of tenants (N=37)

Type of housing	Living costs per head	Rent per room 1989	Rent per room 1988	Rooms per head
	Mean K	Mean K	Mean K	Mean
Mud-brick housing	180.95	25.02	19.65	0.86
Concrete house	226.67	45.56	30.00	0.73

Another argument voiced against landlordism is that it leads to poor maintenance of the housing stock. Although some isolated cases of unduly high rent rates were found for dilapidated housing, our general Kalingalinga survey of physical standards of housing showed only a minor inferiority of rented housing stock in the respective housing categories compared to that of owner-occupiers. Moreover, the range of rents demanded largely corresponds to the physical state of the housing offered. Thus, an incentive is given to maintain and improve housing standards, as investments can be recouped from the equivalent rates on the rental market. The danger may be that commodification of housing will gradually disrupt the present structures of market provisions and withdraw capacities of cheap housing stock.

In 1989 there was no indication that regularization was pushing up the rent ceiling. Despite the benefits of legalization and new service provisions, rent rates for comparative housing in Kalingalinga are still approx. 10% lower than in the illegal, but more centrally disposed area of Kanyama surveyed in the same period. Nonetheless, the process of housing commodification is slowly advancing - particularly with housing stock that complies with the new minimum housing standard introduced in the mid 1970s for housing in legally declared areas. An indicator of the emerging commodity character in Kalingalinga of this type of rental housing is expressed by the close relationship between rent increases and overall consumer price developments. The annual 1988-89 rises in rent of 25% for mud-brick and 50% for concrete-block housing largely correspond with the annual inflation rate of 51.2% for 1988 consumer prices for low-income groups (CSO, 2/1989). In comparison to this, wage increases for labourers were estimated at 31% while tradesmen had achieved an annual 47% increase in income (NHA, 1989). Therefore developments on the rental market for lower income groups are now placing constraints on access to affordable housing similar to those on achieving home ownership of newly constructed housing. In all newly built housing complying with official housing standards, minimum construction costs had risen in 1989

297

to K5,000 for a two-room housing unit. According to estimates by local UNCHS experts, investments of this size require monthly incomes of K1,000, double the monthly minimum wage, which is a prohibitive level for most low-income households. If price and income discrepancies continue further along these lines, the commodification process in housing will indeed force new low-income households to satisfy their housing demand in squatter areas that provide or allow them to build cheap mud-brick housing. For the growing fraction of those presently accommodated in rental housing, pressures towards displacement are building up in two ways: either in that concrete block housing is becoming unaffordable for income groups earning the minimal wage rates, or that currently provided cheap mud-brick housing is gradually transformed by landlords into more profitable concrete-block style housing.

At least in Kalingalinga the council practice of tolerating petty-scale absentee landlordism is still helping to serve the housing demand of low-income households. But the indulgence shown towards affluent multi-occupiers of housing should be extended to poorer owner-occupiers as well. If space and infrastructure capacities permit, the council should allow or even encourage the construction of additional rooms for subletting within the terms proposed earlier (cf. page 142). In the absence of adequate housing programmes, efforts in this direction would be a welcome contribution to reducing the housing shortage in Lusaka and would help to subdue price developments. Simultaneously, the provision of a secondary income from rent would for many owner-occupiers strengthen their economic position and curb the potential encroachment of gentrification. While an outright process of gentrification did not seem to be imminent in 1989, excepting the post-upgrading plot allocations by the council in the new extension areas, a certain rise in the socioeconomic entry threshold to Kalingalinga was already observable on the rental market. Local leaders quite rightly perceive this residential mix as a strengthening of the local economy offering new potentials for all residents. Also the price/income disparities have not risen to a level that gives concern about distortions of the socioeconomic homogeneity or displacement of poorer households. But in the end it would be important that local leaders reaffirm their policies of control over in-migration in order to maintain the crucial social balance between the new, more affluent, and the older, but generally poorer households.

In view of the 1995 situation, this 1989 account needs some updating with respect to the claim of limited attraction of plots in Old Kalingalinga for a commercial housing market. Five years later the demographic pressure on urban housing markets in Lusaka had risen considerably, and in times of high inflation rates, capital investments in real estate are a viable strategy to preserve monetary values. Market demand is now reaching the old parts of Kalingalinga that formerly appeared reasonably protected through their physical and spatial conditions, offering little attraction for home ownership to affluent buyers. The situation is, no doubt, aggravated by a growing economic vulnerability of low-income households who are forced to sell out and move to peripheral housing areas in Lusaka. The price for standard plots with mud-brick housing is now approx. K500,000, which is still comparatively cheap for a serviced housing area in Lusaka. The outcome of this process is however not gentrification. Apparently a large part of this housing has been bought by commercial housing agencies and private companies who are converting complete parcels of old mud-brick structures into large concrete-brick housing units for rentals or for their employees. This explains why the earlier described 'deterrent' mechanisms fail to apply for this particular type of development since housing is bought not for middle-class home ownership but for the provision of middle-standard lodgings that are in high demand on the rental market.

a) Physical housing developments in Kalingalinga

The fact that Kalingalinga's housing structure falls into two very different categories in the old area and the overspill, made it necessary to consider the question whether or not to treat it as a single survey unit. On the one hand, the newly built housing stock in the overspill was achieved with the financial and labour inputs of residents and, thus, represents their genuine housing aspirations. On the other hand, it seems doubtful if the specific decisions taken on housing standards, financial obligations etc. truly reflect household dispositions beyond the given frame of project. While physical and spatial developments in the old area concern factors such as socioeconomic and sociocultural constituents, space use, housing preferences and ownership, the basic standard of housing in the overspill is the direct result of the legal and physical terms of project agreed upon. All residents resettled in the overspill were obliged to construct their new housing within the standard terms laid down by the building codes for site and service areas (cf. Figure 10.3). To this end, all residents affected by 'essential resettlement' due to the building of infrastructure lines or road clearances received a free plot and a building material credit sufficient to build a two-roomed concrete brick house with foundation, a roof for one room and one door. Credits were repayable after a grace period of one year into a revolving housing fund at a modest interest rate of 2% p.a.[20] Building materials were drawn from a local project-unit store and, if required, advisory support on construction was given. For residents reluctant to move, resettlement to the overspill was not compulsory. By swapping of houses with neighbours willing to move, hardships were usually avoided.

However, swapping has obviously had the side-effect of transferring a large part of potential improvers to the new area, who - when the areas are investigated separately - no longer show up in the analysis of housing determinants and development potentials of Old Kalingalinga. Nevertheless, due to the strong channelling of housing activities by the project arrangements, I have decided to make a clear division between the old area and the new housing stock built in the overspill area.

For the general survey of housing conditions in a representative sample of 133 household units in *both* parts of Kalingalinga, a classification scheme was used based on the rating of two sets of factors: (1) the basic physical housing standards, i.e. foundations, walls and roofing, which were considered the most significant components in determining basic physical housing standards; (2) to allow further differentiation of the basic standards, additional selective 'house developments' were considered like the existence of window and door frames, painting, plastering, etc. Thus, according to the combination of different materials used in construction, its state of maintenance, its finish and the 'additional developments', the housing stock was grouped into six major categories as presented below in Table 11.16.

Table 11.16
Standards of housing by area and in total housing stock (N=133)

Standard of housing	Total percentage for areas		Percentage of total housing stock	
	Old area	Overspill	Old area	Overspill
Mud-brick, undeveloped	37.5%	-	22.6%	-
Mud-brick with developments	21.3%	-	12.8%	-
Mixed materials, undeveloped	11.3%	1.9%	6.8%	0.8%
Mixed materials, with developments	3.8%	1.9%	2.3%	0.8%
Concrete house, undeveloped	12.5%	43.4%	7.5%	17.3%
Concrete house, developed	13.8%	52.8%	8.3%	21.1%
Totals	100 %	100 %	100%	

b) Determinants of housing standards and improvements in Old Kalingalinga

In identifying the most significant single factor for housing standards not much statistical analysis is required. Quite obviously the ownership status of residents is the major single incentive for housing improvements. Nearly half (46.7%) of the undeveloped mud-brick housing stock was rented out, with landlords living either in or outside the area but never in the same house. In all the more developed forms of housing, conversely, home ownership becomes the predominant proprietary status. The highest rate of owner-occupancy is found in fully developed concrete-brick housing with only 18.2% in this category owned by landlords. Impressively these results demonstrate the mobilizing capacities of low-income households to improve housing if legal home ownership or plot security is conferred. In this context it is noteworthy that all owner-occupiers who lived in concrete-brick houses had named 'getting a house and plot' as the major reason for coming to Kalingalinga.

300

Table 11.17
Old Kalingalinga housing standards and ownership status

Standard of housing	Landlord	Resident owned
Mud-brick, undeveloped	46.7%	53.3%
Mud-brick with developments	23.5%	76.5%
Mixed materials, undeveloped	22.2%	77.8%
Mixed materials, with developments	-	100.0%
Concrete house, undeveloped	30.0%	70.0%
Concrete house, developed	18.2%	81.8%

According to information given by local council housing officers, 98% of mud-brick housing cannot be upgraded due to lack of foundations. This is confirmed by the survey, where there is a close correspondence between the 53.8% of cases with no foundation and the 58.8% of housing classified as 'mud-brick' structures. Partial foundations were found in 15.2% of housing that had been extended or partially rebuilt using either concrete, laterite cement, or burnt-brick. 26.3% of the stock in Old Kalingalinga can already be classified as concrete-brick housing, with a minority of 3.8% using the newly introduced laterite cement bricks. This leaves only a stock of 37.5% in Old Kalingalinga in the original state of undeveloped mud-brick housing, nearly half of which is owned by absentee landlords. As an indirect effect of upgrading (and legalization), privately financed, individual efforts towards housing improvements have been made since the early 1980s. Approx. 40% of the entire housing stock had been built or rebuilt in the 1980-89 period, half of it in concrete brick, 25% in mud-brick, and 25% with mixed materials.[21] These figures, however, do not represent the real absolute potential for improvements as those cases that had swapped houses with other residents due for essential resettlement no longer show up.

The next table illustrates the terms of house construction and forms of building finance. The impact of LUDC loan schemes is difficult to estimate as there are not enough cases to reliably determine the rate of rebuilding with loans in relation to total rebuilding. In any case, the housing loans from a revolving fund (K650) were only provided for a short span till the mid 1980s when the programme was suspended due to inadequate financial stocks to match the price increases in building. Estimated construction costs for a core house rose from K650 in the early 1980s to K5,000 - 15,000 per unit in 1989, and K300,000 - 350,000 in 1995. To finance this with loans would demand repayments beyond the paying capacities of most Kalingalinga residents. Thus, the great majority of building finance for all forms of housing in Old Kalingalinga was procured through family savings. The commercialization of the construction process, on the other hand, is already fairly advanced irrespective of the building materials used, or the period of construction. Although the most recent builders of concrete-brick housing exclusively used craftsmen, the symmetric distribution of self-help and commercial building modes, apparent in the table below, is already found for housing built 20 years ago. The relatively early emergence of a commercialized building process, supplanting self-help, matches with the already presented information that construction-labour is the cheapest cost component in the building of the house (cf. page 230). Obviously, the trade-off of investing labour-power in other activities and hiring craftsmen for building is often more beneficial than investing it in self-help housing.

Table 11.18
Builders in Old Kalingalinga

Building material	Building finance		Form of building	
	Savings/ wages	Loan	Self-help	Paid craftsmen
Mud-brick housing	100.0%	-	50.0%	50.0%
Mixed materials	100.0%	-	50.0%	50.0%
Concrete housing	80.0%	20.0%*	40.0%	60.0%

*) Only one case

To judge from the dominant patterns of house construction since upgrading took effect, mud-brick housing is now generally viewed as substandard. Since the GTZ/GRZ scheme started in the early 1980s, only 9.1% of newly built houses in Kalingalinga (both areas) were made of mud-brick. Instead, like in the squatter areas upgraded by the HPU project, concrete brick has become the new *de facto* locally desired housing standard - even if partially reinforced by the dwellers' erroneous impression that all new or rebuilt housing must comply with building regulations or that such a directive might be forthcoming (while in fact all housing in the old area is legally exempted from building codes). Another important factor adding to the preference for concrete blocks is the growing crime rate in Lusaka, since mud-brick housing is unable to safeguard domestic possessions. These findings are underscored by observations in an extra subsample of six houses in Old Kalingalinga under reconstruction or being extended during the period May/June 1989. Here only an exceptional case (a very poor single old lady) was still using mud-brick as material to rebuild her house that had been severely damaged in the last rainy season. All other cases were rebuilding on an adjoining site or were progressively transforming the old structures room-by-room with concrete bricks. In the housing sample the reported duration of the building process was a maximum of 30 days for mud-brick buildings. Building of houses in concrete brick by construction workers was taking between 45 and 270 days in the overspill while building of concrete houses by self-help in the old area was a more incremental process taking 500-700 days.

New momentum to improving the as yet undeveloped mud-brick housing stock had been added by the severity of damage during the 1988/89 rainy season: 137 houses collapsed completely, representing 5.7% of the total housing stock or 7% of that in Old Kalingalinga. In the survey as many as 40% of households reported in both areas that they had suffered from partial damage (such as damage to walls, outside toilets and kitchens). Costs of repair were estimated by households at an average of K640, with a median value of K360. The urgency of improving housing to durable standards is also expressed in the rate of planned improvements in Table 11.19: according to owners, approx. 50% of the undeveloped stock is due for complete reconstruction or upgrading as soon as financial means become available.

The socioeconomic potential of households to actually carrying out these planned improvements is difficult to assess, as the determinants of housing improvements in the past may no longer be valid due to escalating building prices. Nevertheless, the following table indi-

Picture 11.5   A 25-year-old mud-brick house in Old Kalingalinga

cates how housing strategies link up with the household situation and reproduction strategies, even if the reduced sample size may set limits to generalizations. Findings, however, do not add up to a straightforward definite pattern showing what type of household is inclined to improve. Moreover, social dispositions and individual motivations play a difficult to assess role in the final housing accomplishment. For example, all residents living in concrete housing stated as their main reason for coming to Kalingalinga that they came exclusively for 'house and plot'. For households living in mud-brick housing, conversely, 'family reasons' and others like 'education for children' or unspecific reasons were strongly represented. Evidently, the determination to get a plot and house figures as a vital motivation to improve housing. But dispositions to improve housing also evolve from specific household, occupational or demographic situations. Even with the reservation that the actual household situation at the time of interview may be different from that at the time of house-building, we can observe *five* relatively direct impacts of the socioeconomic household situation on housing standards:

1   House developers in both the mud-brick and concrete-brick categories are households that have higher per capita living costs than the non-developers in their respective housing categories.

303

Table 11.19
Socioeconomic determinants of housing standards
in Old Kalingalinga for house owners

House development	Years in township Mean	Years in house Mean	Size of household Mean	Children under 12 years Mean	Living costs per capita Mean K	Employment rate Mean
Mud-brick, undeveloped	18.75	7.25	6.75	1.75	97.32	0.2
Mud-brick, with developments	22.0	14.76	8.67	2.00	127.78	0.15
Mixed materials, undeveloped	8.0	8.0	14.0	9.0	142.86	0.20
Mixed materials, with developments	13.0	7.00	8.0	3.0	76.59	0.38
Concrete house, undeveloped	13.0	13.00	7.0	4.0	114.29	0.33
Concrete house, developed	16.0	16.33	9.25	4.75	134.72	0.42

continued....

| House development | Job sector head of household | | | | | Living satisfaction*) | Old area — Planned improvements (number of cases in brackets) | | | | |
	Employed by government	Employed by company	Employed privately	Informal business	Total	Mean	Rebuild	Extend	Upgrade	None	Total
Mud-brick, undeveloped	-	-	6.7%	13.3%	20.0%	1.25	40% (2)	-	20% (1)	40% (2)	100%
Mud-brick, with developments	-	6.7%	-	13.3%	20.0%	1.67	66% (2)	-	-	33% (1)	100%
Mixed materials, undeveloped	-	-	-	6.7%	6.7%	1.00	100% (1)	-	-	-	100%
Mixed materials, with developments	-	20.0%	-	-	20.0%	1.67	-	66% (2)	-	33% (1)	100%
Concrete house, undeveloped	6.7%	-	-	-	6.7%	2.00	-	-	-	100% (1)	100%
Concrete house, developed	13.3%	6.7%	-	6.7%	26.7%	2.00	20% (1)	40% (2)	20% (1)	20% (1)	100%
					100%						

*) Scale: 1 = dissatisfied 2 = satisfied about living conditions in Kalingalinga

2   This first pattern is overlaid by that of the size of households that works in the same direction, i.e. due to their extended income base, larger households can either afford housing improvements or their household situation gives them greater security and incentives to improve. In this respect we can note that independent of family size and type of housing, all households tend to realize near identical standards of space-use in housing.

3   Another obvious pattern is that dwellers in mud-brick housing are older residents who typically have lived in Kalingalinga for some 20 or more years and naturally have considerably fewer children under 12 years of age than all other household groups. There is also a high concentration of informal sector workers in this type of housing. Approx. 66% of the total heads of household in this occupational group live in mud-brick housing with and without developments.

4   The distribution of employment rates of household members is distinctly skewed with respect to their housing standards: for families living in housing of at least partially durable building materials or fully consolidated housing, the employment rate of dwellers is nearly twice as good as for those in mud-brick housing.

5   Finally, the occupational sector of heads of household seems to be the strongest overall determining factor for owner-occupied housing. A reinforcing factor is, of course, that occupations in government and some private firms qualify for housing allowances.[22] Accordingly, the spectrum of occupational patterns is almost perfectly reproduced in housing diversity. No government employee was living in mud-brick and only one informal sector worker was living in concrete brick dwellings. Importantly the occupational effect occurs to some extent independent of income levels. While only 16.7% of informal sector workers had built concrete-brick housing, the income-situation of dwellers in mixed and mud-brick housing 'with developments' would not seem prohibitive to this aim. This is underscored by the high rate of cases in these categories planning 'complete rebuilding'. However, it must be assumed that formal occupational categories are closely associated with job security and the predictability of incomes that enhance long-term household investments. Moreover, for those in formal occupations, in particular with the government, thresholds are likely to be lowered in dealing with official and administrative matters attached to construction according to building codes.

In conclusion, achievements in housing-standards are not simply determined by a given rate of income-to-housing value. While income and employment levels are important factors, decisions to invest in housing are made for more complex reasons. Absolute income levels, the security of household sustainment, and the extent of familial networking are all mediated with certain dispositions of households related to their stage in demographic life cycles and future perspectives. In view of these results, conclusions concerning the potentiality of improvements or rebuilding can only be drawn tentatively for Old Kalingalinga. In general we can distinguish four household types with distinctly different prospects for housing development:

- impoverished older households
- incremental developers
- struggling consolidators
- consolidated dwellers

The *impoverished older households* seem to have the lowest potential for future house development. As long-term residents their traditional housing strategy has been not to invest much in the durability of housing. Owing to this, they have been compelled to renew the mud-brick structures at regular intervals of six years on average.[23] They are the most dissatisfied group, but lacking alternatives seem unlikely to decide to move away. Although 40% in this group plan to rebuild with concrete, their low income situation does not make this prospect very likely in the near future. Besides, they lack the demographic incentive to improve that was shown to correlate with having young children in the household and with the prospects of a long-term sustainment of achievements by the next generation.

The *incremental developers* are groups living in improved mud-brick or partially rebuilt housing of mixed materials. The comparison of years of stay in Kalingalinga and the year of building of the present house shows that successful steps have been taken to make housing durable and to protect the investments made in developments. Their level of living satisfaction is considerably higher, and this group has the highest rate of planned rebuilding. Despite a low employment rate, incomes are in the range of consolidated dwellers. This relatively positive rate of income-to-housing value seems to yield prospects for incremental improvement and could be enhanced if small loan programmes were available for step-by-step development. In view of this, the official decision to suspend the housing loan programme (since loans were no longer sufficient to finance *complete* rebuilding) should be reconsidered. Instead petty loans should be disbursed in accordance with the household housing strategy of protecting investments by incremental improvements or extensions. These programmes should also address the group of large households only planning extensions to reduce household living densities.

Small groups of *struggling consolidators* are found both in Old Kalingalinga and in the overspill, representing 15-20% of the incompletely developed concrete housing stock. Their predicament results from the fact that they made major investments in housing in the early 1980s when building was reasonably cheap but are now faced with inadequate incomes to continue building at the present prices for building materials. As the approximate per capita income to sustain this type of housing is at least K150, these dwellers with incomes below this level seem potential candidates for displacement through the housing market. Market values for concrete brick housing of K5,000 in the old area and K10,000 in the overspill (1989) may provide a considerable enticement to sell if no financial support is given. Here too, small housing loan programmes should be granted to overcome the discrepancy between incomes and the housing value. In view of rent rates that can be achieved in this type of housing, some part of these loans might be dedicated to the construction of additional rooms for subletting that would help in improving the rate of income-to-housing value.

Finally, the *consolidated dwellers* demonstrate the superior potential of larger households in conjunction with high employment rates, reliable formal incomes, and the presence of young children. The pooling of resources of the extended family and the broadening of the household's economic base enables housing investments that are beyond the means of nuclear families or would be considered by them as 'risky' in times of uncertain economic prospects. The relatively high figure for young children in the households of consolidated dwellers is also a vital aspect of household reproduction strategies: only the existence of young children safeguards the long-term sustainment of achievements in terms of a 'contract' between two generations. This agreement will secure housing standards even when the parent generation is no longer able to contribute to housing investments or to maintenance.

c) Determinants of housing standards and improvements in Kalingalinga overspill

Due to the obligatory project terms, the physical standards of housing are naturally much better in the overspill area although, as we shall see, there is no great difference in the economic situation of households. Standard plot sizes are 22 x 18 metres, and all plots have direct access to tarmac roads within a general geometric layout (see Figure 11.1 *eastern overspill area*). Noteworthy is that while the average of 3.58 roomed-structures is nearly the same as in the old area (3.65), housing in the overspill potentially offers lower occupancy densities. In Old Kalingalinga no owner-occupied housing existed with better than 0.55 rooms per person while 32.3% of overspill residents achieved densities of 0.56 and better, 20% had 0.71 and better, and 10% of households even had a ratio of 1 and more rooms to one person. Provision of facilities like kitchens and toilets was, too, slightly better in the overspill: 30.8% had kitchens inside the house compared to 20.8% in the old area; but 61.5% still had no kitchen at all (75% in the old area), with the residual cases made up of semi-permanent mud-brick or temporary straw shacks outside the house for kitchens. As pit latrines are a compulsory component of the building code, 92.3% in the overspill had their own pit latrine and 7.7% even had a flush toilet inside the house. This compares to the old area where 54.2% of households had their own pit latrine and 25% were sharing it with other households. The rest either had none at all (4.2%) or their latrines had collapsed in the rainy season.[24]

But data on the overspill also conveys that more than half the resettled residents have been unable or hesitant to develop their site & service house beyond the basic state enabled by the provision of building materials and the initial loans for two rooms (see Picture 11.6). According to the housing sample (N=133), 63.6% of the housing stock was undeveloped or not yet completed concrete-brick, 27.3% was completely consolidated, and 9.1% was built of mixed materials. The latter cases were apparently households not affected by resettlement but officially tolerated in the overspill despite the applicability of building codes in this area.

The main cost-saving procedures adopted in undeveloped site & service housing stock were to save inside and outside plastering (both 80% of cases), the blocking up of window openings (42%), omitting door frames (27.3%), and only temporary fastening

Picture 11.6   Incomplete site & service housing in Kalingalinga overspill

of roofs (13.2%) - in particular by using stones as a roof-anchorage instead of nails. The economic logic behind this is that these components add little to the use-value of the house but incur very high costs. A metal door frame in 1989 alone cost K690, i.e. represented a saving equivalent to the value of the entire house just a few years back. However, the socioeconomic background of households portrayed in the next table conveys that failure to complete housing is related more to household priorities in expenditure than to absolute constraints on living costs. In fact, except for 20% of cases with absolute income constraints, households living in undeveloped houses had relatively high average per capita living costs, but they also were the largest families with the highest number of young children. Therefore, smaller households with fewer children, that put priorities on housing, were able to complete their house at an early stage at low cost. Conversely, families that gave housing only lower priority were not only hesitant to complete; they now face prohibitive costs of building in compliance with building codes and seem unable to develop space-use according to their actual needs. Irrespective of their increased needs, the vast majority of this grouping is still living in the original two-room core house. In this respect, average values for space-use presented in Table 11.20 are misleading as in reality there is a polarized situation: a relatively high-income minority was able to build quite spacious housing with up to 9 rooms; but 71%

of dwellers in undeveloped concrete housing are, due to family growth, now living under conditions of relatively high occupancy density in their core houses, i.e. less than or equal to 0.33 rooms per person, while this applies to only 33% of households in fully developed housing. Not surprisingly, these households have appropriately given 'extending the house' priority for their planned improvements.

Table 11.20
Socioeconomic determinants of housing standards in Kalingalinga overspill for house owners

House development	Years in township	Years in house	Size of household	Children under 12	Rooms per head
	Mean	Mean	Mean	Mean	Mean
Mixed materials, undeveloped	20.00	9.00	4.00	-	0.50
Concrete house, undeveloped	11.86	8.00	7.57	4.29	0.43
Concrete house, developed	14.00	9.67	6.33	2.00	0.47

(continued)

House development	Living costs per head	Employment rate	Living satisfaction*	Type of planned improvement	
	Mean K	Mean	Mean	Extend	Upgrade
Mixed materials, undeveloped	100.00	0.50	2.00	-	9.1 %
Concrete house, undeveloped	173.36	0.33	2.00	45.5 %	18.2 %
Concrete house, developed	130.95	0.38	2.00	18.2 %	9.1 %

*) Scale: 1 = dissatisfied 2 = satisfied about living conditions in Kalingalinga

In comparing household data between the two residential areas it is noteworthy that the socioeconomic situation of owner-occupied households in the overspill is slightly better in terms of income and employment than in the old area. This effect, however, is not due to a positive impact of housing conditions on occupational opportunities. Rather it is the obvious result of selectivity and preferentialism on the part of those who, in the end, were able to decide the terms of the resettlement process. The decision of the project planners to open this part of the scheme to dwellers' participation seems to have produced irregularities. In the first case, resettlement was largely biased towards formal sector workers. The occupational distribution in the overspill showed that 30% of owner-occupiers were employed by government, 30% were working with companies, 20% were pieceworkers, and only 10% were economically active in the informal sector (10% were retired). Secondly, in view of the intention to resettle households that had to make way for infrastructure lines, the number of former house owners in the present stock of owner-occupiers is quite low (below 20%). Instead the bulk of resettled households from Old Kalingalinga were former renters (approx. 30%), an even larger group of households that formerly lived with relatives (approx. 40%), and finally households that had lived in employers' housing (approx. 10%). Of the group formerly living with relatives, the great majority had only moved to Kalingalinga in the 1979-83 period, apparently with the intention of qualifying for home ownership in the resettlement programme. Preferentialism along Party lines seems less explicit than might have been expected. While the overall level of Party organization was much higher in the overspill (90.8% compared to 68.8% in Old Kalingalinga), the highest rate of non-organized owner-occupiers in specific housing types was found in the fully developed housing stock (33%).

Another form of preferentialism in housing allocation becomes evident from the relatively high rate of tenancy in the overspill. According to the housing sample (N=133), 30.4% of undeveloped and 46.4% of the fully developed housing stock in the overspill was rented out, of which at least one-third of all cases were classified by the tenants as absentee landlordism. The impression is, therefore, that a substantial part of resettlement (and thus the housing credit programme) was used by influential community members to acquire illicit multiple ownership for renting-out with no intention of living in this housing. This new rental stock does not benefit residents from Kalingalinga, as tenants are exclusively coming from outside: the overspill renter population is made up in equal measure of people from unauthorized housing areas, who came in the 1979-85 period, and of movers from Lusaka site and service areas after 1986, formerly living with relatives.

In the end, therefore, the project decision to leave procedures of resettlement to residents and leadership was not a very efficacious example of participation. For the old-established Kalingalinga residents the benefits of the overspill are mixed considering that an over-proportional part of project means for infrastructure (e.g. roads, street lighting) and for housing credit programmes was dedicated to it. Only a few long-term Kalingalinga residents have been resettled there, and it has also to some extent created home ownership for relatives of Kalingalinga dwellers. But more than half the overspill housing stock either accommodates residents who had merely lived in Old Kalingalinga briefly in order to use the resettlement programme as a stepping stone to home ownership, or was used by influential Kalingalinga proprietors (some of them not even living in the area) as an opportunity to establish commercial interests in rental housing.

In contrast to the situation in the new extension areas opened by the council after the project completion (cf. page 134), the preferential terms of allocation in the overspill have at least ensured that resident households were able to sustain their acquisitions. By 1989 there had been no (or very few) housing sales in this area, and the probability of displacement by housing market mechanisms seemed low as diligent efforts had been made by this residential group to acquire home ownership. However, the situation may be different for poorer residents resettled in the overspill. Besides their noted low priorities in respect of housing standards, the stagnation of progressive developments on the part of this group may indicate a mismatch between living in concrete-brick style building and the capacity of relocated households to actually afford this. With growing pressure on the housing market and continuing economic crisis, this group already appeared in 1989 the most likely to sell out in the future. In fact, by 1995 nearly all cases of undeveloped overspill housing had, according to information from the local housing officers, sold their dwellings.

The overall picture of Kalingalinga's development in 1995 shows a recommencement of the developments already depicted in 1989. In accordance with the general slump in economic growth, Kalingalinga's informal sector has continued its slow course of growth. Small scale businesses on the two marketplaces go on unchanged. The only notable difference in commercial activities concerns the new line of informal businesses taken up with self-produced building materials. The general scale of commercial operations has, no doubt, been negatively affected by the reduction in the credit volume of the EPU. The main residual function of the EPU is apparently to support female marketeers by micro loans. Importantly, this organization has been able to sustain its business advisory function out of the running funds. Facilities provided by the GTZ project like schools, the clinic and the community centre were still in operation. The communal water taps were running, but were not free from occasional vandalizing of installations. The innovative plans of 1989 for the self-organization of waste disposal and a scheme to redeem service charge arrears by communal works were not implemented by the council. This decision had already been taken before the change of government. However, some of these components have now been adopted by the CARE community development and food-for-work programmes in Kalingalinga. Solid waste disposal and the unblocking of storm drainage is carried out in this way, although mobilizing support for non-remunerated forms of self-help remains a problem for the new RDC. Kalingalinga has also remained a reasonably cheap housing area without much gentrification. As most of the site and service housing in the overspill and the post-project extension areas, initially reserved for Kalingalinga residents, has already been sold to outside buyers, the housing market demand is now concentrating on Old Kalingalinga. Rates of house transactions are on the rise as very few owners of mud-brick housing have been able to carry out their plans for rebuilding in concrete style. Many are now tempted to capitalize the increased land value. Prices for plots with mud-brick structures are in the range of K500,000 (US$500) compared to K5,000 (US$310) in 1989, which in both periods is equivalent to approximately ten minimal wages.

Notes

1   The GTZ suggests that this is explained by the lack of thatching material in an urban environment (GTZ, 1987, p. 4). But as thatched housing is still found in rural areas not far from Lusaka, another explanation might be that urban dwellers in the 1960s were already making conspicuous efforts to reject rural style housing - a process that seems to have been further encouraged by the newly introduced housing standard of the World Bank/GRZ housing project. Therefore thatch, although a possible candidate for cheaper, appropriate roofing material (that is waterproof if done by craftsmen from western Zambia), would in fact not be accepted by the authorities or by urban dwellers due to its 'rural' image.

2   This assumption is confirmed by observations in 1989 where new council plots had been allocated along the northern edge of Kalingalinga, i.e. moving into the marsh. Here water-logging was persistent even months after the rainy season was over, therefore obviously making the area unsuitable for mud-brick housing.

3   According to urban bye-laws, cultivation of vacant land is not permitted. The former council practice of slashing crops was, however, stopped at the end of the 1970s since government entomologists disproved the assumption that maize fields are breeding grounds for mosquitoes. As distant gardening on vacant plots is merely tolerated by the council, the access to and the use of plots is governed entirely by prescriptive right, i.e. by the 'rights of the first' or by kinship ties. This fits with the observation that distant gardening is mainly an activity of long-term urban residents and not one of recent arrivers from rural areas (Jaeger/Huckabay, 1986, p. 270; Sanyal, 1984).

4   The 'model' character also applies to the type of project itself. Together with a similar project in Santo Domingo, Ecuador, Kalingalinga was the first integrated upgrading project, combining physical upgrading with the improvement of the local economic and employment situation.

5   Exchange rates in 1980 were K1.27 to US$1, and K0.80 after devaluation in 1983. In the following, unless stated otherwise prices and costs are given in the 1989 actual prices with an exchange rate of K0.062. It was not in all cases possible to establish the new prices of commodities, rates, and costs at the 1995 level. The exchange rate in 1995 was K0.001 to US$1. As a rule, most wages and prices seem to have increased by a factor of 100 from 1989 to the end of 1995.

6   Despite their merits, this set of leaders was not reelected after the community reformation due to incidents of unlawful enrichment in office. The new leadership in office until 1991 appeared very much more integrated into UNIP structures.

7   I am aware of the fact that any notion of 'tribalism' is officially strongly rejected in contemporary Zambia and is not very manifest in political life. The prolonged struggle for independence in the confrontation with South Rhodesia and South Africa may indeed have heightened genuine Zambian nationalism. But given the worldwide renaissance of ethnic conflicts, it is difficult to imagine that Zambia's multiethnic society will be an exception (cf. Adam, 1980). Now that external threats to national unity no longer exist, these conflicts may reemerge in the wake of the new multi-party system. An example is the present public debate as to whether Kaunda should be allowed to re-run for presidency following accusations that he is formally still of Malawian nationality. This controversy is enmeshed with allegations that the UNIP strongly favoured public office holders from Eastern Province, i.e. indicating ethnical closeness to Malawians.

8   In the organizational division of self-management and decision-making, the *ward* was, besides general supervision, responsible for infrastructure, the community centre, the use of commercial and industrial plots as well for EPU policies; the *branch* decided the use of its area, it organized the preschool association, the market cooperative, and was responsible for the nurses' and teachers' house. The *section*, finally, was responsible for the spacing of plots and houses, and supervised refuse, taps and drainage in its area (see Oestereich, 1987, p. 33). This division of responsibilities has been adopted by the new RDC structure.

9   As is to be expected with this type of question, the empirical substantiation of opinions is not very reliable even if shows seemingly definite tendencies. In my own study, using a nearly identical question just one year later, responses differed considerably, now resulting in three major clusters: besides 35% 'don't knows', 35% claimed 'not enough money', and 17.5% thought that people were 'taking advantage of the council as it did not apply sanctions'. The latter category had not even appeared under the insignificant answers in Osei-Hwedie/Mijere's study. An additional verification of responses by gender showed no major difference excepting a higher rate of 'don't knows' on the part of women (47.1%) compared to men (26.1%).

10 cf. Osei-Hwedie/Mijere (1989), *Kalingalinga Community Based Work Programme: An Alternative for Service Charge Arrears*, Lusaka; Maembe, E. (1989), *Refuse Collection and Disposal in Kalingalinga, Lusaka - A Strategy for Community Participation*, Lusaka; Maembe, E. (1989), *Expansion of the Economic Promotion Unit's Revolving Fund in the Peri-Urban Areas of Lusaka*, Lusaka.

11 Local leaders had become aware of this problem and reported that plots in the north had been surreptitiously obtained by 'tricking' the council. But with respect to the council, this statement seems questionable as plots had been officially demarcated

314

without names on the register list. It was also found that some beneficiaries were in fact council employees. However, since then no further allocations have taken place in this area. Some irregularities in plot allocation by housing officers and leaders were also disclosed in the housing survey, as well as many cases of illegal absentee landlordism.

12 Refuse collection and works on drainage improvement are now done by residents through the food-for-work PUSH programme.

13 This suggestion, as with the community-based refuse disposal programme, initially goes back to proposals from the GTZ.

14 No cases of unemployment of heads of household were found, but Osei-Hwedie/Mijere (1988), in their much larger sample, put unemployment at approx. 3%. Otherwise, general employment data from both studies correspond: Osei-Hwedie/Mijere put self-employment at 25% with a further 2% engaged in both formal and informal occupations without, however, providing further details concerning occupational distribution (ibid., p. 9).

15 According to Maembe/Sibbuku, of the 48 legally recognized markets in Lusaka 14 are owned by the council, 23 are built and run by cooperatives, and 11 are owned by private self-help groups. Council services (work sites, water, health inspections, refuse disposal, sanitation) are extended to most of these markets besides those run by the council itself (Maembe/Sibbuku, 1987, p. 17).

16 cf. also Maembe/Tomecko (1987) and Maembe/Sibbuku (1987).

17 This information was provided by Mr Chiila, the EPU officer responsible in Kalingalinga. The difference between this and the assessment of job sectors of main income earners given in Table 11.2 is explained by the circumstance that the EPU census also included supplementary income activities of women who alone make up 80% of small business entrepreneurs and 93% of marketeers.

18 According to inquiries on Kalingalinga markets, a limited amount of locally-produced charcoal was available in 1989 at K50 for a 90-kg sack.

19 By Regulation 32 of CAP. 441 of the Statutory Housing and Improvement Areas Act, subletting (excepting to relatives) without council permission is a breach of law liable to a fine of K500 or even imprisonment. While the council is aware of frequent violations of this regulation, it has in practice not imposed any sanctions due to the vague legal situation. (i) Various Statutory Housing and Improvement Areas in Lusaka have not yet been legally declared and thus do not fall under the regulation. (ii) Even in legally declared areas like Kalingalinga, only very few residents have actually applied for the occupancy licence. In the strict sense of the Housing Act they are still illegal residents. (iii) The imposition of housing regulations derived from a First World setting (i.e. the British Town and Country Planning Legislation) is not appropriate to the informal terms of tenancy usually agreed upon. Thus, any council allegation of breach of contract is easily evaded by the claim of absentee landlords that his tenants are in

fact 'relatives'. Lacking legal protection of their tenancy status, tenants would hardly be inclined to contradict the landlord's statement.

20   According to plans, these funds were to be made available to Kalingalinga households as credits for house improvements. However, due to high inflation in building costs, implementation has been postponed since the original lending terms (K650) are no longer regarded as being financially adequate.

21   This specific information should be considered an approximation as not enough cases were left in the subsample of Old Kalingalinga builders in 1980-89 to give statistically reliable data. To compensate for the lack of findings on the building process, an extra survey of six active builders in May/June 1989 was carried out.

22   In Old Kalingalinga our cases of workers in private firms who were dwelling in housing of mixed materials (developed) received an average of K210 monthly housing allowance while the government employees in developed concrete housing received K227.

23   A factor difficult to control in the sample was a disadvantageous topographical location of the housing site. Due to a slight elevation in the northern part of the central area, not all parts of Kalingalinga are equally exposed to flooding and erosion.

24   Dissatisfaction about the hygiene conditions was near identical in both parts of Kalingalinga. But although between 65 and 69% belonged to this group, improvements to the WC, like making it a permanent building with a roof, did not receive high priority in household upgrading plans.

XII   Kanyama: thirty years of unauthorized development

1   The historical background

Kanyama is today the largest and most populous unauthorized housing area in Lusaka. In 1989 it consisted of approx. 3,250 housing units and, according to an estimate by the Ward Councillor, had a population of about 79,000 (36,920 in the last 1980 census). Not much is known about the early history of Kanyama. It appears to have come into existence in the late 1940s or early 1950s. The first official reference to the area is found in the 1963 colonial census of Africans counting 2,961 inhabitants (Collins, 1986, p. 125). Information on the settlement's development rests entirely on a 1966 sample survey by the Dept. of Community Development in New Kanyama (Okada, 1966), a brief comment on this survey by Collins (1986), interviews with Mr Mwanza, a Senior Housing Officer of the LUDC, who in the 1960s was responsible for the Provincial Government's squatting control in Kanyama, and finally on the knowledge of the Ward Councillor Mr Phirie, in office since 1983.

Chinika, that appears on the map below as the adjoining settlement to the north of New Kanyama, no longer exists in this form. It was the former site of the second African workers' compound, the other being Chibolya. Its function as a municipal housing area had decreased continuously in the 1950s, gradually reducing its territorial expansion. The area, that in 1963 still had a population of 2,158, was cleared entirely by 1969 due to unsuitable living conditions, which in 1989 left an open space between Kanyama and the central business area (CBO). As mentioned earlier, growing demographic pressure has in the 1990s led to partial resettlement of this area by squatters.

The major territorial developments of Kanyama can be seen in the map below. Two parts need to be distinguished. *New Kanyama* in the northwest is an officially planned self-help site and service area opened in 1963. Although it is probably the settlement nucleus, for practical reasons it is referred to as the 'new' part distinguished by its modern-style physical developments. It has a grid-iron style layout composed of relatively spacious sites (12.2 x

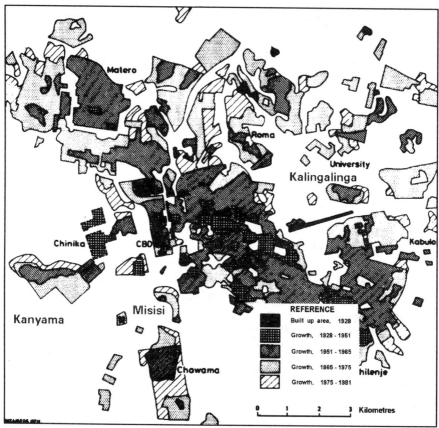

**Figure 12.1   Territorial developments of Kanyama and growth of Lusaka 1928-
1981** *Source: Adapted from Williams, 1986, p. 149*

21.3m in the southern and 16.7 x 21.3m in the northern part), dissected by eight east-west
and three north-south untarred roads (for more physical details see Figure 12.2). For various
reasons explored later, it never received official recognition by the urban authorities although
social infrastructure that was added by 1975 (a school, two cooperative markets with
municipal installations, a civic centre) gave it a permanent, semi-legal status. *Old Kanyama*
to the southeast displays the typical haphazard pattern of plot allocations in unauthorized
housing areas. The early growth axis of the 1951-65 period follows an east-west track that
connects Old Kanyama with the new part (and the Lusaka business area) and from the western
tip branches north, leading to Mumbwa Road. Densities vary from highly built-up sections
of approx. 29 units/ha in areas close to New Kanyama and much less intensive forms of land-
use in the hinterland (17 units/ha). In the wake of New Kanyama's development, considerable
expansions of Old Kanyama have took place in 1965-75, fostered by the semi-legal status

318

of the area and by participation in the new water and road infrastructure provisions. This occurred despite squatting control that seems to have concentrated on New Kanyama, preventing any occupation of the space reserved for public facilities.[1] Thereafter, territorial development slowed down considerably. Only minor growth has taken place since 1975, and in 1989 the area was still practically within the boundaries of 1981, even though some infilling has taken place in Old Kanyama. Excepting the sites for social infrastructure on its northeastern tip, there had been no expansions of New Kanyama at all until the early 1990s.

After the citywide upgrading programme in the 1970s, Kanyama remained the last centrally disposed squatter area with a predictable 'permanent'

Figure 12.2 Aerial map of New Kanyama (1987)
Source: Survey Department, Lusaka

status, and it was the only one that had vast areas of vacant space surrounding it.[2] Considering this potential, and that it was initiated as a site and service scheme, the near complete neglect of Kanyama by the authorities in the 1970s and 1980s is astonishing. Not even installed municipal infrastructure was maintained, the only tarred road to town is now after 30 years completely devastated. These discrepancies point to various underlying developmental problems that are partially physical and demographical constraints (as officially claimed), but are perhaps even more related to political circumstances and to general administrative policies towards low-income groups.

319

In its present state Kanyama makes an unsuitable and potentially unhealthy housing area. Rock outcrops and a high water table approx. one metre under the surface make it an extremely difficult to service terrain that would require a complex and extensive drainage system to prevent flooding and subsequent health hazards caused by over-flowing pit latrines. Few toilet constructions are built with adequate elevation to provide sanitary conditions (cf. Picture 12.1). The same rock outcrops throughout the area prevent the construction of adequate housing foundations, and most are no more than 10cm below grade (NHA, 1978, p. 10). In the unprecedented flood disaster of 1977/78 many casualties were caused by the bad state of foundations when houses collapsed on top of their residents. These geomorphologic conditions also make it nearly impossible for dwellers to sink properly sealed pit latrines to prevent the pollution of ground water. The

Picture 12.1   Pit latrine raised above flood level

numerous wells that exist no longer contain potable water. For many years the supply from public water taps was not ensured in the dry season when the water pressure dropped in Lusaka's inadequate water supply system. The only official steps to address these problems were taken under the immediate impact of the flood disaster in 1977/78. Commissioned by the Ministry of Local Government and Housing, a feasibility study was undertaken by the NHA on surface drainage as part of a hypothetical upgrading programme in Kanyama (NHA, 1978). This detailed study came to the conclusion that the water table in the Lusaka area was rising continuously, making similar future events probable in Kanyama. However, water-logging could be avoided by 'providing a network of storm drains deep enough to intercept the ground water flow' (NHA, 1978, p. 20). Costs for drainage in 1978 were estimated at K2.2 million, as 80% of excavations would be on hard rock (equivalent to 70% of the costs for the entire upgrading of Kalingalinga). Additional costs would arise for the compensation of farm owners as half of the main drains leading to a stream in the south would run through their lands.

As of 1995, no action has been taken, and expectations expressed by the Ward Councillor that Kanyama would be next in line for upgrading if financial means become available do not fit with the plans of the LUDC: in a project proposal to the GTZ it apparently gave upgrading priority to Bauleni (Mapala, 1987), which in fact eventually received basic servicing in the 1990s by an NGO project. This preference given to a newer squatting area 11 km southeast of the city centre is a good indicator of the revival of official policies towards low-income groups that seek to channel this population into the urban periphery. With respect to Kanyama the impression is, therefore, that the LUDC refrained for political reasons from any attempt to resettle Kanyama residents - but at the same time deprived the area of infrastructure and services to systematically discourage further settlement.

Perhaps no less significant for political decision-making is that Kanyama's position within the council is not very strong and is not free from political friction between local leadership and the municipality. In its demographic composition Kanyama is one of the poorer areas in Lusaka with a high proportion of informal sector workers, even if per capita income levels are approx. 70% above those in Kalingalinga. Thus, prospects of cost-recovery for any kind of service improvement are not considered good, and any official measures taken would require subsidization. Additionally it accommodates a considerable number of foreigners (but probably not more than 3 to 5%), mainly from Zaire. Both these factors tend to reinforce the traditional prejudices against dwellers of illicit housing areas that question their capacity for social integration. Despite the formal integration of the local leadership into the Party system and a near 90% UNIP-membership rate of households in 1989, council control over the former ANC stronghold has been fragile. Conflicts between local leaders and the council have occurred over violations of the squatter containment policy in Kanyama. Various Branch and Section Chairmen were suspended following illegal plot allocations; and like in the World Bank/GRZ housing project, local leadership has encouraged people not to pay charges for inadequate service provisions.[3] Corresponding to this, the council representation in Kanyama has decreased. A land-control warden was withdrawn in 1986, and the township is now administered from the Matero site and service office some 5 km away. There remains, however, a police station, and some council social workers who are still active in New Kanyama civic centre.

Very much in contrast to its exclusion from the city's planned development is Kanyama's de facto commercial integration into the urban housing and rental market where residents have taken an active part in developing informal sector activities in this field. The background to this development appears to have been laid in the early stages of its inauguration. In the transition period between the end of the Federation with Southern Rhodesia and Nyasaland in 1963 and Zambia's independence in 1964, the assumption was that the council would eventually be able to provide housing for all in employment, following the colonial tradition of 'tied housing'. With the bulk of government and council resources going into high-cost housing for its own employees, a housing gap emerged for lower-income employees of the private sector whose employers had been dispensed from actual housing provision by its substitution through a system of 'housing allowance'. This was fixed by government in 1964 at K5.50 per month for all employees earning less than K40 a month. To provide housing in this low income range, the government responded with officially sponsored site and service and informal settlements, both using informal methods of house building.

New Kanyama was the first of the serviced site schemes, provided in July 1963 on land zoned 'undetermined'. With a view to the intended future regular housing of all employees, the 720 sites were allocated on a *temporary* basis designated for the intermediate resettlement of dwellers from the town's informal settlements (Collins, 1986, p. 130). As in all early site and service schemes, no sewerage was planned, and the only form of service provided was public water taps disposed at regular intervals on east-west streets. To the north one strip of stands 250 feet in width was left vacant for future non-residential use (churches, shops).

> The most interesting result of the New Kanyama project was that instead of 720 households in 720 owner-occupied self-built houses, there were by 1966 7,960 people in 2,960 rooms, 53% of which were for renting, at between K4 and K6 a month - i.e., the amount of the housing allowance or very close to it. The informal system was responding to demand by creating, for the first time on this scale, a pool of rented dwellings as an alternative to the formal housing sector. By the time of the 1969 census there were 3,056 households in 2,514 dwellings on the same 720 plots (Collins, 1986, p. 130).

Due to various developments the initially 'temporary' status of Kanyama became more and more permanent. In the 1963-70 period Kanyama came under the administration of the Provincial Government that merely exercised squatting control and service charge collection for water, but was responsible neither for planning nor for provision of new services. This anomaly was removed in 1970 when Lusaka's boundaries were expanded to incorporate all peri-urban areas. However, by the time the LUDC became responsible for Kanyama, the major territorial and physical consolidation had already taken place and population had increased within six years by 613% to 18,157 (1969).[4] Although plans were in preparation that would have turned Kanyama into an administrative district (the Doxiadis Plan for Greater Lusaka), experiences with relocating squatters to the urban periphery (e.g. Kaunda Square) in the late 1960s had been discouraging and lacked the political backing of local councillors. Thus, the pressure to find a solution to post-independence mass migration to Lusaka left no other alternative but to abandon this part of the Doxiadis Plan in 1972/73 and to upgrade the existing squatter areas originally designated for relocation. The ambition of the World Bank to demonstrate cost-recovery in its projects, for all the reasons mentioned, inevitably led to the exclusion of Kanyama. However, as a corollary to the decision to include the neighbouring squatter area of Chawama in the programme, matters were implicitly finally settled for Kanyama as well.

The indirect stabilizing effect on Kanyama of this shift in policies is evident from the subsequent demographic and commercial development. While population growth rates from

1969-1980 stagnated at 1.1% for the other neighbouring unauthorized areas John Laing and Chibolya - both potentially in the direction of central business area expansion - people's confidence in Kanyama's perseverance is expressed by a growth rate of 6.7%, equal to Lusaka's average in 1969-1980 (Wood, 1986, p. 179). Moreover, if the Councillor's estimates of population in 1989 are correct, demographic growth has gone on at similar rate during the 1980s.

Parallel to this, substantial commercial development has begun. While the 1966 survey counted only 1 shop in New Kanyama, a few houses with street vending, and some pedlar activities, there are today 150 shops, 4 markets (2 recognized as cooperatives), and a number of informal workshops (car repair, furniture making, tin-smithing, building materials producers, etc.). Kanyama also has the advantage of being within close walking distance to the town's largest informal wholesale market ('Soveto'), situated 2 km away on the southeastern edge of the central business area.

An incident in 1977/78 known as the 'Kanyama funds scandal' put the policies of local leadership on a new trajectory oriented towards communal self-help. Following the floods of 1977/78 that left thousands homeless in Kanyama, Misisi and Makeni, these locations were declared 'disaster areas' by the Prime Minister, and an international relief programme was started. The administration of donations was put in the hands of a joint committee formed by the Cabinet Minister of Provincial Government, the Permanent Secretary Lusaka Province, the Permanent Secretary Local Government and Housing, and the Lusaka City Council Engineer. Due to mishandling of these funds, apparently nothing reached the disaster areas. According to a confidential report by an administrative inquiry convened by the Prime Minister in 1980, most of the donated goods (including blankets, medicine, tinned milk, concrete blocks, diesel fuel) were 'sold' at giveaway prices to the members of the relief committee or disappeared unaccounted for. The same applies to K40,000 in cash (Times of Zambia, 20.9.81 and 17.12.81). In the end the report was never published, and no political or administrative action was taken against the accused.

It was against this background that the present Ward Councillor set up his political election campaign to promote self-help activities with the help of NGOs - a policy opposed by his predecessor in office. After his successful election in 1983, several major projects have been accomplished with a good response on the part of inhabitants in the form of self-help labour contributions.

- With the help of a Canadian church-related NGO and by donations of MPs and local businessmen, the building of a clinic was started in 1983 by self-help work. By 1989 it was nearly completed. A sister was in charge; but it was planned to transform this into a public clinic to be run by the Ministry of Health.

- In 1988 a preschool has been built in a former branch office, and the old ward office has been transformed into a primary school for 800 pupils. Another ward office is to be extended by self-help to function as a new civic centre. Approximate costs will be K100,000.

- Four markets had already been constructed entirely by self-help in 1968, 1973, and 1978. A consumers' cooperative was formed in 1982 by organized street vendors.

- The most ambitious project, however, has been dedicated to overcoming the acute water shortage in the dry season and to providing public water-taps in the unserviced parts of Old Kanyama and in the neighbouring John Laing compound. With the active participation of HUZA, £35,000 were provided by the British NGO 'UK Water Aid' to drill a 60-metre deep borehole, tapping the area's abundant ground water reserves that are protected from surface pollution by an intermediate stratum of limestone. Except for the actual drilling of the two boreholes, no heavy machinery was required. The excavation of 1 km of trenches for pipes was completed by self-help in 1987, including unconventional methods of breaking up very large rocks: these were made red hot by burning tyres and then cracked by sudden cooling down by water. After completion of the water line, it took three years for the council engineers to finally give their technical approval for the installation of the pressure storage tanks and the electric pumps. On completion in 1990 the scheme was handed over to the council.

- Also with technical advice and training by HUZA, there exists a pilot scheme for the production of appropriate building materials. Among other items, the self-help group has been particularly successful in producing sisal-cement roofing tiles of good quality, something not achieved in the Kalingalinga upgrading project. Several houses in Old Kanyama have been equipped with these tiles. So far, production is 'on demand' only, displaying once more the typical weakness of informal business in Lusaka that lacks working capital and does not receive adequate support to build up knowledge in the field of marketing.

By the standards of Lusaka, these communal self-help achievements in Kanyama were outstanding for the 1980s. While most other badly serviced low-income housing areas continue to rely entirely on the council, efforts in Kanyama demonstrate that residents' self-help may also have a potential for attaining more official recognition. It appears that the water project served as a catalyst in that the council, following the solution to the water problem, has begun to allocate new low density plots in the southeast of Old Kanyama. With this revival of official planning measures, it might, as a corollary, be expected that other deficits in infrastructure provision will eventually receive the required attention.

2 The household and housing survey

Research procedures for the survey were the same as in Kalingalinga using a slightly modified questionnaire to cope with the greater variety of housing standards and other specific features (e.g. residents' distinct efforts to demarcate boundaries between houses by fences). In both parts of Kanyama 37 households were included in the 'household sample', and altogether 80 additional houses were selected for the briefer 'housing sample', giving a total of 117 cases. Sampling methods in New Kanyama posed no problems as the grid style layout made it possible to define a plot numbering system and random selection of cases. In Old Kanyama, however, sampling methods had to be unorthodox due to various methodological and technical problems. With limited research capacities, the large housing stock for which no exact figures existed and the lack of any physical mapping or house numbering system in Old Kanyama prevented a representative survey for the whole settlement in strict statistical terms. Additionally, the Councillor advised against conducting the long household interviews in the more remote parts of Old Kanyama where his influence might not be comprehensively established. Following his proposal, a group of 21 houses was finally selected that met the requirements for physical security for research, and which, with its mix of housing standards, appeared typical for the purpose of the 'household sample'. The house group in question was situated some 300m into Old Kanyama along the early development axis previously described (cf. Figure 12.2). As the required nominal proportioning of houses between Old and New Kanyama of approx. 4:1 would have given too small a sub-sample for New Kanyama, a weighted sample of 16 houses was selected by conventional random methods to assure better representativeness of data in this area.

In designing the larger sequel 'housing sample' with 80 additional households, various aspects required consideration. Firstly, a reliable representativeness for the whole of Kanyama seemed questionable under the mentioned circumstances given that the survey was based only on approx. 3% of the entire housing stock. Secondly, housing standards in New Kanyama were obviously much more homogeneous, which moved the priority in research to the lesser known situation of Old Kanyama. Thirdly, the selection of another house group in a delimited territorial section (as in the household sample) involved a possible bias in the sample. For all these reasons it was decided to concentrate efforts in the 'housing sample' entirely on Old Kanyama, with the aim of establishing reasonably reliable survey data for this part. This decision was backed by the increased acceptance of the research team by Kanyama residents, encouraging the extension of field work to the entire area. Finally, eight evenly spaced apart locations, which supplied ten cases each, were determined with the help of aerial photography. On reaching these predetermined points in the field, the interviewers spread out in different directions. Selecting every fifth house, moving approx. in a straight line, this gave an area coverage in the style of concentric circles.

325

a) Settlement and housing

As the survey data clearly shows, the early specialization of New Kanyama in providing an extensive informal rental housing market was more than a secondary aspect in the use of the housing stock. The commercialization of rental housing has advanced considerably and become a dominant function for entire Kanyama. According to Table 12.1, a mere 12.5% of houses in New Kanyama are *not* now used for renting while owner-occupancy still prevails in 37.6% of Old Kanyama's housing stock. Demand for rental accommodation is mainly for small dwellings of two or three rooms. This has been served by subdividing the original large houses into subunits and providing these with separate doors. The overall average is 2.2 rented rooms per household with an occupancy density between 2.2 and 2.5 persons per room.

Table 12.1
House occupancy in New and Old Kanyama (N=117)

	House occupancy				
	Resident landlord	Absentee landlord	No subletting	Employers' house	Total
Old Kanyama	27.7%	33.7%	37.6%	1.0%	100%
New Kanyama	43.8%	43.8%	12.5%	-	100%

As owner-occupied houses in both areas are smaller than the averages (3 rooms compared to 9.4 in the new, and 4 rooms compared to 5.8 in the old part), available space for expanding houses obviously was and still is an important factor in the unfolding of the rental market. The 43.8% of the housing stock in New Kanyama that is exclusively used for lodging (i.e. with an absentee landlord) comprises the largest housing units with an average of 13 rooms while housing with a resident landlord had an average of only 8 rooms. In this respect the relatively spacious plot allocations in New Kanyama, with one-storey houses of up to 18 rooms on the northern stands, and up to 13 in the southern part, have provided an ideal setting for commercialization. Combined with its locational advantages like the closeness to town, water provision, and an orderly layout with road access, the rental market in New Kanyama is clearly the more diversified and advanced: while rent rates per room for old housing only show minor differences (K43 in the old and K54 in the new part), upgraded rental accommodation in New Kanyama, on average, achieves K116 compared to K46 in Old Kanyama. A few recently built middle-class accommodations with individual water supply, flush toilets, and surrounding walls achieve rates of up to K900 for one unit (cf. next picture). Although Old Kanyama also provides a small stock of higher-quality rental housing, rent ceilings even then do not exceed K75 per room, giving little incentive for owners to improve housing. Accordingly, approx. 80% of accommodation there is provided in lower standard

326

houses built in the 1960s and early 1970s. However, the high rate of absentee landlordism in New Kanyama indicates that scope for transferring further housing stock into rental tenancy is nearly exhausted in this part. With the solution of the water problem it is to be expected that Old Kanyama will gradually be able to respond to the demand for higher-quality rental accommodation by expanding and rebuilding houses accordingly. In contrast to the situation in New Kanyama, plots in the old part usually have ample surrounding space to make extensions. The occasional example of recently built, large middle-class lodger accommodation could already be observed in Old Kanyama in 1989.

The imprint of the rental market on the local economy and the dynamics of housing development is evident everywhere - but of lower commercial importance than might be expected. Besides that, housing in Kanyama reflects specific local idiosyncrasies in the way it is valorized in terms of use-value and exchange-value. Reproductive strategies of households and preferential aspects of local networking interact with purely commercial aspects. This has effects on the way access to and the utilization of housing is mediated within the community. As we shall see from the household data and the detailed survey of the housing stock, Kanyama, although somewhat more affluent than Kalingalinga, has a higher rate of informal activities. Also, there is a higher proportion of women contributing to household incomes.

Most of the housing stock built in the 1960s and early 1970s is now showing signs of dilapidation since apparently little has been done to maintain or improve housing standards. For the 81% of landlords who are in this category of old, dilapidating housing, incomes from rent (due to the differential rates between 'good' and 'low-cost' housing) are merely a subsidiary to some other kind of main family earnings.

Picture 12.2   Middle-class lodgings in New Kanyama

Even the larger houses that allow ten or more rooms to be rented out only yield total rents in the range of one minimal wage. This yield will be even less for landlords in Old Kanyama who, on average, can only rent out six to seven rooms at lower rates. The dilapidation of housing is probably reinforced by the low number of resident landlords (20.7%) in the old housing stock.

327

As to the 19% of upgraded housing stock that can achieve a differential rent, there is a near equal division between house developers for the exclusive purpose of renting and a figure of 45.5% of landlords who reside in their dwellings with additional subletting. As a rule, upgraded houses are substantially larger than the old housing stock, which is particularly true for Old Kanyama where low-cost houses had an average of 5 rooms compared to 9 in the upgraded stock. In New Kanyama the difference was less distinct with an average of 9 rooms in the old and 11 rooms in the newer upgraded stock.

An important aspect of the 'local idiosyncrasies' mentioned is that absentee landlordism in Kanyama apparently has a quite different connotation than in Kalingalinga where it was largely associated with housing speculation by outside owners. According to informa-

Picture 12.3   Early (1960's) housing in New Kanyama

tion from lodgers, only 31% of their non-resident landlords lived outside Kanyama. Therefore, the dominant aspect of absentee landlordism is, rather, a maximizing strategy in the use and the valorization of the house.[5] Most likely, house owners' decisions to vacate or not will focus on the location of their house and its potential on the rental market. If the house location is suited for rental tenancy, a marginal benefit is gained if the landlord vacates the house and moves somewhere else. Similarly, when a family has the means to build a new house for its own use (plus subletting), it is preferable to do this on a new site and transform the old family rooms into lodgings. Complying with the preferential rental market of New Kanyama, the percentage of absentee landlords from this part who are living outside Kanyama is higher (40%) than in Old Kanyama (27%). Conversely, more absentee landlords from Old Kanyama (39.6%) live in another part of Kanyama than those running a lodger house in New Kanyama (30%). These terms of housing valorization correspond to a relatively 'closed' housing market for the stock suited for rental tenancy. 81.3% of owners were the original builders of the house with an average occupancy of 21 years. Of the 18.7% in the remaining category of bought housing, most of the transactions concerned either houses in Old Kanyama that were improved or extended by their new owners, or were small houses with two to three rooms in New Kanyama. Out of the three cases that fell in the category of bought housing, there was only one of a large house in New Kanyama recently bought. Another notable feature of the housing market is its operation along local and personal networks. Nearly all buyers had previously been renters in Kanyama for a few years before they were able to realize home ownership. As to the process of housing construction, there is a slight majority of commercial building by craftsmen (61.5% of total housing stock). However, this average is due to a preponderance of commercial construction in the 1966-77 period (i.e., 71.4% of construction in this period). In all following periods there is an equal distribution of family self-help and commercial building by paid craftsmen. Practically all building was done without planning assistance from the council. Over 90% of housing finance was provided by family savings, and only one case out of 13 had taken out a buildings loan from the Zambian National Provident Fund. The building costs per room for concrete block housing reflect the accelerated inflation of building material prices: while one room cost approx. K500 in 1966-70, costs had risen to K750 in the mid-1970s and to K1,800 in the early 1980s.

Data for the settlement process in all Kanyama shows an average house-owner residence of 16.3 years. Quite a considerable fraction of 32.1% house owners had already settled in the early development stage of the 1960s and had now been living in Kanyama for at least 20 years. The oldest population group is found in the low-cost housing of New Kanyama that shows an average residence of 22 years. Only 21.4% of owners had been living in Kanyama for less than 10 years. With tenants, residential averages were 8.66 years, composed of long-term tenants in New Kanyama (12-13 years), and a mean value of 6 years tenancy for Old Kanyama. As there has not been much expansion of the housing stock, the figure of 14.8% tenants living in Kanyama for one year or less suggests that there is also some short-term turnover in rental housing.

The common practice of house sharing between landlords and tenants complicated the sampling for the household survey. Unlike Kalingalinga where a house was usually inhabited by one household, a selected house in Kanyama would not automatically be representative of housing and households at the same time. Moreover, a representative sampling of households would have required a ratio of approx. 4:1 between renters and landlords, which would not have appropriately reflected priorities of research into the housing process. Therefore, a weighted sampling method was used in the large housing survey to give an equal representation of both types of households. For each selected house this, in practice, meant that the landlord was interviewed if he was resident, and in all other cases the interview was done with one of the tenant households. Accordingly all tables based on the household survey (N=37) are representative for households of owner-occupiers and for households of tenants separately but *not* for all households.

Reasons stated for coming to Kanyama were investigated in the 'household sample'. Answers grouped into three major categories. Most important was the availability of plots or accommodation named by 47.6% of respondents, followed by 27% for whom employment or the closeness to place of work was most important. A final group of 18.9% had come or were living there for family reasons, like joining relatives, marriage, or had already been there from childhood. Access to urban infrastructure played no important part as being mentioned by only 2.7%. The next table combines the previous place of residence in a breakdown into two periods. This is to indicate possible changes in mobility patterns between the early settlement period up to 1978 and the recent one of the last ten years. Looking first at owner-occupiers, the total of various groups shows that Kanyama was and to some extent still is a recipient housing area for migrants coming to Lusaka. Those coming from outside Lusaka, including foreign countries, made up a total of 56.4% of owner households while inner city mobility of movers within Lusaka totalled only 20%. The largest single group of 43.6% were those that had previously lived in another town while direct moves from a rural area into home ownership were the exception.

Table 12.2
Former place of residence and period of arrival
for tenants and owner-occupiers (N=37)

Old place of residence	Tenants		Owner-occupiers	
	Settlement before 1979	Settlement 1979-89	Settlement before 1979	Settlement 1979-89
Lusaka site & service (low-cost)	3.7%	14.8%	7.3%	1.8%
Lusaka upgraded	-	3.7%	3.6%	-
Lusaka unauthorized	1.9%	1.9%	7.3%	-
Kanyama	20.4%	16.7%	12.7%	3.6%
Other town	3.7%	14.8%	30.9%	12.7%
Foreign country	-	3.7%	-	3.6%
Employers' housing	1.9%	1.9%	7.3%	-
Total	33.3%	66.7%	72.7%	27.3%

With tenants, the intake from other housing areas in Lusaka is slightly higher with a total of 26%. In particular the proportion of households coming from Lusaka site & service areas in the last 10 years has risen to 14.8%. But again, direct migration to Kanyama from outside is more significant accounting for 33.4% of total tenants, including a higher representation of migrants from rural areas. What is striking in both the owner-occupier and the tenant sample is the high proportion of internal resettlement from within Kanyama. This points to the existence of a self-supplying and self-centred network that gives local residents privileged access to housing. This agrees with the findings that 50% of tenancy arrangements were between relatives and friends while the other half were the result of 'personal enquiries'. This system appears to have been capable of accommodating most of Kanyama's own population growth and the subsequent housing demand of young families. No less than 37.1% of rental tenancies were given to 'locals' although competition with movers from Lusaka, as also shown in Table 12.2, has risen in the last 10 years. Statistically, mean rent per dwelling had risen from K116.4 in 1988 to K146.7 in 1989, i.e. by 26%. This seems to signify a growing economic pressure on the housing stock utilized for renting, with landlords now seeking to serve a more solvent demand on the housing market. This shift from local to outside demand is probably also related to the consolidation of Kanyama as a housing area and the growing housing demand left unsatisfied by the very low municipal provision of low-cost housing.

As the sequence of Pictures 12.2 to 12.4 illustrates, there is considerable variety in housing styles. It ranges from adaptations of colonial housing in the early, individually styled buildings of the sixties - using burnt-bricks - to the functional uniformity introduced by the site and service house plans in the 1970s - using concrete blocks. Related to incremental steps in stabilizing housing structures, there is a considerable portion of 'mixed' building materials combining adobe bricks with burnt-bricks and concrete blocks. Additionally there is some 'inconsistency in structure' as houses with stable wall materials may not have adequate foundations and vice versa. Thus, in view of the geophysical problems with flooding, it is difficult to give a reliable classification of these heterogeneous

Picture 12.4   **House under construction on the northern fringe of Old Kanyama (with city centre in the background)**

housing standards in terms of potentially stable or unstable structures. Looking first at wall building materials, we suggest grouping housing into three types: (1) the quota of potentially '*unstable housing*' is not more than 5.1%. It is predominantly made of mud-bricks (adobe), usually in combination with a smaller part of the house built from more stable materials, i.e. either burnt-bricks or concrete blocks; (2) an intermediate group of 22.1% belongs to the category of '*relatively stable*' houses. These have burnt-bricks as the main building material; (3) finally, 77.8% of housing is considered '*stable*' with walls made of concrete blocks. In assessing foundations, information had to rely on statements from residents as to their construction. According to this, 43.6% had concrete slabs, 42.7% laterite cement, 5.1% rammed earth with concrete, 2.6% partial foundation, 0.9% stones only, and 5.1% had no foundation. For the purpose of an overview presented in Table 12.3, we suggest a grouping of foundations into a) 'foundations with concrete', b) 'partial foundations' (including stones), and c) 'no foundations'. This leads to a typology of housing distinguished according to the materials and assumed stability of their wall materials, i.e. 'partially solid', 'solid with burnt-bricks' and 'concrete'. By finally adding the information on roofing conditions, this gives the following Table 12.3 on the absolute distribution of housing standards by type of housing separately for roofing standards and foundations.

Table 12.3
Housing conditions in Kanyama by roofing and foundations (N=117)

Housing type	Roofing standard		Foundation		
	Temporary fixing	Permanent fixing	No foundation	Partial foundation	Concrete foundation
Adobe or partially solid	2.6%	2.6%	-	0.9%	4.3%
Solid / part burnt-brick	8.5%	8.5%	1.7%	1.7%	13.7%
Concrete	24.8%	53.0%	3.4%	0.9%	73.5%
Column total	35.9%	64.1%	5.1%	3.4%	91.5%
Total	100 %		100 %		

According to this, approx. 2.6% of unstable housing requires acute rehabilitation. This is made up of the 0.9% of mud-brick buildings with partial foundations and of the 1.7% of burnt-brick constructions without foundations. If all mud-brick housing and the burnt-brick housing with partial foundations are included, this puts the proportion of housing requiring upgrading, to make it less vulnerable to flooding damage, at approx. 8.6% of the total housing stock. However, the problems caused by bad foundations seem to affect an even larger number of cases: a damage report compiled from the household survey showed that 18.9% of housing had been affected by the torrential rains of 1988/89, including one-third with damage to walls and plastering but two-thirds with various problems caused by water seeping through holes in foundations. This damage occurred at an equal rate in New and Old Kanyama.

Although all of the housing classified as needing acute rehabilitation is found in Old Kanyama, this result is not indicative of the standard of the entire housing stock of this area. In fact, the overall standards of housing in this part are better than in New Kanyama. Because the larger part of Old Kanyama was built up in the 1970s, replacing all of the old rural style housing (pole and dagga) along the early growth axis, 82.1% of its housing is now made of concrete blocks, 13.9% of burnt-brick, and only 4% is made of mud-brick. In comparison the figures for New Kanyama are 50% concrete block, 37.5% burnt-brick, and 12.5% mud-brick buildings.

Compared to the basic style of housing in Kalingalinga, two final observations suggest a stronger urban image in Kanyama's housing stock. On the part of 43.6% house owners we find distinct efforts to individualize and demarcate plots by some kind of physical boundary, even if these are seldom well maintained. The exception is the brick walls (5.1%), which inevitably arise with middle-class style housing to screen off and to protect possessions. The usual forms of fence are metal sheets (7.7%), wire (16.2%), mixed materials (2.7%), or at least shrubs (12%) and 56.4% no fence at all. A strong touch of urbanity is also found in the prestige of glazed and barred windows. While glazed windows were rare exceptions in Kalingalinga, 31.2% of houses in Kanyama had window panes in all windows and 16.5% in some windows. As to bars, 15.1% had them in all windows and 11% in some of the windows. Moreover, there was a near equal distribution of glazed windows and bars in all types of housing. Only in burnt-brick style housing were the proportions lower: i.e. 22% window panes in all windows compared to 33% in both mud-brick and concrete block housing, and 90% of burnt-brick housing having no bars compared to the 50% of mud-brick and the 73% of concrete block housing.

b) The household survey

The household survey comprised an entire house group in Old Kanyama (N=21) and a random sample in New Kanyama (N=16). In terms of house occupancy, the house group consisted of 10 tenant and 11 owner households; in New Kanyama there were 10 tenants and 6 owner-occupiers. For the reasons stated earlier, representativeness of figures is for housing and for household types only, but not for all households. This deficiency, however, appears well

Table 12.4
Living costs by area and tenancy (N=37)

	Living costs per capita	
	Tenants	Owners
	Mean K	Mean K
Old Kanyama	214.88	254.99
New Kanyama	291.71	240.28

compensated in that owners and tenants, by their social stratification, belong to the same income and consumption-standard groups. Mean per capita living costs including children under 12 years are K253 for renters and K249 for house owners, compared to K205 (renters) and K130 (owners) in Kalingalinga. Minor differentiations among income groups appear for living areas (cf. Table 12.4): tenants are the highest and lowest income groups, reflecting high rent rates in New and lower ones in Old Kanyama.

Higher living costs for renters in the higher-standard living quarters express the same tendency as in Kalingalinga where the expenditure of renters in 'good housing' was higher than those of house owners. The gap between renters and owners is, however, considerably smaller in Kanyama. Only the tenant fraction in the cheap housing market of Old Kanyama had a low expense level, comparable to that of renters in Kalingalinga.

Compared to the averages in Kalingalinga, per capita living expenses are approx. 70% higher in Kanyama despite very similar total household living costs of K1,164 in Kanyama and K1,116 in Kalingalinga. This difference in per capita expenditure is explained by the different demographic and occupational situation. Despite occasional cases of very large households in which several families were pooling their resources, there is a distinct tendency towards the formation of nuclear family structures in Kanyama. With an average of 5.23 members, family sizes were relatively smaller in Kanyama compared to 7.84 in Kalingalinga, and there were fewer children under 12 years of age (1.92) than in Kalingalinga (3.3).[6] The essential point, however, is the much higher employment rate. In an average household in Kanyama 1.38 workers support only 3.97 dependent family members (Kalingalinga: 1.35 workers to 6.43 dependents). According to Table 12.5, Kanyama also appears to have an advantage with regard to the qualification profile of its labour force. While the domain of Kalingalinga was services (guards, waiters), nearly 25% of activities in Kanyama are

Table 12.5
Occupations by sector (N=37)

Occupational categories	Formal sector	Informal sector
Retailing	5.9%	17.6%
Building crafts	-	2.9%
Services	5.9%	-
Technicians	20.6%	5.9%
Other crafts	-	8.8%
Qualified office jobs	11.8%	-
Labourer, unqualified	11.8%	-
Domestic servants	2.9%	-
Others (e.g. soldier)	5.9%	-
Total	64.7%	35.3%

technical (drivers, mechanics, etc.), and a sizable 12% had qualified office jobs. Nearly 20% of workers were employed by the government. Kanyama's higher employment rate also seems attributable to the greater potential of its informal sector, which was larger (35.3% of total occupations of the head of household) than in Kalingalinga (28.4%). One of its advantages is that it is much less local based as only 53% of informal business was conducted exclusively in Kanyama.

Despite the higher income levels compared to Kalingalinga (where economic activities of women were associated with lower income levels), women in Kanyama are generally more economically active. In total 63.6% are economically active, of which 54.2% are in marketeering, 25% are home producers, 12% have regular formal employment, and 8.3% are running their own businesses. This high activity rate may also be explained by the low significance of subsistence gardening, usually an important field of women's activities in other low-income housing areas of Lusaka. Only 10% of households had either a local or a distant garden, as suitable areas in the vicinity of Kanyama are already used for this purpose by commercial farmers and house gardens could only be maintained in the low-density parts of Old Kanyama.

The prominent role of women as contributors to income features strongly in the household decision-making structure. The same 63% of active women also stated that 'the husband does not decide all matters', and 15% of the active women had their own budget. Although, as shown, there are no absolute income thresholds for women to take up economic activities, this is closely related to the relative household situation: as Table 12.6 shows, women become active in households with below average per capita living costs and with a relatively

Table 12.6
Socioeconomic circumstances of households with
economically active women (N=37)

Women economi- cally active	Number of family workers	Dependent household members	Children under 12 years	Per capita living costs in Kwacha	Job sector of head of household	
	Mean	Mean	Mean	Mean K	Formal sector	Informal sector
Yes	1.48	7.29	4.33	211.02	40.0%	23.3%
No	1.08	4.08	1.83	315.29	30.0%	6.7%

high dependency rate including children under 12 years of age. The country's economic crisis obviously adds to the pressure on women to perform complementary work. Nearly a quarter of households named 'selling on the market' as a means of improving the household budget situation. Finally, the job sector of the partner also plays an important role since seven out of nine women whose partner had an informal sector occupation took on income-generating activities. In this respect there was, however, no significant difference between the two residential areas of Kanyama.

Networking activities amongst neighbours play an important part in economic survival. Of all households 65.5% borrowed and 71.4% lent money regularly. However, 36.8% of borrowing and lending was 'kaloba', a credit arrangement with interest, which involves tenant and informal sector households more than those of house owners or those of formal sector workers. The main borrowing/lending groups were nearby friends (57.9%) and relatives in Kanyama (21.1%). Only 20% of networking was done with outside groups, like friends or relatives in Lusaka or in another town, including 5.3% who borrowed from employers. A slight majority of households that depended on borrowing money were from Old Kanyama, or belonged to households with a lower employment rate. Informal sector households (44.4% borrowing) seemed to be less dependent on borrowing than families working in formal employment (71.6%). Lending, on the other hand, is a far more common practice with households living in New Kanyama (100%) than in Old Kanyama (53.8%), and it is also far more usual for informal sector families than for those working in the formal sector.

In correlating household data with the standard/style of owner-occupiers' housing, apparently neither the economic nor the demographic situation of households had any direct influence on the development of housing style. The supposedly lower-standard burnt-brick housing is, in fact, inhabited by families with slightly above average living costs and with a better employment situation.[7] The only significant difference appearing in Table 12.7,

Table 12.7
Socioeconomic features of house-owners by type of housing (N=17)

Housing type	Per capita living costs	Workers in household	Dependent family members	Informal family workers	Children under 12 years
	Mean K	Mean	Mean	Per cent	Mean
Solid / mainly burnt-brick	269.84	1.75	3.75	93.75%	2.5
Concrete block	243.92	1.31	5.0	19.23%	2.08

continued ...

Housing Type	Rooms in household	Standard of facilities *)	Years in Kanyama	Years in present house
	Mean	Mean	Mean	Mean
Solid / mainly burnt-brick	3.0	8.25	19.0	17.5
Concrete block	3.18	9.46	21.69	17.0

*) Scale for domestic facilities: no glazed windows, no kitchen, no WC = 3; all windows with glass, kitchen in a separate room, and WC inside house = 15

above, concerns the dominant employment sector of household workers. Here considerable polarization is to be observed between *formal sector* workers and employees who are mainly living in concrete block housing, and *informal sector workers* who are mainly living in burnt-brick style housing. This polarization can be attributed to two factors: (1) the relative priority assigned to housing within the reproductive strategies of informal sector workers, and (2) the prestige attached to a particular style of housing on the part of formal sector workers, especially since concrete housing has become the preferred standard in Lusaka. These tendencies are reinforced if we consider additional components that define domestic housing quality such as the standard of kitchen and WC and the number of glazed windows. Combining these into a scale of 'standards of domestic facilities', the score is somewhat higher for concrete block housing, emphasizing the importance of 'prestigious' attributes in housing. In conclusion, we find lower priority being given to the standard of housing in those households in which less secure informal sector occupations are preponderant, even if their income situation would allow them to make improvements. These divergent priorities are to some extent also reflected in the planned improvements to the house shown in Table 12.8.

Table 12.8
Planned house improvements by owners (N=17)

Planned improvements	Housing type	
	Solid / partially burnt-brick	Concrete block
External plastering	-	6.3%
Internal plastering	14.3%	-
Improve roof	-	6.3%
Improve doors	14.3%	6.3%
Improve or renew latrine	-	12.5%
Build kitchen	14.3%	6.3%
Rebuild house on same site	14.3%	6.3%
Install electricity	-	6.3%
Build wall fence	-	6.3%
Build rooms for renting	-	12.5%
Build more rooms	42.9%	31.3%
Total	100 %	100 %

While priority planning of informal sector households appears more basic and directed to internal living qualities of the house (more rooms, rebuild house, build kitchen, improve doors, internal plaster), formal sector households show a tendency towards prestigious

337

improvements like a wall fence, electricity, and latrines[8] and favour visual improvements on the outside of the house (roof and external plaster).

Finally, people's perceptions of community problems and possible solutions were explored by a series of questions including the following: (1) What is the biggest problem in the community? (2) Who is going to solve these problems? (3) Is the council going to help Kanyama? If yes, what should it do first? (4) Could more be done in self-help? And if yes, what could be done? (5) What is best in Kanyama? Although responses to these questions were fairly unanimous on the part of all individual groups, crosschecks were made for those factors that had already appeared to reflect particularized interests. These were the residential status (owners or tenants), the job sector of the household (formal or informal), and the residential area (New or Old Kanyama).

Starting with the community problems, three outstanding issues were named, uniting 88.9% of all responses: 41.7% said that water provision in the dry season was the biggest problem, followed by flooding/drainage (27.8%), and the condition of roads (19.4%). Other items like security problems, availability of plots, housing standards, and generally high prices were mentioned by 2.8% each. There was some disagreement on the part of informal sector households as to the importance of flooding/drainage. In this group it was named only by 9.1%, and not considered more important than security, housing, plots and living costs. Being the more affected, residents of Old Kanyama put more emphasis on the significance of water provision problems (50%) than those in New Kanyama (31.3%).

Considering people's experiences with the council, it may come as a surprise that it was still looked upon by 64.9% of respondents as the major problem-solving agency. UNIP and self-help only received 5.6% of nominations, local leadership even less (2.7%). However, 18.9% hoped for money and assistance from outside - a reflection of the engagement of the international NGO in the well-drilling project. Again informal sector households deviated slightly by their near exclusive reference to the council (83.3%) to solve problems. On the other hand, confidence in council action lags behind the voiced expectations. Only 25% believed that the council was actually going to help, 31.3% thought not, and 37.8% were undecided. Formal sector households as well as residents in New Kanyama were slightly more optimistic than their informal counterparts or residents of Old Kanyama. In specifying what the council could do, potential fields of council activity were seen in tap water provision (40.6%) and road repair (27%). The third major problem of flooding and drainage does not appear to be specifically considered a council field of action. It was only mentioned by 5.4% of respondents and not given a higher preference than street lighting. An area-specific exception from the general pattern of potential council action was the demand for new plots by New Kanyama residents (18.8%).

People's participation in communal self-help was considerably higher than in Kalingalinga. In Kanyama 51.4% had made some kind of contribution to self-help projects; 48.6% had not taken part, but 5.6% of these claimed that they had 'not been informed' and would have

338

liked to have taken part. This high participation rate is unexpected in view of the high proportion of tenant households in Kanyama's population. Since owners have more long-term interests in improvements to the living area than tenants, participation rates of tenants in housing projects are usually lower. Typically this finding is only counterbalanced when the provision of basic needs is involved (e.g. water, electricity, roads), leading to an overall better participation (Gilbert/Ward, 1984a and 1984b). Since one of the recent major projects was dedicated to water provision, this might help to explain why the self-help contributions of tenant households in Kanyama (55%) were in fact even higher than those of owners (47.1%). Adding to this, the fraction of tenants contains a high proportion of long-term permanent residents. At the same time there was no difference in participation levels between Old and New Kanyama. However, the highest mobilization rate for any particular group is found for informal sector households, 83.3% of which participated in self-help activities while less than one-third of formal sector households had made any contributions. 70.3% of respondents believed that even more could be done by self-help. The most enthusiastic advocates were residents in Old Kanyama (87.5%), the informal sector households (83.3%), and the tenant fraction (80%). Suggestions for possible fields of self-help action were far less unanimous than the problem assessment. Only road repair (22.2%) and digging drainage trenches (11.1%) received some wider acceptance, followed by refuse collection, mutual funds, and drilling of boreholes (all 7.4%). All other concrete suggestions were particularistic such as plot allocations, forming cooperatives, building for subletting, building schools, raising house foundations (3.7% each). Informal sector households, probably for business reasons, put the highest priority on repairing roads (36%).

People's reasons for living in Kanyama ('what is best?') are varied. The proximity to town and to workplaces took the leading position (35.1%), but was closely followed by 32.4% who were unable to see any particular benefit from living in Kanyama at all. Availability of housing and accommodation was named by 13.5%. The least significant factors were living with friends and good security in their housing area (8.1% each), and finally 'cheap rent' (2.7%). As expected, dissatisfaction (i.e. the percentage of those seeing no benefits) was more pronounced with residential groups living in rental tenancy (40%), most of which are still looking for a plot,[9] and residents living in Old Kanyama (42.8%) lacking adequate service provision.

3   Conclusions

Since the expectations of most residents that the council will not upgrade Kanyama in the near future are probably realistic, this raises the question of viable community development policies. There are various arguments in favour of continuing the present self-reliance oriented approach.

-   As shown, Kanyama's high proportion of renter households has not been detrimental to self-help activities. On the contrary, renters have been particularly responsive to the call for participation and appear motivated to do more. Besides, self-help instead of council provision of services allows renters to enjoy the benefits of their work without service charges being passed on to rent rates, which might make living in Kanyama unaffordable for those depending on cheap accommodation.

-   Considering the policy of international NGOs of working with active community organizations, Kanyama is, due to its history, probably the settlement in Lusaka best qualified for further support by this type of programme. Projects that might be initiated in this way are road repair and possible extension of road connections into Old Kanyama. Since the water project included the provision of an electric power line, this might also be used to provide street lighting and lights for markets. An important side-effect of street lighting would be more security at night as Kanyama is notoriously a dangerous place.

-   The problem of adequate drainage cannot be solved without the LUDC due to the magnitude of the legal and technical problems involved. According to the NHA study, trenches that could be dug by self-help would be inadequate. However, not even the implementation of the proposed NHA scheme would prevent temporary flooding as complete drainage after heavy rains would still take 24 hours (NHA, 1978, p. 19). Consequently, improvements to the existing housing stock or innovative solutions to new housing are inevitable. Here, either the Lusaka Council or an NGO should come forward with appropriate architectural plans for improving the situation for dwellers. These plans should include suggestions for improving foundations and the construction of hygienic latrines.

-   According to the household survey, house owners in Old Kanyama were in 1989 prepared to pay K28 per month for more services, in New Kanyama as much as K76. That was considerably more than the rates for site and service and upgraded housing areas at that time. Judging by the financial obligations people would be prepared to take on for improvements, there appears to be a potential for operable loan or savings schemes. With the decline in real incomes due to Zambia's structural adjustment programme and the economic crisis, building material price inflation makes the conventional form of housing finance by family savings near impossible. To stop the dilapidation of the old housing stock and to rehabilitate housing with dangerous deficiencies, a revolving housing fund like that in Kalingalinga is urgently needed. In view of the physical problems of the area, lending priority should be given initially to houses lacking stability or requiring improvements to foundations. As investments in housing may to a large extent be recouped from rents, there seems only a low probability of defaults in repayment. Following the negative

340

experiences in the past, the council may not be the appropriate implementor for such schemes. Instead churches already active in Kanyama may be the suitable trustworthy agents or guarantors for the administration of funds if a seed fund donor can be found.

- In view of its apparently successful informal sector and the high proportion of women's income generating activities, the extension of the council EPU-programme to Kanyama should be considered. At present the LUDC makes a point of only including legalized or declared Development Areas in its programmes. Considering the Zambian Government's commitment to more promotion of the informal sector, the council should approach the implementation of an EPU programme independently of the question of upgrading Kanyama or not. Granting loans to informal producers in Kanyama would involve no obligations in respect of housing issues, and it would remove the present bias against the probably largest and most thriving part of the city's informal sector.

With the continuing controversies over inner city land use, all these potentials and opportunities are presently lying idle. To avert political conflicts with the LUDC, HUZA has withdrawn from Kanyama and like the international NGOs is concentrating its activities in low-income settlements on the peripheral areas of the city that are politically less sensitive with respect to land-use. In view of the lack of action on the part of authorities to prevent squatting in the critical zone between the north of the settlement and the city centre, it seems highly unfair to Kanyama residents to imply a de facto collective responsibility for these developments. In the planned council study of the alternative options of upgrading or resettlement, a distinction should be made between the overwhelmingly long-term residents in New and Old Kanyama who have obtained prescriptive rights within the 1989 boundaries, on the one hand, and the desperate plot seekers who have recently squatted outside this area, causing the encroachment, on the other. While resettlement of recent squatters to alternative sites may seem inevitable to yield space for city expansion, the Lusaka Council should finally recognize the rights of Kanyama in its *old boundaries* and thereby make it eligible for support from authorities and NGOs.

Notes

1   This area was, as intended, partially used by two churches. As can be seen from Figure 12.2 the rest is, however, still vacant as planned shops were allocated to the market areas instead. According to its present designation, it is to become the future bus station.

341

2   The three adjoining smaller unauthorized areas to the west, John Laing, Chibolya, and Misisi, are all in the potential direction of future inner city expansions and are unlikely to receive official recognition - even if the present slow city expansion is moving to vacant areas in the east and not to the south.

3   In the household sample 11.8% of residents stated that they had received their plot from local leaders. These cases occurred after 1966.

4   The advancement of physical consolidation of housing was already apparent in the 1966 survey of housing standards in New Kanyama. According to this only 3.4% were classified as 'temporary', 7.8% were 'excellent', at least 19.4% were permanent, made of cement block, the rest being semi-permanent. As the sample survey of Old Kanyama will show, the early housing stock, there too, displays parallel tendencies towards deploying permanent building techniques.

5   Probably, absentee ownership also signifies cases of multiple ownership of more than two houses. However, due to the legal ban on multiple ownership, landlords were not inclined to disclose this information. Contrary to the facts, only one landlord actually admitted having another house in Kanyama.

6   In the housing sample with 117 cases, average family sizes are larger, at 7.39. This was partially explained by two cases with exceptionally large joint households with 80 and more members, which may not be representative. If these cases are excluded, the mean value for family households of 5.98 is in the same range as the household survey.

7   All mud-brick housing in the household sample was exclusively used for renting.

8   The classification of improving latrines as 'prestigious' needs explaining. While by European standards the condition of latrines would appear to be a vital issue, this is much less the case with low-income dwellers in Lusaka. This is demonstrated by the findings that 44% of residents in Kanyama are unhappy with their latrines, and 32% have to share them with other households. Nonetheless, a real high priority on improving latrines would show up more strongly in the preferences made for future improvements. Like in Kalingalinga, this was generally not the case among Kanyama residents.

9   80% of tenants stated that they were trying to get their own plot, but only 20% had actually applied for one on the council list.

XIII African perspectives in housing and urban development

In reviewing research findings from other African countries, most of the issues and problems of Lusaka's urban development appear typical of postcolonial urbanization on that continent (cf. Stren, 1993). Key elements that shaped the course of African urban development were the persistency of colonial heritages and social stereotypes underpinning planning approaches, the unprecedented urban growth rates, and the disparities in the peripheral capitalist growth model that have led cities into 'urban crisis and organizational debacle' (Mabogunje, 1990, p. 361). As Mabogunje has further pointed out, the capitalist transformation of African cities has, independent of different colonial patterns, generally not been as substantial as expected, with 'pre-capitalist formations' playing an important part in the urban structuring. In particular the mass of low-income migrants has 'overwhelmed' many cities by the way they have created informal methods of provision in housing and employment (ibid., p. 160). In looking to the European urban culture, administrators and researchers have failed to analyse and adapt to these aspects as manifestations of a specific logic of African urban areas with their own 'needs, means and aspirations in a modern world' (Coquery-Vidrovitch, 1991, p. 74). Another typical feature that Zambia shares with the rest of Africa is the weakness of local administration, which with the pervasiveness of clientelism has resulted in widely ineffective urban planning. With the indifference of political linkages between important urban groups there is also a strong lack of urban social movements to articulate political demands in urban affairs (Mabogunje, 1990, p. 173). Furthermore, bureaucrats have failed to reverse colonial patterns of exploitation and instead used them to gain opportunities for themselves (Wallis, 1989, p. 17).

Within this political setting even major international housing schemes like those of the World Bank have only achieved limited impact on national policy formulation. Usually taking physical planning into their own hands, the World Bank and bilateral aid housing programmes (as in Zambia) have been unable to raise political support among the strategic urban classes for the development of appropriate housing policies for low-income groups. Instead, a lasting

343

effect of large World Bank upgrading schemes (e.g. in Kenya and Zambia) has been the accelerated commodification of low-cost housing, the discouragement of use of traditional building materials, and the supplantation of local building materials supply. Their place has been taken up by more capital-intensive forms of retailing with imported materials, in compliance with the demand created by newly introduced building standards (Macoloo, 1991). The complex regulations involved in such large-scale schemes have also proliferated bureaucracy and reinforced the patronage of the state over the poor in Tanzania (Campbell, 1990, p. 213). Collaterally with the orientation to new urban housing standards and the shift to 'modern' building materials there is wide agreement that commercialization of low-income housing has become the dominant process throughout African cities, including illegal informal markets (Amis/Lloyd, 1990, p. 20). The contemporary building process usually involves professional contract-workers in an 'articulation of the formal and the informal sector', with owners' self-help construction becoming the exception (Coquery, 1991). As in Lusaka, the use of permanent building materials is advancing all over Africa, either as a reflection of growing de facto security of tenure (and thus investments), or as the most effective means of securing the right to urban land in view of the often unsettled legal problems (Canel et al., 1990, p. 162).

These tendencies have been reinforced by the disengagement of the African state, particularly following the debt crisis in 1980s. With declining political commitment and the failure of planners to address the problems of urban poverty, mass low-income housing, and infrastructure provision, most states now implicitly accept unauthorized settlements as a 'relatively painless, and potentially profitable' way to appease the urban poor (Amis, 1990, p. 19): after an early phase of state-built housing, followed by programmes of aided self-help housing, the contemporary concern of the state is reduced to 'management' of infrastructure and services (Stren, 1990, p. 49). The urban populations living in absolute poverty, which in 1985 according to the UN made up 29% of residents in African cities, are hit hardest by these developments (UN, 1989, p. 39). With rising levels of physical housing consolidation in unauthorized settlements and with the bureaucratic formalization of the building process, even access to this type of housing is becoming socially selective. As Canel et al. note for their case studies in Douala and Kinshasa, it is no longer the poorest who are able to build in these housing areas (ibid., 1990, p. 163). At the same time, the informal means of cheap or free access to urban land by traditional forms of allocation are now virtually closed due to either growing state control over land markets or the formation of illegal land markets (Amis/Lloyd, 1990).

A sideline to upgrading and commodification has been the expanded supply of rental accommodation. In view of the potential of rental tenancy to raise urban productivity, surprisingly little attention has been paid by African governments to the promotion of this sector as a means of alleviating urban poverty. Its expedient role as provider of accommodation is underscored by the absence of exploitative relations between landlords and tenants. Although there have been rent increases due to upgrading programmes, most landlords, having similar

344

socioeconomic characteristics to their tenants, operate on a very small scale with little tendency towards speculation in housing or evictions of tenants (Amis/Lloyd, 1990).[1]

The economic recession and the effects of structural-adjustment programmes in Africa have greatly reduced the capacities of governments to intervene against rising poverty and to mitigate unsatisfied basic needs in housing and infrastructure. In rural areas recession has encouraged permanent migration to cities as a 'destiny of last resort' (Stren/White, 1989; Gilbert/Gugler, 1992). The absorptive capacities of cities have been further reduced by the fall in real incomes and the inflation of building prices that make house construction unaffordable for earners in the minimal wage income-brackets. Competition over scarce land (or leasehold in the case of Zambia) has intensified following the widespread seizure of urban land in Africa by the middle classes as a hedge against inflation and recession (Amis/Lloyd, 1990, p. 19).

Growing informalization of cities and new strategies of survival within household networks have been the response to the crisis of the urban economy and declining public service provisions. It seems that very few African governments have reacted by policy adjustments to support informal sector initiatives (Stren, 1993, p. 220). For example, as in Lusaka, urban agriculture plays an important role in food provision for low-income groups in African cities. This potential could be greatly fostered if authorities liberated and regulated access to land reserves for this purpose (ibid., p. 221). As to informal production, small-scale enterprises attain growing importance for the urban economy after the rapid decline of formal sector occupations. It is particularly important for the productive involvement of African women who generally have very limited access to formal sector occupations. Nonetheless, legal restrictions on conducting informal activities in inner city or statutory residential areas are the rule in Africa.

Against the background of single-party states as the dominant political culture and the only recent emergence of democratization in Africa, there are, so far, only limited prospects of rising political awareness and more participation in political decision-making. A single exception is reported from Abidjan where municipal democratization and decentralization in 1980 have raised people's concern over their own living circumstances, urban management, and the quality of life in the urban environment (Attahi, 1989, p. 146). Other states like Uganda, Malawi and Zambia have only recently implemented decentralization policies but lack adequate planning capacities to effectively carry through these programmes (Tait/ Shihembetsa, 1995). Although there have been mass responses by protests and riots to austerity programmes in various African countries, there seems little hope that the effects of recession will politically mobilize the urban poor who suffer most. Instead clientelism appears reinforced and not undermined by recession. For sub-Saharan Africa, Mabogunje has explained that clientelism traditionally far outweighs class struggle in political action (Mabogunje, 1990, p. 169). Therefore, in times of recession it is probable that African politicians will find ways of channelling available resources to their supporters, forestalling the emergence of social movements (Gilbert, 1993, p. 127).

Hopes of solutions to the urban crisis thus come to rest heavily on administrative reforms and programmes to improve urban productivity.[2] In its structural-adjustment lending programmes the World Bank has identified four major areas of constraint.

(1) Infrastructure deficiencies, which restrict productivity of private investment; (2) inappropriate regulations; (3) the dominant role of government in planning and financing urban infrastructure, starving local governments of financial resources; and (4) poorly developed financial sectors that hinder investment in infrastructure, housing, and other urban activities (Gilbert, 1993, p. 123).

As shown earlier (cf. 119 pp.), the World Bank sees a key to raising urban productivity and financial resources in the introduction of cost-recovery and market pricing of urban services, as well as the removal of subsidies 'that undermine the health of public agencies' (Linn, 1983). While governments have adopted this approach for housing and infrastructure provision for the poor, they have for political reasons been reluctant to remove subsidies awarded to strategic groups in this field. As Mabogunje has observed, this tends to make urban services unaffordable for the poor, which in turn produces corruption and a 'counterculture' of illegal means of securing and 'hoarding' these services (Mabogunje, 1990, p. 146).

Additionally the World Bank advocates the privatization of public services as a means to create competition and to increase productivity (World Bank, 1983a, p. 22; Stein, 1991). Since the 1960s this has already de facto taken place by privatization of a 'third kind', with informal business filling gaps in urban service provision, e.g. in housing, public transport, water supply, and waste disposal (Stren, 1988, p. 243). But with respect to urban infrastructure, experiences with privatization are ambiguous. According to Stren, the poor have in part benefited as services are now provided, even if for a price, that were formerly not available. Like in Lusaka, most of the deprived would also be prepared to pay for certain additional services (Stren, 1988, p. 219). While privatization has in practice occurred in certain areas due to the breakdown of state provisions, it would carry the issue too far if the state were released from its responsibility to supply basic services. In particular the urban very poor would be seriously disadvantaged as the supply of services to this group at market prices seems impracticable without a certain amount of cross-subsidization (Stren, 1990, p. 50). In a recent international evaluation of the impact of its structural-adjustment policies (including Lusaka) the World Bank has identified growing poverty and vulnerability among urban groups who are disadvantaged in responding to the new opportunities and incentives offered by economic liberalization. The Bank implicitly acknowledges that poverty reduction policies will be inevitable for the very poor, who, for example comprise 31% of the population in the Lusaka low-income settlement studied (Moser, 1994).

Finally, turning to urban development and planning in Lusaka, it is apparent that feasible strategies to service low-income groups have been seriously impaired by Zambia's debt crisis. But urban reforms are perhaps even more blocked by the political culture and power structures that have emerged from the state-centred postcolonial development. In suggesting proposals for Lusaka it therefore seems pertinent to distinguish between the *problem assessment* under the political dominance of a single-party system and the *developmental potential* after democratization in 1991. The short history of democracy in Africa has not yet nourished hopes of radical reforms or the breaking up of monolithic structures in the state apparatus and in its bureaucracies. In Zambia the heritage of the single-party state is a highly concentrated and centralized decision-making structure that has made district councils highly dependent on directives and financial resources from central government. The influence of central government in affairs of urban councils has been reinforced by its interest in state housing provision as a sensitive political issue directly related to the class privileges bestowed on government and parastatal employees. As a result, the new decentralization policies have not been backed by an effective devolution of powers to the district level. Moreover, local government authorities have neither enough professional capacities nor sufficient independent revenue sources to carry through the new policy effectively. In fact, after the introduction of the new decentralization policy, central government has continued to grow as the largest national employer while employment in local government has been steadily declining.[3] Public-private partnerships are the designated remedy to mobilize local resources for the improvement of urban infrastructure. While potentials of the private sector exist to enter into such partnerships, hesitation on their part is due to a lack of cooperative approaches of planning authorities that are failing to open themselves to local needs and priorities and to participative planning. The newly institutionalized committees at district and community level (DDCCs, RDCs, etc.) currently represent a top-down approach to decentralization advocated by the Ministry of Local Government and Housing. Decentralization measures have not been able to involve the local political structures and the local planning authorities, nor are they fully coordinated with and supported by other responsible ministries or the provincial governments.[4]

Seen from this vantage point, it seems unrealistic to suppose that the state and its supportive class base will come forward to support radical administrative and planning reforms that will enable participation and public-private partnerships. What is required for a structural change in the Zambian context is *political planning* that incorporates the political circumstances and conflicts of planning issues. To achieve innovations, urban actors must raise resonance and support outside of institutionalized politics (cf. p. 105). Actors that are capable of devising poverty-oriented programmes and raising political support for their benefit are available in and outside of Zambia.

- Although the NHA has for some time concentrated on commercial housing activities, it has capacities for town planning and architectural design in low-income settlements. The organization has recently reengaged in the construction of appropriate housing and intermediate building technology and has built low-cost demonstration houses in Bauleni and Kamanga. In the planned cooperation with international organizations (i.e. Shelter Afrique, African Housing Fund, UNDP) these house designs might be developed further into truly affordable solutions.

- International NGOs (INGOs) working with low-income communities have become the most vigorous advocates of participation at this level. Due to their international financial backing and adherence to First-World-devised concepts, these organizations are deploying independent approaches, perhaps in advance of a national supportive political framework. With further adaptation of INGOs to the Zambian context and the creation of more indigenous NGOs, the potential of non-government organizations in urban development is certain to grow. They may, for example, play an important role in unblocking the present 'deadlock' between government authorities and the private sector in moving towards mutual action. Like in Peru, once the integrity of NGOs is generally accepted, they can function as impartial mediators and facilitators at round tables, bringing together all those groups that are responsible for urban development or interested in participating in it.

- Nationally, the biggest critical potential is found at the University of Zambia in Lusaka and at the Copperbelt University in Kitwe. The University in Lusaka has already been commissioned to carry out various urban studies and could play an important role as advisor in urban policy development. Consultancy from the academic field may also come from various international researchers with profound experience and practical long-term involvement in Lusaka's development (e.g. A. Schlyter, C. Rakodi, K. Hansen, R. Martin).

- The UNCHS has until recently maintained an office in Lusaka and with DANIDA has already staged a training programme for government staff and community leaders in human settlement. This organization has shown interest in supporting Zambia in a national low-income housing programme and has broad experience in designing appropriate housing and settlement schemes.

- HUZA, the only active indigenous NGO in Lusaka in human settlement, could contribute to implementing new approaches by drawing on its own experiences from educational work in low-income settlements and from the recent 'upgrading' in Bauleni. HUZA has paid particular attention to the aspect of appropriate communication and dissemination procedures with its target groups, an aspect that was crucially ignored in most previous programmes.

348

The future frame of action will be defined by the new government housing policy draft of 1995 prepared by the MLGH. It states as its main policy goal 'to provide adequate affordable housing for all income groups in Zambia' (GRZ, 1995b, p. 14). The main objectives to achieve this are (ibid):

(a)   an allocation of a minimum of 15% of the national annual budget to housing to support a sustainable housing development programme;

(b)   making serviced land available for housing development and streamlining the land allocation system;

(c)   streamlining of building standards, regulations and other controls so that they accord with the capabilities, needs and aspirations of the various sections of the population;

(d)   encouraging the production and use of local and affordable building materials;

(e)   assisting the poor to acquire decent shelter through alleviation of their affordability problems;

(f)   fostering housing areas that are functional, healthy, aesthetically pleasant and environmentally friendly; and

(g)   the preparation of a national housing implementation strategy.

The general approach to implementing these objectives will be the encouragement of home ownership through private investments on a deregulated housing market. The growth of the housing market is to be stimulated by adequate land and service delivery and the promotion of housing finance jointly by the public sector, building societies, capital markets and international agencies. Investment in rental housing is also to be promoted through the removal of rent control. To complement this process the state and employers are to withdraw completely from tied employers' housing. Tax incentives to the private sector are to make manufactured building materials cheaper and popularize the use of local building materials and appropriate technology. The full implementation of this policy will be a lengthy process, requiring review of the presently fragmented and inconsistent legal framework in the housing sector. For the creation of an enabling legal environment, amendments to no less than 13 different Acts are earmarked.

While suggestions for restructuring the formal housing sector display a comprehensive problem assessment and differentiated policy measures, this is much less the case with the informal housing sector. Beyond the general postulate that the poor and the vulnerable are

349

to be assisted in their affordability problems, the policy draft is much less explicit as to how this will be realized for the 69% of national households who are presently living in poorly services or unserviced informal housing in urban and rural areas. It also remains unclear whether low-cost housing will be affected by the new provisions of minimum approved building standards that are to be controlled by a building inspectorate. Only four cursory suggestions are put forward as to how low-income groups are to be supported in their housing provision.

1   The provision of conventional site and service programmes with a minimal level of basic services.

2   For settlement upgrading and squatting a 'discretionary approach' will be applied involving the adoption of self-help and community participation in the provision and maintenance of infrastructure. These communities will also be encouraged to articulate their shelter needs through residents' assemblies.

3   To encourage the provision of adequately serviced land with secure tenure for all income groups, especially the poor and the vulnerable.

4   The encouragement of township layouts that are functional and economical.

No further suggestions are made as to how the general policy framework is to be adapted to the special conditions in an informal environment and housing market. Considering the present housing problems of low-income dwellers such as lack of access to credits, lack of correlation between building standards and paying capacities, legal insecurity, limited potential of self-help solutions, growing displacement of vulnerable households, etc., strong lobbying will be required to ensure that these aspects are addressed in the forthcoming national housing implementation strategy. Particular attention must also be paid to the foreseeable spillover effects of a restructured formal housing market that will have a negative effect on the proposed solutions for the informal housing sector. For instance, in the past, site and service schemes already had a reputation of being unaffordable for low-income groups. With the planned reforms of economic costs in housing and the deregulation of rents, overall rising housing costs are bound to create competition between formal and informal residents for the newly planned site and service schemes. Without careful control of terms of eligibility it seems unlikely that low-income households will be able to match the financial capabilities of displaced formal sector residents in qualifying for these schemes. Necessary elements of appropriate urban development policies, adjusted to the realities of poverty and informalization, are proposed in the following.

Of course it would be impossible to implement new policies and programmes without the active involvement of local councils, the elected councillors, local leadership, and residents.

Here, too, structural changes in the relationships are necessary to reach agreement over a realistic assessment of priorities and needs. The present situation is characterized by considerable alienation between these different parties that blocks effective cooperation.

At the level of the *council*, political leadership and municipal bureaucracies have for a long time clung to the illusion of state patronage and hierarchical decision-making as the exclusive method of managing urban provision systems. They have also failed to realize that economic development impedes large-scale and overzealous solutions. In this respect, planning is still trapped in the legal and physical framework of British Town and Country Planning that has produced highly inflexible and inappropriately formalized planning procedures in dealing with urban development. Adaptations to the current situation would, for example, require acceptance of and support for the informal sector, not as a subsidiary, but as a vital sustainer of the urban economy and accordingly amend planning legislation and bye-laws. In housing and settlement of low-income populations, planning and legislation require more pragmatic and less bureaucratic procedures and more consideration of people's real paying capacities. Communication structures have added to the rupture between low-income residents and authorities. English, the official administrative language, is spoken by only very few residents, and hardly any manuals on settlement topics are available in a form or language that is understood by residents.

The elected *councillors* may play a more important intermediate role as negotiators between the settlements they represent and the political decision-making bodies. In the past the practice of party nomination of eligible candidates has in part prevented true representation of communal and residential interests. This, for instance, was the case when politically influential persons without ties to the communities they represented were nominated for councillorship. The new multi-party system may help to divest councillors of their traditional alignment to party politics or bring forth a new generation of councillors dedicated to democratic principles. Until now, councillors with popular backing have often lacked the articulation or political standing to be influential in the parliamentary system or have not been taken seriously by the political executive. The future enhancement of their political powers would, therefore, depend on a far greater mobilization and political awareness amongst communities in backing their representatives.

The relationship between *local leaders* and the council has often been characterized by mutual mistrust and friction, particularly when leadership has used its mandate to 'intervene' in territorial affairs, such as illegal plot allocations, or has encouraged residents not to pay for service charges (GRZ/CDG, 1989). Although these problems in part result from vested interests of local leaders, they are also corollaries of discriminatory council policies and disparities in urban provision. While the council has heavily subsidised middle-class housing, it obliged the urban poor to contribute self-help labour for the building of infrastructure and to pay for services rendered. As to the cases of misuse of office that have occurred over plot allocations (e.g. in Kalingalinga and Kanyama), it should also be conceded that the council and its representatives, too, have not refrained from such practice, and that informal methods of plot allocation are a logical response to the immense deficits in official land delivery. Moreover, land-use plans in Lusaka seriously lack realistic assessments of actual developments (e.g. as shown in the case of settlements south of the city centre). Compliance with essential town planning could be more readily ensured by integrating local informal planning into urban development policies. This would require determined efforts to train local leadership. But even more essentially, if the aim is to achieve judicious leadership, constructive cooperation with the council must be rewarded in the form of benefits for community development, since otherwise leaders will seek 'illicit' ways of achieving this to secure political support. A scheme based on these principles of rewarding collaborating communities might be a starting point in the rehabilitation of council-leadership cooperation.

The political engagement and awareness of *residents* in communal and urban affairs in Lusaka have been low for various reasons. Traditionally, urban settlement has been an individualized process, negotiated between local leaders and settlers without the collective component as is the case with land invasions. This pattern has been reinforced by the African tradition of delegating matters to leaders, a system entrenched by the party system for the urban situation. In this respect, the World Bank housing project was an important step in the inculcation of principles of state patronage, and it had an important political sideline in extending UNIP party control to informal residential areas that were strongholds of the opposition. However, with the decline of popular programmes and welfare functions, the old political hierarchy has become impervious to public demands or criticism, leaving a situation of growing alienation and anomie amongst low-income residents. The somewhat different situation in Kanyama, where neglect by authorities has given rise to self-help potentials, merely illustrates this point. Even under the new democratic order it will be difficult to recover from this situation as the lasting economic crisis is a serious restraint to social transformation. At community level, residents must react and no longer wait for municipalities to become active. Much will depend on the change of political climate brought about by the newly formed parties and a fresh approach to urban policies that removes inappropriate restrictions to an enlarged self-organization in local and private habitat issues.

Among the elements of appropriate urban development policies, adjusted to the realities of poverty and informalization, four issues are preeminent.

a) Housing and infrastructure provision. Despite expectations that the HABITAT 2 conference in 1996 would bring forth new solutions and priorities in sustainable urban development and housing, a shift in international development policies is already evident that will not exempt the UNCHS. While emphasis on urban development ('engines of development') has been restored, sectoral concepts are now directed to building up urban productivity and management capacities, and will support privatization, market deregulation, economic costs in urban services and enabling strategies for its provision. But multilateral or bilateral organizations will generally no longer finance housing programmes requiring subsidization (Burgess/Carmona/Kolstee, 1994; DSE, 1994). With the minor exception of NGO support for the upgrading of a few low-income settlements, no further international large-scale support can be expected for housing schemes in Zambia. At the same time, the national potential in housing provision has suffered considerably as the result of the dramatic rise in construction costs of housing in the 1980s and '90s, which has slowed down self-help housing provision and the improvement of old structures by owner-occupiers. Moreover, Zambian building legislation has made access to home ownership socially selective in serviced housing areas. The building codes in site and service and Development Areas introduced in the mid-1970s require that a basic house must be built according to council house plans within 6-12 months. As these plans impose minimally the building of two rooms with foundation, doors, roof, and wall construction in permanent materials (i.e. cement-block or burnt brick), this effectively prohibits building by lower-income households in these areas. Even if credit schemes were available, the estimated minimum income to finance housing of this standard would have to be in the range of two minimum wages (K1,000 in 1989 or K100,000 in 1995) or even higher. Therefore the revision of building codes and schedules is imperative to overcome stagnation in housing provision and to allow progressive building in accordance with the financial capacities of low-income households.[5] Detailed guidelines for 'extendable and upgradable' constructions, using stabilized traditional building materials (adobe, bamboo, wood) for the initial basic house, have been developed by the Zambian architect F. Ndilila (1980). His design of the basic unit allows the flexible and incremental conversion of the entire structure or of individual elements into stabile and durable forms. By virtue of its spatial layout it can also be easily extended horizontally or vertically. The LUDC should commission the NHA, which has already experimented with alternative basic house forms, to carry out a feasibility study on the introduction of this model.

The city's current space-use patterns have aggravated the problems of urban infrastructure provision. Vertical house extensions that lower unit costs of construction and intensify the use of existing infrastructure have not yet been used in low-income housing in Lusaka. In view of the financial constraints on providing new infrastructure, vertical expansions of housing should be encouraged as a novel approach that makes better use of the existing facilities and at the same time provides new housing capacities. As an incentive to make this possible for home owners in the existing stock, the official restrictions on rental tenancy should be reconsidered, allowing new building by residents for this purpose. As an alternative approach for home owners who lack capital for extensions, new residents (or housing agencies) could upgrade the existing house in exchange for the right to share the premises with the original resident under the new 'Second Title' legislation. The NHA might extend its efforts in the design of low-cost housing to the development of plans for a cheap conversion of old houses into multi-storey constructions.

b) Land delivery. The current land delivery for low-income residents, serving approx. some ten per cent or less of the actual demand and exclusively dedicated to site and service housing, is a disguised deterrent policy towards potential migration from rural areas. But as economic recession tends to affect rural more than urban areas, there is little alternative but to face inevitable developments and to draw up plans for coping with uncurbed demographic growth. For the same reason, money put into programmes of repatriating urban dwellers back to the countryside is wasted and should be invested in urban programmes instead. As already suggested by an international consultancy, land 'shortages' are the self-made consequence of the planning paradigm of low-density development leading to urban sprawl.[6] Following surveying of the carrying capacities of existing infrastructure or the local potentials (e.g. for boreholes), some demographic growth could be sustained by selected extensions of existing areas, requiring close cooperation with local leadership. The present policies of channelling low-income populations to the urban periphery are in conflict with Lusaka's spatially centralized commercial and industrial areas. Within revised citywide space-use plans, a stronger mix of residential and commercial areas should be envisaged. Meanwhile, new low-income residential areas should be planned in suitable inner-city areas to the east, leaving enough space for city expansions, but remaining within reasonable distance to places of work. As already successfully practised in the Copperbelt town of Kabwe, the approach of preplanning would guide and control the incipient settlement process by anticipating the requirements of future regularization and infrastructure provision. In view of interminable constraints in cadastral surveying and low manpower capacities for proper land registration, land administration could be minimized by introducing collective leasehold, shifting part of the formal responsibility over land use to locally formed dwellers' organizations.

c) Finance of housing and infrastructure. A crucial problem in restructuring council expenditure is the present disparity between enlarged council functions and the insufficient revenue base imposed by the 1980 Local Administration Act amended in 1991.[7] Amendments to this Act are required to restore vital council functions and to give more priority to urban management. However, as a complete recovery of council budgets from within the old finance-providing sources seems improbable, restructuring of public spending and measures of cost-reduction including privatization are inevitable. As a first step, the Lusaka Council has begun to privatize the highly subsidized high-cost council housing. Statutory obstructions should be removed in order to encourage private commercial activities in housing that strengthen home-ownership - as suggested in the promotion of rental tenancy. Indirect support for private investments in unauthorized areas could be given in the form of security of tenure and the provision of affordable basic infrastructure. In the event of future privatization of these services, the terms of public-private contracts should ensure that special rates are made available for vulnerable groups so as not to exclude them from provisions. At present, various unauthorized housing areas in Lusaka are held in a state of indeterminacy due to lack of means to declare them Development Areas and to provide infrastructure. If no conflicts over space use exist, declarations of 'intent' should be considered as an intermediate solution to give security and to promote investments in housing and commerce. As to the actual financing of housing and infrastructure, our two surveys in low-income housing areas in Lusaka have shown that there is a potential for cost-recovery in publicly or privately provided services if new institutional forms of administration and collection are introduced. The politicization of financial aspects in past housing projects implies that it would be essential to keep these institutions free from state or political interference. Making cooperatives responsible for the running of specific urban services would be an example of this kind of scheme (cf. p. 275). An alternative form now viable under the Decentralization Act would be to entrust the RDCs with this function. The model of locally controlled revolving funds, successfully tried in Kalingalinga, seems the most promising comprehensive approach that might be used jointly to finance housing and infrastructure improvements. New projects should set up a seed fund and provide infrastructure at basic standards, like in the previous upgrading schemes. Further improvements in standards should then be left to residents' self-determination *and* to their financial capacities of maintaining and expanding the revolving fund. The terms of repayment to the council (or to other donor organizations) should be carefully adapted to the micro-economic situation of the settlement involved and, if necessary, incorporate an element of cross-subsidization or offering of preferential rates.

d) Economic promotion of the informal sector with consultancy. The expansion of Kalingalinga's economic promotion programme to authorized housing areas would be an important step towards acceptance of the urban informal sector in Lusaka. Fresh momentum has been provided by the EPU support of individual initiatives, which seem more enterprising than cooperatives in adapting to urban informalization. This programme should be implemented citywide as fast as possible, whatever the legal residential status. Another key to its success was the compulsory provision of business consultancy. While essential formal advice on financial planning, accountancy, etc. was made available by EPU management, there were deficiencies of knowledge relating to the commercial operations of the informal sector. In this respect, valuable information would be gained by incorporating successful informal entrepreneurs in the advisory on marketing aspects. Although interference with informal activities should be kept to a minimum, certain steering measures might be conducive to achieving more diversification. For example, EPU lending priorities should be put on business expansions creating new employment, or on activities that structurally improve local commerce, decentralize the urban economy or protect the environment. In more capital-intensive lines of business the council or private companies should participate in joint ventures with the informal sector to improve urban services. The promotion of local building materials supply would be an appropriate scheme as their present acquisition in the town centre incurs excessive transport costs to bring materials to the settlements. Economic promotion should also be extended to semi-legal urban gardening, which might be intensified by a declaration of its official toleration in defined areas and by allowing usufruct of vacant council lands. Inappropriate municipal regulations also restrict the potential of informal activities. In the general policies towards the informal sector, local authority bye-laws and the Town and Country Planning Act still impose territorial restrictions on activities outside of markets or in the vicinity of areas zoned for housing. The relaxation of legal restrictions would reduce the present spatial (and social) division between informal traders and producers and their potential customers in middle-class housing areas. Town planning could contribute to this development by a flexible allocation of marketplaces and facilities according to the needs of informal business. But revised laws will be useless without a change in the social stereotypes and paternalistic attitudes of bureaucrats. Solutions to the present urban problems require a partnership attitude of mutual learning among low-income residents and planners. Finally, they require the full recognition of poor residents as citizens by an urban authority that dedicates itself to professionalism and to democratic principles in creating the enabling environment for community development.

Notes

1   An exception to this rule is Kenya.
2   This position has now been accepted by all major international development agencies. For its 1996 HABITAT 2 conference in Istanbul, the UNCHS considers the repercussions of this issue on housing and infrastructure provision for the poor to be one of the major points of the agenda.
3   In 1994 central government accounted for 26.6% (133,600 jobs) of total formal employment, 1.4% more than in 1993. In the same period formal employment in local government declined from 4.2% to 3.5%. This is a loss of 18.5% of jobs in local government from 21,600 down to 17,600 within one year (GRZ, 1995b, p. 5).
4   This analysis is based on observations in Lusaka and in Livingstone, the capital of Southern Province. It may misrepresent the situation in other parts of Zambia, in particular in the Copperbelt where - according to information from the UNCHS/ DANIDA in Nairobi - more progress in reforming urban structures has been achieved.
5   According to MLGH information, minimum standards may be reduced to one room but no revision of the building schedule is envisaged.
6   cf. page 245.
7   cf. page 240.

Bibliography

Abrams, C. (1964), *Housing in the Modern World*, London.

Adam, E. (1977), *Zambia. Reflektionen zu Partei und Gesellschaft im Entwicklungsstaat*, Bonn.

Adam, E. (1980), *Tribalismus und Ungleiche Entwicklung in Zambia*, Bad Honnef.

Amin, S. (1980), *Class and Nation, Historically and in the Current Crisis*, London.

Amin, S. (1974), *Modern Migrations in Western Africa*, London.

Amin, S. (1978), *The Law of Value and Historical Materialism*, New York/London.

Albers, G. (1989), 'Stadtplanung und Kommunalwissenschaften', in Hesse, J. (ed.), *Kommunalwissenschaften in der Bundesrepublik Deutschland*, Baden-Baden.

Amis, P. (1990), 'Introduction: Key Themes in Contemporary African Urbanisation', in Amis/Lloyd (eds.), *Housing Africa's Urban Poor*, Manchester.

Amis/Lloyd (eds.) (1990), *Housing Africa's Urban Poor*, Manchester.

Angel, S. (1983), 'Upgrading Slum Infrastructure. Divergent Objectives in Search of a Consensus', *Third World Planning Review*, Vol.5 (1).

Angel/Archer/Tanphiphat/Wegelin (eds.) (1983), *Land for Housing the Poor*, Singapore.

Arrighi, G. (1973), 'Labour Supplies in Historical Perspective: A Study of the Proletarianization of the African Peasantry in Rhodesia', in Arrighi/Saul, *Essays on the Political Economy in Tropical Africa*, New York.

Attahi, K. (1989), 'Côte d'Ivoire: An Evaluation of Urban Management Reforms', in Stren/White (eds.), *African Cities in Crisis*, Boulder.

Baer, W. (1991), 'Filtering and Third World Housing Policy', *Third World Planning Review*, Vol. 13, No. 1.

Bairoch, P. (1973), *Urban Unemployment in Developing Countries: The Nature of the Problem and Proposals for its Solution*, Geneva.

Balies/Szeftel (1982), 'The Rise of Zambian Capitalist Class in the 1970s', *Journal of Southern African Studies*, Vol. 8 (2).

Baldwin, R. (1966), *Economic Development and Export Growth. A Study of Northern Rhodesia*, 1920-1960, Berkeley.

Bamberger, M. (1981), 'Shelter Programs for the Urban Poor: A Comparative Review', *ITCC Review*, No. 38.

Bamberger/Hewitt (1986), *Monitoring and Evaluating Urban Development Programs. A Handbook for Program Managers and Researchers*, Washington.

Bamberger/Sanyal/Valverde (1982), *Evaluation of Site and Services Projects. The Experience from Lusaka, Zambia*, Washington.

357

Banaji, J. (1977), 'Modes of Production in a Materialist Conception of History', *Capital & Class*, No. 3.

Banda, M. (1979.), *People Buying Plots and Houses in Chawama Overspill and Chawama Existing, the 'Newcomers'*. Lusaka Housing Project Evaluation Team, Lusaka.

Baran, P.A. (1957), *Politische Ökonomie des Wachstums*, Berlin.

Bardouille, R. (1981), *The Sexual Division of Labour in the Lusaka Informal Sector: A Case Study of Lusaka*, Lusaka.

Baross, P. (1983), 'The Articulation of Land Supply for Popular Settlements in Third World Cities', in Angel et al., *Land for Housing the Poor*, Singapore.

Baylies/Szeftel (1982), 'The Rise of Zambian Capitalist Class in the 1970s', *Journal of Southern African Studies*, 8 (2).

Berger, E. (1974), *Labour, Race and Colonial Rule - The Copperbelt from 1924 to Independence*, Oxford.

Bettison, D. (1959), 'Numerical Data on African Dwellers in Lusaka', *Rhodes-Livingstone Communication* 16, Lusaka.

Beuter/Späth (1984). 'Der informelle Sektor: Eine Perspektive für Frauen? Beispiele aus Jamaika und Sambia', in Berlinghausen/Kerstan (eds.), *Die unsichtbare Stärke: Frauenarbeit in der 3. Welt, Entwicklungsprojekte und Selbsthilfe*, Saarbrücken.

Biermann, W. (1980), *Zambia - Ein Frontstaat zwischen Befreiungskampf und postkolonialer Abhängigkeit*, Bonn.

Biermann, W. (1979), 'The Development of Underdevelopment: The Historical Perspective', in Turok, B. (ed.), *Development in Zambia*, London.

Blankhart, S. (1986), 'Urban Transport in Lusaka', in Williams (ed.), *Lusaka and its Environs*, Lusaka.

Bley/Tetzlaff (eds.) (1978), *Afrika und Bonn - Versäumnisse und Zwänge deutscher Afrika-Politik*, Reinbek.

BMZ (ed.) (1986), *Wohnungsversorgung und Selbsthilfe*, Bonn.

Bodemeyer, R. (1986), *Bürokratie und Politik in Sambia*, Giesen.

Bodemeyer, R. (1983), 'Verwaltung und grundbedürfnisorientierte Entwicklung: Das Beispiel Sambia'. *Verfassung und Recht in Übersssee*, 16.

Borst/Krätke (1993), 'Die sozialräumliche Ausdifferenzierung 'metropolitaner' Stadtregionen', *Zeitschrift für sozialistische Politik und Wirtschaft*, No. 72.

Boserup, E. (1982), *Die ökonomische Rolle der Frau in Afrika, Asien, Lateinamerika*, Stuttgart.

Bose, A. (1973), *Studies in India's Urbanization 1901-1970* , McGraw Hill.

Bose, A. (1974), *The Informal Sector of the Calcutta Metropolitan Economy*, World Employment Programme Research Working Paper, Geneva.

Boswell, D. (1967), *Community Care and the African Family in Lusaka*, London.

Boswell, D. (1975a), *The Growth and Socio-Political Development in Chawama*, (Working Paper B.7 in the set Planning Urban Growth: The Lusaka Experience 1957-1973), London.

Boswell, D. (1975b), *Buildings & Households in Roberts's/Chawama. A Comparison of the situation in 1965 and in 1974*, London University College, Planning Unit (Working Paper B.7), London 1975(b).

Boswell, D. (1975c), *Business & Petty-Trading in Robert's Compound in 1965 and Reflections on the Situation in 1974*, London University College, Development Planning Unit (Working Paper B.7), London.

Boswell, D.M. (1969), 'Personal Crisis and the Mobilization of the Social Network', in Mitchell (ed.), *Social Networks in Urban Situations*, Manchester.

Bowa *et al.* (1979), *Gardening in the City*, University of Zambia, Institute for African Studies (typescript report), Lusaka.

358

Bowles/Gintis (1977), 'The Marxian Theory of Value and Heterogeneous Labour: A Critique and Reformulation', *Cambridge Journal of Economics*, No.1.

Böhm/Stürzbecher (1981), 'Das Integrierte Projekt aus der Sicht einer Beratungsfirma', in Gesellschaft für Umweltforschung (ed.), *Möglichkeiten und Grenzen Integrierter Entwicklungsprojekte*, Saarbrücken.

Braverman, H. (1974), *Labour and Monopoly Capital*, New York.

Bromley, R. (1978), 'Organization, Regulation and Exploitation of the So-Called 'Urban Informal Sector': The Street Traders of Cali, Colombia', *World Development*, 6.

Browett, J. (1984), 'On the Necessity and Inevitability of Uneven Spatial Development under Capitalism' *International Journal of Urban and Regional Research*, Vol. 8, No. 2.

Browning/Roberts (1982), 'Urbanization, Sectoral Transformation and the Utilization of Labour in LatinAmerica', *Comparative Urban Research*, No.8.

Bruno/Körte/Mathéy (1984), *Umgang mit städtischen Wohnquartieren unterer Einkommensgruppen in Entwicklungsländern*, Darmstadt.

Bryant, C. (1980), 'Squatters, Collective Action and Participation: Learning from Lusaka', *World Development*, Vol. 8 (1).

Bryant/White (1982), Managing Development in the Third World, Boulder.

Burawoy, M. (1982), 'The hidden abode of underdevelopment: labour process and the state in Zambia', *Politics and Society*, 11(2), pp.123-166.

Burdette, M. (1988), *Zambia: Between Two Worlds*, Aldershot.

Burdette, M. (1984), 'The Mines, Class Power, and Foreign Policy in Zambia', *Journal of Southern African Studies*, Vol. 10, No. 2, 1984.

Burgess, R. (1984), 'The Limits of State Self-Help Housing Programmes', in Bruno/Körte/Mathéy (eds.), *Umgang mit städtischen Wohnquartieren unterer Einkommensgruppen in Entwicklungsländern*, Darmstadt.

Burgess, R. (1987), 'The International Sponsorship of Self-Help Housing and the Reproduction of Labour Power Theory', in Harms/Zschaebitz (eds.), *International Conference Urban Renewal and Housing for Low-Income Groups in Metropolitan Areas of Latin America*, Vol. 3. Hamburg.

Burgess, R. (1988), 'Helping Some to Help Themselves - Third World Housing Policies and Development Strategies', *TRIALOG*, No. 18.

Burgess, R. (1982), 'Self-Help Housing Advocacy: A Curious Form of Radicalism. A Critique of the Work of John F. C. Turner', in Ward, M. (ed.), *Self-Help Housing. A Critique*, Oxford.

Burgess/Ramirez (1988), 'Affordability - and no Cost Recovery. Or: How to Transform World Bank Housing Policies', *TRIALOG*, No. 18.

Burgess/Carmona/Kolstee (1994), Contemporary Urban Strategies and Urban Design in Developing Countries - A critical review, Publiatieburo Bouwkunde, Faculty of Architecture TU Delft.

Cabannes, Y. (1983), 'Die Urbanisierungspolitik der Weltbank', *TRIALOG*, No.1.

Campbell, J. (1990), 'World Bank Shelter Projects in East Africa: Some matching needs with appropriate responses?', in Amis/Lloyd (eds.), *Housing Africa's Urban Poor*, Manchester.

Canel/Delis/Girard (1984), *Construire la ville africaine: Histoire comparée de chantiers d'habitation auto-produit á Duala et á Kinshasa*, Paris.

Canel/Delis/Girard (1990), *Construire la ville africaine: Chroniques du citadin promteur*, Paris.

Carter/O'Meara (eds.) (1985), *African Independence. The First 25 Years*, Bloomington.

Castells, M. (1972), *La Question Urbaine*, Paris.

Castells, M. (1979), *City, Class and Power*, London.

Castells, M. (1983), *The City and the Grassroots*, London.

CDG (1987), *Workshop "Participation and Self-Help" within HABITAT FORUM BERLIN '87*, Cologne.

CDG/DESWOS (eds.) (1983), Self-Help Housing Groups in Squatter Settlements of Zambia - Legal Aspects,. Cologne.

CDG/GRZ (1989), *Legal Aspects of Organized Self-Help in Low Income Informal Settlements - "Training Material" - Workshop Report: Lusaka/Zambia 13. - 15.04.1989*, Cologne.

Chakravorty, U.N. (1981), *Calcutta's Slum Improvement: A Myth?*, Information Service on Science and Society-related Issues, Centre for Science & Development.

Chikulo, B. (1981), 'The Zambian Administrative Reforms: An Alternative View', *Public Administration and Development*, No. 1, pp. 55-65.

Chikulo, B. (1985), 'Re-organization for local Administration in Zambia. An Analysis of the Local Administration Act, 1980', *Public Administration and Development*, No. 5,1.

Chipungu, S. (1988), *The State, Technology and Peasant Differentiation in Zambia - A Case Study of the Southern Province 1930-1986*, Lusaka.

Cliffe, L. (1976), 'Rural Political Economy of Africa', in Gutkind/Wallerstein (eds.), *The Political Economy of Contemporary Africa*, Beverly Hills.

Cliffe, L. (1979), 'Labour Migration and Peasant Differentiation: Zambian Experiences', in Turok, B. (ed.), *Development in Zambia*, London.

Cohen, G. A. (1978), *Karl Marx's Theory of History: A Defence*, Oxford.

Cohen, R. (1972), 'Class in Africa: Analytical Problems and Perspectives', *The Socialist Register*, London.

Colletti, L. (1976a), *Hegel und der Marxismus*, Frankfurt/M.

Colletti, L. (1976), *Marxismus und Dialektik*, Frankfurt/M.

Collier, D. (1976), Squatters and Oligarchs: Authoritarian Rule and Political Change in Peru, John Hopkins Press.

Collins, J. (1969), *The Myth of the Garden City*. Zambia Urban Studies 2, Lusaka.

Collins, J. (1970), *The Evolution of Urban Housing Policy in Zambia with particular reference to Lusaka*, New York.

Collins, J. (1980), 'Lusaka: Urban planning in a British Colony, 1931-64', in Cherry, G. E. (ed.), *Shaping an Urban World*, London.

Collins, J. (1986), 'Lusaka: The historical Perspective of a Planned Capital, 1931-1970', in Williams, G. (ed.), Lusaka and its Environs,. Lusaka.

Collins/Muller (1974), *Economic Activity, the Informal Sector and Household Income* (Mimeo). Lusaka.

Connolly, P. (1982), 'Uncontrolled Settlements and Self-Build: What kind of Solution? The Mexico City Case', in Ward, P. M. (ed.): *Self-Help Housing. A Critique*, Oxford.

Coquery, M. (1991), 'Secteur informal et production de l'espace urbanisé en Afrique', in Coquery-Vidrovitch/Nedelec (eds.), *Tiers-Mondes: L'informel en question?*, Paris.

Coquery-Vidrovitch, C. (1991), 'The Process of Urbanisation in Africa (from the origins to the beginning of independence)', *African Studies Review*, Vol. 34 (1).

Cordova, A. (1973), *Strukturelle Heterogenität*, Frankfurt/M.

CSO (Central Statistical Office), Republic of Zambia (1987), *Lusaka Urban Labour Force Survey 1985*, Lusaka.

CSO (Central Statistical Office), Republic of Zambia (1985), *1980 Population and Housing Census of Zambia. (Analytical Report Volume III) Major Findings and Conclusions*, Lusaka.

CSO (Central Statistical Office), Republic of Zambia (1986), *Country Profile Zambia 1985*, Lusaka.

CSO (Central Statistical Office), Republic of Zambia, *Consumer Price Statistics 5/1987, 8/1988 and 2/1989*, Lusaka.

DAC-OECD (1988), *Sustainability in Development Programmes: A Compendium of Donor Experience*,. Paris.

Dallas, R. (1995), *Pocket Africa. Profiles, facts and figures about Africa today*, London.

DANIDA/UNCHS (1989), *Final Evaluation Report for a Training programme in Community Participation*, Lusaka.

Daniel, P. (1985), 'Zambia, Structural adjustment or downward spiral', *IDS Bulletin*, 16 No.3.

Davies, D. H. (1971), *Zambia in Maps*, London.

Davidson, F. (1992), *Community Participation in Zambia: the DANIDA/UNCHS Training Programme*, UNCHS, Nairobi.

Davidson, F. (1994), *Monitoring and Evaluation: From Project to Programme. The Community Participation Training Programme in Zambia*, UNCHS, Nairobi.

Davis, J.M. (ed.) (1933), *Modern Industry and the African*, London.

Davis, K. (1972), 'The Urbanization of the Human Population', in Breese, G. (ed.), *The City in Newly Developing Countries*, London.

De Kadt, E. (1982), 'Community Participation for Health: The Case of Latin America' *World Development*, Vol. 10.

Della Volpe, G. (1973), *Schlüssel zur historischen Dialektik* ('The Key to Historical Dialectics'), Berlin.

Doebele, W. (1987), 'The Evolution of Concepts of Urban Land Tenure in Developing Countries', *HABITAT International*, Vol. 11, No. 1.

Drakakis-Smith, D. (1981), *Urbanization, Housing and the Development Process*, London.

Drakakis-Smith, D. (1986), *Urbanisation in the Developing World*, Dover.

DSE (German Foundation for International Development) (1994), *International Round Table. Sustainable Urban Development*, Berlin.

Dwyer, D. (1975), *People and Housing in Third World Cities: Perspectives on the Problem of Spontaneous Settlements*, London.

Eccles (1944), *Report of the Commission appointed to enquire into the Administration and Finances of Native Locations in Urban Areas (Eccles Report)*, Northern Rhodesian Government, Lusaka.

Economic Promotion Unit (EPU), *Final Report on a Two-Stages Consultancy for the Lusaka Urban District Council. Kalingalinga Integrated Upgrading Project, Economic Promotion*, Undated internal report, Lusaka.

Elliott, C. (ed.) (1971), *Constraints on the Economic Development of Zambia*, Nairobi.

Elsenhans, H. (1981), *Abhängiger Kapitalismus oder bürokratische Entwicklungsgesellschaft. Versuch über den Staat in der Dritten Welt*, Frankfurt/M.

Elwert/Evers/Wilkens (1982), *Die Suche nach Sicherheit - Kombinierte Produktionsformen im sogenannten 'informellen Sektor'*, Bielefeld.

Engelhardt, R. (1988), 'Verdrängungstendenzen im Konsolidierungsprozeß randstädtischer Elendsviertel', *TRIALOG*, No. 18.

Engelhardt, R. (1991), 'Konsolidierung und Verdrängung', in Augel, J. (ed.), *Zentrum und Peripherie*, Saarbrücken.

Engels, F. (1975), *The Housing Question*, Moscow.

Epstein, A. L. (1958), *Politics in an Urban African Community*, Manchester.

Eriksen, K. (1977), 'Zambia: Class Formation and Detente', *Review of African Political Economy*, No. 9.

Etzioni, A. (1973), 'Mixed Scanning: A "Third" Approach to Decision Making', in Falundi (ed.), *A Reader in Planning Theory*, Oxford.

European Economic Community (EEC) (1988), *Assisted Low Income Extendable, Core Housing Project - Report of the Handover Seminar Held at Mazabuka 27 - 29 July 1988*. Lusaka.

Evers, H. D. (1981), 'Zur Theorie der urbanen Entwicklung', *Dritte Welt*, Vol. 1-2, No. 9.

Evers, T. (1980), 'Reproduktion der Arbeitskraft und städtische Bewegungen: Der Fall der illegalen Parzellierung in São Paulo', *Peripherie*, No. 2, 1980.

Evers, T. (1977), *Bürgerliche Herrschaft in der Dritten Welt*, Frankfurt/M.

Evers/Wogau (1973), 'Lateinamerikanische Theorien zur Unterentwicklung', *Das Argument*, No. 79.

Feagin/Smith (eds.) (1987), *The Capitalist City*, London.

Feder, E. (1978), *Strawberry Imperialism*, London.

Ferchiou, R. (1982), 'The Indirect Effects of New Housing Construction in Developing Countries', *Urban Studies*, Vol. 19.

Fickert/Wetter (1981), *Squatter und informeller Sektor in Lusaka*, Berlin.

Fiori/Ramirez (1988), 'Towards a conceptual framework for the analysis of self-help housing policies in developing countries - or: A critique of self- help housing critique', *TRIALOG*, No. 18.

Foster-Carter, A. (1978), 'The Modes of Production Controversy', *New Left Review*, No. 107.

Frank, A. G. (1980), *Abhängige Akkumulation und Unterentwicklung*, Frankfurt/M.

Frank, A. G. (1979), 'Über die sogenannte ursprüngliche Akkumulation', in Senghaas (ed.), *Kapitalistische Weltökonomie,* Frankfurt/M.

Frank, A. G. (1981), 'Weltsystem in der Krise', in Fröbel/Heinrichs/Kreye (eds.), *Krisen in der kapitalistischen Weltökonomie*, Hamburg.

Friedman, J. (1974), 'Marxism, Structuralism and Vulgar Materialism', *Man*, No. 9.

Friedmann/Wolff (1976), *The Urban Transition*, London.

Friedmann/Wolff (1982), 'World City Formation: An agenda for research and action', *International Journal of Urban and Regional Research*, Vol. 6, No.3.

Frieling, H. (1984), 'Stadtentwicklung in Industrie- und Entwicklungsländer', *Praxis Geographie*, No. 5, 1984.

Furtado, C. (1970), *Economic Development in Latin America*, Cambridge.

Fröbel/Heinrichs/Kreye (1986), *Umbruch in der Weltwirtschaft*, Hamburg.

Gann, L. (1964), *A History of Northern Rhodesia*, London.

gate (ed.) (1991), 'Integrated Household Energy Supply', *gate*, No. 1.

Gerry, C. (1974), *Petty Producers and the Urban Economy. A Case Study of Dakar*, ILO/WEP Working Papers, Geneva.

Gilbert, A. (1986), 'Self-Help Housing and State Intervention: Illustrative Reflections on the Petty Commodity Debate', in Drakakis-Smith (ed.), *Urbanisation in the Developing World*, Beckenham.

Gilbert, A. (1993), 'Third World Cities: Housing, Infrastructure and Servicing', in Paddison/ Lever/Money (eds.), *International Perspectives in Urban Studies 1*, London.

Gilbert/Gugler (1992), *Cities, Poverty and Development: Urbanization in the Third World*, Oxford.

Gilbert/Van der Linden (1987), 'The Limits of a Marxist Theoretical Framework for Explaining State Self-Help Housing', *Development and Change*, Vol. 18, No.1.

Gilbert/Ward (1985), *Housing, the State and the Poor*, Cambridge.

Gilbert/Ward (1984a), 'Community Action by the Urban Poor: Democratic Involvement, Community Self-Help or a Means of Social Control?', *World Development*, Vol.12, No. 8.

Gilbert/Ward (1984b), 'Community Participation in Upgrading Irregular Settlements: The Community Response', *World Development*, Vol.12, No.9.

Glade, W. (1986), 'Sources and Forms of Privatization', in Glade, W. (ed.), *State Shrinking. A Comparative Inquiry into Privatization*, Institute of Latin American Studies, University of Texas, Austin.

Gluckman, M. (1960), 'Tribalism in Modern British Central Africa', *Cahiers d'études africaine*, I. Paris.

Godehart, S. (1986), 'Vom Squattergebiet zum Stadtteil - Beobachtungen in einem erfolgreichen Upgrading-Projekt in Sambia', in Augel/Hillen/Ramalho (eds.), *Die verplante Wohnmisere*, Saarbrücken.

Godelier, M. (1972), *Rationality and Irrationality in Economics*, London.

Goethert/Oestereich (1987), *Kalingalinga - Community on the Move*, Eschborn.

Good, K. (1988), Zambia, back into the future, *Third World Quarterly*, 10 1.

Good, K. (1989), Debt and the One-Party State in Zambia. *The Journal of Modern African Studies*, 27,2.

Gore, C. (1994), 'The State, Development and Policy Formation in Developmentalist States' University College Swansea, *Centre for Development Studies Newsletter*, 9 (April).

Gramsci, A. (1975), *The Modern Prince and other Writings*, New York.

Gram/Person/Skarendahl (1984), *Natural Fibre Concrete. Report from a SAREC-financed Research and Development Project*, Stockholm.

Greenwood/Howell (1984), 'Urban Local Authorities', in Tordoff, W. (ed.), *Government and Politics in Africa*, London.

Grimes, O. F. (1976), *Housing for Low-Income Urban Families. Economics and Policy in the Developing World*, Baltimore.

GRZ (Government of Zambia) (1972), *Second National Development Plan*, Lusaka.

GRZ (Government of Zambia) (1973), *Mwanziona: A Study of Unofficial Housing Area*, Lusaka.

GRZ (Government of Zambia) (1974), *The Housing Statutory and Improvement Areas Act: Schedule to Regulations*, Lusaka.

GRZ (Government of Zambia) (1979), *Third National Development Plan 1978-1983*, Lusaka.

GRZ (Government of Zambia) (1985). *Report of the Committee on Local Administration*, Lusaka.

GRZ (Government of Zambia) (1985), *Report of the Committee on Local Administration for the Second Session of the Fifth National Assembly - Appointed on 16th January*, 1985, Lusaka.

GRZ (Government of Zambia) (1989), *New Economic Recovery Programme. Fourth National Development Plan 1989-1993*, Office of the President, National Commission for Development Planning, Lusaka.

GRZ (Government of Zambia) (1995a) *Cabinet Office Circular No. 1 of 1995. Institutional Framework for Planning, Co-ordinating and Monitoring of Development in the Districts and Provinces*, Lusaka.

GRZ (Government of Zambia/Ministry of Local Government and Housing) (1995b), *National Housing Policy (draft)*, Lusaka.

GTZ (ed.) (1979), *Kalingalinga Integrated Upgrading. Report of the Preparatory Mission*, Eschborn.

GTZ (ed.) (1984), *An Integrated Approach to the Housing Problems of Low-income Groups*, Eschborn.

Gugler, J. (ed.) (1970), *Urbanization in Sub-Saharan Africa*, Kampala.

Guldager, R. (1983), *Planen wir an den Bedürfnissen der Dritten Welt vorbei? - Probleme der Verstädterung. Stadtprobleme der Dritten Welt - Möglichkeiten zur Verbesserung der Lebensbedingungen*, 2. Tübinger Gespräch zu Entwicklungsfragen, Stuttgart.

Gumede/Shumba (1976), *SAIL in Perspective*, Lusaka.

Gutkind/Wallerstein (eds.) (1976), *The Political economy of Contemporary Africa*, London.

HABITAT International Forum (1988), *Workshop on Self-Help and Participation held by the CDG in Berlin 1987*, Cologne.

HABITAT (United Nations Centre for Human Settlement) (1982), *Survey of Slum & Squatter Settlements*, Nairobi.

Hall, R. (1965), *Zambia*, London.

Hammock/Lubell/Sethuraman/Rafsky (1981), 'Low-income Settlement Improvement through Income and Employment Generation and Integrated Housing Programmes', in Habitat (ed.), *The Residential Circumstances of the Urban Poor in Developing Countries*, New York.

Hansen, K. (1982), 'Lusaka's Squatters: Past and Present,' *African Studies Review*, Vol. 15 (2&3).

Hansen, K. T. (1984), 'Negotiating Sex and Gender in Urban Zambia,' *Journal of Southern African Studies*, Vol. 10, No. 2.

Hansen, K. (1985), 'Budgeting against Uncertainty: Cross-Class and Transethnic Redistribution Mechanisms in Urban Zambia', *African Urban Studies*, 21 (Spring).

Hansen, K. (1987), 'Urban Woman and Work in Africa: A Zambian Case', *Transafrica Forum*, Vol. 4, No. 3.

Hansen, K. (1989), 'The Black Market and Woman Traders in Lusaka, Zambia', in Parpart/Staudt (eds.), *Woman and the State in Africa*, London.

Hansen, K. (1989a), *Distant Companions. Servants and Employers in Zambia, 1900-1985*, Ithaca.

Hansen, K. (1990), 'Domestic Trials: Power and Autonomy in Domestic Service in Zambia', *American Ethnologist*, 17 (2).

Hansen, K. (1990a), *Gender and Domestic Service: The Case of Housing in Postcolonial Lusaka, Zambia*. National Swedish Institute for Building Research, University of Lund, Lund.

Hardoy/Satterthwaite (1989), *Squatter Citizen. Life in the Urban Third World*, London.

Harms, H. (1982), 'Historical Perspectives on the Practice and Politics of Self-Help Housing', in Ward, P. (ed.): *Self-Help Housing. A Critique*, Oxford.

Harms, H. (1989), *Changes in Self-Help Housing in Developed and Third World Countries*, (mimeo), Hamburg.

Harris, B. (1960), 'Plan or Projection?', *Journal of the American Institute of Planners*, Vol. 26.

Hart, K. (1973), 'Informal Income Opportunities and Urban Employment in Ghana', *Journal of Modern African Studies*, 11.

Harvey, D. (1973), *Social Justice and the City*, London.

Harvey, D. (1974), 'Class-Monopoly Rent, Finance Capital and the Urban Revolution', *Regional Studies*.

Harvey, D. (1978), 'Klassenmonopolrente, Finanzkapital und Urbanisierung', in Mayer/Roth/ Brandes (eds.), *Stadtkrise und soziale Bewegungen*, Frankfurt/M.

Häußermann/Siebel (1978), 'Thesen zur Soziologie der Stadt', *Leviathan*, 4.

Heinrich, T. (1987), *Technologietransfer in der Stadtplanung. Masterplanung in Dar es Salaam/Tansania durch internationale Consultings*, Darmstadt.

Hein/Simonis (1977), 'Entwicklungspolitik, Staatsfunktionen und Klassenauseinandersetzungen im peripheren Kapitalismus', in Schmidt (ed.), *Strategien gegen Unterentwicklung - Zwischen Weltmarkt und Eigenständigkeit*, Frankfurt/M.

Heisler, H. (1971), 'The Creation of a Stabilized Urban Society. A Turning Point in the Development of Northern Rhodesia/Zambia', *African Affairs*, Vol. 79, No. 279.

Heisler, H. (1974), *Urbanisation and the Government of Migration*, London.

Hoek-Smit, M. (1982), *Community Participation in Squatter Upgrading*, Philadelphia.

Hughes, A. (1985), 'Alternative Forms and Levels of Popular Participation: A General Survey', in Lisk, F. (ed.), *Popular Participation in Planning for Basic Needs: Concepts, Methods, Practices*, Aldershot.

HUZA (1989), *Participatory Evaluation Report November 1989*, Lusaka.

ILO (1970), *Employment, Incomes and Equity: A Strategy for Increasing Productive Employment in Kenya*, Geneva.

ILO (1976), *Narrowing the Gaps, Planning for Basic Needs and Productive Employment in Zambia*, Geneva.

ILO (1981), *Zambia: Basic Needs in an Economy Under Pressure*, Addis Ababa.

ILO (1982), *Southern African Team for Employment Promotion (SATEP), The Urban Informal Sector in Zambia - a Programme for Action*, Lusaka.

Institute for African Studies (IAS) (1989), *Analysis of the 1989 Budget of Zambia*. Working Papers of the Economic Research Group, Division for Development Research, Lusaka.

Issak, T. (1981), *Housing Policies in Zambia 1960-1981: A Critical Perspective*. Columbia University.

IYSH NGO Forum (1987), *Limuru Declaration by the Global IYSH NGO Forum in Nairobi, April 1987*, Limuru.

Jaeger/Huckabay (1986), 'The Garden City of Lusaka: Urban Agriculture', in Williams (ed.), *Lusaka and its Environs*, Lusaka.

Janvry/Garramón (1977), 'Laws of Motion of Capital in the Center-Periphery Structure', *Review of Radical Political Economics*, No. 9.

Jere, H. (1984), 'Lusaka: Local Participation in Planning and Decision-Making', in Payne, G. (ed.), *Low Income Housing in the Developing World*, Chichester.

Jere/Muyaba/Ndilila (1988), 'NGO Promotes Community Development', in Turner, B. (ed.), *Building Community: A Third World Case Book*. Habitat International Coalition.

Johnson, T. (1987), 'Upward Filtering of Housing Stock. A Study on Upward Filtering of Housing Stock as a Consequence of Settlement Upgrading', *Habitat International*, Vol. 11, No. 1 pp. 173-190.

Jules-Rosette, B. (1975), 'Marrapodi: An Independent Religious Community in Transition', *African Studies Review*, 18.

Kajoba, G. (1986), 'Land Tenure as a Development Constraint in Lusaka', in Williams (ed.), *Lusaka and its Environs*, Lusaka.

Kasfir, N. (1983), 'Designs and Dilemmas: An Overview', in Mawhood, P. (ed.), *Local Government in the Third World: The Experience of Tropical Africa*, Chichester.

Kasongo/Tipple (1990), 'An Analysis of Policy Towards Squatters in Kitwe, Zambia', *Third World Planning Review*, Vol. 12, No.2.

Kaunda, K. (1988), *State of the Nation. Vol. 1: Politics and Government*. Edited by C. Mphaisha, Lusaka.

Kautsky, K. (1970), *La Question agraire*, Paris.

Kay, G. (1967), *A Social Geography of Zambia*, London.

Keare/Jimenez (1983), *Progressive Development and Affordability in the Design of Urban Shelter Projects*. World Bank Staff Working Papers Vol. 560, Washington D. C.

Keare/Parris (1982), *Evaluation of Shelter Programs for the Urban Poor*, Washington D. C.

King, A. D. (1976), *Colonial Urban Development*, London.

King, A. D. (1980), 'Exporting Planning: the Colonial and Neo-Colonial Experience', in Cherry, G. E. (ed.), *Shaping an Urban World*, London.

Kinsey, B. (1981), *Planning and Implementation: problems of parallel hierarchies in local development in Zambia*, Norwich.

Knauder, S. (1982), *Shacks and Mansions - An Analysis of the Integrated Housing Policy in Zambia*, Lusaka.

Koenigsberger, O. (1982), 'Action Planning', in Mumtaz (ed.), *Readings in Action Planning*, London.

Kool/Verboom/Van der Linden (1989), 'Squatter Settlement Improvement and Displacement. A Review of Concepts, Theory and Comparative Evidence', *Habitat International*, Vol.13, No. 3.

Korten, D. (1987), 'Third Generation NGO Strategies: A Key to People-Centered Development', *World Development*, No. 15.

Krätke, S. (1989), *Wohnungsbau-Finanzierung in der Dritten Welt: Zur Funktionsweise und Reichweite 'Revolvierender Fonds'*, Berlin.

Kunzmann, K. (1981), *Integrierte Entwicklung durch sektorale Projektbausteine*. Gesellschaft für Umweltforschung (ed.), Möglichkeiten und Grenzen Integrierter Entwicklungsprojekte, Saarbrücken.

Kurbjuweit, D. (1989), 'Billiges Geld vom weißen Mann', *Die ZEIT*, No. 21, May 1989.

Küpper, U. (1990), 'Zum Wandel der Verfahren und Entscheidungsstrukturen in Stadtentwicklung und Stadtplanung', in Sieverts, T. (ed.), *Zukunftsaufgaben der Stadtplanung*, Düsseldorf.

Larson, A. (1989), 'Traditional Tswana Housing', *TRIALOG*, No. 19.

Läpple, D. (1985), 'Internationalization of Capital and the Regional Problem', in Walton (ed.), *Capital and Labour in the Urbanized World*, London.

Läpple, D. (1978), 'Gesellschaftlicher Reproduktionsprozeß und Stadtstrukturen', in Mayer/Roth/ Brandes (eds.), *Stadtkrise und soziale Bewegungen*, Frankfurt/M.

Lea, J. (1979), 'Self-Help and Autonomy in Housing: Theoretical Critics and Empirical Investigation', in Murison/Lea (eds.), *Housing in Third World Countries. Perspectives on Policy and Practice*, London.

Lebrun/Gerry (1975), 'Petty Producers and Capitalism' *Review of African Political Economy*, No. 3.

Lee, M. (1985), 'Myths of Affordability', *Third World Planning Review*, 7, 2, pp. 131-142.

Lefèbvre, H. (1972), *Die Revolution der Städte*, Munich.

Lefèbvre, H. (1972), *Die Stadt im marxistischen Denken*, Ravensburg.

Lemarchand, R. (1981), 'Comparative Political Clientelism: Structure, Process and Optic', in Eisenstadt/Lemarchand (eds.), *Political Clientelism, Patronage and Development*, London.

Lenin, V.I. (1957), *Collected Works*, Moscow.

Lerner, D. (1958), *The Passing of Traditional Society - Modernizing the Middle East*, New York.

Lewin, A. C. (1981), *Housing Co-operatives in Developing Countries*, London.

LHPET (Lusaka Housing Project Evaluation Team) (1977), *Community Development and Change: The Community Development Process in Chawama and George*, Lusaka.

LHPET (Lusaka Housing Project Evaluation Team) (1978), *Survey Methodology Vol. II.* Working Paper No. 19, Lusaka.

Lilly, T. (1982), 'A Research Note on the Importation of British Town Planning in the 1930s: A Legacy for Modern Zambia', *African Urban Studies*, 12.

Linn, J. (1983), *Cities in the developing World*, Washington D. C.

Lloyd, P. (1972), *Africa in Social Change*, Harmondsworth.

Lloyd, P. (1979), *Slums of Hope? Shanty Towns of the Third World*, Oxford.

Lloyd, P. (1980), *The 'Young Towns' of Lima - Aspects of Urbanization in Peru*, London.

Loches/Guenzel/Wolf (1976), *Housing - Kenya - Sambia. Politische und wirtschaftliche Determinanten für die Wohnungsversorgung der unteren Einkommensschichten von Kenya und Zambia.* Berlin, Fachgebiet Bauen und Planen in Entwicklungsländer, Berlin.

Lomnitz, L. (1977), *Networks and Marginality - Life in a Mexican Shantytown*, New York.

LUDC (Lusaka Urban District Council) (undated), *Site and Service Briefing Material and Building Regulations for Site and Service Areas*, Lusaka.

LUDC (Lusaka Urban District Council) (1987), *Self Help Housing. Are You Aware?* Lusaka.

LUDC (Lusaka Urban District Council) (1988), *Research Report: In Search of another Step Towards the Promotion of Small Business in Kalingalinga*, Lusaka.

Lundgren/Schlyter/Schlyter (1969), *Zambia, Kapwepwe Compound. A Study of Unauthorized Settlement*, Lund.

Lungu, G. (1985), *Administrative Decentralization in the Zambian Bureaucracy*, University of Zambia, Lusaka, Lusaka.

Lungu, G. (1986), 'Mission impossible: integrating central and local administration in Zambia', *Planning and Administration*, 13 (1), pp. 52-57.

Mabogunje, A. L. (1990), 'Urban Planning and the post-colonial state in Africa: a research overview', *African Studies Review*, 33.

Macoloo, C. (1991), 'The Transformation of the Production and Retail of Building Materials for Low-Income Housing in Mombasa, Kenya', *Development and Change*, 22.

Maembe, E. (1989), *Refuse Collection and Disposal in Kalingalinga, Lusaka - A Strategy for Community Participation*. Institute for African Studies: Research Reports No. 4, Lusaka.

Maembe, E. (1989a), *Expansion of the Economic Promotion Unit's Revolving Fund in the Peri-Urban Areas of Lusaka*, Lusaka.

Maembe/Sibbuku (1987), *An Assessment of Policies and Programmes for the Improvement of Working Conditions and Welfare of Urban Informal Sector Workers and Their Families in Lusaka*, Lusaka.

Maembe/Tomecko (1987), *Economic Promotion in an Integrated Upgrading Project: The Case of the Kalingalinga Township, Lusaka*, Lusaka.

Maennling, W. (1984), 'Grundelemente zu einem Paradigma des überlebensökonomischen Territorismus'. *TRIALOG, No. 2.*

Maimbolwa, M. M. (1990), *Unauthorized Developments in the Urban Areas - Problems and Opportunities*. Decentralisation Division. Office of the Prime Minister, Lusaka.

Mangin, W. (1967), 'Latin American Squatter Settlements: A Problem and a Solution', *Latin American Research Review*, Vol. 2.

Mangin, W. (ed.) (1970), *Peasants in Cities*, Boston.

Makgetla, N. S. (1986), 'Theoretical and Practical Implications of IMF Conditionality in Zambia', *Journal of Modern African Studies*, 24, 3.

Mapala, H. J. (1987), *An Outline for Eventual Extension of GTZ/LUDC Co-Operation Beyond 1987: Summery of the Proposed Bauleni Integrated Project for Project Preparation*, Lusaka.

Marcuse, P. (1990), 'Why Self-Help Won't Work', *TRIALOG*, No. 23/24.

Martin, R. J. (1972), *Gardens and outdoor living: Plot use in low cost housing areas of Lusaka*, Lusaka.

Martin, R. J. (1974), *Government in Lusaka*, Lusaka.

Martin, R. J. (1976), 'Institutional Involvements in Squatter Settlements', *Architectural Design*, Vol. XLVI.

Martin, R. J. (1977), 'Housing Options, Lusaka, Zambia', *Ekistics*, 261 (8), pp. 89-95.

Martin, R. J. (1982), 'The Formulation of a Self-Help Housing Project', in Ward (ed.), *Self-Help Housing: A Critique*, London.

Martin, R. J. (1983), *Land Tenure in Zambia and Security*, London.

Martin, R. J. (1987), 'Experiences with Monitoring and Evaluation in Lusaka', in Skinner/Taylor/ Wegelin (eds.), *Shelter Upgrading for the Urban Poor; Evaluation of Third World Experience*, Manila.

Marx, K. (1961), *Capital Vol. I-III*, Moscow.

Marx, K. (1939/41), *Grundrisse der Kritik der politischen Ökonomie*. Moscow 1939/41. Undated reprint Frankfurt/M.

Marx/Engels (1962), *The Manifesto of the Communist Party*. Selected Works Vol. I., Moscow.

Mathéy, K. (1984), 'Basis and Methodology for the Design of an Integrated Development Project in Ciudad Sandino, Nicaragua', in Bruno/Körte/Mathéy (eds.), *Umgang mit Städtischen Wohnquartieren unterer Einkommensgruppen in Entwicklungsländern*, Darmstadt.

Mathéy, K. (1992), *Selbsthilfestrategien als Element der Wohnungspolitik in Entwicklungsländern - Bibliographie mit Anmerkungen zum Stand der Forschung*, Kassel.

Mathéy/Sampat (1987), 'Comparative Evaluation of Case Studies on Slum- and Squatter Upgrading', *TRIALOG*, No. 13/14.

Matibini, P. (undated), *Land Tenure and Legal Aspects of Sites and Services and Upgrading*, Lusaka.

Mawhood, P. (ed.) (1983), *Local Government in the Third World: The Experience of Tropical Africa*, Chichester.

Mayo, S. (1985), 'How much will Households spend for Shelter?', *The Urban Edge*, Vol.9, No.10.

Mayo/Gross (1987), 'Sites and Service and Subsidies: The Economics of Low-cost Housing in Developing Countries', *The World Bank Economic Review*, Vol. 1, 2.

Mayo/Malpezzi/Gross (1986), 'Shelter Strategies for the Urban Poor in Developing Countries', *The World Bank Research Observer*, Vol. 1, No.2.

Mazumdar, D. (1975), *The Informal Sector*. World Bank Staff Working Paper No. 211. Washington D. C.

Mbavu, C. M. (1984), 'Learning from Lusaka', in Bruno/Körte/Mathéy: *Umgang mit städtischen Wohnquartieren unterer Einkommensgruppen in Entwicklungsländern*, Darmstadt.

McGee, T. G. (1971), *The Urbanization Process in the Third World*, London.

McGee, T. G. (1986), 'Circuits and Networks of Capital: Internationalisation of the World Economy and National Urbanisation', in Drakakis-Smith (ed.), *Urbanisation in the Developing World*, Dover.

Meewissen, J. (1991), *Training for Community Participation in Zambia*. (unpublished mimeo) UNCHS, Nairobi.

Meyns/Nabudere/Wadada (eds.) (1989), *Democracy and the One-Party State in Africa*, Hamburg.

Mezger, D. (1989), 'Zambia: das Scheitern einer Entwicklungsstrategie als ökologische Herausforderung', *Afrika Spectrum*, No. 1.

Mingione, E. (1983), 'Informalization, Restructuring and the Survival Strategies of the Working Class', *International Journal of Urban and Regional Research*, No. 3.

Mitchell, J. C. (1969), *Social Networks in Urban Situations*, Manchester.

Mitchell, J. C. (1973), 'Distance, Transport and Urban Involvement in Zambia', in Southall (ed.), *Urban Anthropology. Cross-Cultural Studies of Urbanisation*, New York.

MLGH (Ministry of Local Government and Housing) (1995), *Decentralisation Policy*. Mimeo, Lusaka.

Molina, H. (1976), *La Vivienda y el Problema de la Vivienda. El Problema de la Vivienda en Colombia. Informe Final*. Tomo I (3 tomos. SIAP-CIID-CPU. Universidad de los Andes, Bogota D. E.

Momba, J. C. (1989), 'The State, Rural Class Formation and Peasant Participation in Zambia: The Case of Southern Province', *African Affairs*, Vol. 88, No. 352.

Moser, C. (1978), 'The Informal Sector or Petty-Commodity Production: Dualism or Dependence in Urban Development?', *World Development*, Vol. 6, No. 9/10.

Moser, C. (1994), *Urban Poverty and Social Policy in the Context of Adjustment. Preliminary Results from Lusaka, Metro Manila and Guayaquil*. Paper presented to the International Seminar 'The Hidden Assignment', Rotterdam 5-7 October 1994.

Mulenga, S. (1989), *An Outline Procedure Required for Obtaining Lease and Declaration of Non-authorized Settlements as Statutory and Improvement Areas*. UNCHS/DANIDA Community Participation Training Programme, Lusaka.

Muller, M. (1974), *Participation: Ward Development, Committees and Party Branches and Sections*, London.

Muller, M. (1978), 'Chawama, A Good Place in Lusaka: A Description of an Informal Settlement', in Westley, S. (ed.), *The Informal Sector in Kenya*, Nairobi.

Muller, M. (1979), *Chawama - To make a Good Place Better. The Socio-Economic History of a Squatter Settlement in Lusaka*, Zambia, London.

Mwanamwambwa, C. (1979), *Kalingalinga: A Socio-economic survey of an unauthorized compound*, Lusaka (mimeo).

Mwanamwambwa/Rakodi (1977), *Community Development and Change: The Community Development Process in Chawama and George*, Lusaka.

Mwenda/Nyirongo (1988), *A Review of Incomes and Price Policies in Zambia*. Paper presented at the joint EAZ/PIC on incomes policy in Zambia, Lusaka.

Mwanza, E. (ed.) (1992), *Structural Adjustment Programmes in SADC. Experiences and Lessons from Malawi, Tanzania, Zambia and Zimbabwe*, Harare.

Mwanza/Mwamba/Kakuwa (1992), 'The Structural Adjustment Programme in Zambia: Lessons from Experience', in Mwanza (ed.), *Structural Adjustment Programmes in SADC. Experiences and Lessons from Malawi, Tanzania, Zambia and Zimbabwe*, Harare.

Myrdal, G. (1972), *Politisches Manifest über die Armut der Welt*, Frankfurt/M.

Nagel, E. (1961), *The Structure of Science*, London.

Ndilila, F. (1987), *Shelter With Economic Promotion Through Organized Self-Help and Participation*, Lusaka.

Ndilila, F. (1980), *Entwicklungsfähige Wohnbaukonstruktionen für Sambia*, Frankfurt/M.

Nelson, J. M. (1979), *Access to Power: Politics and the Urban Poor in Developing Nations*, Princeton.

NHA (National Housing Authority, Zambia) (1978), *Kanyama Upgrading Feasibility Study: Surface Drainage*, Lusaka.

NHA (National Housing Authority) (1989), *European Community (EEC) Assisted Low Income Extendable Core Housing Project - Report of the Handover Seminar Held at Mazabuka 27. - 29. July 1988*, Lusaka.

NHA (National Housing Authority) (1989), *Annual Report for 1989*, Lusaka.

Nienhuys, S. (1989), *Letter to the CDG 7.12.89: Comments on the Workshop Report "Legal Aspects of Self-Help Housing" in Lusaka*.

Nienhuys/Matibini (1990), *Manual of Procedures Required to Declare Settlements as Statutory and Improvement Areas*. Zambia UNCHS/DANIDA Community Participation Training Programme, Lusaka.

Nientied/van der Linden (1987), 'Approaches to low-income Housing in the Third World', *International Journal of Urban and Regional Research*, Vol. 9, No. 3.

Nuscheler/Ziemer (1980), *Politische Herrschaft in Schwarzafrika*, Munich.

Nzula/Potekhin/Zusmanovich (1979), *Forced Labour in Colonial Africa*, London.

Obudho/Mhlanga (eds.) (1988), *Slum and Squatter Settlements in Sub-Saharan Africa*, New York.

OECD (1988), *Voluntary Aid for Development: The Role of Non-Governmental Organizations*, Paris.

Oesterdiekhoff/Tait (1979), 'Kapitalisierung und Proletarisierung in den Agrarsektoren des Sudan: Eine Fallstudie über Entwicklungstendenzen kleinbäuerlicher und nomadischer Produktionsverhältnisse', in Hanisch/Tetzlaff (eds.), *Die Überwindung der ländlichen Armut in der Dritten Welt*, Hamburg.

Oestereich, J. (1986), *Community Upgrading. The Kalingalinga Project in Lusaka, Zambia*, (mimeo) Ratingen.

Oestereich, J. (1987), 'The Upgrading of a Squatter Community: Some Conclusions drawn from the Kalingalinga Integrated Upgrading Project in Lusaka, Zambia', *TRIALOG*, 13/14.

Oestereich, J. (1978), 'Wohnungsbau als Sozialtechnologie', *Die Verwaltung*, Bd. 11, No. 3.

Ohadike, P. (1981), *Demographic Perspectives in Zambia*, Lusaka.

Okada, F. E. (1966), *Lodgers and Houses in New Kanyama: A Survey*, Lusaka.

Okada, F. E. (1967), *A Socio-economic Survey of Kalingalinga*, Lusaka.

Ollawa, P. E. (1979), *Participatory Democracy in Zambia, The Political Economy of National Development*, Devon.

Osei-Hwedie/Mijere (1989), *Kalingalinga Community Based Work Programme: An Alternative for Service Charge Arrears*. Social Development Studies, University of Zambia, Lusaka.

Pasteur, D. (1979), *The Management of Squatter Upgrading. A Case Study of Organization, Procedures and Participation*, Farnborough.

Pasteur, D. (1974), *Urban Management in Lusaka*. University College, London: Development Planning Unit, Planned Urban Growth: The Lusaka Experience 1957-1973, London.

Paul, S. (1987), *Community Participation in Development Projects. The World Bank Experience*. World Bank Discussion Paper No. 6, Washington D. C.

Paul/Israel (1991) (eds.), *Nongovernmental Organizations and the World Bank. Cooperation for Development*, Washington D. C.

PCU (Water Supply and Sanitation Sector Programme Coordination Unit) (1994), *Proposed Institutional Framework for the Water and Sanitation Sector*, Lusaka.

Pearse/Stiefel (1979), *Inquiry into participation - A Research Approach*, Geneva.

Peattie, L. (1979), 'Housing Policy in Developing Countries: Two Puzzles', *World Development*, 7, pp. 1017-22.

Peattie, L. (1982), 'Some Second Thoughts on Sites and Services', *Habitat International*, Vol. 6, No. 1/2.

Perlman, J. (1976), *The Myth of Marginality, Urban Poverty and Politics in Rio de Janeiro*, Berkely.

Perlman, J. (1981), 'Strategies for Squatter Settlements: The State of the Art as of 1977', in UN/Habitat (ed.), *The Residential Circumstances of Urban Poor in Developing Countries*, New York.

Perlman, J. (1987), 'Misconceptions About the Urban Poor and the Dynamics of Housing Policy Evolution', *Journal of Planning Education and Research*, Vol. 6.

Peters, C. (1989), 'Politische Stabilität im wirtschaftlichen Niedergang. Eine Untersuchung zum zambischen Wahlsystem', *Afrika Spectrum*, No. 1.

Pfeiffer, P. (1986), *Urbanizcao Sim, Remocao Nunca! Politische, sozio-ökonomische und urbanistische Aspekte der Favelas und ihre soziale Organisation in Rio de Janeiro: Entwicklung - Tendenzen - Perspektiven*, Berlin.

Pinto, A. (1973), *La "Heterogenidad Estructural": Aspecto Fundamental del Desarollo Latinoamericano*, Santiago de Chile.

Polanyi, K. (1978), *The Great Transformation*, Frankfurt/M.

Portes, A. (1985), 'Urbanization, Migration and Models of Development in Latin America', in Walton, J. (ed.), *Capital and Labour in the Urbanized World*, London.

Portes/Walton (1976), *Urban Latin America: The political condition from above and below*. University of Texas.

Portes/Walton (1981), *Labour, Class and the International System*, New York.

Pottier, J. (1988), *Migrants no more. Settlement and Survival in Mambwe Villages, Zambia*, Manchester.

Poulantzas, N. (1975), *Classes in contemporary Capitalism*, London.

Pradilla, E. (1976), *Notes on the 'Housing Problem'*. Unpublished translation by R. Burgess, 1979. From Journal *Ideologia y Sociedad*, No. 16.

Pradilla, E. (1984), 'Selbsthilfe, Ausbeutung der Arbeitskraft und staatliche Politik in Lateinamerika', *Urbs et Regio*, Sonderband 31.

Quijano, A. (1980), 'The Marginal Pole of the Economy and the Marginalized Labour Force', in Wolpe (ed.), *The Articulation of Modes of Production*, London.

Rakodi, C. (1980), *Housing and the Urban Poor in Lusaka*. Papers in Planning Research No. 12; University of Wales Institute of Science and technology, Department of Town Planning, Cardiff.

Rakodi, C. (1986a), 'State and Class in Africa: A Case for extending analyses of the form and functions of the national state to the urban local state', *Society and Space*, No. 4, pp. 419-446.

Rakodi, C. (1986b), 'Colonial Urban Policy and Planning in Northern Rhodesia and its Legacy', *Third World Planning Review*, 8 (3) pp. 193-217.

370

Rakodi, C. (1986c), 'Housing in Lusaka - Policies and Progress', in Williams (ed.), *Lusaka and its Environs*, Lusaka.

Rakodi, C. (1987), 'Land, Layouts and Infrastructure in Squatter Upgrading: The Case of Lusaka', *Cities*, Vol. 4, 4.

Rakodi, C. (1988a), 'The Local State and Urban Local Government in Zambia', *Public Administration and Development*, No. 8.

Rakodi, C. (1988b), 'Urban Agriculture: Research Questions and Zambian Evidence', *Journal of Modern African Studies*, 26,3 pp. 495-515.

Rakodi, C., Upgrading in Chawama, Lusaka: Displacement or Differentiation? *Urban Studies*, 25, 4 (1988c).

Rakodi, C. (1990), 'Urban Development and Planning in Tanzania, Zambia and Zimbabwe in the late 1980s: Some Issues', in Drakakis-Smith (ed.), *Urban and Regional Change in Southern Africa*, London.

Rakodi, C. (1990a), *Housing Markets in Third World Cities: Research and Policy into the 1990s*. Paper presented to the Inter-schools Conference on emerging Trends in Third World Housing Policies 1990s and beyond, Sheffield.

Rakodi, C. (1991), 'Developing Institutional Capacity for Meeting the Housing Needs of the Urban Poor', in Skinner, R. (ed.), *Shelter, Settlements, Policy and the Urban Poor*, London.

Rakodi/Schlyter (1981), *Upgrading in Lusaka: Participation and Social Changes*, Gävle.

Rey, Pierre-Philippe (1973), *Les Alliances de Classes*, Paris.

Reichert, H. (1983), *Elendsviertel und Spontansiedlungen als Bestandteile von Metropolen der Dritten Welt*. Materialien zum internationalen Kulturaustausch Bd. 18. Stuttgart.

Richards, A. (1951), *Land, Labour and Diet in Northern Rhodesia*, London.

Roberts, B. (1978), *Cities of Peasants, The Political Economy of Urbanization in the Third World*, London.

Roberts, A. D. (1976), *A History of Zambia*, London.

Rodenstein, M. (1982), 'Planungstheorie in der Stadt- und Regionalplanunng - Ein Überblick über die Entwicklung verschiedener Ansätze seit Ende der 60er Jahre', in Rodenstein, H. (ed.), *Diskussion zum Stand der Theorie in der Stadt- und Regionalplanung*, Berlin.

Romero, M. (1980), *Neuvas perspectivas ocupacionales y cambios en la estrategia de reproduccion de la fuerza de tabajo*. ILO, Technical Mission to the Ministry of Labor and Social Security, Bogota.

Rothman, N., *African Urban Development in the Colonial Period: A Study of Lusaka 1905-1964*. Unpublished PhD, Northwestern University.

Rowland, L. (1967), *Report on National Housing Policy in Zambia. Ministry of Local Government and Housing*, Lusaka.

Ruiz, M. (1989), 'Delivering Services for the Urban Poor: Governments versus Non-Government Organizations (NGOs)', *TRIALOG*, No. 22.

Saasa, O. (1987), *Zambia's Policies Towards Foreign Investment. The Case of the Mining and Non-Mining Sectors*, Uppsala.

Safferey, A. L. (1943), *A Report on Some Aspects of African living Conditions on the Copperbelt of Northern Rhodesia*, Lusaka.

Safier, M. (1972), 'Urban Problems, Planning Possibilities and Housing Policies', in Hutton (ed.), *Urban Challenge in East Africa*, Nairobi.

Sampson, R. (1982), *So This was Lusaakas - The Story of the Capital of Zambia*, Lusaka.

Sandbrook, R. (1982), *The Politics of Basic Needs: Urban Aspects of Assaulting Poverty in Africa*, London.

Sano, H.-O. (1988), 'The IMF and Zambia: The Contradiction of Exchange Rate Auctioning and De-Subsidization of Agriculture', *African Affairs*, Vol. 349 No. 87.

Santos, Milton (1979), *The Shared Space: Two Circuits of Urban Economy in the Underdeveloped Countries*, London.

Sanyal, B. (1981), 'Who gets what, where, why and how: A critical look at the housing subsidies in Zambia', *Development and Change*, No. 12.

Sanyal, B. (1984), *Urban Agriculture: a Strategy for Survival in Zambia*, Los Angeles.

Sanyal, B. (1987), 'Problems of Cost Recovery in Development Projects: Experience of the Lusaka Squatter Upgrading and Sites/Service Project', *Urban Studies*, No. 24, 4, pp 285-295.

Sanyal, B. (1989), 'Does Development Trickle Up?' *TRIALOG*, No. 23/24.

Sartre, J. P. (1967), *Kritik der dialektischen Vernunft*, Reinbek.

Saunders, P., Urban Politics. A Sociological Interpretation. London 1979.

Scharpf, F. W. (1971), 'Planung als politischer Prozeß', *Zeitschrift für Verwaltungswissenschaften*, Vol. 4, No. 1.

Schlyter, A. (1985), *Upgrading Reconsidered: The George Study in Retrospective*, Gävle.

Schlyter, A. (1987), 'Commercialization of housing in upgraded squatter Areas in Lusaka', *TRIALOG*, 13/14.

Schlyter, A. (1988), *Woman Householders and Housing Strategies. The Case of George, Lusaka*, Gävle.

Schlyter, A. (1991), *Twenty Years of Development in George, Zambia*, Stockholm.

Schlyter/Chanda (1982), *Bibliography on Human Settlements with emphasis on households and residential environment - Zambia*, Lusaka.

Schlyter/Schlyter (1980), *George - The Development of a Squatter Settlement in Lusaka, Zambia*, Stockholm.

Schmetzer, H. (1987), 'Slum Upgrading and Sites-and-Service Schemes under Different Political Circumstances', *TRIALOG*, No. 13/14.

Schmetzer, H. (1989), 'Traditionelle Architektur in Sambia' *TRIALOG*, No. 19.

Schmetzer, H. (1990), *Municipal Planning and Management in Lusaka*. Paper presented to the international congress "Sustainable habitat on an urbanized planet?", Berlin.

Schmidt, A. (ed.) (1976), *Strategien gegen Unterentwicklung - Zwischen Weltmarkt und Eigenständigkeit*, Frankfurt/M.

Schmukler, B. (1979), 'Diversidad de formas de las relaciones capitalistas en la industria Argentina', in Tokman/Klein (eds.), *El subempleo en America Latina*, Buenos Aires.

Schoeller, W. (1976), *Weltmarkt und Reproduktion des Kapitals*, Frankfurt/M.

Schoorl/Van der Linden/Yap (eds.) (1983), *Between Basti Dweller and Bureaucrats: Lessons in Squatter Settlement Upgrading*, Oxford.

Scott, I. (1984), 'Party and Administration under the one-party State', in Tordoff, W. (ed.), *Government and Politics in Africa*, London.

Seidman, A. (1979a), 'The Economics of Eliminating Rural Poverty', in Turok, B. (ed.), *Development in Zambia*, London.

Seidman, A. (1979b), 'The Distorted Growth of Import Substitution: The Zambian Case', in Turok, B. (ed.), *Development in Zambia*, London.

Senghaas-Knobloch, E. (1979), *Reproduktion von Arbeitskraft in der Weltgesellschaft*, Frankfurt/M.

Sethuraman, S.V. (1976), 'The Urban Informal Sektor: Concept, Measurement and Policy', *International Labour Review*, 144, No. 1.

Seymour, T. (1975), 'Squatter Settlement and Class Relations in Zambia', *Review of African Political Economy*, No. 3.

Seymour, T. (1976), *Squatters, Migrants and the Urban Poor: A Study of Attitudes towards Inequity, with special reference to a Squatter Settlement*. Unpublished PhD, University of Sussex.

Shivji, I. (1974), *The Silent Class Struggle*, Dar es Salaam.

Sichone, O. (1989), 'One-Party Participatory Democracy and Socialist Orientation. The De-Politicization of the Masses in Post-Colonial Zambia', in Meyns/Nabudere (eds.), *Democracy and the One-Party State in Africa*, Hamburg.

Siddle, D. (1970), 'Rural Development in Zambia: A Spatial Analysis', *Journal of Modern African Studies*, 8, 2.

Simmance, A. (1974), 'The Structure of Local Government in Zambia', in Hawkesworth, N. (ed.), *Local Government in Zambia*, Lusaka.

Simoko, P. (1981), 'Kanyama Funds Scandal', *Times of Zambia*, 20.9.81.

Simons, H. J. (1979), 'Zambia's Urban Situation', in Turok, B. (ed.), *Development in Zambia*, London.

Simson, H. (1985), *Zambia. A Country Study*, Uppsala.

Sina (Settlements Information Network Africa), *Newsletter* No. 13, Nairobi 1987.

Singer, P. (1985), 'Capital and the National State', in Walton, J. (ed.), *Capital and Labour in the Urbanized World*, London.

Skinner, R. (1983), 'Community Participation: its scope and organization', in Skinner/Rodell (eds.), *People, Poverty and Shelter: Problems of Self-Help Housing in Third World Countries*, Methuen.

Skinner/Taylor/Wegelin (eds.) (1987), *Shelter Upgrading for the Urban Poor. Evaluation of Third World Experience*, Manila.

Slater, D. (1989), 'Territorial Power and the Peripheral State: The Issue of Decentralisation', *Development and Change*, Vol. 20.

Slater, D. (1986), 'Capitalism and Urbanization at the Periphery: Problems of Interpretation and Analysis with Reference to Latin America', in Drakakis-Smith (ed.), *Urbanisation in the Developing World*, Beckenham.

Somma, P. (1989), 'New Towns in Independent Africa', *TRIALOG*, No. 20.

Somma, P. (1990), 'Ethnic Segregation: A Heritage of the Colonial Past or Model for all Future Cities?' *TRIALOG*, No. 23/24.

Southall, A. (1971), 'The Impact of Imperialism upon Urban Development in Africa', in Turner, V. (ed.), *Colonialism in Africa 1870-1960*, Cambridge.

Southall, T. (1980), 'Zambia: Class Formation and the Government Policy in the 1970s'. *Journal of Southern African Studies*, 7 (1).

Southern African Economist (1992), 'Cover Story: Who is planning the cities?' *Southern African Economist*, November 1992.

Stein, A. (1991) 'A Critical Review of the Main Approaches to Self-Help Housing Programmes'. *DPU-Working Paper*, No. 27, London.

Steinberg, F. (1986), 'Mit angepaßter Ausbildung gegen die Wohnungsnot: Ein Plädoyer für partizipatorische Stadtteilentwicklung', *TRIALOG*, No. 10.

Steinberg/Mathéy (1987), 'Upgrading: The Proof of the Pudding is in the Eating', *TRIALOG*, No. 13/14.

Stiens, G. (1982), 'Langfristszenarien zur Raumentwicklung', *Informationen zur Raumentwicklung*, Heft 8.

Stokes, C. (1962), 'A Theory of Slums', *Land Economics*, Vol. 38, No. 5.

Stockmann, R. (1993), 'Langfristige Wirkungen - bisher wenig untersucht', *E+Z*, No. 2/1993.

Stockmann/Gaebe (eds.) (1993), *Hilft die Entwicklungshilfe langfristig?* Opladen.

Sträb, H. (1986), 'Verstädterungsprobleme in Afrika - Stadtplanung als Krisen- management', *TRIALOG*, No. 10.

Sträb, H. (1990), 'Stadtentwicklung und Infrastruktur in Afrika', *TRIALOG*, No. 27.

Strassmann, W. (1977), 'Housing Priorities in Developing Countries: A Planning Model', *Land Economics*, Vol. 53, No. 3.

Stren, R. (1986), 'The Ruralization of African Cities: Learning to live with Poverty', in Stren/Letemendia, *Coping with rapid Urban Growth in Africa: An Annotated Bibliography*, Montreal.

Stren, R. (1988), 'Urban Services in Africa: public management or privatization?', in Cook/Kirkpatrick (eds.), *Privatization in less developed Countries*, Brighton.

Stren, R. (1990), 'Urban Housing in Africa: the changing role of government policy', in Amis/Lloyd (eds.), *Housing Africa's Urban Poor*, Manchester.

Stren, R. (1991), 'Old Wine in New Bottles? An Overview of Africa's Urban Problems and the 'Urban Management' Approach to dealing with them', *Environment and Urbanization*, 3 (1), pp. 9-22.

Stren, R. (1993), 'African Urban Research since the Late 1980s: Responses to Poverty and Urban Growth', in: Paddison/Lever/Money (eds.), *International Perspectives in Urban Studies 1*, London.

Stren/White (eds.) (1989), *African Cities in Crisis: Managing Rapid Urban Growth*, Boulder.

Stuckey/Fay (1980), *Produktion, Reproduktion und Zerstörung billiger Arbeitskraft: Ländliche Subsistenz, Migration und Urbanisierung*. Starnberger Studien 4, Frankfurt/M.

Sundra, T. (1976), *Low-Income Housing Systems in Mexico City*. Massachusetts Institute of Technology.

Szeftel, M. (1982), 'Political Graft and the Spoils System in Zambia - The State as a Resource in Itself', *Review of African Political Economy*, No. 24.

Tait, J. (1979), 'Interner Kolonialismus und ethnisch-soziale Segregation im Sudan', *Africa Spectrum*, No. 3.

Tait, J. (1983), 'The Modernization of the Colonial Mode of Production in the Gezira Scheme', in Oesterdiekhoff/Wohlmuth (eds.), *The developmental Perspectives of the Democratic Republic of Sudan*, Munich.

Tait, J. (1987), 'How to Survive Capitalist Development in Third World Metropolis - Housing, Subsistence and Simple Commodity Production in Theories of Urban Reproduction', in Harms/Zschaebitz (eds.), *International Conference Urban Renewal and Housing for Low-Income Groups in Metropolitan Areas of Latin America*. Vol. 3, Hamburg.

Tait, J. (1989), *Report on the Workshop "Legal Aspects of Organized Self-Help Housing" held in Lusaka, Zambia 13-15 April 1989*, Lusaka.

Tait, J. (1996), *Consolidation of Squatter Settlements in the Barrios of Caracas, Venezuela, 1960-1985*, Hamburg.

Tait/Shihembetsa (1995), *Country Reports and Recommendations on Training Needs for Urban Planners in Uganda, Zambia and Malawi*. Unpublished Report for the CDG, Cologne.

Taylor, J. L. (1983), *An Evaluation of Selected Impacts of Jakarta's Kampong Improvement Programme*, Los Angeles.

Tetzlaff, R. (1977), 'Staat und Klasse in peripher-kapitalistischen Gesellschaftsformationen: Die Entwicklung des abhängigen Staatskapitalismus in Afrika', *VRÜ*, Bd. 10.

Tetzlaff, R. (1975), 'Krisen, Staat und Krisenmanagement in einer Entwicklungsgesellschaft am Beispiel Sambias', in Elsenhans/Jänicke (eds.), *Innere Systemkrisen der Gegenwart*, Reinbek.

Tetzlaff, R. (1980), *Die Weltbank: Machtinstrument der USA oder Hilfe für die Entwicklungsländer?* Munich.

Tetzlaff, R. (1989), 'The Social Basis of Political Rule in Africa: Problems of Legitimacy and Prospects for Democracy', in Meyns/Nabudere (eds.), *Democracy and the One-Party State in Africa*, Hamburg.

Todd, D. (1979), *Housing Costs. Lusaka Housing Project Evaluation Team*, Lusaka.

Todd, D. (1987), 'Constraints on the Development of Appropriate Sanitation Policies in Zambia', *Habitat International*, Vol. 11, No. 1.

Todd/Mulenga/Mupimpila (1979), 'Markets and Vendors in Lusaka, Zambia', *African Urban Studies*, 5.

Todd/Mulimbwa (1979), *An Evaluation of the Legal Framework of Public Participation in the Management of Human Settlements of Zambia*, Lusaka.

Todd/Shaw (undated), *Education, Employment, and the Informal sector in Zambia*. Urban Community Research Unit. Institute for African Studies. Lusaka (approx. 1979).

Tokman, V. (1978), 'An Exploration into the Nature of Informal-Formal Sector Relationships', *World Development*, 6.

Tordoff, W. (ed.) (1980), *Administration in Zambia*. Manchester.

Tordoff, W. (1984), *Government and Politics in Africa*, London.

Tordoff, W. (ed.) (1974), *Politics in Zambia*, Manchester.

Turnbull, S. (1983), 'Co-operative Land Banks for Low-Income Housing', in Angel et al., *Land for Housing the Poor*, Singapore.

Turner, B. (ed.) (1988), Building Community. *A Third World Case Book*, Habitat International Coalition.

Turner, J. (1968), 'The Squatter Settlement. An Architecture that works', *Architectural Design*, Vol. 8.

Turner, J. (1969), 'Uncontrolled Urban Settlements: Problems and Policies', in Breese, G. (ed.), *The City in Newly Developing Countries*, Eaglewood Cliffs.

Turner/Turner (1986), 'Geology of the Lusaka Area', in Williams (ed.), *Lusaka and its Environs*, Lusaka.

Turok, B. (1979a), 'The Penalties of Zambia's Mixed Economy', in Turok, B. (ed.), *Development in Zambia*, London.

Turok, B. (1979b), 'State Capitalism: The Role of Parastatals in Zambia' *Africa Development*, No. 4, 2/3.

Turok, B. (1980), 'Zambia's System of State Capitalism', *Development and Change*, 11 (3), pp. 455-478.

Turok, B. (ed.) (1979), *Development in Zambia*, London.

Turok/Sanyal (1978), *Lusaka Housing Project: A Critical Overview of Low-Cost Housing in Zambia. World Employment Programme Research*. Working Paper No. 92, International Labour Office, Geneva.

UN (1989), *1989 Report of the World Social Situation*, New York.

UNCHS (1982) , *Survey of Slums and Squatter Settlements*, Dublin.

UNCHS (1987a), *Global Report on Human Settlements 1986*, Oxford.

UNCHS (1987b), *Shelter for the Homeless: the Role of Non Governmental Organizations*, Nairobi.

UNCHS (1993), *Strategies for the Provision of Facilities, Service and Housing Improvements in Ghana, Uganda and Zambia*, Nairobi.

UNFPA (1986), *State of World Population Report 1986*, New York.

United Nations (1976), *United Nations Conference on Human Settlements, Vancouver, Canada 31 May - 11 June 1976*, New York.

United Nations (1978), *Non-Conventional Financing of Housing for Low-Income Households*, New York.

United Nations (1975), *The Social Impact of Housing. Goals, Standards, Indicators and Popular Participation*, New York.

van den Berg, L. (1986), 'Between the City and the Farms', in Williams (ed.), *Lusaka and its Environs*, Lusaka.

van den Berg, L. (ed.) (1982), *In the Shadow of Lusaka: land and people under pressure of urban growth*, Lusaka.

Van Der Linden, J. (1987), *The Sites and Service Approach Reviewed: Solution or Stopgap to the Third World Housing Shortage?* Aldershot.

Van Velsen, J. (1975), 'Urban Squatters: Problem or Solution?', in Parkin, D. (ed.), *Town and Country in Central and Eastern Africa*, London.

Vergopoulos, K. (1974), 'Capitalisme deforme (Le cas de l' agriculture dans le capitalisme)', in Amin, S. (ed.), *La question paysanne et le capitalisme*, Paris.

Wakely, P. (1990), 'The Devolution of Housing Production: Support and Management', *TRIALOG*, No. 23/24.

Waldeck, W. (1986), 'Lusaka: A First Attempt at Socio-Spatial Modelling', in Williams (ed.), Lusaka and its Environs, Lusaka.

Walker, R. (1974), 'Urban Ground Rent. Building a new Conceptual Framework', *Antipode*, No. 6.

Wallace, I. (1990), *The Global Economic System*, London.

Wallerstein, I. (1974), *The Modern World System*, New York.

Wallerstein/Martin/Dickensen (1989), *Household Structures and Production Processes. Theoretical Concerns, plus data from Southern Africa and nineteenth century United States*, Birmingham (N. Y.).

Wallis, M. (1989), *Bureaucracy: Its Role in Third World Development*, London.

Walton, J. (ed.) (1985), *Capital and Labour in the Urbanized World*, Beverly Hills.

Ward, P. (ed.) (1982), *Self-Help Housing - A Critique*, London.

Weeks, J. (1975), 'Politics for Expanding Employment in the Informal Urban Sector of Developing Economies', *International Labour Review*, Vol. 111, pp. 1-13.

Wegener, R. (1982), *Wohnungsbau-Finanzierung in Entwicklungsländern: ein integrierter Ansatz*, Bonn.

Werlin, H. (1988), 'Improving Squatter Settlements in Africa: The World Bank Experience', in Obudho/Mhlanga (eds.), *Slum and Squatter Settlements in Sub-Saharan Africa*, New York.

Wetter, M. (1984), *Der Mythos der Selbsthilfe - Illegale Siedlungen und informeller Sektor in Nairobi*, Berlin.

White, B. (1989), 'International Experiences with NGO's Active in Developing Countries', *TRIALOG*, No. 22.

Williams, D. (1984), 'The Role of International Agencies: The World Bank', in Payne (ed.), *Low-Income Housing in the developing World*, Chichester.

Williams, G. (1986a), 'Landforms and Landscape Evolution', in Williams (ed.), *Lusaka and its Environs*, Lusaka.

Williams, G. (1986b), 'The Early Years of the Township', in Williams (ed.), *Lusaka and its Environs*. Lusaka.

Williams, G. (1986c), 'The Physical Growth of Lusaka: Past and Projected', in Williams (ed.), *Lusaka and its Environs*, Lusaka.

Willkomm, W. (1981), *Selbstbau in Entwicklungsländern*, Hannover.

Wilson, G. (1947), *An Essay on the Economics of Detribalization in Northern Rhodesia*. Rhodes-Livingstone Papers No.5, Livingstone.

Wohlmuth, K. (1973), Sambia - 'Modell einer gescheiterten Dekolonisation', in Grohs/Tibi (eds.), *Zur Soziologie der Dekolonisation*, Frankfurt/M.

Wohlmuth et al. (eds.) (1990), *Yearbook on African Development Perspectives. Vol I: Human Dimensions of Adjustment*, Berlin.

Woldring, K. (ed.) (1984), *Beyond Political Independence: Zambia's Development Predicament in the 1980s*, Berlin.

Wood, A. (1986), 'Agriculture in Lusaka Province', in Williams (ed.), *Lusaka and its Environs*, Lusaka.

Wood, A. with Banda/Mundene (1986), 'The Population of Lusaka', in Williams (ed.), *Lusaka and its Environs*, Lusaka.

World Bank (1982), *Evaluation of Shelter Programs for the Urban Poor. Principal Findings*, Washington.

World Bank (1983), *Learning by Doing: World Bank Lending for Urban Development, 1972-1982*, Washington D. C.

World Bank (1983a), *World Development Report 1983*, Washington D. C.

World Commission on Environment and Development (1987), *Our Common Future (The 'Brundtland Report')*, Oxford.

WSDG (Water Sector Development Group) (1994), *Proposed Institutional Framework for Water Supply and Sanitation Sector/Discussion Paper for the Cabinet established 'Programme Coordination Unit'*, Lusaka.

Wulf, J. (1988), 'Zambia under the IMF Regime', *African Affairs*, Vol. 349, No. 87.

Young, R. (1988), *Zambia - Adjusting to Poverty*, Ottawa

Zambia UNCHS/DANIDA (1990), *Administrative Procedures for Declaring a Site as a Statutory Housing Area or an Improvement Area*. Ministry of Decentralisation, Lusaka.

Zambia UNCHS/DANIDA (1988), *Community Participation Training Programme: Introduction to the Training of Government Staff and Community Leaders for the Improvement of Human Settlements through Community Participation*. Ministry of Decentralisation, Lusaka.

Zambia UNCHS/DANIDA (1989a), *Final Evaluation Report for a Training Programme in Community Participation*, Lusaka.

Zambia UNCHS/DANIDA (1989b), *Target Outcome of the Community Participation Training Programme for the Improvement of Human Settlement*, Lusaka.

Zelter/Witola (1967), *A Socio-Economic Survey of Kalingalinga*. Ministry of Cooperatives, Youth and Social Development, Dept. of Community Development, Lusaka.

Ziss, R. (1986), 'Projekte der Wohnversorgung - Eine entwicklungspolitische Herausforderung', *TRIALOG*, No. 10.

Ziss, R. (1987), 'Settlement Upgrading in Latin America and the Leverage of Technical Cooperation - The Process of Upgrading', *TRIALOG*, No. 13/14.

Ziss/Kotowski-Ziss (1986), *Baumaterialien und Selbsthilfe*, Saarbrücken.